Macroeconomic Policy Regimes in Western Industrial Countries

This book analyses how the economic crisis in the 1970s led to the erosion of the regulated type of capitalism that came to be in place after the Second World War, and paved the way to a Neoliberal Globalisation. Deep structural institutional changes especially in the field of financial markets, labour markets and the international economy became the basis for a liberal type of capitalism which included financial markets in a dominant role. The new neoliberal model fundamentally changed the conditions for all macroeconomic policies. In this book, these macroeconomic policy regimes are discussed on a theoretical level.

Macroeconomic Policy Regimes in Western Industrial Countries explains how certain countries have created a more liberal and market-based type of capitalism. The emphasis throughout is on how understanding macroeconomic policies, and the institutional framework in which they operate, is vital to understanding the long-run dynamics of a capitalist economy. The policy regimes that are examined consist of changes in the financial system, monetary policy, fiscal policy, wage policy changes in distribution, and foreign economic policy. The argument emerges that this deregulated type of capitalism is unacceptably unstable and is only preferable to a minority.

Moving on from the finance-driven development of recent decades, the authors take a look at the need for fundamental reforms, including institutional reforms in the areas of national and international financial and labour markets. Case studies from the United States, the United Kingdom, Germany and Japan dating from the 1970s up to today provide the reader with clear examples and analysis of the development in question. This book will be of interest to postgraduates and researchers of economics and political science.

Hansjörg Herr is Professor for Supranational Integration at the Berlin School of Economics and Law, Germany.

Milka Kazandziska is a lecturer at the Berlin School of Economics and Law, Germany.

Routledge frontiers of political economy

1 **Equilibrium Versus Understanding**
Towards the rehumanization of economics within social theory
Mark Addleson

2 **Evolution, Order and Complexity**
Edited by Elias L. Khalil and Kenneth E. Boulding

3 **Interactions in Political Economy**
Malvern after ten years
Edited by Steven Pressman

4 **The End of Economics**
Michael Perelman

5 **Probability in Economics**
Omar F. Hamouda and Robin Rowley

6 **Capital Controversy, Post Keynesian Economics and the History of Economics**
Essays in honour of Geoff Harcourt, volume one
Edited by Philip Arestis, Gabriel Palma and Malcolm Sawyer

7 **Markets, Unemployment and Economic Policy**
Essays in honour of Geoff Harcourt, volume two
Edited by Philip Arestis, Gabriel Palma and Malcolm Sawyer

8 **Social Economy**
The logic of capitalist development
Clark Everling

9 **New Keynesian Economics/ Post Keynesian Alternatives**
Edited by Roy J. Rotheim

10 **The Representative Agent in Macroeconomics**
James E. Hartley

11 **Borderlands of Economics**
Essays in honour of Daniel R. Fusfeld
Edited by Nahid Aslanbeigui and Young Back Choi

12 **Value, Distribution and Capital**
Essays in honour of Pierangelo Garegnani
Edited by Gary Mongiovi and Fabio Petri

13 **The Economics of Science**
Methodology and epistemology as if economics really mattered
James R. Wible

14 **Competitiveness, Localised Learning and Regional Development**
Specialisation and prosperity in small open economies
Peter Maskell, Heikki Eskelinen, Ingjaldur Hannibalsson, Anders Malmberg and Eirik Vatne

15 **Labour Market Theory**
A constructive reassessment
Ben J. Fine

16 **Women and European Employment**
Jill Rubery, Mark Smith, Colette Fagan and Damian Grimshaw

17 **Explorations in Economic Methodology**
From Lakatos to empirical philosophy of science
Roger Backhouse

18 **Subjectivity in Political Economy**
Essays on wanting and choosing
David P. Levine

19 **The Political Economy of Middle East Peace**
The impact of competing trade agendas
Edited by J.W. Wright, Jnr

20 **The Active Consumer**
Novelty and surprise in consumer choice
Edited by Marina Bianchi

21 **Subjectivism and Economic Analysis**
Essays in memory of Ludwig Lachmann
Edited by Roger Koppl and Gary Mongiovi

22 **Themes in Post-Keynesian Economics**
Essays in honour of Geoff Harcourt, volume three
Edited by Claudio Sardoni and Peter Kriesler

23 **The Dynamics of Technological Knowledge**
Cristiano Antonelli

24 **The Political Economy of Diet, Health and Food Policy**
Ben J. Fine

25 **The End of Finance**
Capital market inflation, financial derivatives and pension fund capitalism
Jan Toporowski

26 **Political Economy and the New Capitalism**
Edited by Jan Toporowski

27 **Growth Theory**
A philosophical perspective
Patricia Northover

28 **The Political Economy of the Small Firm**
Edited by Charlie Dannreuther

29 **Hahn and Economic Methodology**
Edited by Thomas Boylan and Paschal F. O'Gorman

30 **Gender, Growth and Trade**
The miracle economies of the postwar years
David Kucera

31 **Normative Political Economy**
Subjective freedom, the market and the state
David Levine

32 **Economist with a Public Purpose**
Essays in honour of John Kenneth Galbraith
Edited by Michael Keaney

33 **Involuntary Unemployment**
The elusive quest for a theory
Michel De Vroey

34 **The Fundamental Institutions of Capitalism**
Ernesto Screpanti

35 **Transcending Transaction**
The search for self-generating markets
Alan Shipman

36 **Power in Business and the State**
An historical analysis of its concentration
Frank Bealey

37 **Editing Economics**
Essays in honour of Mark Perlman
Edited by Hank Lim, Ungsuh K. Park and Geoff Harcourt

38 **Money, Macroeconomics and Keynes**
Essays in honour of Victoria Chick, volume one
Edited by Philip Arestis, Meghnad Desai and Sheila Dow

39 **Methodology, Microeconomics and Keynes**
Essays in honour of Victoria Chick, volume two
Edited by Philip Arestis, Meghnad Desai and Sheila Dow

40 **Market Drive and Governance**
Reexamining the rules for economic and commercial contest
Ralf Boscheck

41 **The Value of Marx**
Political economy for contemporary capitalism
Alfredo Saad-Filho

42 **Issues in Positive Political Economy**
S. Mansoob Murshed

43 **The Enigma of Globalisation**
A journey to a new stage of capitalism
Robert Went

44 **The Market**
Equilibrium, stability, mythology
S.N. Afriat

45 The Political Economy of Rule Evasion and Policy Reform
Jim Leitzel

46 Unpaid Work and the Economy
Edited by Antonella Picchio

47 Distributional Justice
Theory and measurement
Hilde Bojer

48 Cognitive Developments in Economics
Edited by Salvatore Rizzello

49 Social Foundations of Markets, Money and Credit
Costas Lapavitsas

50 Rethinking Capitalist Development
Essays on the economics of Josef Steindl
Edited by Tracy Mott and Nina Shapiro

51 An Evolutionary Approach to Social Welfare
Christian Sartorius

52 Kalecki's Economics Today
Edited by Zdzislaw L. Sadowski and Adam Szeworski

53 Fiscal Policy from Reagan to Blair
The left veers right
Ravi K. Roy and Arthur T. Denzau

54 The Cognitive Mechanics of Economic Development and Institutional Change
Bertin Martens

55 Individualism and the Social Order
The social element in liberal thought
Charles R. McCann Jnr

56 Affirmative Action in the United States and India
A comparative perspective
Thomas E. Weisskopf

57 Global Political Economy and the Wealth of Nations
Performance, institutions, problems and policies
Edited by Phillip Anthony O'Hara

58 Structural Economics
Thijs ten Raa

59 Macroeconomic Theory and Economic Policy
Essays in honour of Jean-Paul Fitoussi
Edited by K. Vela Velupillai

60 The Struggle over Work
The "end of work" and employment alternatives in post-industrial societies
Shaun Wilson

61 The Political Economy of Global Sporting Organisations
John Forster and Nigel Pope

62 The Flawed Foundations of General Equilibrium Theory
Critical essays on economic theory
Frank Ackerman and Alejandro Nadal

63 **Uncertainty in Economic Theory**
Essays in honor of David Schmeidler's 65th birthday
Edited by Itzhak Gilboa

64 **The New Institutional Economics of Corruption**
Edited by Johann Graf Lambsdorff, Markus Taube and Matthias Schramm

65 **The Price Index and its Extension**
A chapter in economic measurement
S.N. Afriat

66 **Reduction, Rationality and Game Theory in Marxian Economics**
Bruce Philp

67 **Culture and Politics in Economic Development**
Volker Bornschier

68 **Modern Applications of Austrian Thought**
Edited by Jürgen G. Backhaus

69 **Ordinary Choices**
Individuals, incommensurability, and democracy
Robert Urquhart

70 **Labour Theory of Value**
Peter C. Dooley

71 **Capitalism**
Victor D. Lippit

72 **Macroeconomic Foundations of Macroeconomics**
Alvaro Cencini

73 **Marx for the 21st Century**
Edited by Hiroshi Uchida

74 **Growth and Development in the Global Political Economy**
Social structures of accumulation and modes of regulation
Phillip Anthony O'Hara

75 **The New Economy and Macroeconomic Stability**
A neo-modern perspective drawing on the complexity approach and Keynesian economics
Teodoro Dario Togati

76 **The Future of Social Security Policy**
Women, work and a citizens' basic income
Ailsa McKay

77 **Clinton and Blair**
The political economy of the third way
Flavio Romano

78 **Marxian Reproduction Schema**
Money and aggregate demand in a capitalist economy
A.B. Trigg

79 **The Core Theory in Economics**
Problems and solutions
Lester G. Telser

80 **Economics, Ethics and the Market**
Introduction and applications
Johan J. Graafland

81 **Social Costs and Public Action in Modern Capitalism**
Essays inspired by Karl William Kapp's theory of social costs
Edited by Wolfram Elsner, Pietro Frigato and Paolo Ramazzotti

82 **Globalization and the Myths of Free Trade**
History, theory and empirical evidence
Edited by Anwar Shaikh

83 **Equilibrium in Economics**
Scope and limits
Edited by Valeria Mosini

84 **Globalization**
State of the art and perspectives
Edited by Stefan A. Schirm

85 **Neoliberalism**
National and regional experiments with global ideas
Edited by Ravi K. Roy, Arthur T. Denzau and Thomas D. Willett

86 **Post-Keynesian Macroeconomics**
Essays in honour of Ingrid Rima
Edited by Mathew Forstater, Gary Mongiovi and Steven Pressman

87 **Consumer Capitalism**
Anastasios S. Korkotsides

88 **Remapping Gender in the New Global Order**
Edited by Marjorie Griffin Cohen and Janine Brodie

89 **Hayek and Natural Law**
Eric Angner

90 **Race and Economic Opportunity in the Twenty-First Century**
Edited by Marlene Kim

91 **Renaissance in Behavioural Economics**
Harvey Leibenstein's impact on contemporary economic analysis
Edited by Roger Frantz

92 **Human Ecology Economics**
A new framework for global sustainability
Edited by Roy E. Allen

93 **Imagining Economics Otherwise**
Encounters with identity/difference
Nitasha Kaul

94 **Reigniting the Labor Movement**
Restoring means to ends in a democratic labor movement
Gerald Friedman

95 **The Spatial Model of Politics**
Norman Schofield

96 **The Economics of American Judaism**
Carmel Ullman Chiswick

97 **Critical Political Economy**
Christian Arnsperger

98 **Culture and Economic Explanation**
Economics in the US and Japan
Donald W. Katzner

99 **Feminism, Economics and Utopia**
Time travelling through paradigms
Karin Schönpflug

100 **Risk in International Finance**
Vikash Yadav

101 **Economic Policy and Performance in Industrial Democracies**
Party governments, central banks and the fiscal–monetary policy mix
Takayuki Sakamoto

102 **Advances on Income Inequality and Concentration Measures**
Edited by Gianni Betti and Achille Lemmi

103 **Economic Representations**
Academic and everyday
Edited by David F. Ruccio

104 **Mathematical Economics and the Dynamics of Capitalism**
Goodwin's legacy continued
Edited by Peter Flaschel and Michael Landesmann

105 **The Keynesian Multiplier**
Edited by Claude Gnos and Louis-Philippe Rochon

106 **Money, Enterprise and Income Distribution**
Towards a macroeconomic theory of capitalism
John Smithin

107 **Fiscal Decentralization and Local Public Finance in Japan**
Nobuki Mochida

108 **The 'Uncertain' Foundations of Post-Keynesian Economics**
Essays in exploration
Stephen P. Dunn

109 **Karl Marx's *Grundrisse***
Foundations of the critique of political economy 150 years later
Edited by Marcello Musto

110 **Economics and the Price Index**
S.N. Afriat and Carlo Milana

111 **Sublime Economy**
On the intersection of art and economics
Edited by Jack Amariglio, Joseph W. Childers and Stephen E. Cullenberg

112 **Popper, Hayek and the Open Society**
Calvin Hayes

113 **The Political Economy of Work**
David Spencer

114 **Institutional Economics**
Bernard Chavance

115 **Religion, Economics and Demography**
The effects of religion on education, work, and the family
Evelyn L. Lehrer

116 **Economics, Rational Choice and Normative Philosophy**
Edited by Thomas A. Boylan and Ruvin Gekker

117 **Economics Versus Human Rights**
Manuel Couret Branco

118 **Hayek Versus Marx and Today's Challenges**
Eric Aarons

119 **Work Time Regulation as Sustainable Full Employment Policy**
Robert LaJeunesse

120 **Equilibrium, Welfare and Uncertainty**
Mukul Majumdar

121 **Capitalism, Institutions and Economic Development**
Michael Heller

122 **Economic Pluralism**
Robert Garnett, Erik Olsen and Martha Starr

123 **Dialectics of Class Struggle in the Global Economy**
Clark Everling

124 **Political Economy and Globalization**
Richard Westra

125 **Full-Spectrum Economics**
Toward an inclusive and emancipatory social science
Christian Arnsperger

126 **Computable, Constructive and Behavioural Economic Dynamics**
Essays in honour of Kumaraswamy (Vela) Velupillai
Stefano Zambelli

127 **Monetary Macrodynamics**
Toichiro Asada, Carl Chiarella, Peter Flaschel and Reiner Franke

128 **Rationality and Explanation in Economics**
Maurice Lagueux

129 **The Market, Happiness, and Solidarity**
A Christian perspective
Johan J. Graafland

130 **Economic Complexity and Equilibrium Illusion**
Essays on market instability and macro vitality
Ping Chen

131 **Economic Theory and Social Change**
Problems and revisions
Hasse Ekstedt and Angelo Fusari

132 **The Practices of Happiness**
Political economy, religion and wellbeing
Edited by John Atherton, Elaine Graham and Ian Steedman

133 **The Measurement of Individual Well-Being and Group Inequalities**
Essays in memory of Z. M. Berrebi
Edited by Joseph Deutsch and Jacques Silber

134 **Wage Policy, Income Distribution, and Democratic Theory**
Oren M. Levin-Waldman

135 **The Political Economy of Bureaucracy**
Steven O. Richardson

Macroeconomic Policy Regimes in Western Industrial Countries

Hansjörg Herr and Milka Kazandziska

Routledge
Taylor & Francis Group
LONDON AND NEW YORK

First published 2011
by Routledge
2 Park Square, Milton Park, Abingdon, Oxfordshire OX14 4RN

Simultaneously published in the USA and Canada
by Routledge
711 Third Avenue, New York, NY 10017

First issued in paperback 2014

Routledge is an imprint of the Taylor and Francis Group, an informa business

Typeset in Times by Wearset Ltd, Boldon, Tyne and Wear

British Library Cataloguing in Publication Data
A catalogue record for this book is available from the British Library

Library of Congress Cataloging in Publication Data
Herr, Hansjörg, 1951–
Macroeconomic policy regimes in Western industrial countries/by Hansjörg Herr and Milka Kazandziska.
p. cm.
Includes bibliographical references and index.
1. Western countries–Economic policy. 2. Developed countries–Economic policy. 3. Macroeconomics–Western countries. 4. Macroeconomics–Developed countries. 5. Neoliberalism–Western countries. 6. Neoliberalism–Developed countries. I. Kazandziska, Milka. II. Title.
HC59.15.H48 2010
339.509182'1–dc22 2010035286

ISBN 978-0-415-56173-0 (hbk)
ISBN 978-1-138-80725-9 (pbk)
ISBN 978-0-203-83034-5 (ebk)

Contents

Foreword

The world economy is still suffering the consequences of the crisis which erupted in the US financial system in 2007 and subsequently spread to all countries. True, the world economy is growing again. But the economic recovery is still too weak and fragile to overcome the damage made in terms of employment losses, growing job precariousness and major business failures. According to ILO's *World of Work Report 2010*, it will take several more years for employment to return to the pre-crisis situation. Importantly, the brunt of the crisis is borne by those groups that had not benefited much from the earlier expansionary period.

Despite the gravity of the situation, much of the policy action to date has focused on addressing the consequences of the crisis – and not its causes. In 2009, major fiscal stimulus plans were launched to boost aggregate demand. As part of these plans, social protection was reinforced in many countries in order to ensure adequate income support to the innocent victims of the economic slump. The measures helped put a floor on the crisis and kick-start economic recovery. Millions of jobs were saved or created as a result. And yet they are now being challenged as policy attention has shifted to reducing fiscal deficits.

This volume provides a comprehensive assessment of the origins of the crisis and, thereby, helps understand the limits in crisis responses so far. It examines in detail the structural weaknesses that led to the crisis, including the growing disconnect between the financial system and the needs of the real economy. Interestingly, the volume goes further and analyses the impact of the financial system on corporate governance, notably as regards the search for ever higher short-term profits. It provides examples where such a short-termism goes against the longer term interest of society and the environment, while also affecting real investment and therefore the economy itself.

The authors also point to the unsustainability of the globalisation process. Export-led growth strategies have led to growing current account imbalances. More generally, globalisation has gone hand-in-hand with a widening of income inequalities without precedent in recent economic history. According to the authors, the view that greater income inequalities were the price to pay for higher economic growth has proved to be a major policy mistake.

Finally, the authors present a set of policies to achieve a New Globalisation which gives prominence to the real economy and emphasises a more balanced growth path. The approach covers an impressive range of policies – macroeconomic, trade, financial markets, taxes and social protection, employment and corporate governance. In this respect, the volume is full of thought-provocative ideas.

In short, this is an impressive piece and a timely contribution to the debate on the post-crisis economic model.

Raymond Torres
Director, International Institute for Labour Studies, ILO

1 Introduction

The years following the Second World War are generally perceived as a period of steady economic development until structural change was adopted in the 1970s and 1980s. Before that break a regulated capitalism had existed, sometimes called the 'Golden Age of Capitalism' or 'Fordism'. The break in the 1970s led to a much more market-based type of capitalism in nearly all western countries and to a specific type of globalisation. What we call 'Neoliberal Globalisation' shaped the world economy and national economies. With regard to economic purposes the key elements of Neoliberal Globalisation involve the liberalisation of national and international financial markets, the liberalisation of national labour markets including reforms in the social safety net, and a change in corporate governance structure following the shareholder principle. These developments increased the power of the financial system and of the agents acting in the financial spheres.

Compared with the 1950s and 1960s, economic development in the 1990s and 2000s became much more unstable and volatile. GDP growth rates declined and unemployment figures increased. A long sequence of currency crises and domestic financial crises developed. The subprime financial crisis, which in 2008/09 triggered the deepest crisis in the world economy after the 1930s, is only the latest example. Moreover, the neoliberal development went along with an increasingly unequal income distribution.

In this book we set out to explain how countries created a more liberal and market-based type of capitalism and how they adjusted to the era of Neoliberal Globalisation, which for most countries was beyond control. We do not analyse in depth the political processes that led to these changes. We rather concentrate on the economic policies that were carried out, and the effects these policies have had. We furthermore focus on policies on the macroeconomic level including the institutional changes that have had significant macroeconomic repercussions. Together with the school of rational expectations, developed mainly in the 1970 and 1980s, and later the New Keynesians, who now dominate economic thinking, the microfoundation of macroeconomics became popular. In these approaches representative households and companies are analysed, and their behaviour is directly transferred to the macroeconomic level as if one single agent represented the whole household sector or the businesses of a country. Our approach is to analyse the macroeconomic level, which gives single households and companies the parameters for their actions. We endorse a macrofoundation of microeconomics.

Macroeconomic policy is traditionally characterised by monetary policy, fiscal policy, wage policy and foreign economic policy as well as their interaction. We support this view. These policies and their interaction are of paramount importance for the development of an economy. However, macroeconomic polices cannot be analysed on a theoretical level that does not take into account the very specific institutional framework of a country. For example, wage policy on a macroeconomic level means a policy that enables the realisation of a certain increase in the level of nominal wages. Obviously, to achieve such an aim wage policy must be very much supported by an adequate institutional framework like strong trade unions and/or strong employers' associations, which in many countries do not exist or are very weak. Referring to monetary policy, it makes a world of a difference if a central bank is equipped with only one policy instrument, the interest rate, or whether it can use capital controls as a second instrument or even direct restrictions on credit expansion as a possible third instrument to achieve its monetary goals.

Institutions can be actively changed by policy actions. Abandoning control over international capital flows, forcing employers to become members of employers' associations or allowing commercial banks to use their own risk models to calculate legal equity requirements are all political decisions with the aim of changing institutions. But institutions can also change beyond the control of policy-makers. The breakdown of the Bretton Woods System in 1973 and the switch to flexible exchange rates between the key currencies in the world was an example of institutional change that could not be influenced, at least not by smaller countries.

Taking everything into account we define a macroeconomic policy regime as the interaction between monetary policy, fiscal policy, wage policy and foreign economic policy within a framework of both, macroeconomic institutions which can be actively changed by policy-makers and become part of economic policy, and institutions which are beyond the control of policy-makers.

To analyse macroeconomic policy regimes we follow a qualitative analysis that considers the many institutional changes that characterise the development of the past decades and that paved the way for the macroeconomic policies. In our opinion econometric tools are not suitable for capturing the deep qualitative changes or the interactions between monetary policy, fiscal policy, wage policy and foreign economic policy, which to a great extent also depend on institutional changes. Keeping in mind what has been mentioned above, we argue that the macroeconomic policy regime is a broad concept in which we attempt to incorporate macroeconomic policies and the relevant institutions as well as their changes – a wide range of factors which can hardly be captured by quantitative econometric analyses that only focus on a very few variables. Consequently, the empirical part of this book rests upon qualitative analyses combined with numerical investigations. By illustrating the use of macroeconomic policies and the country-specific institutional development, case studies will be presented in order to explain the different types of macroeconomic regimes.

A complex analysis of the economic development throughout the 1950s and 1960s and the breakdown of the regulated capitalism of that time period is beyond the scope of this book. Instead, we concentrate on how countries acted and reacted in the era of Neoliberal Globalisation. Considering their role as the engines of the change in the neoliberal era we decided to confine our analysis to the developed western economies. There is a big chance that countries like China, India or Brazil will shape the world, but only in future decades. Given their major importance, we focus on the four biggest countries in the western world as cases: the United States, United Kingdom, Germany and Japan. As the largest country, the United States deeply influences the world's economic development including fundamental institutional changes in all of these countries. President Ronald Reagan who was elected US President in 1980 headed one of the governments who actively and radically changed domestic and international institutions, and gave birth to the Neoliberal Globalisation. Almost equally important in triggering neoliberal development was the United Kingdom. Margaret Thatcher, elected Prime Minister in Great Britain in 1979, introduced policies no less radical than the ones followed by Ronald Reagan. However, the economic size of countries is not the only deciding factor. Following the neoliberal changes very hesitantly at first, Germany and Japan are the latecomers in the neoliberal era. Both countries are characterised by particularly interesting developments. While the German case also highlights the problems of the European Monetary Union, Japan suffered from deflation – a phenomenon thought to be dead after the Great Depression in the 1930s. In addition, we would like to stress that our approach can serve as a blueprint for analyses of other countries, such as Italy, France or the Scandinavian countries, and even developing countries. The countries we have chosen can therefore be considered exemplary despite their respective country-specific conditions.

The structure of the book is straightforward. First, we analyse the macroeconomic policy regime in detail to clarify our theoretical approach. Then the case studies are presented. We finish with the outline of a reform strategy with the aim to overcome the Neoliberal Globalisation.

A German version of this book was published in 2006 (Heine *et al.* 2006). Therefore we would especially like to thank Michael Heine and Cornelia Kaiser who could not join the publication of the English version. We are indebted to the Hans Böckler Foundation and especially Frank Gerlach for their financial support for the German publication, as well as the Berlin School of Economics and Law where we work. Last but not least, we thank Peter Bofinger, Trevor Evans, Eckhard Hein, Ulrich Fritsche, Arne Heise, Dierk Hirschel, Jürgen Kromphardt, Jan Priewe, Wolfgang Scheremet, Dieter Scholz, Achim Truger, Rudolf Welzmüller, as well as Florian Zinsmeister who gave their invaluable contributions to the development of this project. Most of them were members of the Academic Advisory Board of the project, which led to the German publication. As research projects are never identical, this English publication is now substantially different from the German original. In the meantime, the subprime financial crisis and its effect on the world economy have improved the understanding of Neoliberal Globalisation and led to different judgements on policies. For providing data research for the English publication we are grateful to Marco Scheufel, Bea Ruoff and Stefanie Marie Scholz.

2 Macroeconomic policy regimes and their assessment

This chapter begins with a more detailed description of a macroeconomic policy regime concept. In the first section we analyse the general characteristics of a macroeconomic policy regime. In the second section the different elements of macroeconomic policy regime are examined individually. Finally, the last section deals with the typical theoretical constellations of a macroeconomic policy regime.

2.1 The general characteristics of a macroeconomic policy regime

2.1.1 'Ordnungspolitik' and process policy

The macroeconomic policy regime concept stands for the recognition that macroeconomic policies and the institutional framework in which they operate play a paramount role in understanding the short-run, and much more importantly, the long-run dynamics of a capitalist economy. The macroeconomic policies that will be examined here consist of monetary policy, fiscal policy, wage policy and foreign economic policy. Economic development of a country cannot be understood by analysing one policy area in an economy exclusively. For example, the economic development in the US, Japan or in Germany during the 1990s cannot be explained by a specific monetary policy alone. Rather, it is the interaction of the different elements of the policy regime that is important to explain economic development. Essentially, the outcome of a macroeconomic policy regime is more than the sum of its individual parts. For example, wage policy is of vital importance for monetary policy in a way that excessively high wage increases over productivity gains pose inflationary dangers to the economy and will trigger restrictive monetary policy. On the other hand, the case of Japan shows that nominal wage cuts reduce unit labour costs and thus cause a deflationary development, making monetary policy less successful in controlling price development. The idea of the importance of a policy mix is not spectacular in itself. However, different economic paradigms stimulate the emergence of different opinions about a good or a bad macroeconomic policy regime.[1] It is therefore essential in this study to define in more detail what we understand by macroeconomic policy regime.

Macroeconomic policies and their effects are not entirely independent of institutions. In fact, institutions can set the basis for and/or limit the policy mix of a macroeconomic policy regime. An illustration: in countries where labour market institutions (employment protection, unemployment benefits, coordination of collective bargaining, etc.) are sufficiently developed and where trade unions and employers' associations are strong and internalise the macroeconomic effects of their action, a macroeconomic wage policy is potentially possible. In the opposite case, the lack of agents who could carry out such a policy renders macroeconomic wage policy impossible; we can only talk of wage development. To offer another example: if asset markets are strictly controlled and separated from the commercial banking system, asset price inflations and deflations do not fundamentally disturb monetary policy. Macroeconomic policies depend on the institutional framework in which they are executed. Without understanding institutions that shape macroeconomic policies, the economic development of a country is difficult to understand.

Institutions are not fixed; they can change, while politics cannot easily shape all institutions. However, there is an important area of politics that changes institutions intentionally. It is a German tradition to label such a policy Ordnungspolitik.[2] We define Ordnungspolitik as a policy to change institutions with the explicit aim to influence the behaviour of (macroeconomic) agents and create certain economic results. These policies also provide the framework in which macroeconomic policies operate. For instance, making a central bank independent of direct government interventions may aim at gearing the monetary policy exclusively towards price level stability; changing laws which weaken trade unions may strive to create wage moderation; a law to enforce balanced public budgets may be proposed to prevent increasing public indebtedness.

However, policies to change institutions may have effects that are not intended. Institutions may also be a subject of change without a government's interference and beyond its control. For example, the collapse of the Bretton Woods System and the introduction of flexible exchange rates were beyond the control of many governments and at the same time fundamentally changed the framework for economic policy.

Thus, we make a distinction between policies that change institutions (Ordnungspolitik) and process policies. The latter cover the traditional macroeconomic policies that strive to influence macroeconomic variables like GDP growth, inflation rates or exchange rates. Of key importance is monetary policy, which is the most direct process policy. An increase or decrease of the refinancing rate dictated by the central bank influences GDP growth and/or the price level. No less significant is fiscal policy as a process policy. An active expansionary fiscal policy, for example, targets an increase in GDP growth. As explained above, wage policy is possible in some countries, whereas in other countries institutions for wage policy are missing. Foreign economic policy can also become an important process policy. It depends on the exchange rate system and the embeddedness of a country in the world market whether the exchange rate can be used as a policy instrument or not. If possible, a country can use the exchange rate to foster export-driven growth. The stabilisation of the exchange rate can also be used to give the domestic price level an anchor and to fight against inflationary processes. From the long list of asset market bubbles and financial crises in developing and developed countries – for example the asset price deflation in Japan in the early 1990s, the worldwide stock market crisis after the end of the dot-com bubble in 2000–2001, or the subprime crisis in the United States after 2007 – it becomes clear that the financial system has many important macroeconomic dimensions that influence process policies deeply. Therefore, the financial system is an important part of a macroeconomic policy regime.

If we take the institutional dimension and process policies into account we arrive at the following five elements of a macroeconomic policy regime (see Figure 2.1): monetary policy, fiscal policy, wage policy, foreign economic policy and the financial system. The monetary, fiscal and foreign economic policies of a country always involve institutional dimension and process policies. Wage development always has an institutional dimension. However, whether wage policy is possible depends on the specific situation of a country. Finally, the structure of the financial system thus far only has an institutional dimension. Usually, each element of an economic policy regime influences all other elements of the regime.

In this book we first describe and analyse the different macroeconomic policies in a country, including their interaction. Theoretically and empirically we find successful and unsuccessful types of policy mix leading to positive and negative economic results. A simple measure of a positive performance of a country is high GDP growth combined with low unemployment. We are

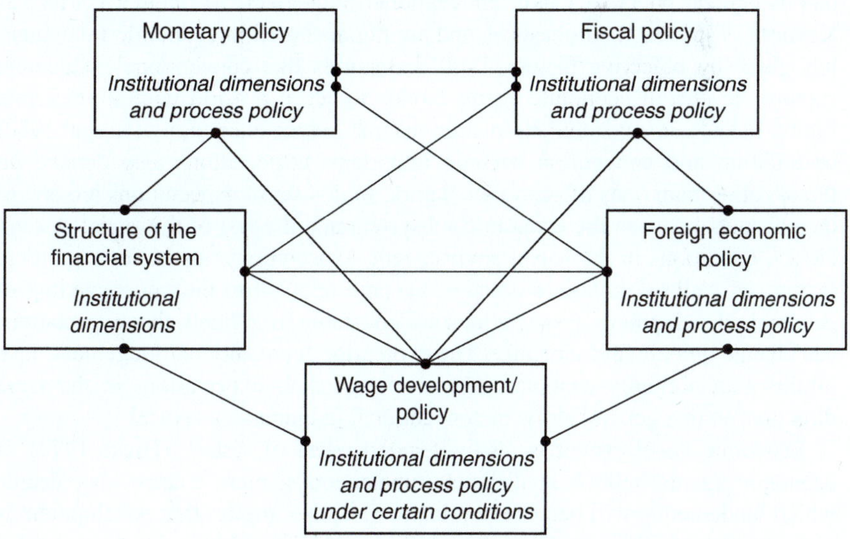

Figure 2.1 Elements of a macroeconomic policy regime (source: authors' illustration).

certainly aware of the fact that GDP and even GDP per capita is not a perfect welfare measure as it ignores especially ecological effects and income distribution. However, the elites in all of the countries we analyse were and are still attempting to achieve high sustainable growth and higher employment through GDP growth. We look to see how the different countries have managed to control the capitalist process in their economies to achieve these results.

We do not argue for permanent high growth for developed countries as a target as such. Instead, we believe that in the long run industrial countries should use their increasing productivity for shorter working hours and not for higher output (Keynes 1930a). But we also hope to contribute to an understanding of how to control and how to manage a capitalist economy. The better this is understood, the higher the chances will be of avoiding crises and also of following a conscious policy for full employment even without growth.

Economies are characterised by uncertainties. This means that not all future events are known and even for known events it is difficult to find probabilities. With such an approach there are no models available that can fully explain expectations. There are no axiomatic foundations to determine expectations and there is also no sound psychological model to solve the problem. The only solution is to assume that expectations are given for the economy exogenously. The other 'solution', i.e. following rational expectations and assuming that expectations are identical with the equilibrium outcome of the model and in this way disappear as independent variables, lacks plausibility.[3] This argument requires further explanation: it does not mean that economists cannot say anything about expectations. The point is that expectations also depend on historical time and place and cannot be discussed without taking into account the institutional, social and political constellation in countries and in the world economy. Expectations depend on factors like 'conventional judgement' or 'animal spirits', as Keynes (1936, 1937) emphasised, and are not anchored in economic fundamentals given by objective factors. 'Soft' categories like conventional judgement capture the idea of economic agents having to act in a world with an uncertain future. In such an environment institutions that reduce uncertainty (Kregel 1980) or tradition and convention become important. Expectations also depend on factors other than ones of economic nature. In this sense expectations are one of the channels between the economic subsystem and the rest of the social system. Hence, conditions in the social environment, expectations, institutions, political factors, as well as economic policies, become relevant to the understanding of economic development. Expectations are not stable. It is likely that expectations can change quickly and violently. The expression 'conventional judgement' also implies that normally economic agents change their expectations in the same direction, so that general shifts in conventional judgment are typical.[4]

Economic development is also not independent of history (Hicks 1979). If economic agents believe in different fundamentals, mere chance may decide which fundamental will become dominant. This also implies that development is path dependent. George Akerlof and Robert Shiller (2008: 12) give a nice example. After Hurricane Katrina in 2005 destroyed large parts of New Orleans it was questionable as to whether New Orleans would be rebuilt or not. If the opinion prevailed that many people would rebuild their homes in New Orleans, it would be rebuilt. If, on the other hand, it were a common belief that many people would not go back to New Orleans, it would not be rebuilt, as nobody would like to live without neighbours or shops. In such cases we can speak of a self-fulfilling prophecy, an expression coined by the sociologist Robert Merton (1949). The economy is full of such phenomena. Shocks like a financial crisis can change the long-run development path of an economy. Expressed in a formal way, various equilibria can come into being, including undesirable ones (New Orleans is not rebuild, long-term stagnation, etc.). Market forces do not necessarily have to tend towards equilibrium. Markets can create processes that bring the economy into a more and more fragile and unstable constellation. We use equilibrium as an analytical tool. However, we do not assume that markets by default tend towards equilibrium. Instead, we assume that stabilising institutions and adequate process policies are needed to prevent a market economy from suffering from permanent instability.

Under the conditions of uncertainty and unanchored expectations economic fluctuations do not follow any long-term trend that can be set objectively. Trends arise solely as a statistical result of the previous development. Thus, we reject ideas of fundamental factors that determine long-term growth and a business cycle moving around this long-term trend without changing it. We consider growth models on the basis of production functions such as those in the tradition of Robert Solow not very helpful in explaining economic developments.[5] Rather, we assume a sequence economy with a succession of phases (Hahn 1981). The respective phases depend on the corresponding specific historical constellation including the macroeconomic policy regime of a country.

A macroeconomic policy regime possesses certain durability because the relevant institutions, traditions and macroeconomic policy strategies of a country do not normally change 'overnight'. Thus, they affect the medium-term, or, if they are stable over a long period, the long-term prospects of a national economy. Therefore, an economic policy regime generally consists of a number of sequences and is usually longer than a business cycle.

Since an economic policy regime is embedded in various specific institutional frameworks and based on strategies followed by economic agents and policymakers with certain inertia, it cannot, as mentioned above, be solely created by economic policies. Also, positive economic policy regimes can arise without resulting from coordinated or deliberate policies. They simply reflect luck. Equally, in almost all cases a negative economic policy regime is not a planned outcome.

Our approach implies that there are different types of capitalism depending on the institutions in place and the economic policies followed. Of course, certain types of macroeconomic policies are only possible if a certain type of capitalism exists. If, for example, international capital flows are regulated, the banking system is state-owned and the interest rates of the banking system are dictated by the central bank, different policy options are possible than in a country with an unregulated domestic financial market and full integration into the international capital market. However, given certain institutions there is room to choose between different macroeconomic policy mixes.

Analysing institutions and policies that change them and process policies is not very common. In many regime analyses the emphasis lies on institutions as building blocks of regimes (see for example Hall and Soskice 2001). Process policies and the analysis of a policy mix to influence macroeconomic variables are usually excluded in institutional economics. Or, there are analyses of a macroeconomic policy mix, but the institutional changes and backgrounds are not made as clear as necessary.

2.1.2 Rational expectations and efficient financial market hypothesis

The dominant schools of thought in today's economic theories are to a certain extent all based on the neoclassical paradigm (the new classical model, the New Consensus macroeconomics).[6] The neoclassical paradigm is guided by the idea that the economy is a kind of machine which, as long it is not disturbed by misled policies, works properly and leads to welfare gains for all. Models used in this approach are methodologically based on the classical Newtonian physics. This is because the founders of the neoclassical school were strongly influenced by Isaac Newton in forming their theories. The essence of this methodical approach has remained unchanged to this day. The models developed in the neoclassical tradition are thus independent of the historical situation of a country. Differences in national institutions, unique national or regional features, traditions or historical situations do not play a significant role here. Even economic policy is unimportant or of secondary importance for the long-term economic development of a country.

This viewpoint was most radically emphasised in the new classical model with its basic assumption of 'rational expectations' (see for example Muth 1961; Lucas 1973 and 1981; Barro 1974 or Sargent 1979). John Muth (1961: 316), the father of rational expectations, gave the definition: 'I would like to suggest that expectations, since they are informed predictions of future events, are essentially the same as the predictions of the relevant economic theory.' We have to savour this. It means that expectations disappear as independent variables from economic models as economic agents expect the equilibrium outcome of the economic model. For the model builder rational expectations are of great help. The proponents of this theory can build their models without being disturbed by such nasty problems as time and expectations. Economic models capture fundamentals and it is simply assumed that economic agents expect these fundamentals. In this way, expectations are made endogenous and at the same time removed as independent factors in explaining economic development.

Later Muth's model of rational expectations was made more complicated without changing its substance. It was argued, for example, that there is no perfect foresight and economic agents only in a probabilistic sense are able to predict future variables. However, the probabilities that are important for economic models are assumed to be objective probabilities. As probabilities of future events simply do not exist, past probabilities were used under the assumption that in a probabilistic sense developments in the future are identical with developments in the past – a perfect Newtonian world (Davidson 1991).

Different versions of rational expectations exist which also became the assumption behind the efficient financial market hypothesis (Fama 1970). First, it can be assumed that all economic agents have subjective probabilities and that these probabilities are all identical with the objective probabilities. In this case the subjective-probability distribution of economic actors is identical with the true objective-probability distribution of the economic system. Second, it can be accepted that some agents have wrong expectations. However, wrong expectations have normal distribution and cancel out. Third, it can even be assumed that wrong expectations are biased and do not have normal distribution. In this case the arbitrage processes of informed economic agents will realise the equilibrium and lead to the same result as if all economic agents had subjective probabilities identical to the objective probability. In any case, expectations of economic agents do not disturb the equilibrium given by the fundamentals of the economic model.

The twin of rational expectations is the microfoundation of macroeconomics. Microfoundation simply means that the rational optimisation of a representative agent, a household, a firm or a worker is analysed; the outcome of the optimisation is then set to be identical with the macroeconomic behaviour of all households, all firms or all workers.

This kind of model creation does not seem to be very plausible to us since there is no way in which all economic agents will attach credibility to the same economic model, nor, moreover, can their expectations be established on the basis of objective probabilities. Even experts in economics do not base their arguments on the same model and give different predictions about future economic development. The microfoundation of macroeconomics ignores one of the basic outcomes of macroeconomic thinking: the phenomenon that rational microeconomic behaviour of individuals can lead to suboptimal and even disastrous macroeconomic results. And there are plenty of examples to show that rational individual behaviour can lead to bad macroeconomic results (Shiller 1978; Palley 1996: 87ff.).

Neoclassical models and approaches in their tradition tend to stress the role of flexible and liberalised markets, good incentive structures, optimal allocation and innovation-friendly economic policy for economic development. Macroeconomic policies are considered to be of secondary importance. Macroeconomic polices should not disturb the microeconomic process of optimal allocation – this is the best macroeconomic policy can do. We are sceptical about such arguments. This is because improving allocation does not automatically lead to economic dynamics. If an economy is characterised by a lack of demand, a better allocation and even a jump in productivity will not increase GDP growth and employment – in fact, unemployment can be the result. Thus, a policy of allocation improvement and productivity increases leads to a dead-end when the macroeconomic constellation does not provide a sufficient increase in demand and output. This of course is not an argument against improving allocation and productivity. But there is no way around the recognition that without active and good macroeconomic policies, microeconomic improvements will become meagre in the end. And it also should be seen that high investment stimulates productivity as new technologies are nearly always incorporated in new investment goods.

Our rejection of 'Say's law', which assumes that the supply side of the economy determines output and creates sufficient aggregate demand, is reflected in this conclusion. The neoclassical postulate that there is a market between current savings and current net investment and that the interest-rate mechanism always channels all ex-ante savings into investment does not hold (Heine and Herr 2003). Output in most historical constellations, i.e. all constellations with unused capacities and unemployment, depends on aggregate goods demand and is not restricted by supply factors. If Say's law does not hold true, the neoclassical (and classical) dichotomy of the economy between a monetary sphere and a real sphere is not sustainable. We assume that money or monetary policy and economic policy in general are not neutral in the short, or in the long term.

New Keynesian economics, which has gained dominance in recent years at the expense of new classical thinking, assumed the concept of rational expectations and the microfoundation of economics. The difference between New Keynesians and new classical economists is that the former find imperfections on the microlevel, which disturb the economy. Such imperfections are based on rational behaviour and optimisation and, in this spirit, are part of markets. Such examples are: If menu costs exist to change price lists, prices may become sticky for some time and disturb the economy. If firms try to prevent shirking, they pay higher real wages than market wages to motivate employees or expose them to the risk of losing well paid jobs. If all companies follow such a strategy, the real wage level is above the equilibrium level and unemployment can result (efficiency wage theory). Given such imperfections, macroeconomic policy becomes important in the realisation of high employment – this is the important difference from the new classical model (Mankiw and Romer 1991). However, the New Keynesian model is completely different from the approach followed in this book.

In the following sections we analyse the different elements of the economic policy regime in detail. Our departure point is the financial system.

2.2 Financial system

2.2.1 Prototypes of financial systems

Financial systems can be regulated and function in completely different ways. We will present two prototypes.

Bank-based highly regulated financial systems

One extreme would be a bank-based regulated financial system under strict control of the central bank and the banking supervisory institution. In such a system, stock markets and capital markets in general play an as unimportant role as non-bank financial institutions of all types (investment banks, hedge funds, private equity funds, etc.) do. The financial system could be generally divided into commercial banks and non-bank financial institutions. There are also no or only a limited number of credit relationships between commercial banks and non-bank financial institutions, as commercial banks are not allowed to give credits to non-bank financial institutions. Commercial banks are also prohibited to hold shares. Such a regulation implies that there is a big wall between commercial banks, being the major source of finance for the firms, and more speculative and risk-oriented non-bank financial institutions. In addition, real estate financing could be considered a special case and allowed to be carried out only by special institutions. The real estate market can be made a special segment with regulated credit relationships with the rest of the financial system.

If non-bank financial institutions exist at all and if they want to attract funds for their businesses, they are forced to attract part of the monetary wealth held by households (or the public). Private wealth owners can keep their wealth in the form of bank deposits of different maturity or in the form of shares and debt-securities. Speculation in the stock market is generally limited because credits from commercial banks are not available and the real estate market is a special segment in the financial market. However, speculative activities can be undertaken by private households or by non-bank financial institutions, which attract a household's monetary wealth like saving accounts. Of course, households may suffer losses and even non-bank financial institutions may break down, but losses in the stock market have no systemic character.

Derivative markets do not exist or only to a very limited extent. For example, all derivatives are sold and bought in organised markets. Only certain products are allowed and only certain agents with licences can take part in the market.

The system creates sufficient funds for bold adventures as every household could directly or indirectly invest in risky businesses via non-bank financial institutions. That means investment projects that are considered too risky for commercial banks can obtain funds from non-bank financial institutions.

Commercial banks and insurance companies are more strictly regulated than other financial institutions. The key argument is that these institutions hold deposits or insure risks that are of paramount importance for the majority of citizens and for the stability and coherence of the economy and society. The most common regulation of banks is to force them to keep a certain percentage of the loans they grant as equity. This restricts their credit expansion. The most common regulation of insurance companies is to strictly regulate the quality of assets they are allowed to buy. Credit for speculation, as for all non-bank financial institutions, is also not allowed for insurance companies.

In a highly regulated financial system the central bank could use credit controls as the main policy instrument to directly control the credit volume of the banking system. Interest rate policy plays a subordinate role in such a system. The central bank could even fix banks' deposit rate to prevent de-stabilising competition in the financial system. Also lending rates could be controlled by the central bank (Hellmann *et al.* 2000). In such a system the central bank would determine the rate at which the credit volume of the banking system, and accordingly of every bank, is allowed to increase. Under such a rule a single bank has an incentive to utilise the given room for credit expansion – otherwise it would lose its market share during the next round of credit expansion.

In addition, the allocation of credit can be regulated. For example, loans to the real estate sector can be quantitatively restricted. Under this condition real estate bubbles become very unlikely and easy to control. The same can happen for credit to consumers or credits for speculative purposes in the stock market and to non-bank financial institutions. Within such a framework credit allocation can be left to commercial banks. They decide which enterprises get credit and which ones do not; they finance innovative entrepreneurs and they decide to stop giving loans to loss-making enterprises that consequently go bankrupt. Such a system is perfectly compatible with a hard budget constraint that is typical for capitalist economies.

In the financial system too much competition can lead to risky behaviour. Banks in a very competitive environment have the incentive to follow an aggressive and risky business strategy to defend or increase their market share. Within the scope of a highly regulated financial system, however, competition among commercial banks is limited as it is not possible for them to compete via interest rates for deposits from other banks and to expand faster than competitor banks.

Obviously this type of financial system implies strict capital inflow controls. Otherwise credit ceilings fixed by the central bank can be penetrated by foreign credit inflow. Capital inflow controls are also desirable to prevent asset price bubbles in the real estate sector and the stock market, which may both be stimulated by foreign investment.[7]

The banking system outlined above is not imaginary. It existed in different versions in all East Asian miracle countries (Japan, South Korea, Malaysia, Taiwan, etc.) after the Second World War (Stiglitz 1996; Stiglitz and Uy 1996). In Japan, for example, this system was only abolished in the early 1990s. The Chinese financial system after 1978, when the reform process started, equally fits the financial system described.[8] Even without any relevant non-bank financial institutions and without derivative markets, there is no doubt that a bank-based highly regulated financial system can support high GDP growth or even become the most important engine for a long-term growth process.[9] It offers sufficient and cheap credit for the enterprise sector and thus stimulates growth and employment. This task can be perfectly fulfilled without assigning an important role to stock markets, investment funds of all types or derivative markets.

Of course window guidance systems of the above type lead to credit rationing. There are unsatisfied credit demanders and the interest rate will not equalise credit demand and credit supply. However, such an ideal equilibrium case never exists as banks always ration credit even in the most extremely market-based financial systems (Stiglitz and Greenwald 2003).[10] If we have this in mind, financial systems with window guidance look much less anti-market than initially thought.

The financial system becomes more liberalised when the central bank only sets the refinancing rate in the money market and allows commercial banks to decide about the credit volume. Under such conditions it is more difficult for central banks to control credit volumes. For example, they may have to increase interest rates to very high levels to slow down credit expansion. However, contrary to the liberalised system (see below), as long as all of the other regulations are in place there is at least no conflict between consumer price inflation/deflation and asset price inflation/deflation. Credit expansion and credit contraction of commercial banks is focused on the enterprise sector and there is no direct channel from central bank refinancing via credit expansion of commercial banks to speculative activities. After the Second World War the US and the UK had financial systems along these lines. Of special importance in the US was the Glass–Steagall Act from the early 1930s, which separated commercial banking from investment banking.[11] Real estate financing was also highly regulated. In the US, for example, banks which gave mortgage loans could sell these loans to a state-owned bank, the Federal National Mortgage Association (Fannie Mae) that was founded in 1938 by US President F.D. Roosevelt to support housing for a large part of the population. Fannie Mae could indirectly control the quality of mortgage loans by not buying subprime loans. It also regulated the quantity of real estate credit by fixing the quantity of loans it bought from mortgage banks (for real estate markets see Cardarelli *et al.* 2008).

In continental Europe a different type of a highly regulated financial system existed. Compared with the Anglo-Saxon financial system after the Second World War commercial banks were permitted to invest directly in asset markets, like stock markets, and were principally allowed to carry out all types of businesses in the financial markets. In these so-called universal banking systems investment banks, hedge funds and other risk-oriented institutions more or less did not exist. Commercial banks were strictly controlled; an unregulated shadow banking system could not develop. Competition among financial institutions in these systems was usually low. In addition, a long-term orientation of banks using shareholding and credit expansion to influence the long-term strategies of big companies dominated. Real estate financing was largely taken over by special non-bank financial institutions like building societies. Originators did not sell their credits in secondary markets. Households could speculate in stock markets, but speculation was limited.

Liberalised financial system

The contrary extreme is an extensively market-based system, which we call a liberalised financial system. In such a system non-bank financial institutions like investment banks, private-equity funds and hedge funds play an important role. Firms finance themselves in the capital market by issuing debt-securities and shares. There is no segmentation in the financial system. Commercial banks and non-bank financial institutions engage in all types of activities. There is no restriction for commercial banks to give credit to non-bank financial institutions, speculators and real estate investors or to consumers. The difference between commercial banks and other financial institutions becomes blurred as non-bank financial institutions take over the function of commercial banks and commercial banks expand in any business they want.

There are close interrelations between commercial banks that interact with the central bank and non-bank financial institutions. Non-bank financial institutions can get credit from commercial banks to invest in the real estate sector or in the stock market. For example, a private equity firm can take huge amounts of credit from commercial banks to take over a firm, cut it into pieces, sell them for a profit and pay back the loan. Hedge funds, to give another example, can take credit from commercial banks and speculate with extreme leverage. Commercial banks can sell their credit given to firms and households to non-bank financial institutions. By transferring credits including the default risk of their debtors to other institutions commercial banks then become more brokers than banks. As the banks sell credit they do not use as much of their equity during a phase of credit expansion as they might otherwise, and can go on expanding credit and selling it without any hard equity constraint.

In a liberal financial system non-bank financial institutions are traditionally not as strictly regulated as commercial banks. This also means that compared with a regulated system a bigger part of the financial system has no or a low level of regulation. A so-called shadow banking system expands. Non-bank financial institutions are – partly, but not only as a result of laxer regulation – more risk- and speculation-oriented than commercial banks. They can use very high leverage to finance their activities.

Compared with the bank-based regulated financial system, in liberal financial systems there is an additional layer. The accordion of credit expansion and credit contraction is much more complex in such a system. During a period of credit expansion not only do the commercial banks give additional credits to firms and households and increase their leverage, they also give credit to non-bank financial institutions, which increase their leverage too, grant credit to all kinds of economic units and engage in speculative activities. During an expansion the credit accordion pumps enormous amounts of air (credit) into its lungs. Leverages of all agents increase. During periods of credit contraction the opposite takes place. In such a case financial institutions reduce their leverage and ration credit, as uncertainty is high. Institutions with high leverage break down and the financial system comes under stress (Minsky 1975, 1982).

Derivative markets are future markets and play an important role in liberalised financial systems. In asset markets expectations drive spot prices. If, for example, most agents believe that share prices will fall, they will do so. In the extreme case of a change in expectations of all agents in the same direction, prices will change even without any transaction. If, for example, all agents expect that share prices will fall by 20 per cent, all of them will try to sell shares. As there is no buyer, the price of shares will immediately fall by 20 per cent in spite of the fact that no shareholder is able to sell her or his shares. This mechanism explains the quantitatively big and very abrupt changes of prices in all asset markets. Derivative markets express all market expectations about the future. This also implies that price changes in derivative markets will move prices in spot markets. This effect may be significant as agents in derivative markets usually use a very high leverage and derivative markets consequently have huge volumes. All types of assets can become the object of speculation in future markets: shares, currencies, natural resources like oil and gold or even food.

In liberal financial systems extensive credit expansion and credit contraction are accompanied by asset price inflation, followed by asset price deflation. Asset markets are characterised by a low price elasticity of supply. If, for example, the share price goes up, there is an incentive by firms to issue new shares. However, the amount of newly issued shares will be relatively small. To give another example, high real estate prices without a doubt stimulate the construction industry. But the reaction will be slow. A period of high real estate prices in the medium and long term typically leads to a construction boom and later even to overcapacities in the real estate sector, but this takes several years. In contrast to supply, the demand for assets can change quickly and substantially. Also, after an increase in prices, the rise in gold production or the production of oil and even wheat needs time. There are two sources of sudden jumps in demand in asset markets. First, especially private wealth owners and non-bank financial institutions keep huge portfolios of monetary and other wealth. These enormous stocks of wealth can be shifted from liquidity holdings (short-term time deposits, money market papers, short-term government bonds, etc.) to long-term investment (shares, real estate, etc.) and back. These are exactly the portfolio shifts Keynes (1930b: 127ff.) pointed out. Second, private wealth owners and non-bank financial institutions can tap the commercial banking system to take credit and buy assets. In this case the central bank finances commercial banks and the latter private wealth owners and non-bank financial institutions and all agents can buy and later sell assets. Taking portfolio shifts and credit expansion together, it is obvious that demand for assets can potentially change in such a way that huge asset price bubbles and the disastrous asset price deflations that follow are possible.

It could be argued that asset prices are driven by objective fundamentals. According to the financial market efficiency hypothesis investors evaluate the value of an asset, for example a share, by calculating the net present value of the future cash flows produced by the asset. The cash flows will be discounted with a risk-adjusted discount rate to calculate the asset price. Let us use the following example: the price of shares of a steel factory is calculated by estimating all future net cash flows which can be expected from the operation of the steel factory, let us say for the next 30 years. As a discount rate the long-term interest rate for government bonds plus a specific risk premium for the steel factory is used. According to the efficient financial market hypothesis all agents will make this calculation and come to the same result on the basis of objective probabilities or at least mistakes by agents will cancel each other out or will be eliminated by arbitrage. But, asset markets have no anchor in fundamentals. It is not possible to calculate the future cash flow of a long-term investment project in an objective way, as there is simply no information available which could tell us the future. And the past is not a good guide for future developments. Who believes that the performance of steel factories in the last 30 years would deliver a good basis for finding out what would happen in the next 30 years? Expectations are subjective and the probability apparatus in many cases does not work even in calculating subjective probabilities. In addition, expectations depend on more than economic factors and can fluctuate between optimism and pessimism (see above).

This allows us to understand a typical asset price bubble: expectations become more and more optimistic – in some cases due to economic factors like a new innovation or a shortage of housing, in other cases due to political factors, in again other cases because of no plausible explanation – and asset prices increase. Irrational exuberance, as Shiller (2001) called it, can lead to portfolio shifts and a credit expansion that drives asset prices to unsustainable levels. A cumulative cycle starts. Credit expansion increases asset prices; at the same time higher asset prices increase the value of collateral, which stimulates even cautious creditors to grant additional credit. Increasing asset prices also raise the equity of financial institutions, which furthermore stimulates additional credit expansion. This can happen even without speculation and despite a long-term orientation of economic agents. However, during a period of increasing asset prices short-term oriented speculation typically sets in and drives asset prices to even higher levels. Derivative markets move future markets and drive the speculation.

The end of a bubble can be triggered by restrictive monetary policy, overcapacities, factors which lay beyond the economic sphere or by unknown factors.[12] The combination of high leverages of economic units and asset price deflations has disastrous effects. An asset price deflation reduces the value of the assets of firms, banks and private households and destroys collateral and equity. Distress selling of assets leads to a cumulative asset price deflation and makes the situation worse. Typically, a liquidity and insolvency crisis spreads. Bankruptcies of firms and private households create non-performing loans in the banking system. An asset price deflation can thus change a healthy financial system into one with unsustainably high non-performing loans overnight. As mentioned before, in a sharp asset price deflation a credit crunch is unavoidable as equity of financial institutions as well as collateral of debtors is destroyed and the level of uncertainty increases. Real GDP drops and unemployment increases. These two factors lead to additional non-performing loans and a further reduction of output and employment. Even a goods market deflation may be triggered by the asset price deflation. This story of bubbles and their consequences is not new. Fisher (1933) and Kindleberger (1996) have told it as forcefully as Minsky (1975, 1982).

The central bank in a liberalised financial system has a relatively weak position. It has only one policy instrument at its disposal, the refinancing rate in the money market. The credit volume as well as the volume of central bank money is determined endogenously. Of course, the central bank can change its refinancing rate to influence credit volumes or the volume of central bank money, but this is a difficult task. A cut in interest rates may not lead to credit expansion; a rather slight increase in interest rates may not lead to the wanted reduction in credit volumes. However, a central bank can theoretically increase interest rates to astronomic levels to stop credit expansion. In this sense restrictive monetary policy always works. But expansionary monetary policy can fail, as even a zero-interest-rate policy is not a sufficient condition to stimulate credit expansion.

There is an additional fundamental problem for central banks in a liberalised financial system: they have no control over the structure of credit allocation. We do not mean here that the central bank cannot decide to give credit to a car manufacturer A or to a chemical factory B. We mean that the central bank cannot avoid asset price bubbles in the real estate sector, the stock market, the market of natural resources or an unsustainable consumption-credit boom. Central banks in a liberal financial system simply cannot prevent the commercial banking system from expanding credit to consumers and/or highly risk and speculative oriented non-bank financial institutions that invest in asset markets and create or substantially add to bubbles. Monetary policy is confronted with dilemmas. Asset price inflations can develop in a constellation of low consumer price inflation, low GDP growth and high unemployment. Interest rate policy, which fights against asset price inflations in such a constellation, may lead to a recession and even goods market deflation. It is also possible that an asset price deflation has to be fought by the central bank by cutting interest rates to very low levels. This can trigger a new asset price bubble, which then is difficult to control by the central bank. In a liberalised financial system central banks are confronted with much more market-based shocks than in a regulated financial system and at the same time have fewer instruments to stabilise the economy.

2.2.2 The type of financial system prevailing today

During and after the Great Depression in the 1930s a regulated type of capitalism was introduced – in the US this was formally called the New Deal, but in modified versions it was created in all capitalist states. After the Second World War, in addition to domestic regulations the Bretton Woods System was established and gave the western world a stable institutional framework. The Bretton Woods System broke down at the end of the 1960s/early 1970s. Many western countries suffered in the 1970s from high inflation rates and currency crises. The UK and the US were two of these countries. The governments in power at that time could not solve the economic turbulences during this period, which also led to political turbulences. The development in the 1970s formed the basis for the political success of radical conservative governments. In 1979 Margret Thatcher became Prime Minister in the UK and in 1980 Ronald Reagan was elected

President of the US. Both politicians had a radical neoliberal reform agenda, which was immediately enforced. Later, more or less all western countries followed these neoliberal reforms. From the 1970s a neoliberal type of globalisation developed which shaped the world economy that exists today. Key elements of the neoliberal agenda were the deregulation of domestic and international financial markets and the deregulation of labour markets (Dullien *et al.* 2009).

The International Monetary Fund constructs a financial reform index to measure the degree of liberalisation of financial markets. Figure 2.2 shows the development of the index since 1973. It comprises seven dimensions of financial regulation with equal weight, namely credit controls and reserve requirements, interest rate controls, entry barriers to the banking sector, banking supervision, privatisation, international capital flows and the development of security markets. An index value of zero would refer to a completely regulated financial system; an index value of one gives a completely deregulated system. From the Figure it becomes clear that in the early 1970s in the US, in the UK, in Japan and in Germany financial systems were relatively strictly regulated. During the 1970s and 1980s this changed quickly, whereas the Japanese financial system was deregulated somewhat later than the other countries. It is also noteworthy that the US and the UK switched to completely liberalised financial systems in

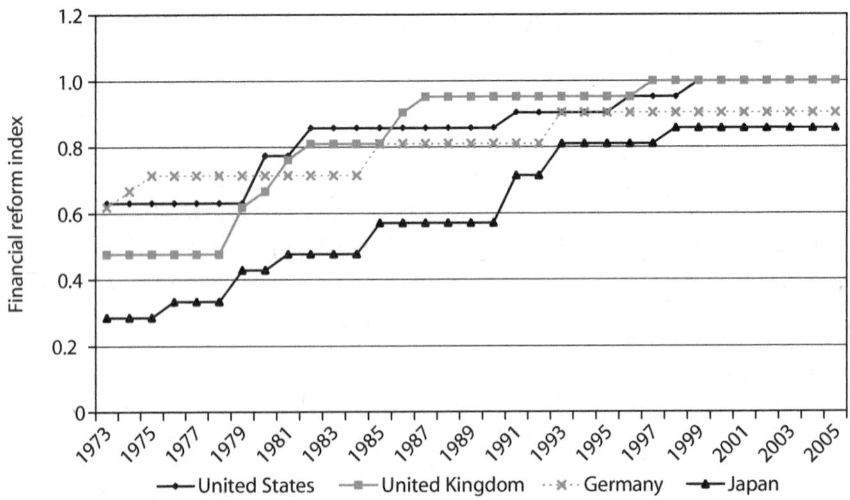

Figure 2.2 Financial Reform Index for the US, UK, Japan and Germany, 1973–2005[1] (source: Abdul *et al.* 2008, also see IMF 2010a).

Note

1 The index is an aggregate index of seven dimensions of financial regulation, namely credit controls and reserve requirements, interest rate controls, entry barriers to the banking sector, banking supervision, privatisation, international capital flows, and development of security markets. Each of the dimensions was given a score on a 0–3 scale. Assigning equal weight to each dimension, the sum of the seven components was normalised to be between 0 and 1.

the late 1990s, whereas Japan and Germany still have a slightly less deregulated financial market. In all four countries the deregulation wave in the financial system is a major institutional change and a prime example of neoliberal Ordnungspolitik.

The financial system that has been developing over the past 30 years more or less fits the liberalised financial system described above. Important elements of the new systems are: an increasing role of non-bank financial institutions, a greater role of securitisation, financial innovations and the explosion of derivative markets.

Due to financial deregulation non-bank financial institutions became more and more important and the traditional banking system lost importance. In Anglo-Saxon countries the previously existing wall between commercial banks and non-bank financial institutions broke down. In countries with universal banking systems non-bank financial institutions, which had been unimportant or even non-existent, started to play a bigger and bigger role. In addition, sheltered segments of the financial market like the real estate sector had become fully integrated in the financial market, and a shadow banking system had flourished and become an important part of the financial system (see Figure 2.3).

Agents in the shadow-banking sector are highly risk loving, have a speculative orientation, look for high short-term returns and work partly with extreme leverages. As analysed, in the case of the liberalised financial system these agents can not only use their own huge stocks of monetary wealth to speculate. Furthermore they can tap the commercial banking system to mobilise additional huge funds for investment in the financial sphere.

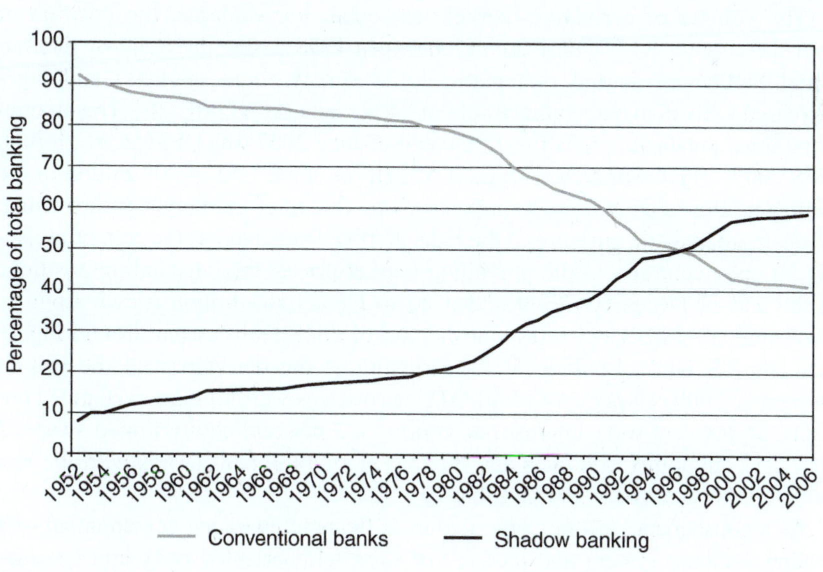

Figure 2.3 The development of the shadow banking system in the US, 1950–2007 (source: Krugman 2009).

In the shadow banking system securitisation plays an important role. Securitisation is a very old financial instrument and as such harmless. It simply means that a credit is sold in the secondary market to another agent and that the originator of the credit does not hold the credit until it is paid back. Securitisation exploded after the 1970s: especially firms preferred to hold short-term money market papers instead of bank deposits, economic units of all types issued debt securities to finance themselves and banks sold credits they originated to non-bank financial institutions. Securitisation led to a bulk of financial innovation. For example, a number of debts, be they of one type (for example only real estate debts) or of different types (for example real estate debts and credit card debts), were pooled. Cash flows of debt pools were carved into different tranches with different default risks. In asset-backed securities, for example, the so-called waterfall principle was used, which implies that in case part of the cash flow does not materialise, the so-called equity tranche first has to bear the losses, then the next tranche and so on. The distance between the originator and the final holder of the debt became greater and greater as several levels of pooling and carving up of cash flows became popular. Rating agencies, a cartel of three private firms without government supervision, took over the function of evaluating the quality of such papers.

Derivatives can reduce the risk of asset price changes including those in foreign exchange markets, the risk of interest rate changes and default risks. The problem with these markets is that while they reduce the risk of one of the trading partners, they increase the risk of the contract partner, as in nearly all of the cases the contract partner is a speculator. Most contracts must even be considered contracts between speculators.

The volume of derivative markets exploded. For example, the position of over-the-counter (OTC) derivatives[13] between 1998 (when the Bank of International Settlement started systematically to survey these markets) and 2007 increased with an average annual rate of 24 per cent (BIS 2007: 20). The amount of notional outstanding position at the end of June 2007 was US$516,411 billion (BIS 2007: 21). Compared with the US GDP of about US$14,000 billion in the same year this is an extremely high sum. Looking at gross market values which give a more realistic measure of the risks involved and express the cost of replacing all open contracts at the prevailing market prices, the outstanding positions at the end of December 2009 added up to US$21,583 billion (down from its maximum of US$32,375 billion at the end of 2008), still a sum around bigger than the US GDP. Looking at the structure of the derivatives at the end of December 2009, 10 per cent of all OTC derivatives were foreign exchange contracts, 65 per cent were interest rate contracts, 3 per cent equity-linked swaps, 3 per cent commodity contracts and 8 per cent credit default swaps with the rest being unallocated (BIS 2010b: Table 19).

As a consequence of the deregulation of financial markets, development of a shadow banking system and increase of short-term oriented risky and speculative transactions, asset price bubbles in all kinds of asset markets with partly disastrous economic consequences have become more frequent and much graver.

At the same time the indebtedness in most economies in the world has increased substantially – a trend that follows Minsky's logic of higher leverages during the build-up of a bubble. What we see is a development of a kind of super-bubble over a period of several decades (Soros 2008). Let us look at some instructive indicators of the countries we have chosen as case studies.

Figure 2.4 shows the stock market indices of the four countries, which are the focus of our analysis. In Japan in the second half of the 1980s a huge stock market bubble developed, which came to an end in 1990. Share prices in Japan have never again reached the level they had exhibited before the collapse in the 1990s. Share-price development in the US, in the UK and in Germany has been more or less similar. In the 1980s share prices started to increase substantially. However, the increase in stock markets in the 1980s was nothing compared with the stock market inflations that followed. In the 1990s – the years of the Internet bubble – stories about a new area with jumps in productivity and profits were told until the bubble imploded in the early 2000s. A few years later the next bubble started without a 'plausible' explanation and came to an end together with the subprime crisis in 2007.

Under the rules of liberalised financial markets, real estate prices also became unstable. Beginning in the 1960s real estate prices in Japan increased permanently. In the second half of the 1980s the increase escalated and a bubble developed. The real estate bubble came to an end in 1991 and was followed by a long period of falling real estate prices, which in 2007 reached levels comparable with the early 1970s (see Figure 2.5). In the US (see Figure 2.6) real estate prices were stable from the late 1980s to the late 1990s, as well as in earlier

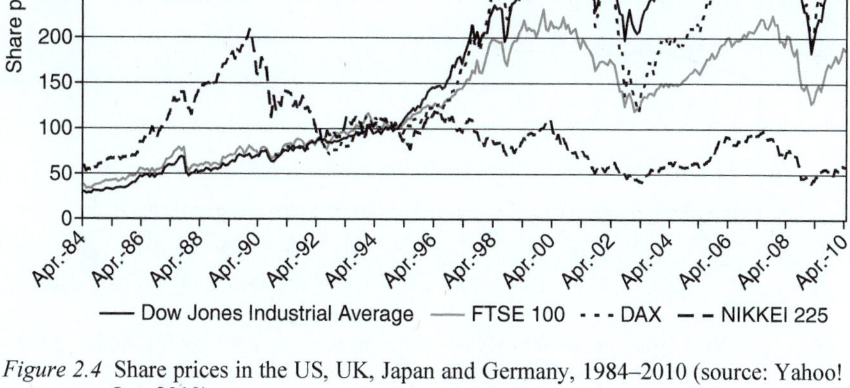

Figure 2.4 Share prices in the US, UK, Japan and Germany, 1984–2010 (source: Yahoo! Inc. 2010).

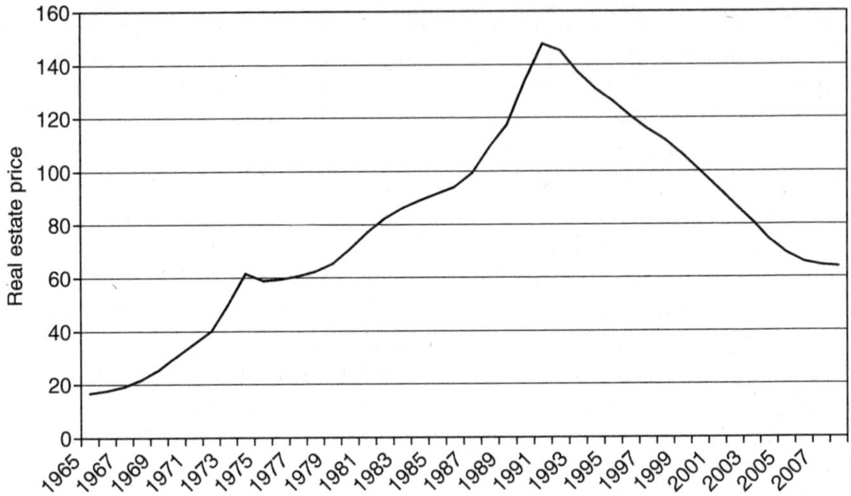

Figure 2.5 Real estate prices in Japan, 1965–2008 (2000 = 100)[1] (source: Japan Real Estate Institute (2009).

Note
1 Urban land price index, total average.

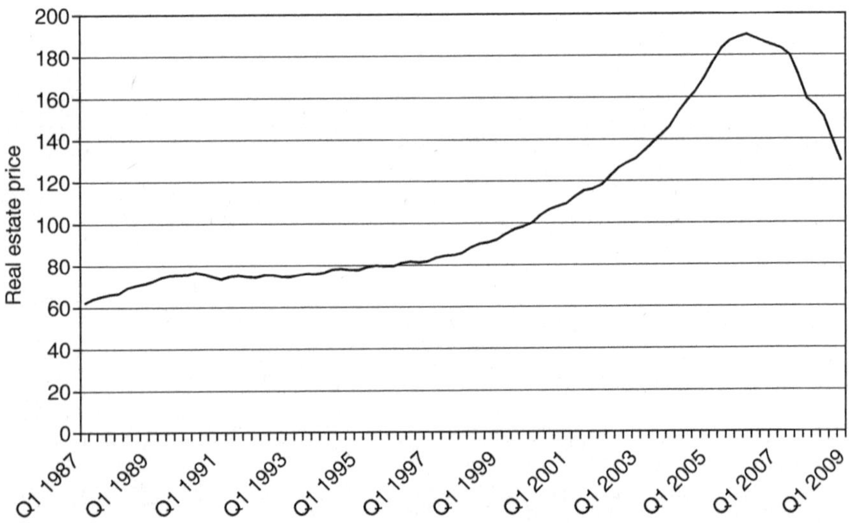

Figure 2.6 Real estate prices for private homes in the US, 1987-2009 (January 2000 = 100) (source: S&P/Case-Shiller Home Price Indices (Composite-10 CSXR) (2009)).

decades (Shiller 2008). Then a bubble started to develop which gained speed after 2003. The result was the subprime mortgage crisis that broke out in 2007 and triggered plummeting real estate prices in the US. The UK (see Figure 2.7) experienced high increases of real estate prices in the late 1980s. However, this was very moderate compared with the explosion of real estate prices that began in the late 1990s. As in the US, the real estate bubble drew to an end with the subprime crisis. In Germany on the other hand increasing real estate prices were recorded in the whole of the 1980s and especially in the early 1990s when Germany experienced the unification boom (see Figure 2.8), but the real estate prices stabilised in the mid-1990s and even fell moderately. In the 2000s Germany did not suffer from a real estate bubble.

It has been mentioned that future markets for natural resources and food can also be used for speculative purposes. Figure 2.9 shows this for the price of oil. The two oil price shocks in 1973 and 1979 were to a large extent caused by the OPEC cartel, which was able to exploit the high oil demand in the 1970s for price increases. In the second half of the 1980s oil prices dropped and remained at this level until around 2000. Afterwards, oil prices increased again and reached extremely high levels, peaking in 2007, and then falling off again. The volatility of oil prices in the 2000s is clearly connected with the speculation of agents who previously had not massively taken part in oil speculation. As dramatic as the oil price volatility in the 2000s was the volatility of food prices.

Financial systems can create credit for different economic sectors, which then become indebted. In Table 2.1 the development of the indebtedness of the non-financial corporation sector, the private household sector (including non government organisations, NGOs) and the total government sector in percentage of

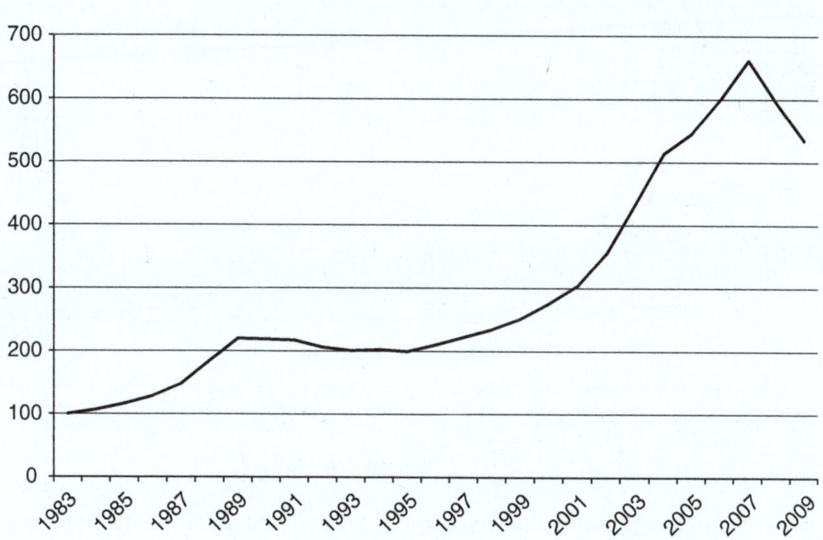

Figure 2.7 Real estate prices in the UK, Q4 1952–Q3 2009 (1954 = 100) (source: Nationwide Building Society 2009).

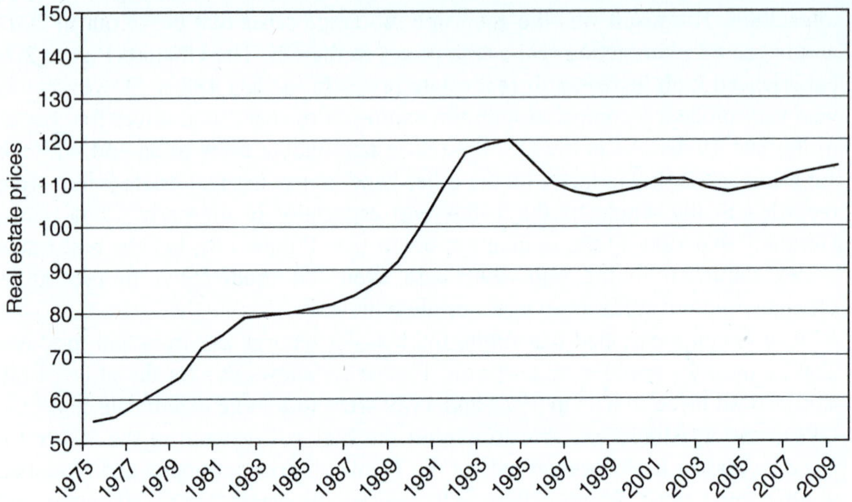

Figure 2.8 Real estate prices in Germany, 1975–2009 (1990 = 100) (source: BulwienGesa AG 2009).

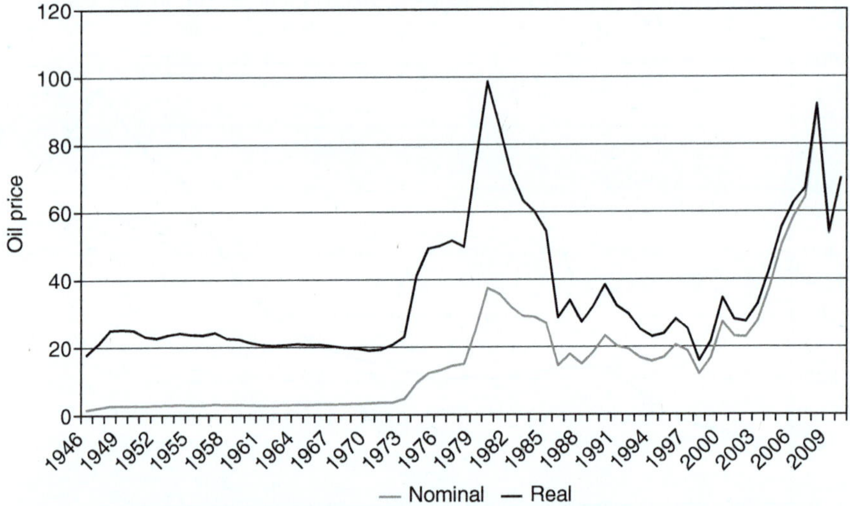

Figure 2.9 Development of the oil price in US dollars, 1946–2009[1] (source: Financial Trend Forecaster 2010).

Note

1 Real price adjusted by US inflation rate.

GDP is shown for the US, the UK, Germany and Japan. The figures show annual averages during the business cycles whereas the cycle is measured as usual in GDP development.[14] The general picture is that indebtedness over the decades in all countries shown increased substantially, sometimes even in an extreme way. We can argue that the deregulation of financial systems starting in the 1970s produced a credit expansion for almost all sectors in all countries. Following Hymen Minsky (1975: 124) it could be argued that the credit expansion reflects that households, firms and financial institutions during a period of credit expansion 'undertake ever more adventuresome position-making activity' and a 'layering of debts occurs' (p. 123). We could argue that a long-term economic boom or even a bubble developed from the 1970s to the subprime crisis at the end of the 2000s. George Soros (2008: 81) speaks about a super-bubble, which developed after the 1970s leading to higher and higher debt quotas (also see Palley 2009). In his model Minsky thought that during a boom phase with higher credit quotas GDP growth would be higher. It actually can be shown that in boom periods of asset markets – for example during the dot.com bubble in the 1990s or the real estate bubble in the 2000s – credit and GDP growth were high and in periods of recessions credit expansion came to an end or even decreased (see the case studies). However, what we see here is an over-cyclical increase in debt quotas, which was not combined with especially high GDP growth at least compared with the 1950s and 1960s. Let us look at the debt quotas in greater detail.

The debt of non-financial corporations in percentage of GDP increased in all countries. In Japan the level of debt is the highest reflecting a bank-based financial system. In such systems firms can afford high debt rations as house banks are closely affiliated with the firms and guarantee stable financing. This also explains why non-financial firms in Germany have a relatively high debt level. In the US, with a more capital-based system providing more equity, debt ratios are at a lower level, although they have increased sharply in recent decades. The UK also has a capital-based financial system. It is astonishing that the non-financial corporate sector in the UK has a very high debt level, comparable with Japan.

Households' debt to GDP also increased in all countries. However, there are big differences. Debt ratios of households are high in the US and in the UK. After the 1970s and especially during the 2000s household debt exploded. Here we can clearly see the households' credit-driven expansions. Real estate credits that led to the subprime crisis but also credit card and consumption credits played a vital role in stimulating GDP growth in these two countries. In Japan households' credits increased especially during the Japanese bubble in the second half of the 1980s. However, in the 1990s and 2000s there was no further increase in households' credit in percentage of GDP. Germany shows the lowest indebtedness of households and only very small increases in household debt quotas. The high increase in households' credit in the US and in the UK and the stagnation of household credit in Germany and Japan very much fit the relatively high GDP growth in the two former countries and the relatively low growth in the two latter countries.

Table 2.1 Indebtedness of different economic sectors in percentage of GDP in the US, the UK, Japan and Germany, 1971–2009

		Yearly averages in business cycles in (%)				
USA	Business cycles	1971–1975	1976–1982	1983–1991	1992–2001	2002–2009
	General government	46.5	44.7	59.5	66.2	64.8
	Non-financial business	75.4	93.2	106.0	109.0	125.2
	Private households and NGOs	46.8	49.8	59.0	69.8	94.8
UK	Business cycles	1971–1975	1976–1981	1982–1991[1]	1992–2002	2003–2009
	General government	66.7	55.7	45.1	44.4	47.1
	Non-financial business	–	–	199.5	243.9	258.5
	Private households and NGOs	–	–	70.0	74.7	103.1
Germany	Business cycles	1971–1975	1976–1982	1983–1993[2]	1994–2003	2004–2009
	General government	19.2	29.8	40.6	58.5	67.5
	Non-financial business	–	–	111.9	149.3	167.1
	Private households and NGOs	–	–	55.5	69.0	66.3
Japan	Business cycles	1971–1974	1975–1986	1987–1993	1994–1999	2000–2009
	General government	15.5	50.7	71.5	106.4	173.4
	Non-financial business	168.9	196.0	312.1	282.1	262.4
	Private households and NGOs	41.5	55.2	74.9	84.7	81.7

Source: AMECO (2010); authors' calculations based on Federal Reserve Flow of Funds Accounts database (2010), UK Office for National Statistics Economic Accounts database (2010), Deutsche Bundesbank time series database (2010), Bank of Japan Flow of Funds database (2010).

Notes

1 Averages for non-financial business and private households & NGOs only refer to data from 1987–1991.

2 Averages for non-financial business and private households & NGOs only refer to data from 1991–1993

Also, general government credit increased in all four countries. An extreme increase of the ratio government debt to GDP can be found in Japan, jumping from about 16 per cent in the early 1970s to over 200 per cent at the end of the 2000s. This mainly reflects the Japanese stagnation after the bubbles in the second half of the 1980s. Germany also increased public debt to GDP substantially to over 70 per cent, albeit not comparable with Japan. In the US government debt to GDP has had about the same level as in Germany in the 2000s, however, the US started from a level of a higher public debt in the 1970s. Public debt in the UK is relatively low and expressed in percentage of GDP has only increased moderately over the past decades. However, in the UK the double-digit budget deficits in percentage of GDP in 2009 and 2010 also increased public debt quotas quickly. The medium-term increase in public debt, which is most pronounced in Japan and also Germany, reflects the low growth rates in these countries, which drove public households into budget deficits. Overall, the increase in public debt to GDP in all countries has to be seen as the outcome of an unsatisfactory development of the economy, which has been compensated by growing budget deficits.

2.3 Foreign economic policy

2.3.1 Institutional changes

The international economic system depends fundamentally on global institutions and the way the global economy is governed. In the international sphere the dominant feature of the 1970s was the breakdown of the Bretton Woods System, closely connected with the deregulation of international capital flows. In addition, in the decades after the Second World War the international monetary system has been changing from complete dominance of the US dollar to a system with more intensive currency competition. In the following we discuss one point at a time.

The breakdown of the Bretton Woods System

The Bretton Woods System, which was bargained in 1944 by the victors of the Second World War, gave western members of the world economy a stable framework. It was a system with fixed but adjustable exchange rates. Capital flows between the developed countries were to a large extent also controlled. The US dollar became the centre of the system as all members of the Bretton Woods System except the US pegged their exchange rates with a narrow band to the US currency. The system was also strengthened by the promise of the US to exchange US dollar reserves of central banks into gold at a fixed conversion rate. Exchange rates during the 1950s and 1960s were stable. After the breakdown of the Bretton Woods System, exchange rate shocks became widespread (see Figure 2.10). Not only did nominal exchange rates start to fluctuate widely, real exchange rates also became unstable (see Figure 2.11). Under the Bretton Woods

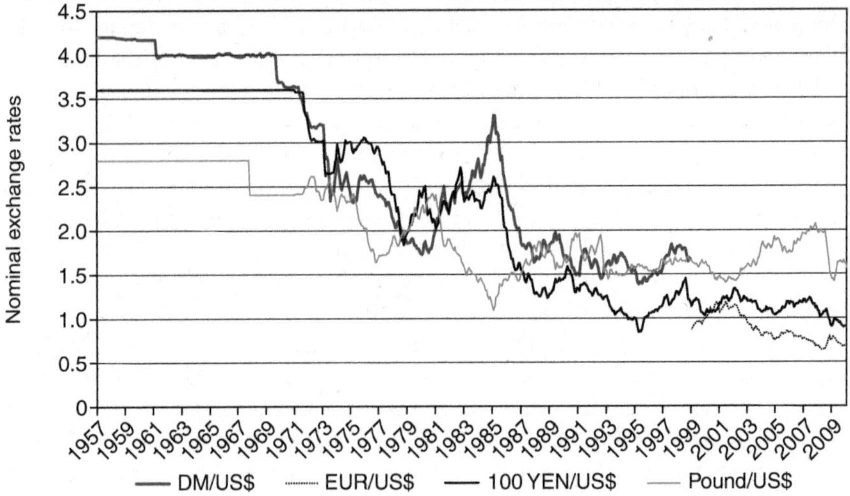

Figure 2.10 Exchange rate movements between the US dollar, Japanese yen, British pound and German mark, 1957–2009 (from 1999 euro)[1] (source: Federal Reserve Bank of St Louis 2010).

Note
1 Increase means appreciation of US dollar.

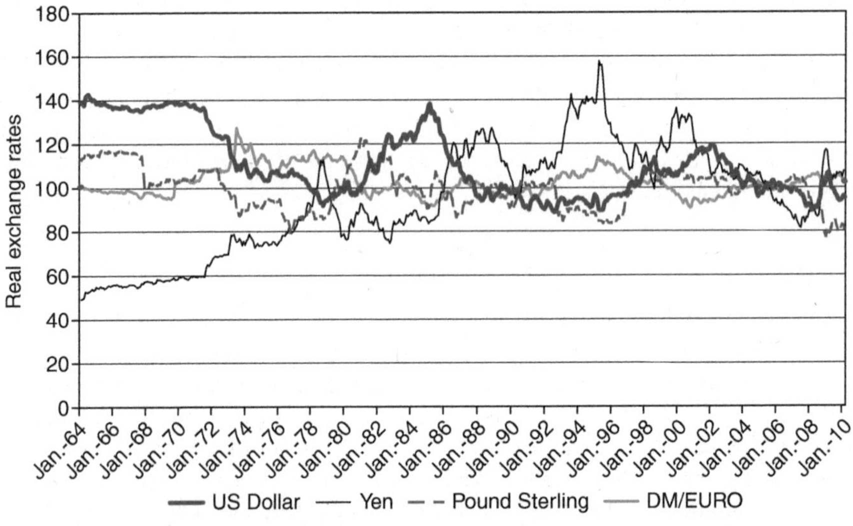

Figure 2.11 Index of real exchange rate movements of US dollar, British pound, Japanese yen and German mark, January 1964–January 2010[1] (from 1999 euro) (source: BIS 2010a).

Note
1 Increase means appreciation.

System some countries realised moderate permanent current account surpluses. Germany is one of the clearest cases for this. The US, the UK and Japan had more or less balanced current accounts during the time the system was in place. Huge current account imbalances typical for the decades after the breakdown of the Bretton Woods System were unknown in the period before (see Figure 2.12).

Underlying all of these developments stands the liberalisation of international capital flows. In its 'Annual Report on Exchange Arrangements and Exchange Restrictions' (IMF 2010a) the International Monetary Fund surveys changes in restrictions of international capital flows and calculates a capital control index.[15] A one in the index would be a completely closed country for capital flows, a zero a completely open country for capital flows. At the end of the 1960s the index for industrial countries was around 0.5 and slowly decreased during the 1970s. From the end of the 1970s deregulation steps became faster and the capital flows in industrial countries became nearly completely liberalised by the 1990s. Traditionally, southern European countries had more capital controls (the index was around 0.8 until the early 1980s, reduced to 0.6 in the 1980s and dropped sharply in the first half of the 1990s). For developing countries the picture is different. The index for all developing countries was slightly above 0.5 during the 1970s, increased to around 0.6 in the 1980s and started to drop very quickly only in the early 1990s (Alfaro 2002: Figures 1 and 2). The UK, Germany and Japan all liberalised their international capital flows during the 1970s, the US even earlier (see Abdul *et al.* 2008: index on international capital flows).

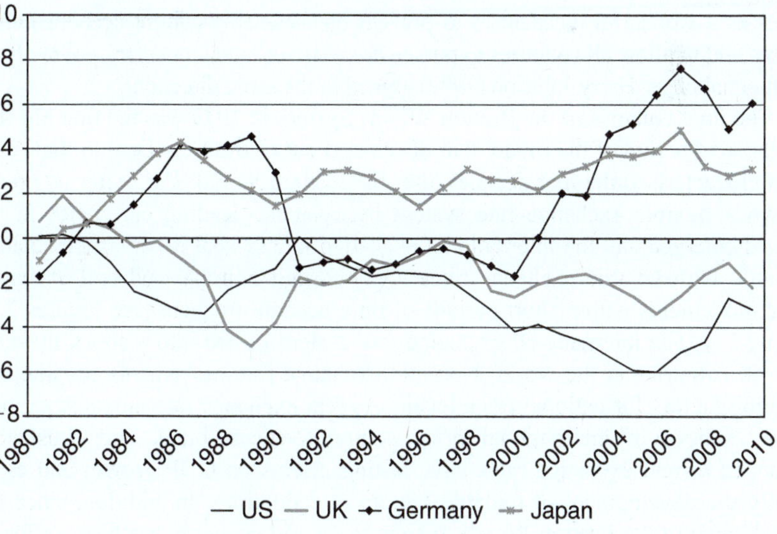

Figure 2.12 Current account balances of the US, the UK, Japan and Germany in percentage of GDP, 1980–2009 (source: OECD (2009c); authors' calculations).

Looking at transactions on foreign exchange markets (see Table 2.2) it becomes clear that capital flows exploded in relation to foreign exchange transactions caused by trade. Total spot transactions in foreign exchange markets are usually more than ten times greater than spot transactions caused by trade. Even more important is the explosion of outright forwards and foreign exchange swaps which, taken together, were nearly 30 times bigger than spot transactions caused by trade in 2007. There is no doubt that capital transactions dominate in the foreign exchange markets.

The Bretton Woods System entered into crisis at the end of the 1960s. The reasons for the breakdown were manifold. First, the system favoured the US. The US central bank, the Federal Reserve (Fed), was not forced to defend the exchange rate of the US dollar; this was the task of all other central banks belonging to the system. During the Gold Standard before the First World War as well as during the later created European Monetary System (EMS) the leading currency of the system was also forced to defend its exchange rate with restrictive monetary policy when necessary (Herr 1992). The US started to exploit its privileged position in the second half of the 1960s. Due to the Vietnam War and the 'war' against domestic poverty, a dollar glut developed and economic policy in the US became very expansionary (Calleo 1981). Capital outflows weakened the US dollar and other central banks had to buy huge amounts of US dollars against their will. It would have been necessary to follow a more restrictive economic policy in the US to stabilise the US dollar and save the Bretton Woods System. But US governments at that time obviously believed that a switch to flexible exchange rates would eliminate the external constraints of US economic policy. Also, the intellectual climate had changed. Most economists favoured flexible exchange rates and judged the Bretton Woods System as a fossil of the past. As early as 1953, Milton Friedman praised flexible exchange rates as a wonderful mechanism to prevent unsustainable current account imbalances and to allow all countries to pursue domestic-oriented monetary policy. In an influential paper Harry Johnson (1972) argued in the same direction.

The final collapse of the Bretton Woods System in 1973 was the first big step in the destruction of the model that developed out of the New Deal in the 1930s and characterised the first decades after the Second World War. After its breakdown a flexible exchange rate system between the leading currencies in the world emerged and the international exchange rate system became immediately chaotic with volatile exchange rates. Double-digit nominal and real exchange rate movements within short periods of time became frequent (see Figures 2.10 and 2.11). The international exchange rate system turned into a shock machine for all countries in the world. Nominal exchange rate movements became disturbing factors for national price levels. As real exchange rate movements indicate changes in international price competitiveness, quick and substantial changes in real exchange rates have lasting effects on GDP growth and especially the development of tradable sectors in economies. In addition, since the breakdown of the Bretton Woods System the world economy has been suffering from the lack of a stable international reserve currency because the US dollar became very unstable.

Table 2.2 Global foreign exchange market turnover in US billion dollars, selected years

	Daily averages in April of the years[1]						
	1989	*1992*	*1995*	*1998*	*2001*	*2004*[2]	*2007*
Spot transactions (1)	317	394	494	568	387	631	1,005
Outright forwards (2)	27	58	97	128	131	209	362
Foreign exchange swaps (3)	190	324	546	734	656	954	1,714
Estimated gaps in reporting (4)	56	44	53	60	26	106	129
Total 'traditional' turnover (1) to (4)	590	820	1,190	1,490	1,200	1,900	3,210
Memo: Turnover at April 2007 exchange rates[3]	–	880	1,150	1,650	1,420	1,970	3,210
Daily trade transactions	17	21	28	31	35	50	74

Source: Bank for International Settlement, Triennial Central Bank Survey 2007. Data for 1989 taken from Triennial Central Bank Survey 2001, data for Daily Trade Transactions are taken from IMF 2009a.

Notes

1 Adjusted for local and cross-border double-counting. Due to incomplete maturity breakdown, components do not always sum to totals.

2 Data for 2004 have been revised.

3 Non-US dollar legs of foreign exchange currency transaction were converted from current US dollar amounts into original currency amounts at average exchange rates for April of each survey year and then reconverted into US dollar amounts at average April 2007 exchange rates.

However, it would be a mistake to claim that flexible exchange rates were common between all currencies. Most countries, including developed countries, pegged to one of the key currencies. Of the entire member states of the IMF in 2001, about a fifth followed a system of flexible exchange rates. The rest practised a policy of controlled floating, unilateral pegging of the exchange rate to a foreign currency, crawling pegs and established even a currency board (Bubula and Ötker-Robe 2002). The US-dollar bloc became the biggest bloc followed by a German-mark bloc. After the breakdown of the Bretton Woods System some countries in Europe immediately pegged unilaterally to the German mark, and the so-called currency snake was created. In 1979 the EMS was founded with the German mark as its leading currency. But there was a big difference between the Bretton Woods System and the EMS. In the Bretton Woods System the leading currency was given by the Bretton Woods treaty whereas in the EMS markets determined the leading currency. In 1999 after a deep crisis in the years 1992/93 the EMS was transformed into the European Monetary Union (EMU). The D-mark bloc became the euro bloc. In all of this time the Japanese yen has never been able to create a currency bloc.

That fact that many countries tried to stabilise their exchange rates mainly by unilateral pegging to a strong currency is also demonstrated by the explosion of official reserve holdings in recent decades (see Figure 2.13). Since the Asian crisis in 1997 central banks in developing countries have increasingly bought hard currencies. Central bank interventions and an increase in reserves can be interpreted as a policy by countries to protect themselves against the instability created by flexible exchange rates and unstable capital flows. In the past few

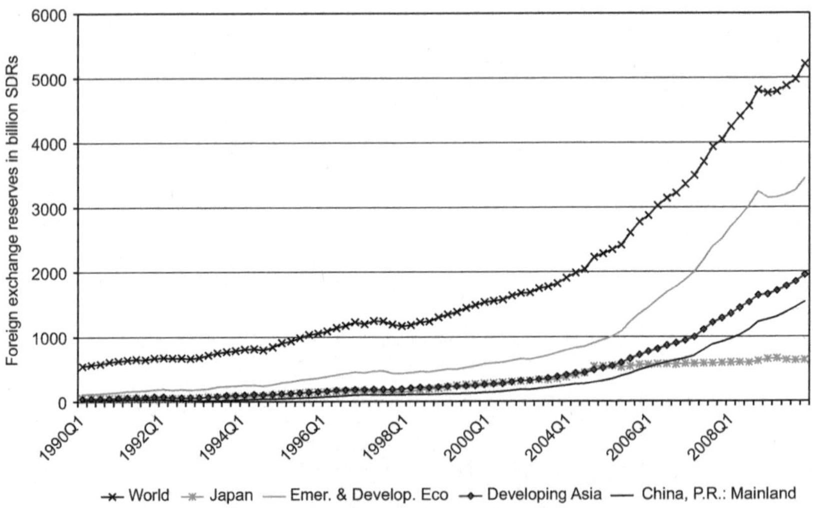

Figure 2.13 Official foreign exchange reserves in million US dollar, Special Drawing Rights, 1990–2009 (source: IMF 2009a).

decades Japan has increased its official reserves substantially. In the second half of 2009 China had the biggest foreign reserves followed by Japan.

The explosion of official international reserves after the Asian crisis in 1997 especially within the US-dollar bloc has led to speculation that the world economy has implicitly fallen back to a revived Bretton Woods System (Dooley *et al.* 2003). The idea is that countries from the periphery formally peg their currencies against the US dollar or at least prevent large exchange rate changes of their currencies vis-à-vis the US dollar and at the same time push for current account surpluses (see below).

The US is passively pushed into a constellation with high current account deficits and can enjoy a high level of consumption. The new system is of mutual interest and can last for decades as the periphery can follow export-led growth and the US can realise high welfare gains due to their overvalued currency. The hypothesis of a revived Bretton Woods System is not very convincing as the constellation is not based on an international treaty; rather it is a kind of private cartel to stabilise the exchange rate of the US dollar (Eichengreen 2004; Palley 2006b). The euro does not take part in the revived Bretton Woods System. Should the external value of the US dollar collapse only the first central bank switching from reserves held in US dollar to reserves held in other currencies will avoid losses. As the number of countries in the revived system is large, the private cartel can break down any time when especially smaller central banks, but also even more important central banks, start to switch from the US dollar to other currencies. There is the danger that the revived system could break down violently and add to worldwide exchange rate instability. For the US the system is a mixed blessing. It increases the current real consumption in the US. However, it also reduces domestic growth and employment.

For the world economy the switch to flexible exchange rates meant a deep change in the global governance regime. Exchange rate movements frequently place a great strain on domestic economic policy – many times greater than under a system of fixed exchange rates. However, the exchange rate could also become a policy variable that increases the freedom of domestic economic policy including aggressive beggar-thy-neighbour policies (see below).

Capital flows and exchange rate movements

Exchange rate movements are driven by capital flows. Of course in a theoretical model with no capital mobility and flexible exchange rates, exchange rate movements are also possible. In such a theoretical case exchange rate movements reflect different inflation rates between countries, changes in consumer preference or technology, shocks of all kinds and so on. However, nominal exchange rate movements, which could be observed after the breakdown of the Bretton Woods System, cannot be explained by such factors.

The key model used to explain exchange rate movements in the neoclassical model is the purchasing-power-parity theory (PPP theory), which states a proportional relationship between changes in the price level between two countries and exchange rate movements. According to the quantity theory of money there is a proportional relationship between money supply and changes in the price level. Milton Friedman (1969) used the parable of a helicopter that throws out exogenously created money over a country, thus increasing money supply. Any increase in money supply increases in the first round ceteris paribus the real stock of money as people gather the money falling from the sky and feel they are wealthier. This triggers a real balance effect as the population tries to get rid of the excessively high real stock of money by buying goods and thereby increasing aggregate demand in the goods market. The real balance effect works via demand inflation until the price level increases in proportion with the increase of the nominal money stock and the inflation has reduced the real stock of money to the old level. As there is a proportional relationship between changes in the money supply and changes in the price level, and also between changes in the price level and changes in the exchange rate, there is a proportional relationship between an increase in money supply and an increase in the exchange rate (nominal depreciation).[16]

Everyone would agree that very high inflation rates cannot be combined with stable nominal exchange rates in the long run. In such a fundamental way there is a relationship between price level changes and exchange rate movements. The problem is, however, that after the breakdown of the Bretton Woods System there were large exchange rate movements between currencies with only minor differences in inflation rates. There is an overriding agreement that all versions of the PPP theory fail to explain short- and medium-term (i.e. periods of up to ten years or so) exchange rate movements. For long-term exchange rate movements, PPP is also highly controversial.[17] We should also have in mind that a correlation between exchange rate movements and price level changes is also compatible, in which the exchange rate influences the price level and not the other way round (see below).

Exchange rate movements are not explainable without taking into account international capital flows. We have seen above that industrialised countries switched from a system of partly controlled capital flows to a system with full capital account liberalisation. International capital flows increased in an extreme way and are far greater than transactions related to international trade.

If future markets for foreign currencies exist, agents like banks can change domestic currency into foreign currency, invest the money in foreign currency and sell the earned foreign currency in the future market to get domestic currency in return. Such arbitrage transactions (foreign exchange swaps) are without exchange rate risk and have increased substantially in past decades (see Table 2.2). They are part of the so-called interest-rate parity theory. This theory states that percentage changes in the nominal exchange rate must be equal to the interest rate differentials between the two countries involved. Thus a depreciation of domestic currency must be compensated by a higher domestic interest rate and vice versa. As long as the interest-rate parity is not fulfilled, arbitrageurs will create international capital flows until the spot exchange rate and the exchange rate in the future market adjust to the equilibrium condition of the interest-rate parity. For currencies with future markets and unregulated capital flows, the interest-rate parity is empirically almost fulfilled. Contract partners in the future markets for foreign exchange are, as always in future markets, usually speculators. The following equation gives the interest-rate parity in a formal way:

$$(1+i_D)=(1+i_F)\frac{e^e}{e}$$

with i_D: domestic interest rate, i_F: foreign interest rate, e: spot exchange rate of domestic currency (increase means nominal depreciation), e^e: future or expected exchange rate of domestic currency.

The gross rate of return for domestic interest bearing titles (the left side of the equation) must in equilibrium have the same value as the gross rate of return for foreign interest bearing titles (the right side of the equation). We can assume that i_D and i_F are given by monetary policy at home and abroad. From asset markets we know that changes in expectations drive asset prices. The foreign exchange market is a typical asset market and the exchange rate is an asset price in spite of the fact that the exchange rate also influences goods and labour markets. The more strongly exchange rate expectations change and the more homogeneous expectations are, the stronger the exchange rates shift. Thus, the spot exchange rate depends on the foreign and domestic interest rate and exchange rate expectations expressed in the exchange rate in the future market.

We get

$$e=\frac{1+i_F}{1+i_D}e^e .$$

According to this equation an increase in the foreign interest rate will lead to depreciation and an increase in the domestic interest rate to appreciation. Without transaction costs and quick adjustment, a realistic model for foreign exchange markets, an expected depreciation (appreciation) will – everything else given – lead to an immediate depreciation (appreciation).

In his famous analysis Ruediger Dornbusch (1976) uses the above sketched approach. He asks the question as to how the future exchange rate e^e can be explained. If the domestic money supply increases in the tradition of neoclassical rational expectations, all rational agents will expect a nominal exchange rate according to the PPP theory. Thus, according to rational expectations, the price level and nominal exchange rate immediately jump to the new equilibrium, the real exchange rate remains unchanged and money stays neutral. It has already been argued above that the PPP theory is not able to explain exchange rate movements.[18] Are other fundamentals, those of the real sphere, able to explain these big exchange rate movements? It is not very plausible that productivity shocks or preference shocks led to the empirically observed exchange rate movements. Empirically, it is simply not possible to find out which of the potential 'fundamentals' should move the exchange rate. 'Economists today still have very limited information about the relationship between equilibrium exchange rates and macroeconomic fundamentals.' (Isard 1995: 182). Dornbusch and

Frankel (1988: 157) found out that: 'The clear conclusion is that exchange rates are moved largely by factors other than the obvious, observable, macroeconomic fundamentals. Econometrically, most of the "action" is in the error term.' Neoclassical exchange rate models meet their Waterloo here.

In the Keynesian paradigm expectations depend on historical time and place and cannot be discussed without taking into account the institutional, social and political constellation in countries (see Section 2.1). For example, in one historical period of time agents may believe that growth differentials in GDPs between countries are important for future exchange rates. In another historical period they may believe that current account imbalances, budget deficits or the productivity or inflation differentials matter. Or they may believe that the political constellation of a country is important and that this will influence exchange rates. Some agents may neglect fundamentals of any type and use, for instance, chart analysis. Different agents or groups of agents may use completely different models to understand the world and may have different opinions about the future exchange rate. Different opinions about future exchange rates leave room for speculation. The latter can also influence exchange rates especially if the time horizon of economic agents is only short term. Last but not the least, economists belonging to different economic schools may influence expectations as well as market leaders, such as influential persons or rating agencies. If this is right, then it should not be a surprise that the search for fundamentals to help explain exchange rate movements has not resulted in anything substantial and never will. It should also be no surprise that exchange rates can change quickly and violently. This is due to the fact that expectations can change abruptly and violently.[19]

To sum up this point: as all asset markets, flexible exchange rates have no endogenous anchor in economic fundamentals. The universe of economic, institutional, social and political factors drives them. Institutions are needed to give expectations and exchange rates an anchor. The key problem is that in the present system of flexible exchange rates there is no centre of gravity for exchange rate expectations able to limit violent capital movements. Economic agents have to act in such an uncertain environment and at the same time increase the uncertainty by their own actions – for example by exchanging their wealth from one currency to another. Large and unstable capital flows and strong exchange rate movements have been inherent elements of the globalisation project gaining speed since the 1970s. The flexible exchange rate system must be considered one of the key destabilising factors in the Neoliberal Globalisation project. For the world economy and all countries the switch to a flexible exchange rate system must be considered a major institutional change.

Capital flows and current account imbalances

Capital flows drive exchange rates and current account imbalances. Sometimes this statement is not understood and it is argued that cheap wages, superior technology or similar factors are responsible for surpluses or deficits of currency areas. It was David Ricardo who taught us that without capital flows the current account must be balanced and that even the most underdeveloped economy is protected by the exchange rate in the sense that it cannot have a current account deficit without capital flows. It is the exchange rate which makes wages so low, for example in a developing country, that the country can compete with countries with much more developed technology. In national accounting a current account deficit must be identical with a net capital import and a current account surplus with a net capital export. The causal link clearly goes from the net capital flow to the current account imbalance. If it were the other way round, a debtor could force a creditor to give credit – for example an importer could force a bank in the exporting country to give credit. Of course, a potential importer can go to a bank in the exporting country and ask for credit, but it is the bank that decides whether the importer receives it or not.

It is safe to argue that net capital flows determine current account imbalances whereas technological factors, consumer preferences, availability of natural resources and tariffs determine the structure of international trade. However, capital flows and flexible exchange rates, both of which are not determined by fundamentals, can become disturbing factors for the allocation of resources. In the case of large real exchange rate swings there will be no optimal allocation of resources reflected in an optimal structure of prices – a key function of markets according to neoclassical thinking – and resources will be wasted.[20] Appreciations can lead to the destruction of international competitiveness of whole industries overnight – a costly destruction of productive wealth. Later depreciations will not lead to the reconstruction of industries destroyed previously.[21]

Capital flows can also be initiated by central banks. If a central bank buys foreign currency, it is implicitly creating a capital export. If central bank reserves are reduced by selling them against domestic currency, implicitly a capital inflow is created. Such interventions can become important elements of foreign economic policies of countries.

The argument developed here is only valid for economic areas with their own currencies. For regions in a currency area the identity between regional current account balances and regional net capital flows also holds. Because there is no exchange rate risk, regional capital flows usually follow – at least in the normal case – regional imbalances. Let us assume region A in a currency area has lost regional competitiveness vis-à-vis region B because unit labour costs have increased substantially in region A but not in region B. In this case, households, companies and so on in region A buy more goods from region B than goods are bought by B from A. A net capital flow from region B to region A will in the simplest case be channelled through the banking system in the currency area. The slightest increase in the interest rate in region A will normally trigger interbank flows to region A. Only if in region A no credible debtors are left, the net capital flow to region A will dry up.

Since all capital flows in general and also net capital flows became bigger after the liberalisation of international capital flows and the switch to flexible exchange rates, one direct consequence was that current account imbalances became more pronounced and in many cases unsustainable. There is not the slightest tendency for flexible exchange rates to balance current accounts in a harmonious way. For example, US capital imports in the 1980s led to a strongly appreciating US dollar and at the same time a huge deficit in the US current account. After 1985 the US dollar collapsed and the current account deficit disappeared. In the 1990s and the 2000s, as a result of high net capital inflows into the US, an even bigger US current account deficit developed, while Japan and Germany realised very high current account surpluses (see Figure 2.12).[22]

Capital flows between developed and developing countries are as unstable as within the group of developed countries. They follow the logic of boom–bust cycles (Williamson 2005; Herr and Priewe 2005). The first of these cycles started in the 1970s and came to an end when Mexico declared bankruptcy in 1982. The next boom phase started in the early 1990s and ended with a sequence of crises from Asia to Latin America. In the 2000s a new and even bigger wave of capital flows to developing countries started and collapsed during the subprime crisis. The boom phase of the cycle takes place on the basis of high confidence of foreign and domestic economic agents in the economic development in the developing countries. Typically, high capital imports lead to a period of stable exchange rates, increasing current account deficits, high domestic credit expansion, high GDP growth and domestic asset price inflation in the stock and real estate market. Fragility increases as the developing countries suffer from increasing maturity and currency mismatch. Currency crises in a fragile constellation can be triggered by many factors such as political shocks, world market shocks, restrictive monetary policy or contagion effects. In all currency crises investors want to secure their wealth and prefer to keep it in high-quality currencies like the US dollar or the euro. In times of crisis foreign creditors stop giving credit and reject the rollover of old stocks of debt. The result is a collapse of the external value of the currency, an increase of the real burden of debt denominated in foreign currency and a domestic asset price deflation. The list of such crises is long: Latin America in the 1980s, Mexico in 1994, the Asian crisis in 1997, Russia in 1998, Argentina in 2001, the Baltic States in 2008 and many others.[23]

From US dollar dominance to a multi-currency system

World currency systems can be divided into hegemonic systems and multi-currency systems. In a hegemonic currency system there is an unchallenged currency that stands at the top of the currency hierarchy. Historically, such a world currency is provided by countries playing an important or even dominant role in the world economy in respect to GDP, financial markets, international trade and other factors that make one currency a leading currency. These countries were also politically and militarily dominant. The absence of competition among different currencies at the top of the currency hierarchy is central to a hegemonic currency system. A hegemonic country has the incentive to provide a stable world economy as an international public good, for example in stabilising international capital flows and exchange rates, and to help countries that undergo a currency crisis. Such policies support the hegemonic position of the dominating country. Within a stable hegemonic currency system the barriers to shift international monetary functions from one currency to another are extremely high, as network effects or positive external effects, created by a widespread use of a currency, stabilise the international function of the leading currency. Only far reaching developments such as prolonged inflationary tendencies or political instability in the country issuing the hegemonic currency can lead to the erosion of the role of a hegemonic currency. However, hegemonic powers can exploit the international role of their currency to a substantial extent and can in this way destabilise the world economy (Kindleberger 1981, 1986). US economic policy during the last period of the Bretton Woods System conforms to this argument. Countries lose dominance if their economic potential in relation to other countries is substantially reduced. Examples of hegemonic currency systems are the Gold Standard before the First World War under the dominance of England and the Bretton Woods System after the Second World War under the dominance of the US.

In a multi-currency system, which includes a bipolar system, more than one currency takes on international functions. Usually the group of important countries in the world economy will provide the currencies at the top of the currency hierarchy. If such a system is combined with completely deregulated international capital flows, it becomes inherently more unstable than a hegemonic system (Herr 1997). In a multi-currency system currency competition at the top of the currency hierarchy can become very intensive. Governments or central banks can actively fight for a dominant position for their national currency within the currency hierarchy. The most decisive economic instruments, besides such dimensions as political stability, policies in the interest of wealth owners and political and military dominance, are a high degree of price stability, the absence of depreciation, current account surpluses and the establishment of a position as an international net-creditor, as well as high growth rates and rising productivity. However, for the purpose of currency competition it is unimportant whether or not countries actively follow a policy to establish their national currency as one of international importance. Wealth owners, banks, investment and pension funds, or companies create competition between currencies. If a country with an international reserve currency does not meet the expected standards concerning price level stability or does not follow an economic policy which strongly promotes currency stability and protects the interest of wealth owners, capital will be withdrawn and relocated to competing currencies.

There is one additional point worth mentioning. In a multi-currency system flexible exchange rates are more likely than under a hegemonic system. This is because with several players it is more difficult to produce the public good of a stable international exchange rate system. In addition, sudden and large capital flows between leading currencies become likely in a multi-currency system and make stable exchange rates more difficult to defend. In a multi-currency system foreign exchange markets with flexible exchange rates function like stock markets. Only the first ones to leave a currency in danger of depreciation will save their wealth. Staying too long in a depreciating currency implies the realisation of losses, just as in the case of a shareholder who loses if she or he has missed the right moment to sell a share whose price has collapsed. To prevent losses, economic agents have to anticipate what other agents expect. As soon as an agent anticipates that other agents expect depreciation, our agent has to sell the currency immediately to protect her- or himself from losing wealth. In this scenario wealth owners especially must be very alert so that they do not miss the crucial time to switch from one currency to another. Periodic shifts of potentially huge funds therefore characterise a multi-currency system with flexible exchange rates. Periodic shifts in the ranking of the currency hierarchy also become likely. The probability of destabilising regroupings of international wealth will thus increase dramatically compared with a system with an unchallenged leading currency. Exchange rate movements create the environment for speculation. A multi-currency system with flexible exchange rates transforms the foreign exchange markets into a casino.

The present world financial system has the characteristics of a bipolar currency system with competition between the US dollar and the euro, with the yen and the pound sterling playing minor roles. Other currencies are not very important in the international sphere. Two indicators can show this development. Table 2.3 gives the currency structure of official foreign exchange reserves.[24] The US dollar plays the biggest role with around 60 per cent of all foreign reserves. This percentage has remained more or less stable since the 1990s. The euro follows as the number two with about 25 per cent and became increasingly important since its introduction. Taken together, the pound sterling and Japanese yen have a share of below 10 per cent.

In Table 2.4 the currency structure of cross-border credit relations in September 2009 are shown.[25] In banks' cross-border asset positions and banks' cross-border liability positions the US dollar has a share clearly less than 50 per cent and the euro is more or less at the same level. However, in local foreign assets

Table 2.3 Currency distribution of official identified foreign currency holdings, selected years (end of year)

	1987[1]	*1990*[1]	*1995*[2]	*1998*[2]	*1999*	*2004*	*2009*
US dollar	56.0	50.3	56.4	65.7	71	65.9	62.2
Euro	–	–	–	–	17.9	24.8	27.3
Japanese yen	7.0	8.2	7.1	5.3	6.4	3.8	3.0
Pound sterling	2.2	3.2	3.4	3.8	2.9	3.4	4.3
Swiss franc	1.8	1.3	0.9	0.7	0.2	0.2	0.1
Unspecified/unallocated	9.5	8.8	11.8	11.8	22.6	29.2	44.1

Source: IMF 2010b.

Note
1 Data from Annual Report 1996.
2 Data from Annual Report 2000.

Table 2.4 Currency structure of selected international assets and liabilities in June 2009

	% of total amount							
	Total amount in billion US dollar	*US dollar*	*Euro*	*Yen*	*Pound sterling*	*Swiss franc*	*Canadian dollar*	*Others plus unallocated*
Banks' cross-border asset positions	30,267.1	38.5	38.9	3.9	6.4	1.5	–	10.8
Banks' cross-border liability position	28,158.7	42.4	33.6	3.7	7.5	1.8	–	11
Banks' local assets in foreign currencies[1,2]	1,946.5	49.6	27.0	5.2	3.9	8.4	–	6.2
Banks' local liabilities in foreign currencies[1,2]	1,872.4	56.5	27.0	3.4	3.9	1.5	–	8.0
International bonds and notes	25,820.1	35.5	48.1	2.8	8.3	1.4	1.1	2.8
International money market instruments	1,077.8	29.5	51.0	1.6	12.1	2.1	0.16	3.54

Source: IMF 2009b.

Notes

Percentages may not add to 100 due to rounding differences.

1 Banks' local asset and liability in foreign currencies vis-à-vis the non-bank sector.

2 Data for June 2009.

and local foreign liabilities of banks the US dollar clearly dominates over the euro.[26] In markets for international debt-securities the euro has the highest share, but this market is relatively small in comparison to banks' cross-border positions.

Overall, the position of the US dollar as number one in the currency competition is unchallenged. Especially with respect to official functions the US dollar dominates. However, in several international functions the euro is now challenging the US dollar, particularly in the area of international bank assets and liabilities and international debt-securities (Galati and Wooldridge 2006). The international role of the euro together with some other smaller currencies is big enough to create the logic of a multi-currency system. Without reforming the international financial system it is likely that in future this competition will become even more intensive. In terms of empirical development all theoretical predictions of a multi-currency system can be found: unstable international capital flows between reserve currency countries, excessive exchange rate fluctuations and huge current account imbalances.

2.3.2 External economic constraints and strategies

After the 1970s the world market became unstable. Unregulated and unstable international capital flows, exchange rate flexibility and current account imbalances can become disturbing and restricting factors for national economic process policy. But, whereas external economic factors can restrict the scope of national economy policies and shape the entire macroeconomic policy regime of a country, they can also influence an economic regime positively. Two economic variables play a pivotal role: the exchange rate and the balance of payments situation.

The exchange rate

Let us assume deregulated capital flows and free trade. In this case it is obvious that countries that take part in a system of *fixed exchange rates* or peg their exchange rate unilaterally to a strong currency have to follow an economic policy to defend the exchange rate. Especially monetary policy must stabilise the exchange rate. Should the exchange rate become weak the central bank in the country with the weak exchange rate has to react. In the short term it has to sell foreign reserves in order to stabilise the exchange rate. However, even with help from an international institution, like the IMF which was founded as part of the Bretton Woods agreements with exactly this purpose, foreign exchange interventions are usually not enough. The central bank in the country with the weak currency must increase its interest rates. If confidence has not already deteriorated, this will lead to capital inflows which help to stabilise the exchange rate. But it also leads to a drop in domestic demand and a so-called stabilisation crisis with a reduction in GDP growth rates and increasing unemployment. This will reduce inflation as well as import demand and both will stabilise the exchange rate.

The situation is different if a central bank has to fight against appreciation. In this case a central bank has two options. First, it can cut the domestic interest rate and stimulate the domestic economy. In the short run capital inflows will be reduced and in the medium term the economy will be stimulated, the price level will probably increase and imports go up. For the country with the weak currency such a policy is preferable as it implies a symmetric adjustment process. But such a policy is not guaranteed. The central bank with the strong currency can simply remain passive and follow the second option not to cut the interest rate. In such a case there is the typical asymmetric adjustment process, which puts the burden of the complete adjustment on the shoulders of the country with the weak currency. In his proposal for the Bretton Woods System, Keynes (1942) recommended a symmetric adjustment process. He did not want the privileges that were given to the US in the Bretton Woods System; he also did not want the asymmetric adjustment process of the Gold Standard before the First World War and the one established again after the war.

A central bank with a strong currency may be institutionally forced to intervene in the foreign exchange market and buy the weak currency.[27] Also, a central bank that pegs its currency unilaterally to another currency may follow such a policy. Since 2000 China has been the best illustrative example. But this does not guarantee a symmetric adjustment process. This is because a central bank can intervene in the foreign exchange market for whatever reasons and at the same time sterilise the liquidity effect of foreign exchange interventions by selling the government bonds it holds, or in case of a lack of government bonds, by issuing own debt-securities. Such a policy can be followed for a long time. Of course, a policy of sterilisation can become difficult. However, the explosion of foreign reserves in recent decades has shown that such a policy has no tightly defined limits. It was the illusion of the so-called 'specie-flow-mechanism' that countries with an increase in international reserves (under the gold standard) must automatically follow an expansionary monetary policy, and in this way must help the country with the weak currency to adjust.

In a hegemonic currency system with fixed exchange rates and liberalised capital flows countries must follow the interest rate policy of the central bank in the hegemonic country. This means that the international key currency country can generally operate an autonomous monetary policy while the other countries are obliged to follow. The international key currency country must, however, defend its international key currency position in times of weakness. But such periods are exceptional cases as otherwise the leading currency would not in fact be the leading currency. We have many historical examples of such a system. The Bank of England usually dictated the world monetary policy under the Gold Standard before the First World War, and the German Bundesbank did the same in the EMS. The less influential countries in both systems had to follow the monetary policy of the leading currency in the system. For example, the monetary policies in France or in the UK were characterised by the need to defend the exchange rate against the German mark over long phases of their membership in the EMS.

Since the breakdown of the Bretton Woods System exchange rates have not been fixed. Let us analyse exchange rate movements and economic policy. We start with *depreciations*. A fall in the external value of a currency can trigger an inflationary process. The reason for this is that depreciations always lead to a price level push because of increasing import prices. The bigger the import quota and the depreciation, the bigger the price level effect. This explains why depreciations for economically small countries with high import quotas are especially difficult and potentially harmful. Without changing nominal incomes in the country real wages and living standards in general are reduced by depreciation. If nominal income in the depreciation country increases in order to compensate for real income losses, a wage–price spiral develops (see Section 2.5). In the extreme case, depreciation can lead to a depreciation–inflation spiral, which leaves the real exchange rate unchanged. Additionally, in this case the logic of the PPP theory is reversed since exchange rate movements dominate the development in price levels and not the other way round. Strong inflationary processes are nearly always driven by periods of strong depreciation, which triggers the inflationary process. Especially when confidence in the domestic currency erodes and capital flight escalates, depreciation and inflation get out of control. A central bank cannot accept such a process and must combat depreciation with restrictive monetary policy to prevent the erosion of the national currency. As soon as depreciations lead to inflationary problems monetary policy has to be subordinated under the stabilisation of the domestic currency system. If a central bank in such a constellation is forced to finance budget deficits the road leading to hyperinflation is open (Robinson 1938; Fischer *et al.* 2002).

Depreciations are successful and thus give rise to a real depreciation when the unavoidable price level push does not trigger an inflationary process. Success means that depreciations increase the price competitiveness of countries and in this way reduce imports and increase exports and, assuming normal elasticities, improve the trade balance. There is a trade-off: a real depreciation stimulates output and employment and in this way the welfare of a country in the long run, but at the same time it reduces the welfare of the population in the short run. How the labour market is constituted is decisive for the success of depreciations. If nominal wage increases after depreciation can be prevented by income policy within the context of a comprehensive stabilisation programme, for example, a depreciation–inflation spiral is then bypassed. Also, high unemployment, which prevents wage increases, raises the probability of successful depreciation. Real depreciation can be used as a macroeconomic policy strategy to stimulate exports and domestic employment. For this case many examples also exist. In 1985 the US wanted to talk the US dollar down to fight against high current account deficits. When the UK left the EMS in 1992 the depreciation of the pound sterling successfully led to a real depreciation and helped to stimulate GDP growth (Herr and Hübner 2005).

Appreciations can also have positive and negative effects. Inflationary processes can be more easily reversed with appreciations. This was the case in the US at the beginning of the 1980s, when, with the help of a sharp dollar appreciation, it was possible to reduce the high inflation rate in the early 1980s within a short period of time (Sachs 1985). Some countries explicitly use a nominal exchange rate anchor to stabilise the domestic price level. In such a case the nominal exchange rate serves as a restriction and orientation of domestic wage and price setting. Southern European countries in the 1980s pegged to the German mark within the EMS exactly with this purpose in mind. Many developing countries have also used a nominal exchange rate anchor including currency boards to stabilise the domestic price level. Such a strategy is not without danger because it can lead to current account deficits, which are not sustainable in the long run. Appreciations can lead to deflationary pressures. For example, the IMF (2003) forecasted deflation dangers for Germany in the spring of 2003 because of the strength of the euro and the already very low inflation rates in Germany at that time. The monetary policy possibilities of central banks are increased by revaluation pressure because a policy of low interest rates becomes possible and stability in terms of price level developments is imported.

Exchange rate movements influence not only price levels and price competitiveness of countries, but they also have effects on assets markets. This is because depreciations lead to asset losses for those who hold their assets in the depreciating currency. Depreciation can undermine the reputation of a currency and trigger a cumulative flight of capital with serious exchange rate consequences. Since such processes are non-linear, a central bank can never know exactly when a massive erosion of an international investor's expectations will occur during a depreciation process. One-time depreciations, which do not lead to an inflation process, can increase the reputation of a currency if previously existing depreciation expectations are removed.

Real depreciation leads to an increase in the real debt burden if the debt is denominated in a foreign currency and debtors realise revenues in domestic currency (businesses, private or public households holding foreign debt in foreign currency and realising revenues in domestic currency). Thus, countries with a high level of debt in a foreign currency must always fear that the domestic financial system will be negatively affected by depreciation.[28] Almost all severe currency crises in countries with a large amount of foreign debt have led to a breakdown of the domestic financial system, triggering so-called twin crises (Kaminsky and Reinhart 1999). Countries with debt in foreign currency must therefore pay careful attention to depreciations. If the debt in foreign currency is high, they simply cannot afford a sharp depreciation without destroying the domestic financial system.[29]

This point shows the fundamental advantage that countries have when their foreign debt is in their own currency. This is because they can depreciate without a negative real-debt effect. Only countries at the top of the currency hierarchy, i.e. the US, the euro area, Japan and a small group of other countries, can incur massive foreign debt in their own currency. This is a valuable privilege for these countries. In this country group, however, it is exclusively the US that until now has built up a very high stock of foreign debt in domestic currency.[30] Barry Eichengreen and Ricardo Hausmann (2005) speak of an 'original sin' most countries in the world suffer from, as they are not able to take foreign debt in domestic currency. The original sin reflects that these currencies have a low reputation and stand in the hierarchy of currencies in the middle group or in the group of lower quality currencies.

We can learn from the above debate that Friedman's (1953) and his followers' argument, that flexible exchange rates allow domestically oriented economic policy without external restrictions and at the same time keep current account balances within sustainable levels, is invalid. This also means that the difference between fixed and flexible exchange rates is less pronounced than thought by the economists in favour of flexible rates. Flexible exchange rates are a double-edged sword. They can give countries an additional instrument for their macroeconomic policy, but they can also add to the destabilisation of countries and can force monetary policy as well as other macroeconomic policies to follow very narrow external constraints. One example is the collapse of the US dollar at the end of the 1970s, which led to an extremely restrictive policy in the US that fought against inflation and depreciation.[31] In spite of flexible exchange rates all countries had to follow the US interest rate hikes to prevent depreciations of their currencies. The result was a world recession.

To sum up: macroeconomic policy regimes of countries depend a great deal on the existence or non-existence of external constraints. Without a doubt, in a situation of unregulated international capital flows the external constraints can be very strict and shape a macroeconomic policy regime. The constraints are especially strict for countries at the bottom of the currency hierarchy, i.e. developing countries, and less strict for countries at the top of the currency hierarchy, such as the US and the euro area. But external constraints in certain historical periods can become tight even for countries at the top of the currency hierarchy.

Balance of payment constellation

A current account surplus represents one of the sources of aggregate demand and thereby of domestic production. As far as net export surpluses of goods (including services like tourism, transportation services, etc.) are concerned, there is a direct demand effect. But net surpluses in income streams or remittances also have indirect positive demand effects as they stimulate consumption demand or other demand elements.[32] Many countries in the world have been following successful medium-term or sometimes long-term strategies of export-led growth.[33] In these countries export demand typically stimulates investment demand and both stimulate consumption demand. From the group of developed countries Japan and Germany are typical for long-lasting current account surpluses. China after 2000 and many of the East-Asian developing countries have been using export-led development strategies successfully over a long period of time.

However, since the 1990s Japan and Germany have shown that permanent export surpluses are not sufficient to guarantee high growth. The link between export surpluses and high domestic demand broke. As long as domestic demand elements are stagnating or even shrinking, high export surpluses do not trigger high GDP growth. Net exports compared with the other elements of aggregate demand cannot become big enough to drive growth alone (see the case studies about Japan and Germany in Chapter 3).

The fact that export surpluses do not automatically trigger a growth process also becomes clear during stabilisation crises. Let us assume a country has experienced a period of high GDP growth, which has led to an unacceptably high inflation rate and high current account deficits. Let us also assume that capital imports suddenly stop, the currency depreciates and the inflation rate becomes even higher. If in such a constellation the central bank increases the interest rate to fight against inflation and depreciation, investment and consumption demand will fall. Typically, imports will be reduced because the domestic currency depreciates and imports fall with falling GDP too. Exports increase as a result of the depreciation. Without a doubt the improvement of the current account will stabilise domestic demand, but this effect will not be sufficient to prevent a stabilisation crisis with falling output.

Which strategies can a country follow to come into a constellation of long-term current account surpluses? Let us start with fixed exchange rates. Under this condition a country is able to follow a policy of domestic cost increases below the ones in other countries. The country with the cost advantage builds up current account surpluses. If labour market institutions allow wage policy, unions and employer's associations can jointly follow a 'mercantilist' strategy to stimulate exports by wage moderation. Of course, the country following a beggar-my-neighbour policy can also try to construct national technological monopolies, exploit economies of scale or other advantages discussed by modern trade theory. One problem of such a strategy is the stimulation of sufficient capital outflows to finance the current account surpluses. The central bank has the option to use low interest rates to stimulate capital exports. However, given inflationary pressures this might not be in the interest of the central bank. Moreover, low interest rates might fail to result in capital outflows. In an exchange rate system where the deficit countries have to stabilise the exchange rate alone, the surplus country can leave it to them to solve the problem. But this may very well create problems for the exchange rate system as a whole. The central bank in the surplus country can intervene in the foreign exchange market and in this way create a capital export. Liquidity effects can be limited by sterilisation policies. That such policies are possible in preventing an appreciation of the national currency and defending current account surpluses (or limiting current account deficits) is shown by the explosion of official foreign exchange reserves in the last few decades. It has been a common practice of developing countries to intervene in foreign exchange markets. But Germany and Japan have also been masters of such policies. Governments can also stimulate capital outflows by giving credit to foreign countries. Actually, development aid in Germany in the late 1950s/early 1960s was founded to create capital exports and Germany via such a policy tried to prevent a revaluation of the German mark in the Bretton Woods System (Emminger 1986). However, a moderate revaluation of the German mark came in 1961.

Under flexible exchange rates the mechanisms are somewhat different. A country can cut interest rates, trigger private capital outflows, depreciate and stimulate the economy via exports (Mundell 1968: chapter 17). Such a policy is possible and can be found in many cases; but due to the problems of depreciation it is not always available. More common is another way to defend current account surpluses. Let us assume that a country realises a current account surplus, but private capital outflows dry up. The result is an appreciation and the destruction of the surplus. Also, here low interest rates can be used to limit the appreciation and trigger sufficient capital outflows. The likelihood of success of low interest rates in the case of slowing down an appreciation is much higher than in the case of a depreciation, which usually weakens the reputation of a currency. An ideal constellation includes domestic unit-labour-cost increases that stay below the increases in competing countries, while the appreciation pressure is reduced by low interest rates which slow down the appreciation and defend the surpluses. The advantage of such a constellation is that exports as a demand engine are stimulated as well as domestic investment. Until the early 1990s Germany was in such a constellation.

In addition, under flexible exchange rates central banks can build-up huge foreign reserves or governments can give foreign credits to fight an unwanted appreciation and to defend current account surpluses. The difference between fixed and flexible exchange rates is smaller than usually anticipated.

Current account deficits reduce aggregate demand. In a situation of unused capacities and unemployment the deficit leads – compared with a situation of a balanced current account – to lower growth and higher unemployment. Only when domestic demand is sufficiently high can negative growth and employment effects be avoided. There is a trade-off: a real exchange rate that leads to domestic unemployment and at the same time to income losses because of low domestic growth increases at the same time as the living standard because of relatively positive terms of trade.

Current account deficits build up a negative net asset position of countries. As in almost all cases capital inflows take the form of credit; a net asset position is combined with high foreign debt.[34] If countries suffer from the 'original sin,' a period of current account deficits leads to high foreign debt denominated in foreign currency.[35] This then leads to a fragile constellation as any breakdown of confidence in the stability of the domestic currency and a strong depreciation will trigger the danger of a twin crisis. As economic agents are familiar with this possibility there is always the latent danger that foreign investors and domestic wealth owners will lose confidence in the ability of a debtor country to pay its debts. However, at least theoretically, some countries with continuous balance of payments deficits may possibly achieve sustained high growth rates. But these will be exceptions to the rule. Finally, it should be mentioned that also for a country like the US a high net asset and debtor position is a negative factor for the reputation of the currency and can lead to the breakdown of confidence in the stability of the currency. But as long as foreign debt is in domestic currency, depreciation is less harmful.

2.4 Monetary policy

2.4.1 Institutional changes

Institutional changes in the 1970s affected monetary policy in two ways. First, the laws under which central banks act changed in many countries. Second, central banks had to conduct monetary policy in a different market environment. We start with the first point.

In contrast with the hybrid neoclassical-Keynesian model, the dominant Neoclassical Synthesis of the 1950s and 1960s, the triumph of monetarism in the 1970s and the neoclassical paradigm were accompanied by rising popularity of the idea that money is neutral and monetary policy should follow strict rules. Monetary policy was considered ineffective in influencing output and employment in the long run. It was argued that in the long-run the monetary sphere could only determine nominal variables. The first generation of monetarists believed that expansionary monetary policy had growth and employment effects in the short term, whereas later during the period of disinflation, it would lead to negative growth and employment effects. It was assumed that fluctuating inflation rates would confuse economic agents, i.e. workers might have money illusions, and this would lead to temporary negative distortions in the real sphere (Friedman 1968). Given this belief it is obvious that monetary policy should be geared only towards guaranteeing a stable inflation rate. To create a situation of short-term inflation and have short-term positive employment effects simply makes no sense. Later the neoclassical school of rational expectations (Lucas 1996) argued that, even in the short run, monetary policy cannot have any systematic effect on output and employment as all economic agents immediately expect the equilibrium outcome of central bank actions. Given this assumption any type of active monetary policy makes no sense.

The best possible monetary policy is a policy that guarantees a *stable* inflation rate, while the level of the inflation rate is of secondary importance. For rather practical reasons a low inflation rate was considered suitable. It was Milton Friedman who made monetary targeting popular as a monetary policy strategy.

> My own prescription is still that the monetary authority go all the way in avoiding such swings by adopting publicly the policy of achieving a steady rate of growth in a specified monetary total. The precise rate of growth, like the precise monetary total, is less important than the adoption of some stated and known rate. I myself have argued for a rate that would on average achieve rough stability in the level of prices of final products, which I have estimated would call for something like a 3 to 5 per cent per year rate of growth in currency plus all commercial bank deposits or a slightly lower rate of growth in currency plus demand deposits only.
>
> (Friedman 1968: 16)

After the breakdown of the Bretton Woods System nearly all central banks in the western world followed monetary targeting, or at least attempted to apply it or told the public they would follow such a rule.

Rule-based monetary policy means that central banks should not have discretionary power to react in the wake of historical developments. Monetarists did see a problem in the incapability of central bankers compared with the professional knowledge of professors, like Milton Friedman. The main argument was that politicians were short sighted. They were considered to be the 'bad guys' exploiting monetary policy to achieve short-term employment effects – especially shortly before elections. At that time a model of so-called 'time inconsistency' of monetary policy was developed (Kydland and Prescott 1977), initiating a broad public discussion. The argument was that it was rational for central banks to take a tough stance concerning a low inflation rate and that they should make this public. However, if the public trusts the central banks' announcements it becomes a rational strategy of central banks to increase the inflation rate, cheat the public and create positive employment effects which, however, are only short term. To avoid such negative short-term oriented policies an independent central bank is helpful.

Rogoff (1985) even argued that central bankers of an independent central bank should be 'conservative', as conservative central bankers have higher preferences for price stability than governments or the public. A lot of empirical studies have been carried out to prove that independent central banks realise lower inflation rates than central banks that were not independent (see for example Cukierman 1992). The studies were highly controversial as it was not clear if the low inflation rates were caused by the independence of central banks or other factors (Hall 1994; Hall and Franzese 1998; Berger *et al.* 2000). In the end, compared with the 1970s, inflation rates in the 1980s went down in countries with and in those without independent central banks (Bofinger 2001: 205).

After the Second World War only the German Bundesbank and the US central bank, the Federal Reserve (Fed), were relatively independent. Starting in the 1980s the number of independent central banks in developed countries became higher. It also has to be taken into consideration that the type of official exchange rate regime in all countries in the world is decided by governments, not by central banks. In the case of fixed exchange rates, governments decide for example about exchange rate realignments. The breakdown of the Bretton Woods System strengthened the role of central banks and took away a policy instrument that was usually in the hands of governments.

Under the influence of neoclassical thinking and the belief of neutrality of money there were also attempts to narrow central banks' targets to low and stable inflation rates as the only aim. Monetary targeting and inflation targeting follow this idea.

Let us now take a closer look at the independence of the central banks in the four countries of our case studies below. For them Peter Bofinger (2001) calculated indices to evaluate their independence (Table 2.5). Of course, the dimensions of independence chosen and the weights given to the different dimensions

Table 2.5 Indices of central bank independence of selected currency areas in the early 2000s (the higher the value of the indices the higher the independence)

	Central bank			
	European Central Bank	*Fed*	*Bank of Japan*	*Bank of England*
Goals independence	2	2	2	1
Instrument independence				
• Interest policy	2	2	2	1
• Exchange rate policy	1	0	0	0
• Explicit limitation of credit to government	1	0	0	0
Total instrument independence	1.33	0.66	0.66	0.33
Political independence of the decision-making body				
• Terms of office	1	2	1	0.3
• Number of members	2	2	1	1
• Staggered nomination	2	2	0	0
• Special status of central bank legislation	2	0	0	0
Total personal independence	1.8	1.2	0.8	0.26
Total independence	1.7	1.3	1.2	0.5

Source: Bofinger (2001: 219).

include subjective judgement.[36] The European Central Bank (ECB), the Fed and the Bank of Japan (BoJ) have full *goal independence*. This means that they can define which inflation rate they are trying to achieve. In the case of the Bank of England (BoE) the government designates the inflation target and the BoE then has to fulfil it. In other words, the BoE is not as independent as the other three (and only gets a 1 instead of a 2 in the table). *Instrument independence* has three dimensions. First, it means that central banks can autonomously set their refinancing rate without restrictions. This is the case in all the above-mentioned countries except in the UK where the government theoretically can override the interest rate policy of the BoE. Second, looking at exchange rate policy in all four countries governments can make decisions pertaining to formal exchange rate arrangements. However, even under flexible exchange rates governments in all counties have some influence, whereby the European Monetary Union (EMU) has the lowest. Third, the ECB is the only central bank that is explicitly not allowed to give direct credits to the government/s. In total, with regard to instrument independence, the ECB is the most independent central bank and the BoE the most dependent one. The *political independence* of the decision-making body includes the terms of office of the members of the decision-making body, the number of members, the diversification in the nomination process (how many different political institutions are involved in the appointment of members, for example upper and lower house), staggered appointments and the specific status of the central bank legislation. In the case of the ECB, for example, it is especially difficult to change central bank legislation as only an EU-wide treaty of the EMU countries can change the legal status of the ECB. Looking at the total personal independence the ECB is by far the most independent central bank. Taking all indicators for independence together the ECB reaches the highest level and undoubtedly has to be considered as the most independent central bank in the world. In many respects the ECB can be seen in the tradition of the German Bundesbank, although the former is much more independent than the latter ever was. The second most independent central bank in the table is the Fed, followed by the BoJ and then the BoE.[37]

Table 2.6 shows further substantial differences which reflect the different official mandates given to the central banks. As their primary objective, the ECB, BoE and BoJ have the maintenance of price stability. In these central banks growth and employment only come into play if the target of price stability is fulfilled. The Fed is an exception. It has officially three targets without prioritisation: stable prices, maximum employment and moderate long-term interest rates. Analysing monetary policy in the case studies below it becomes clear that these official mandates are not only on paper. The Fed cared much more for a policy of compromise between the price level and GDP growth compared with other central banks, which focused on price level stability. Contrary to the Fed and the BoJ, the ECB and the BoE publicly announce quantitative inflation targets. The ECB is the least transparent central bank of all. The BoJ, the Fed and the BoE all publish the minutes of their decision-making bodies but the ECB does not publish minutes. It tells nothing about controversies in meetings, key arguments or voting behaviour.

Compared with the 1950s and 1960s, most central banks in the 1980s became not only more independent, they also had to act in a completely different environment. In addition to interest rate policy central banks had international capital controls as a second policy instrument at their disposal in the 1950s and 1960s. Japan was even able to control the credit volume of commercial banks directly. Central banks at that time were not confronted with huge asset price bubbles, which characterise the economic conditions after the deregulation of financial markets. The real estate sector had been to a large extent disconnected from the rest of the financial system. Monetary policy in former times had much more direct effects on real investment, as the links between monetary policy and asset markets were much looser or more controlled. For example, in the United States the Glass–Steagall Act from 1932/33 introduced the separation of commercial banking from investment banking. Credit expansions financed by the central bank could not directly increase credits to highly speculative and risk loving non-bank financial institutions. In continental Europe and Japan investment banking was completely unimportant and universal banks focused credit expansion towards the enterprise sector. Also, international capital flows were significantly lower and much less important for monetary policy than they are today. Price level and output shocks created by huge exchange rate swings did not exist in the regulated type of capitalism after the Second World War.

Table 2.6 The mandate of central banks in the Euro area, the UK, the US, and Japan in 2002.

	ECB	*Bank of England*	*Federal Reserve System*	*Japan*
Objectives	• Price stability • Without prejudice to price stability, support of the general economic policies of the community	• Price stability • Subject to price stability, support of the economic policy of the Government, including its objectives for growth and employment	• Stable prices • Maximum employment • Moderate long-term interest rates	• Price stability, contributing to the sound development of the national economy
Primary objective	• Maintenance of price stability	• Maintenance of price stability	• No prioritisation	• Maintenance of price stability
Specification of the price stability objective	• Quantified by the ECB	• Quantified by the Treasury	• Qualitative specification provided by the Federal Reserve	• Qualitative specification provided by the Bank of Japan
Legally required reports	• Annual Report • Quarterly reports	• Annual Report • Inflation Reports (quarterly) • Immediate statement after each meeting of the MPC • Minutes	• Annual Report (on operations) • Semi-annual reports (on monetary policy)	• Semi-annual reports • Annual Report (outline of business operations) • Minutes of monetary policy meetings
Selection of other principal communications by the central bank	• Monthly press conference of the President (immediately after the Governing Council meeting) • Monthly Bulletin	• Quarterly Bulletin • Quarterly press conference on the launch of the Inflation Report • Financial Stability Review	• Immediate statement after each meeting of the FOMC • Minutes • Monthly Bulletin	• Immediate statement after each meeting of the Policy Board • Monthly Bulletin • Monthly press conference of the Governor

Source: ECB (2002).

Since the breakdown of the Bretton Woods System and the changes in political power in the United States and the United Kingdom the conditions under which central banks operate changed significantly. Starting with the elections of Margaret Thatcher and Ronald Reagan the conservative revolution increased the power of agents in the financial system. Monetary policy came under the influence of the interests of wealth owners and financial institutions. Without hesitation one can agree with Rogoff (2003: 21): 'I have argued that globalisation and deregulation have been powerful forces supporting the political economy of low inflation. Indeed, the most likely scenario is that these engines of higher competition and productivity will only continue to strengthen in coming decades.' Globalisation and deregulation have promoted a political economy that pushes national economic policies systematically in the direction of the interest of wealth owners. It would be wrong to reduce these developments to the skilful lobbying of holders of financial wealth. The individual economic calculus of securing one's wealth, looking for high returns and the pressure of competition were given more freedom within the current deregulated framework of the world economy. Policies in many countries reflect this changed environment.

Central banks have to act in an environment of currency competition whereas the world economy lacks a stable international reserve currency. The currency competition between the euro and the US dollar not only leads to exchange rate volatility between these two currencies and economic problems for the euro area and US but it also creates shocks for the rest of the world. Sudden and large exchange rate movements have become a challenge for monetary policy all over the world.

Last but not least, compared with the 1950s and 1960s central banks are confronted with more frequent and deeper domestic financial crises. A central bank's function as lender of last resort also shapes monetary policy in many countries not only for short periods. The zero-interest-rate policy in Japan and the liquidity creation in western countries after the outbreak of the subprime crisis are examples of the new environment for monetary policy.

We conclude that central bank independence as such is not a problem. Of course it can be debated whether a central bank under the direct control of government is better than an independent central bank. If the central bank is a department of finance ministries, which was the case for a long time, the coordination of monetary and fiscal policy is easy to organise. On the other hand, there is the danger that political pressure leads to short-sighted monetary policy. We believe that there is no systematic argument stating that governments follow a better monetary policy than an independent central bank. Also, an independent central bank is not isolated from the political sphere as the decision-making bodies of central banks are democratically legitimised. Behind the debate about central bank independence stands the question as to whether power should be concentrated as much as possible in one institution or given to different institutions. Both models have advantages and disadvantages and there are, as shown, different degrees of independence. Central banks do not have to be as independent as the ECB. If central banks are independent, they should be forced to publicly justify their decisions and also to conduct internal debates openly. They should be as transparent as possible. Compared with other central banks, the ECB is much too tight-lipped. At the same time central banks should be embedded in coordination mechanisms, for example by attending regular meetings with the government and other important agents in the field of macroeconomic policy-making like trade unions and employers' associations.

Extremely questionable is the fact that many independent central banks are forced by law to follow only one target, price level stability. Such central bank laws incorporate one specific understanding of how the economy works and reflect the dominance of monetarism in the historical period these laws were introduced. This dominance of monetarism disappeared and many economists, including the New Keynesians, believe that central banks should also target goals other than price level stability. The Fed in this respect has a much better constitution than many other central banks. When central banks limit their target to price level stability and follow their mandate strictly, very negative effects on macroeconomic policy regimes are the result.

2.4.2 Monetary policy options

In this section monetary policy options are discussed in more detail. We start our analysis with the failure of monetary targeting and the rise of inflation targeting. What follows is an investigation in the main theoretical contributions concerning monetary policy options of a central bank. Then we develop our idea about how monetary policy should be carried out.

From monetary targeting to inflation targeting

It was argued above that after the breakdown of the Bretton Woods System monetary targeting became the monetary policy strategy of almost all central banks. The idea was that the interest rate policy of central banks has to guarantee a stable growth rate of a monetary aggregate, and that there was a stable relationship between the growth of the aggregate and the inflation rate. Monetary targeting might have been a good ideological argument in the fight against inflation, but as a monetary policy strategy more often than not it was proven to be a complete failure. Three points are central.

First, the image of a helicopter exogenously controlling the money supply by throwing out money (Friedman 1969: chapter 1) is misleading. The money supply, usually defined as M2 or M3, is endogenously determined by the private sector, while the central bank controls the nominal interest rate on the money market (Kaldor 1985).[38] As the development of monetary aggregates depends on the interaction between the central bank, commercial banks, non-bank financial institutions and the public, it is not possible for central banks to control the money supply. Attempts to control a certain growth rate of a monetary aggregate, let us say of M3, leads to an extreme and destructive volatility of short-term interest rates. When the then Chairman of the Fed Paul Volcker tried to follow monetary targeting in the US at the end of the 1970s this was exactly the problem that came up. Even though the Fed tried hard and interest rate movements became very volatile, M-targets could not be fulfilled. Worse still, M2 and M3 gave different signals as to how monetary policy should be conducted. In the period 1974 to 1998 the German Bundesbank, the central bank most famous for following monetary targeting, failed in its attempts to control the money supply targets in about half of these years (Bofinger 2001).

Second, how to find a suitable definition of a monetary aggregate is completely unclear. M2 or M3 are liquidity aggregates, but how can liquidity be defined? Should short-term money market papers be a part of M2 or M3? Should deposits in domestic currency held abroad, for example in the euro–dollar market, be added to M2 or M3? Especially after the introduction of financial innovations, for instance in the form of securitisation, it was simply not possible to have a precise definition of money supply. Theoretically, the definition of M2 or M3 as money supply was terribly weak. A switch from long-term bond holdings, for example, to short-term bank deposits increases M2 or M3, independent of any central bank action. In this example the public increases 'money supply'!

Third, Milton Friedman argued that the relationship between a monetary aggregate and the price level is stable – the velocity of money is stable, as it was expressed. This was quickly proven to be an illusion. Money supply could grow much higher over years than planned and there was no goods market inflation.

Today, monetary targeting has lost attractiveness and hardly any central bank in the world attempts to fix a stable annual growth rate for a money aggregate such as M3. Thus, inflation targeting became popular as monetary targeting turned out to be impossible to follow. Inflation targeting, as an official monetary policy strategy, was first adopted in New Zealand (1991), then in the UK (1992), in Sweden (1993), Finland (1993 until Finland joined the EMU), Australia (1993) and Spain (1994 until Spain joined the EMU) (Bofinger 2001: 257). The ECB has an explicit inflation target, but it does not officially follow this strategy.[39]

Inflation targeting can be characterised as 'constrained discretion' (Bernanke and Mishkin 1997). Central banks can neglect monetary aggregates but are forced to focus on a stable inflation rate. If i_M is the money market interest rate, which is determined by the central bank, (i^*) a basic interest rate, ($\dot{P}$) the actual inflation rate, ($\dot{P}^*$) the inflation target and α a coefficient, inflation targeting can be described by the following formula:

$$i_M = i^* + \alpha(\dot{P} - \dot{P}^*)$$

As soon as the actual inflation rate $\dot{P}$ is higher than the target inflation rate $\dot{P}^*$ the central bank increases the interest rate. The strength of the interest rate reaction depends on α. The basic interest rate reflects an existing positive interest rate over long periods.[40]

Inflation targeting models usually do not use actual inflation rates to define monetary policy. As the inflation rates are expected to react to changes in interest rates slowly, i.e. after one year or even later, the expected inflation rate ($\dot{P}^e$)

is used. $\dot{P}^e$ is calculated by macroeconomic models fed by all types of variables. In the macroeconomic model, as soon as $\dot{P}^e$ is higher than $\dot{P}^*$ the interest rate is increased to a level that leads to price level changes, which are identical with the inflation target. If the expected inflation rate is below the target, inflation rate interest rates have to be cut.

Inflation targeting follows the monetarist idea that a stable inflation rate is essential for monetary policy. Milton Friedman (1968: 14ff.) discussed inflation targeting as a potential monetary policy strategy, but believed that it was much too complicated. Inflation targeting is a neoclassical monetary policy strategy just like monetary targeting as it assumes that the central bank should only have one target, i.e. a stable inflation rate, and that money in the end is neutral.

From the Keynesian perspective, inflation targeting could be more functional than monetary targeting as Keynesians have always stressed that the velocity of money is not stable. Modern Keynesians are also convinced that central banks have problems controlling monetary aggregates. But this does not necessarily imply that inflation targeting is in line with Keynesian thinking. We do not subscribe to the idea that inflation targeting is a functional monetary policy strategy.

In this respect we disagree with the New Keynesian approach,[41] which assumes inflation targeting as a successful policy option that can ensure a higher credibility for the central bank and lead to a low volatility of price level changes. The dominant New Keynesian approach among economists, the political elites and relevant decision-makers for the past two decades led to what became known as the 'New Consensus'. Three elements characterise this approach: the IS curve (the inverse relationship between interest rates and investment), the Philips curve (or a stable long-run NAIRU curve showing the trade-off between inflation and unemployment) and the monetary policy reaction by the central bank.[42] The New Consensus is based on the assumption that nominal variables have no long-run impact on employment, distribution or growth. Unemployment is explained following the neoclassical paradigm by real wages that are too high (Hein 2001: 3). In this respect the New Keynesians of the 1990s and 2000s as well as the Neoclassical Synthesis Keynesians of the 1950s and 1960s accept in the long run the nucleus of the neoclassical paradigm. They understand Keynesian thinking as modelling diversions and distortions from the neoclassical ideal model. The Neoclassical Synthesis assumed ad hoc a rigidity of nominal wages and usually excessively high real wages; the New Keynesians explain rigidities and real wages that are too high as the outcome of a microeconomic optimisation. They make ad hoc assumptions about market imperfections as, for example, attempted shirking of employees or insider behaviour of trade unionists. The key idea of the Phillips curve is that changes in aggregate demand cause price level effects, and given microeconomic rigidities this leads to movements along the Phillips curve. For example, an increase in the price level, assuming given certain stipulated nominal wages, brings down real wages and increases output and employment. For some time the economy departs from the potential equilibrium output and the equilibrium unemployment rate, both being determined by supply-side factors (Hein and Stockhammer 2007). The concept of potential output and the calculation of a specific equilibrium unemployment rate, both determined by supply-side factors, have nothing to do with Keynesian thinking and are neoclassical concepts (for a more detailed discussion about the NAIRU see Section 2.5).

A different approach was developed by Post-Keynesians.[43] The stream of Post-Keynesian thinking which is interesting for our topic argues that money is an inseparable component of the economy, has an impact on real variables and is not neutral, neither in the short nor in the long run. The supply of money is driven by the credit demand from the private sector and/or credits to be paid back through the banking system.[44] Employment is determined by effective demand, which can be successfully influenced by monetary policy.

Regarding monetary policy, the Post-Keynesians are not unified. Rochon and Setterfield (2007, 2008) distinguish two approaches: the so-called 'activist' approach and the 'parking-it' approach. In the eyes of the parking-it approach advocates (Smithin 2007; Wray 2007) monetary policy has a disturbing effect on output and a significant impact on distribution by changing profit share. Due to the uncertainty as to how interest rates will exactly affect output and employment, they suggest that the interest rate be set at a certain level and changed only infrequently. Fiscal policy should be used to effectively regulate output and combat unemployment. In other words, monetary policy should take on a passive role, whereas fiscal policy will be the main macroeconomic tool to affect aggregate demand. Concerning the level of the interest rate there are three different views: the Smithin view (real interest rates should be maintained at a level very close to zero), the Kansas City view (nominal interest rates are to be set at zero) and the Passineti view (real interest rates should be set according to the growth of productivity).

We are not inclined to this stream of Post-Keynesian thinking. There is certainly no stable relationship between changes in the interest rates by central banks and investment. A situation of an investment trap when cuts in interest rates do not stimulate private demand is possible. It is noteworthy that this Post-Keynesian stream argues for a revival of the Neoclassical Synthesis argument, which means that discretionary monetary policy is often not likely to work and fiscal policy has to take over the guarantee for full employment. A further shortcoming of this approach is that it is doubted if restrictive monetary policy is working. There are thousands and thousands of historical episodes which prove that monetary policy can bring down private demand, increase unemployment and fight inflation by increasing the interest rate. Of course such a policy is costly with respect to growth and employment. But under certain conditions it is the duty of a central bank to prevent inflationary developments and to defend the coherence of a *monetary* production economy. Moreover, looking at the periods of recession in many historical constellations expansionary monetary policy has proven to be functional.

The activist approach stands for an active role of monetary policy in stabilising the economy and influencing employment.[45] In this stream, the interest rate used by central banks as a monetary policy instrument is to be used to control inflation and affect aggregate demand. Such a policy influences output and employment also in the long run. In other words potential output is not independent of monetary policy. For example, a period of high goods market demand can lead to high investment and to an increase in potential output. The same argument counts for the NAIRU, which can shift together with aggregate demand. A long period of high unemployment can reduce labour supply as unemployment leads to the destruction of skills and can lead to a dropout of workers in the so-called 'lumpenproletariat'. As a consequence of such analyses these economists argue that besides inflation central banks should also take into account output growth and employment as targets of monetary policy. Tom Palley (2000, 2006a) recommends that a central bank targets the minimum unemployment rate of inflation, which means that monetary policy should always be as expansionary as possible as long as there are no big inflationary dangers.[46] In our view, the latter Post-Keynesian stream gives more plausible argumentation as to how the various macroeconomic policy instruments should be applied.

The Taylor rule

John Taylor (1993, 1998, 1999) searched for a function to describe past central bank behaviour. The central bank reaction function he found goes beyond inflation targeting and assumes, in line with our argument, that central banks should follow more than one target, i.e. a low inflation rate and high GDP growth (low unemployment). Taylor used the following reaction function for $_F$central banks:

$$i_M = i^* + \alpha(\dot{P} - \dot{P}^*) + \beta(G\dot{D}Pr - G\dot{D}Pr^*)$$

The money market interest rate (i_M) is the policy variable which has to be explained. It depends on a basic interest rate (i^*), the actual inflation rate ($\dot{P}$), the inflation rate target ($\dot{P}^*$), the actual real GDP$_F$ growth rate ($G\dot{D}P_F$), the potential real GDP growth rate ($G\dot{D}Pr^*$) and the two coefficients α and β. FThe coefficients show how strong a central bank reacts if a target is not realised. Changes in the money market interest rate depend on deviations between the inflation rate and the target inflation rate and the deviations between the potential real GDP growth rate and the actual real GDP growth rate. Potential real GDP growth rates are usually calculated by a moving average of past real GDP development. If, for example, the actual inflation rate is higher than the target inflation rate and at the same time the actual real GDP growth rate is below its potential, monetary policy looks for a compromise between the two targets, depending on the size of the deviations and the coefficients. In an econometric model the basic interest rate and the coefficients α and β are calculated in a way that the best fit with the movement of the actual interest rate i_M is given in the above Taylor formula.

The key message of the Taylor formula is that central banks do not only have one aim. They search for a compromise between price level stability and GDP growth. It is no great surprise that investigations in the tradition of Taylor found that in fact all central banks pay attention to the inflation rate and economic growth. But we have to be careful. In an econometric analysis even a central bank that follows strict inflation targeting shows some response to real growth in the above equation. If, for example, in a country with a central bank that follows inflation targeting the (expected) inflation rate is above the inflation target and the central bank increases its interest rate, the economy will fall into recession. This will reduce the (expected) inflation rate and bring down the interest rate. In the interpretation of the above formula it appears that the central bank looks after growth.

However, different central banks can have varying preferences when searching for a compromise between the inflation target and high real GDP growth. Analytically, this is reflected in different weights for the coefficients α and β. Depending on the size of the coefficients, central banks can attach greater weight to (i) price level developments or (ii) to real GDP growth or (iii) weight price level developments and economic developments equally in formulating their monetary policy. Taylor found in his historical explanation of monetary policy in the US that the Fed gave equal weight to inflation and GDP growth.

The Taylor function clearly shows that modern central banks have only *one* instrument, the money market interest rate, and *two* targets, price level change and GDP growth. In many historical constellations the central bank is not able to realise both targets since for this purpose the central bank would need more instruments, in fact one independent instrument for each target. The situation becomes even more complicated when central banks follow a nominal exchange rate target or are compelled to pay attention to the exchange rate, as exchange rate changes may immediately lead to changes in the domestic price level and trigger an inflationary or deflationary process. Even a central bank that follows inflation targeting may be forced to follow a hidden exchange rate target as exchange rate movements have big effects on the price level. There are also attempts to burden a central bank with the task of stabilising asset markets, for example by stopping real estate or stock market bubbles by higher interest rates. Theoretically it would not be a problem to add more variables to the Taylor formula, for example one for an exchange rate target and one for an asset price target. Yet, it is obvious that four targets and one instrument cannot work, and it would be very difficult to find a compromise between four targets (Tinbergen 1956).

The Taylor reaction function, which is calculated from past data, should not be interpreted as a monetary policy rule. A Taylor rule to guide monetary policy has too many weaknesses. To start with, a basic interest rate (i^*) in the Taylor rule is very difficult to calculate. It must be considered as an equilibrium rate of return. A rate calculated from past data does not help as the basic interest rate can change in unpredictable ways (see next section). This is the case for all economic paradigms. In the Keynesian paradigm the basis rate has no anchor in productivity and very much depends on expectations and their changes.[47] In the neoclassical paradigm the basic rate reflects the marginal physical productivity of capital, which can change equally quickly for example when technologies advance. Neither is the interest rate able to reflect possibly varying long-term GDP growth rates. To calculate the basic interest rate theoretically is simply not possible.

The calculation of the deviation of the inflation rate from its target value by the Taylor rule is relatively unproblematic. But there are also controversies as to whether the core inflation rate, consumer price index or GDP deflator should be used as the target inflation rate, and whether an inflation band or a specific inflation rate should be used as a target. The determination of the potential real GDP growth rate is much more problematic. Potential GDP growth in the Keynesian paradigm depends on aggregate demand and the latter on monetary policy. To guide monetary policy by a variable that is dependent on monetary policy makes no sense. In the neoclassical paradigm a macroeconomic production function with the variables labour, physical capital and technology would be the theoretically correct approach to calculate potential output from the supply side. However, a macroeconomic production function is based on methodologically weak grounds and does not help.[48] Because of a lack of theoretical determination, a moving average of the previous development is extrapolated into the future when calculating potential real GDP growth. If there is a sudden increase in the growth trend because of changes within the private sector, the Taylor formula indicates an over-utilisation of the production potential. In accordance with the Taylor rule, the central bank will react with a restrictive monetary policy and prevent an increase in the long-term growth trend. The central bank will even feel justified ex post with its dysfunctional policy when growth turns out to be correspondingly lower because of restrictive monetary policy.

We must assume that the coefficients α and β are not fixed. This does not only reflect historical preference changes by central banks. It is very likely that the coefficients increase the more the targets are not realised. There may even be thresholds when the coefficients jump. For example, for a central bank a certain inflation rate may be too high but still acceptable. In such a case the inflation leads to moderate interest rate increases. If the inflation rate goes above a certain threshold the central banks will fight very hard against inflationary developments, especially if a wage–price spiral starts a cumulative inflationary process.

To sum up: the Taylor reaction formula is a useful instrument to analyse past monetary policy, however, a Taylor monetary policy rule would lead to dysfunctional monetary policy.

Discretionary monetary policy 'on sight'

Central banks must constantly react to changing circumstances in the historical process. Referring to this aspect of monetary policy, we join up the tradition of Knut Wicksell and John Maynard Keynes, who both analysed the dynamics of the economy by the interaction between two rates of return: the money interest rate that is decided upon by the central bank and a rate of return of non-monetary assets. Both emphasised the necessity for discretionary monetary policy to stabilise economic development. Wicksell (1898) argued that the natural real interest rate, which he assumed in the tradition of the neoclassical paradigm to be determined in the real sphere, changes in unpredictable ways.[49] As soon as the natural rate of interest is lower than the money interest rate an inflationary process will start. If the money interest rate is higher than the natural rate, deflation will be the result. The main point is that monetary policy ought to follow the movements of the natural rate, which cannot be predicted in any good way (Fontana 2006a, 2006b). Keynes's argumentation (1930b) showed great resemblance to Wicksell's, but Keynes gave up the idea of a natural rate of return depending on a real sphere in a later stage. In Keynes (1936) the money interest rate has to be compared with the marginal efficiency of capital, which is completely driven by expectations and has nothing to do with a real sphere.[50] Keynes (1936) also argued that equilibrium between the marginal efficiency of capital and the interest rate could be combined with any level of real GDP and employment. Actually, Keynes wanted to overcome the neoclassical dichotomy between a real and monetary sphere, which finds its expression in the neutrality of money. As the marginal efficiency of capital is driven by potentially very unstable expectations it can change in unpredictable ways – as the natural rate in Wicksell's thinking. According to Keynes monetary policy has to compensate for the violent movements of the marginal efficiency of capital.

Keynes (1936, 1937) went beyond Wicksell in a second point. He emphasised, according to the law of effective demand, output essentially depends on investment and consumption demand. Especially investment demand is fundamentally influenced by monetary policy. For Keynes discretionary monetary policy became the most important economic policy to stabilise a capitalist economy, whereby the latter is not only affected by shocks but also suffers from many types of endogenous instability potentials. In the neoclassical monetarist tradition, it is sufficient when central banks provide a stable inflation rate. From such a perspective, this is the best way to avoid money becoming a disturbing factor and to help the market forces to achieve high growth. From a Keynesian perspective money plays an essential role in the short and the long run. If money is not neutral and monetary policy deeply affects economic growth and employment, then this must be considered in the policy of central banks. This does not mean that a low inflation rate should be a subordinate concern of central banks. In principle, every central bank must prevent high inflation rates and the erosion of the monetary system. But central banks have some scope in the definition of price level stability (or better the level of the inflation rate they want to achieve) and in finding a compromise between price level stability and real GDP growth.

Without a doubt monetary policy is of key importance for the stabilisation of a capitalist economy. It is per se a macroeconomic policy and takes macroeconomic effects into account. Monetary policy can react very quickly to macroeconomic developments, much quicker for example than fiscal policy, which needs some time to be implemented. In spite of the high effectiveness in many constellations there are also limitations of monetary policy. The central bank is a market participant, and especially in deregulated capitalist economies cannot force other agents to react in a certain way. High interest rates are always able to reduce private demand, real GDP as well as the inflation rate. But how costly such a method of fighting against inflation becomes in terms of output loss and unemployment is beyond the control of central banks. The power of monetary policy is asymmetric. While reducing inflation with high interest rates is effective, low interest rates may fail to stimulate investment or other demand elements. Deflationary developments are dramatic for monetary policy since nominal interest rates cannot become negative and a deflation can lead to very high real interest rates with all their negative effects. In periods of stagnation or even worse, deflation, the central bank needs allies. Fiscal policy is needed to stabilise demand; and a certain wage development is needed to build a dam against cumulative deflation.

We define a functional discretionary monetary policy as when a central bank operates an active interest rate policy and consistently makes use of the scope of monetary policy for positive economic growth and employment effects. Such a policy includes an interest rate policy operated 'on sight'. Central banks have to analyse the particular historical situation and have to act accordingly in a discretionary way. Any rule would unnecessarily bind central bank actions.

Restrictive monetary policy should only be used if inflationary developments can actually be recognised. However, especially if a cumulative wage–price spiral starts turning and nominal wage increases cannot be controlled, restrictive monetary policy is unavoidable. The Fed in the 1990s gives an example for cautious monetary policy. At that time many economists using historical data estimated that an unemployment rate below 6 per cent would lead to inflation. When the unemployment rate fell to 6 per cent in 1996, restrictive monetary policy was demanded. The Fed, however, refused to comply with this demand. The unemployment rate dropped further, without causing inflationary developments (Blinder and Yellen 2001, as well as the US case study from this book). The Fed increased interest rates only very late in the 1990s when goods market inflation moderately increased.[51] To provide another example, M3 in the euro area exploded after 2001 and rose much faster than planned with respect to the ECB's so-called reference value of 4.5 per cent. The increase in M3 in these years, however, was primarily the result of the portfolio decisions by private investors fleeing from stocks and other long-term investments into liquidity.[52] The increase in M3 had nothing to do with the dangers to inflation. Thus, the ECB was well advised not to follow monetary targeting and instead to lower interest rates (Heine and Herr 2008).

Let us come to expansionary monetary policy. The Keynesian interpretation after the Second World War, the Neoclassical Synthesis, which is still advocated today, considers monetary policy to be a blunt instrument stimulating growth in a recession and long-term growth. It emphasises extreme cases such as the liquidity trap (very high interest rate elasticity in money demand) and the investment trap (very low interest elasticity in investment demand) and thereby points to the ineffectiveness of monetary policy. In addition, the Post-Keynesian parking-it approach is sceptical about the effectiveness of monetary policy. There is also the argument that the option-value of waiting can make it advisable for investors to postpone investment in a situation of high uncertainty (Dixit and Pindyck 1994).[53] Under the constellation of an endogenous money supply the liquidity trap argument does not make much sense. At least wealth owners cannot restrict credit supply when the banking system together with the central bank increases credit supply. But also under the assumption of an endogenous money supply, credit rationing by the banking system can restrict credit supply against the will of central banks (Stiglitz and Greenwald 2003).

Under certain conditions expansionary monetary policy can fail. But we do not share the general assessment that monetary policy is ineffective and of secondary importance in stimulating economic growth compared with fiscal policy.[54] Instead we support the concept that interest rate cuts normally have a strong effect on economic development. The general argument of low monetary policy effectiveness is alien to the basic tenets of Keynes' thinking. He always emphasised the desirability of and necessity for interest rate reductions to attain satisfactory growth:

> The remedy should come, I suggest, from a general recognition that the rate of investment need not be beyond our control, if we are prepared to use our banking system to effect a proper adjustment of the market rate of interest.
>
> (Keynes 1930c: 346)

If needed to bring interest rates down, he demanded open market policies 'á outrance' (Keynes 1930b: 347).

In any case interest rate cuts improve the cash-flow situation in an economy.[55] If the central bank lowers its refinancing rate then short-term interest rates certainly fall and long-term interest rates also generally decrease. Among other things, this has the effect that the cash-flow situation of businesses and private as well as public households improves. This effect will become stronger when a higher proportion of credit has short-term maturity, when credit financing of businesses and other economic entities increases, when more credits have an interest rate indexation and when it becomes easier to refund long-term loan contracts. Additionally, businesses achieve high profits during economic growth periods and finance a large proportion of their investments from profits. In a recession, however, firms typically realise lower profits or even losses. Then they are more strongly dependent on credits. For such firms interest rate cuts relieve their situation.

Interest rate cuts can also stimulate private investment as investors compare the interest rate with the marginal efficiency of capital. It is a very extreme situation when the interest rate elasticity of investment becomes zero. In addition, interest rate cuts increase the value of existing capital such as shares, real estate and fixed-interest debt-securities and thus, on the one hand, can stimulate consumer demand, and, on the other hand, increase the value of collaterals and in this way stimulate credit expansion.

Central banks should lower interest rates rapidly and massively in economic crises. This is because cautious interest rate reductions force market participants into a waiting posture, since they expect a further interest rate reduction and thus postpone their credit-financed investment and purchase of consumer goods. They are even eventually rewarded for this waiting behaviour.

In Germany, as Bofinger (2001: 90) has shown, net interest payments by the firm sector are positively correlated to changes in the money market interest rate. The same effect can be seen in the US (Bernanke and Gertler 1995). Similar processes also occur with consumers. In the US it was feared that the high debt levels of private households would drastically reduce their consumer demand after the stock market crash in 2000/2001. However, consumer demand remained stable because massive interest rate reductions by the Fed improved the cash flows of private households, and the money released was used for consumption. The same effects can be found after the outbreak of the subprime crisis in 2007.[56]

To sum up this point: refinancing interest rates by central banks should be increased in small steps during economic growth phases so as not to burden economic development with an unnecessary overreaction. If, however, the rate of inflation spins out of control and is driven especially by wage inflation, a significant interest rate increase is inevitable. Theoretical considerations and empirical results show that a functional monetary policy decreases interest rates rapidly and strongly if GDP growth goes down. A monetary policy in the described manner increases the probability that unnecessarily restrictive monetary policy is avoided and economic collapses are quickly mastered, while economies are not trapped in phases of stagnation or even be pushed to a lower long-term growth path. Such a monetary policy will increase the long-term growth trend of an economy.

The target rate of inflation and price level fluctuations

Various central banks have chosen different target rates of inflation, whereby some central banks publicly announce their inflation rate target and others only mention price level stability without setting a quantitative amount. Inflation targeting as an official monetary policy strategy became very popular, in that it promoted inflation targets at historically low levels – in many cases at around 2 per cent. But even when a central bank has, apart from the inflation rate, a GDP growth target (or even more targets), it has to have an idea of an optimal inflation rate.

In our opinion, central banks should not choose a too low rate of inflation as optimal. First, the inflation rate target should not be too close to zero, as otherwise a negative economic shock can rapidly lead to deflation. And, of course, no central bank in the world strives for a deflation. It also has to be taken into consideration that official inflation figures tend to be up to 1 per cent too high as quality improvements of products are not completely measurable. Japan is an example of the fact that deflation leads to a disastrous economic development. Germany also found itself on the edge of deflation (IMF 2003). The subprime crisis that hit the world economy in the years 2008 and 2009 increased the danger of global deflation. Central banks should therefore strive for an adequate safety margin against deflation.

Second, the effectiveness of an expansionary monetary policy is increased by a higher rate of inflation. If a central bank decides to provide a strong expansionary impulse, it can lower the nominal refinancing interest rate so as to bring down short-term real interest rates to very low levels or make them even negative. This argument is advocated strongly by the New Keynesians and the New Consensus (Summers 1991; Mankiw 2001). Together with others, Oliver Blanchard, chief economist of the IMF, recently recommended an inflation target of 4 per cent (Blanchard *et al.* 2010). We find this argument quite plausible.

Third, striving for a medium-term inflation target and not an annual target is important. This is not a problem for central banks without an explicit inflation target, since the central bank has not mentioned a particular rate of inflation. Actually, we prefer a qualitative definition of price stability, which defines price stability according to the specific economic situation. But, within an explicit inflation target framework, a medium-term orientation is also possible. The best would be to define the target explicitly over the business cycle. The Australian central bank has, for example, an explicit inflation rate target of between 2 and 3 per cent averaged over an economic cycle (Stone 2003).

Contrary to a common tendency in neoclassical thinking a central bank should not push for the most stable inflation rate possible. A variable inflation rate is needed to give economic development sufficient 'air' over the business cycle. Economic expansions should not be countered by monetary policy too quickly, since the economy is otherwise kept in a state of permanent 'semi-slump' (Keynes 1936: 322). For Keynes (1930b, 1936) as well as for Schumpeter (1926) it was inevitable that strong investment activity, which builds the backbone of an economic expansion, would lead to temporary demand inflation. If a wage–price spiral does not result from the demand inflation, then a temporarily higher rate of inflation is not a problem for the economy at all, but is rather an expression of high growth. Capacities in such a case are increased by strong investment activity, whereby the gap between supply and demand is gradually closed again when new capacities are built up. Then, demand inflation probably fades out. If, however, demand inflation leads to a cumulative wage–price spiral, the central bank is forced to end the inflation process by monetary means.

An exclusively medium-term inflation target is important for a second reason. A rise in the price level can occur because of reasons other than demand and wage increases that are too high. Examples are commodity price increases, changes in the tax system or a single devaluation. In these cases, monetary policy is functional when it is not used to counter these price level increases. The inflation rate then rises temporarily, but falls back again after a certain period of time. It would be extremely costly in terms of growth and employment if a central bank were to respond to such cost increases with a stricter monetary policy. In this case too, monetary policy should only become more restrictive when price increases lead to a wage–price spiral.

2.5 Wage policy

2.5.1 Wages, prices and the wage norm

In this section we first intend to analyse the relationship between wages and prices and then discuss how wages should develop from a macroeconomic perspective. Labour market institutions and wage development are discussed in the next section.

Wages and prices

In long-term equilibrium, the price level in an economy is determined by production costs. Let us show this for a closed economy in the tradition of Keynes' Treatise on Money (1930b) (see also Riese 1986; Herr 2009). With Y as nominal income (identical to net domestic product), W as wage sum and Q_E as equilibrium profit, $Y = W + Q_E$. Nominal income is identical with real income multiplied by the price index, $Y = Y_r \cdot P$, equilibrium profit is identical with equilibrium profit rate q_E multiplied by the stock of capital. With the latter defined as real capital stock (K) multiplied with the price index, $Q_E = q_E \cdot P \cdot K$. Finally, after insertion and isolating P we have:

$$P = \frac{W}{Y_r} + \frac{q_E \cdot P \cdot K}{Y_r}.$$

The first term (W/Y_r) expresses unit labour costs (ULC) and the second term equilibrium profit per unit output. The profit rate or the profit mark-up is mainly given by the financial sector (see Section 2.2). As soon as unit labour costs increase the price level also increases. As a rise in the price level (the first round effect of increasing unit labour costs) also pushes up the value of the nominal capital stock, the second term in the equation above rises too. In a closed economy there is a proportional relationship between increases in unit labour costs and the price level. If percentage changes in unit labour costs are expressed as $U\dot{L}C$ and changes in the price level as $\dot{P}$, the obvious result is: $\dot{P} = U\dot{L}C$.

The money supply is determined endogenously. This then means that a central bank can only reverse an inflationary cost process if it increases the interest rate so that the demand in the goods and labour markets is diminished. Rising unemployment decelerates the rise in wages and thereby reduces the increase in unit labour costs.

Changes in the profit mark-up may indeed affect the price level, but this is a one-time effect. Frequent increases or decreases in the profit mark-up to such an extent that the price level permanently changes are not very likely. Wages are not the single most important factor for the changes in the price level. Price changes for raw materials and agricultural products or increases or decreases in duties and taxes can have an effect on the price level too. For example, a rise in value added tax or in the mineral oil tax raises costs and leads to an increase in prices.

If foreign exchange relationships are taken into account, then depreciations and appreciations influence the price level via changing import prices (see Section 2.3). Severe international competition can prevent the rollover of increasing costs and reduce the profit mark-up. In other constellations international competition may allow higher profit mark-ups.[57] Such modifications can be important in certain historical periods but do not change the general logic of the argument. If over long periods a firm is not able to earn equilibrium profit mark-up, it will disappear.

We can also assume mark-up pricing in a situation of unused capacities and unemployment.[58] Rising wage costs in a situation of unemployment push up prices in the same way as an increase in the oil prices or in value added tax. Should all firms in an industry or even in an economy be confronted with higher costs, it is easy for them to roll over costs to buyers through increasing prices. They can do this in a 'concerted action', which rather quickly adjusts prices to costs. If costs decrease, the competition among firms reduces prices. This typically takes more time than an increase in prices as the competition mechanism usually works slowly.

So far we have only discussed cost inflation or cost deflation and long-run equilibrium. In the short run, imbalances in the goods markets can influence the price level too. Excess demand in a situation of full capacity utilisation increases the price level ceteris paribus, excess supply forces businesses to reduce prices and leads to losses.

Keynes (1930b) also called demand inflation profit inflation as an increasing price level in the described constellation automatically creates undistributed profits.[59] Excess supply and falling prices, on the other hand, lead to losses in the enterprise sector. Quantity and price effects in constellations of demand–supply imbalances are in many cases mixed. In a situation of low capacity utilisation in all industries and unemployment, increasing demand leads to pure quantity effects; if demand goes up and hits some bottlenecks, quantity as well as price increases are triggered; finally, in a situation of full capacity utilisation, rising demand only leads to price effects. Excess supply typically leads to quantity and price reductions. The relative strength of the two effects cannot be determined on a general theoretical level.

Supply–demand imbalances and cost-driven inflation or deflation can be combined into the following four different constellations.

A long period of high demand can lead to excess demand in the goods market and to profit inflation. The combination of exploding profits, inflation-caused declining real wages and falling unemployment is likely to trigger a wage–price spiral. What we have here is an inflationary boom, which periodically can be found to a certain extent in almost all countries in the world.

The second scenario, stagflation, typically describes the combination of restrictive monetary policy in a constellation of cost inflation. The collapse in investment demand and other demand elements leads to falling output, increasing unemployment and demand deflation. At the same time wage-induced inflation or inflation caused by other cost factors like oil prices still continues to rise and these cost rises over-compensate demand deflation. Examples of a situation when both the price level and the unemployment rate increased are the 1970s in many countries.[60]

The combination of continuous wage cuts and a lack of goods market demand leads to a deflationary process and to what is known as a depression. In this scenario falling prices reduce demand and output further and the resulting increasing unemployment leads in turn to further nominal wage cuts and wage deflation.

The fourth constellation, the combination of a cost or wage deflation and high goods market demand is possible but not very likely. It can for example express expansionary fiscal and monetary policy in a situation of labour market pressure and falling wages. In 1997, in the period after the Asian crisis, China fits into this constellation as it combined high GDP growth driven by active macroeconomic policy and falling prices (IMF 2003).

Taking into account all the different cost factors in addition to wages and demand inflation/deflation, one could expect only a loose relationship between unit labour costs and price level changes. However, the relationship between unit labour costs and GDP deflator is surprisingly close. For the US, the UK, Japan and Germany this is revealed in Figures 2.14, 2.15, 2.16 and 2.17. Without overstating we can argue that at least for developed countries nominal unit labour costs are the anchor for the price level. For developing countries the nominal exchange rate can become a second important anchor, but this is not the issue here. In all four countries in the figures relatively high increases in unit labour costs and sharp inflation jumps in the 1970s, which still had some effects in the 1980s, were experienced. In the 1990s unit labour cost increases generally

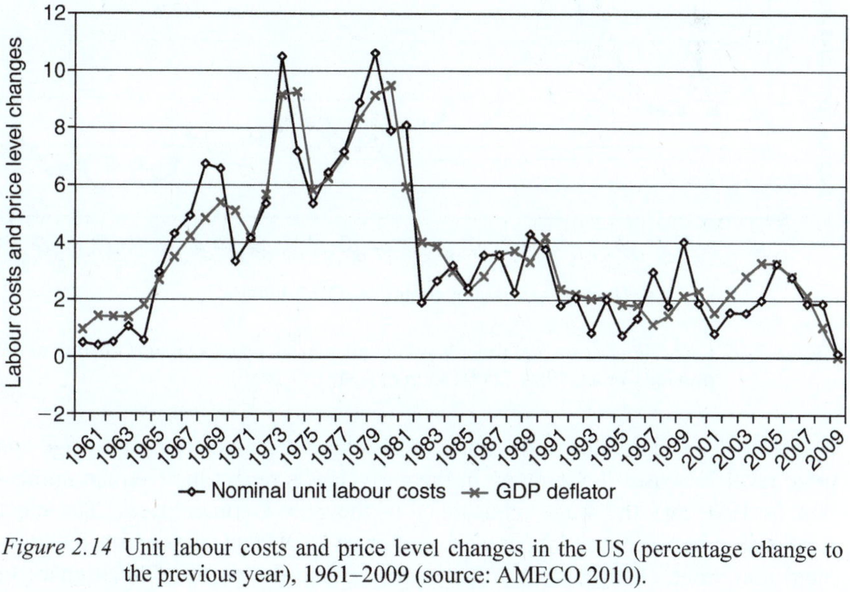

Figure 2.14 Unit labour costs and price level changes in the US (percentage change to the previous year), 1961–2009 (source: AMECO 2010).

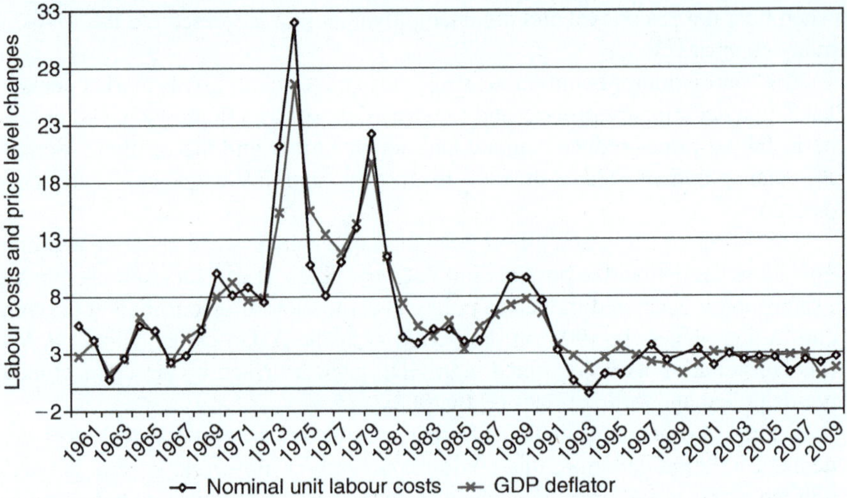

Figure 2.15 Unit labour costs and price level changes in the UK (percentage change to the previous year), 1961–2009 (source: AMECO 2010).

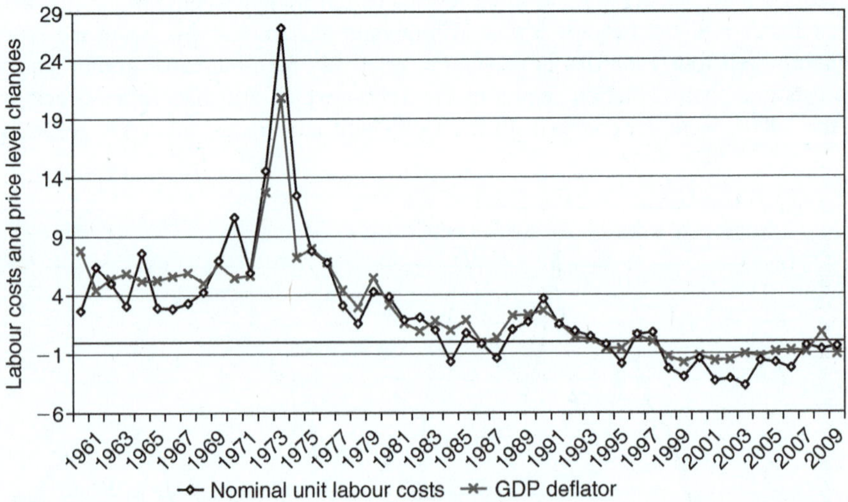

Figure 2.16 Unit labour costs and price level changes in Japan (percentage change to the previous year), 1961–2009 (source: AMECO 2010).

decelerated. In Japan they even started to become negative. The high wage and price level increases in Germany in the early 1990s reflect the German unification in 1990 and the wage adjustment in the new German states. The close relationship between unit labour costs and price level changes supports the argument that wage changes do not necessarily cause the onset of inflationary or

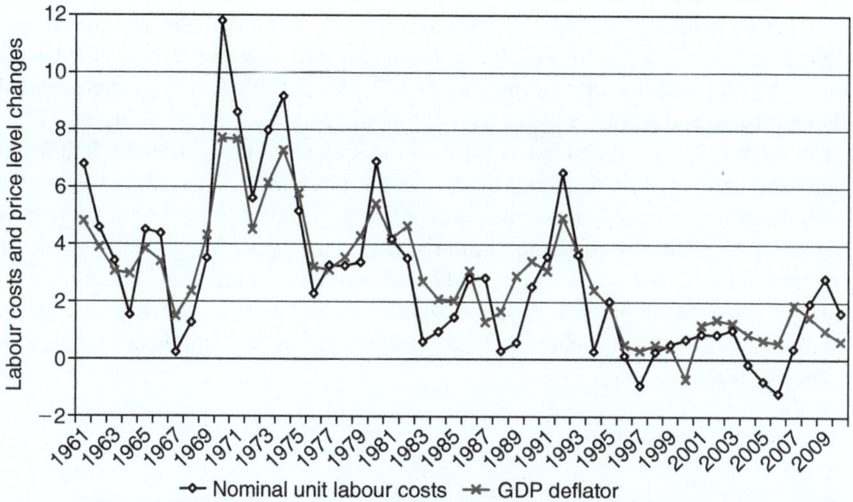

Figure 2.17 Unit labour costs and price level changes in Germany (percentage change to the previous year), 1961–2009 (source: AMECO 2010).

deflationary processes, but strong inflationary or deflationary processes are very closely linked to upward or downward wage–price spirals.

The wage norm

Given the close relationship between unit labour costs and the price level it is obvious that macroeconomic wage development is of key importance for economic development and monetary policy in particular. Wage increases that are too high lead to inflation, which sooner or later has to be combated by the central bank. Wage increases that are too low lead to deflation. A central bank uses restrictive monetary policy to fight against inflation. This may be costly with respect to output and employment, but in this way inflationary developments can be prevented. The central bank is weaker when confronted with deflationary processes, as the nominal interest rate cannot become negative. The rigidity of nominal wages, especially in a situation of high unemployment, becomes one of the key variables in averting deflation. The central bank needs powerful trade unions and a somewhat functional wage bargaining mechanism to prevent falling unit labour costs. Simplified, one can argue that, among other targets, the central bank is responsible for defending price level stability and trade unions are responsible for avoiding deflation by not accepting nominal wages cuts.

The question that arises is how nominal wages should develop to support a stable macroeconomic development. Of course the wage norm we propose is the desired wage development. However, there is no guarantee that wages actually develop according that norm.

Unit labour costs correspond to the relationship between nominal hourly wage and labour productivity. Unit labour costs ($ULC = W/Y_r$) are total nominal wages divided by real output. If we divide nominator and denominator of unit labour costs by the number of working hours (H), we get $W/H = w$ as the nominal hourly wage and $Y_r/H = \pi$ as the average labour productivity, resulting in $W/Y_r = w/\pi$. Above, it was argued that there is in the long run a proportional relationship between changes in unit labour costs and the price level, $\dot{P} = \dot{ULC}$. Taking the definition of unit labour costs into account, then it follows that $\dot{P} = \dot{w} - \dot{\pi}$ with $\dot{w}$ as percentage change of nominal hourly wages and π as the percentage change of productivity. If $\dot{\pi}_{Trend}$ is trend productivity and $\dot{P}_{Target}$ the target inflation rate, and if wage developments should realise wage inflation in line with the target inflation rate, we can define the wage norm $\dot{w}_{Norm}$ as the functional increase in nominal wages:

$$\dot{w}_{Norm} = \dot{\pi}_{Trend} + \dot{P}_{Target}.$$

When we speak about a target inflation rate we do not at all support inflation targeting as a monetary policy strategy. However, the central banks in all countries, even if they are very careful about growth and employment, know quite well what the desired medium-term inflation rates should be. Certainly, it should be positive and high enough to give the central bank the option to reduce real interest rates by cutting nominal rates in case this is needed to stimulate the economy (see Section 2.4.2). It makes no sense to choose a very high inflation rate. For developed countries an inflation rate for a currency area of 3–4 per cent is probably suitable.

A wage development according to such a wage norm serves as a nominal anchor for the price level. If, for example, the target inflation rate is 3 per cent and trend productivity 2 per cent, nominal wages have to increase by 5 per cent to realise the targeted inflation rate. As annual productivity changes with developments during the business cycle, trend productivity has to be used to calculate the desired wage increase. During a recession the number of employees usually cannot be adjusted to reduced production without some time delay. Additionally, businesses can have an interest in holding on to a core workforce even in an economic crisis. Statistically, this leads to a slower increase or even a reduction in productivity. In contrast, during an economic growth phase productivity rises, because production is initially expanded with the existing employment level. The wage norm calls for a nominal wage rigidity or a stable increase in nominal wages per hour. A flexible nominal wage level destabilises the economy, as it leads to disastrous waves of inflation and deflation. Keynes (1936: 269) is right to emphasise: 'To suppose that a flexible wage policy is a right and proper adjunct of a system which on the whole is one of laissez-faire, is the opposite of the truth.'

In many countries trade unions strive for wage increases according to the productivity trend plus compensation for the actual or expected inflation rate, instead of for the target inflation rate. Such a wage setting formula is problematic and

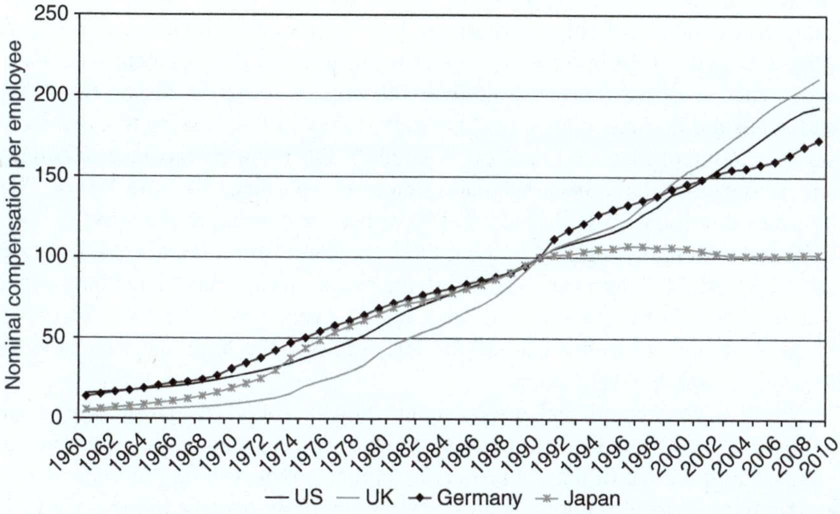

Figure 2.18 Nominal compensation per employee in the US, the UK, Japan and Germany, total economy, 1960–2009 (1991 = 100) (source: AMECO 2010).

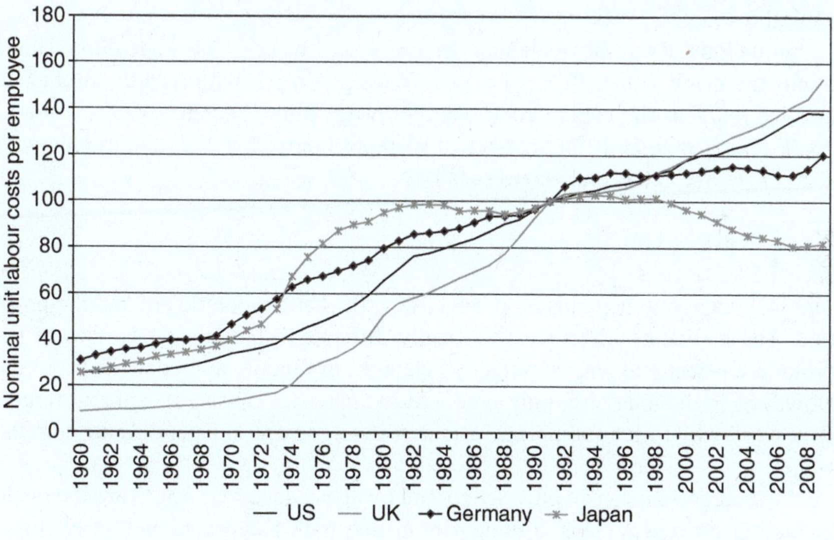

Figure 2.19 Nominal unit labour costs per employee in the US, the UK, Japan and Germany, total economy, 1960–2009 (1991 = 100) (source: AMECO 2010).

likely to trigger inflationary and deflationary processes. An oil price increase, for example, can then trigger a wage–price spiral.

Nominal wages in the US, the UK, Germany and Japan developed in different ways (see Figure 2.18). In Japan and Germany they increased relatively slowly and in Japan even started to decrease slightly in the second half of the 1990s. In contrast, in the UK and especially in the US nominal wages increased continuously and almost without interruptions. Looking at unit labour costs in Figure 2.14–2.17 and 2.19 it becomes clear that in Japan wage development on a macroeconomic level was clearly dysfunctional: unit labour costs during the 1980s and 1990s did increase a great deal but then started to fall, leading to a deflationary development that could not be stopped by the Bank of Japan. In Germany unit labour costs have been stagnating more or less since the mid-1990s. This indicates that nominal wage increases have been according to the trend productivity but without taking into account the European Central Bank's (ECB) target inflation rate of 2 per cent. To fulfil the wage norm, annual nominal wage increases should have been 2 per cent higher every year after the mid-1990s. Wage development in the US and the UK was first too high and then more or less in line with the wage norm.

Nominal wages and real wages should not be confused. To be functional, nominal wages should not respond to changes in real wages. For example, an increase in the price of natural resources implies a reduction in the living standard for the majority of the population. However, if an increase in the price level caused by such a change in the structure of prices is not accepted and leads to higher nominal wages, a wage–price spiral is triggered which in the end will not be able to compensate for the loss in real wages caused by higher prices of natural resources.

Let us look at the factors which determine real wages. The wage quota is one minus the profit quota, $W/Y = 1 - Q/Y$. With $Q = q{\cdot}p{\cdot}\mathrm{k}$ with q as the profit rate and $k = p{\cdot}\mathrm{k}/Y$ as the capital coefficient the wage quota becomes $W/Y = 1 - q{\cdot}\mathrm{k}$. As $W = w{\cdot}H$ with H as the number of working hours, $Y = Y_r{\cdot}P$ and productivity is $\pi = Y_r/H$, we get as real wages (w/P):

$$\frac{w}{P} = \pi(1 - q \cdot k)\,.$$

The real wage rate depends on productivity, the capital coefficient and the profit rate. The capital coefficient is politically difficult to influence. Changes in the profit rate affect real wages, reflecting changes in functional income distribution. However, in the long term only productivity increases cause a rise in real wages. It is worthwhile mentioning again that real wages are independent of nominal wages.

Wage negotiations can only set nominal wages, since real wages are the result of market processes. This argument is in line with Keynes' thinking. Nominal wage cuts cannot bring down real wages. 'There may exist no expedient by which labour as a whole can reduce its *real* wage to a given figure by making revised *money* bargains with the entrepreneurs' (Keynes 1936: 13). Japan is a perfect example of this argument. In spite of reductions of nominal wages real wages in Japan increased (see Figure 2.20).

There is no compromise between neoclassical and Keynesian thinking in the understanding of the macroeconomic role of wages. In the neoclassical world, workers have control over real wages by changing the nominal wage level. The

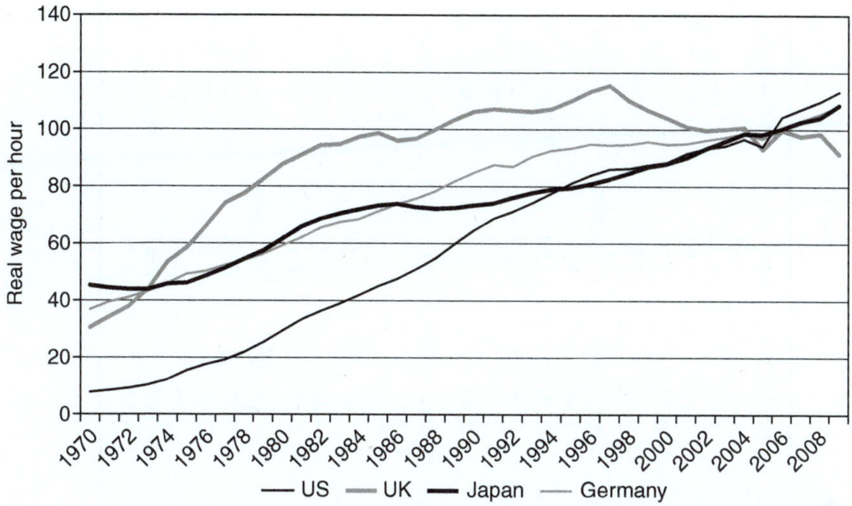

Figure 2.20 Real wage per hour in the US, the UK, Japan and Germany, total economy, 1970–2009 (2005 = 100) (source: AMECO 2010, authors' calculation).

price level is explained by the quantity theory of money. A reduction in real wages is assumed to change not only income distribution in favour of profits, but it also increases labour demand. Classical economists like Adam Smith or David Ricardo and also Karl Marx all argued that changes in wages affect income distribution.

Table 2.7 shows to which extent the US, the UK, Germany and Japan realised the wage norm between the 1970s and today. For each country time periods according to the business cycle are calculated, starting with the first year of an expansion. Then for the periods average labour productivity increases plus the target inflation rate of the central bank are shown. To determine an inflation target involves for some periods and some countries an element of arbitrariness, as an official inflation target is not always given. However, it is safe to assume that all western central banks prefer a small positive inflation rate. For the US we assumed a target inflation rate of 3 per cent.[61] For Germany and Japan, two countries with a history of overall low inflation, we assumed an inflation target of 2 per cent that also corresponds to the official target of the ECB. Following the Bank of England for the UK we assumed 2.5 per cent except for the last period where we took 2 per cent. Given the target inflation rates and the average productivity increases the wage norm is calculated. Finally, given the average nominal wage increases, the deviations between the actual wage development and the wage norm are shown.

Using this simple way to calculate the wage norm it shows that nominal wage increases in the 1970s were too high in all countries. This led to restrictive

Table 2.7 Deviations from the wage norm in the US, the UK, Japan and Germany, 1971–2008

United States	Business cycles	1971–1975	1976–1982	1983–1991	1992–2001	2002–2008
	Average labour productivity increase (%)	1.66	0.69	1.47	1.80	1.77
	Target inflation rate (%)	3.00	3.00	3.00	3.00	3.00
	Wage norm	4.66	3.69	4.47	4.80	4.77
	Average nominal wage increase (%)t	7.76	8.48	4.57	3.70	3.71
	Average deviation from wage norm[1]	3.10	4.79	0.10	–1.10	–1.06
United Kingdom	Business cycles	1971–1975	1976–1981	1982–1991	1992–2002	2003–2008
	Average labour productivity increase (%)	1.91	1.63	1.98	2.20	1.42
	Target inflation rate (%)	2.50	2.50	2.50	2.50	2.00
	Wage norm	4.41	4.12	4.48	4.70	3.42
	Average nominal wage increase (%)	17.52	14.61	8.12	4.26	3.90
	Average deviation from wage norm[1]	13.11	10.49	3.64	–0.44	0.49
Germany	Business cycles	1971–1975	1976–1982	1983–1993	1994–2003	2004–2008
	Average labour productivity increase (%)	2.69	1.89	1.81	2.11	1.35
	Target inflation rate (%)	2.00	2.00	2.00	2.00	2.00
	Wage norm	4.69	3.89	3.81	4.11	3.34
	Average nominal wage increase (%)	10.19	5.76	4.21	2.69	1.33
	Average deviation from wage norm[1]	5.50	1.87	0.40	–1.42	–2.02
Japan	Business cycles	1971–1974	1975–1986	1987–1993	1994–1999	2000–2008
	Average labour productivity increase (%)	4.087	3.34	2.58	1.02	1.71
	Target inflation rate (%)	2.00	2.00	2.00	2.00	2.00
	Wage norm	6.09	5.34	4.58	3.02	3.71
	Average nominal wage increase (%)	18.87	6.61	3.48	0.67	–0.45
	Average Deviation from Wage Norm[1]	12.79	1.28	–1.10	–2.35	–4.16

Source: AMECO (2010), authors' calculations.

Note
1 Difference between the wage norm and the average nominal wage increases.

monetary policies and paved the way for election victories of conservative parties. From the 1990s onwards nominal wage increases in the US were more or less in line with the wage norm, especially if we take into account that a relatively high target inflation rate for the Federal Reserve (Fed) is assumed. To avoid misunderstandings, we are speaking here about the wage level and not about wage dispersion. Nominal wage cuts for certain groups of workers are possible also if the average nominal wage level increases. Wage increases in the UK were much too high in the 1970s and still exceeded the wage norm in the 1980s. Over the following two business cycles until 2008 wage increases were very close to the wage norm. Compared with other countries, Germany had only moderately too high wage increases in the 1970s. In the 1980s the wage norm was realised overall. From the mid-1990s onwards wage increases were far too low, even though the very strict inflation target of the ECB is used. Japan in the early 1970s was confronted with very high wage increases. However, in the cycle starting in 1975 nominal wage increases were not much higher than given by the wage norm. In the 1990s and even more in the 2000s wage increases were consistently below the wage norm, pushing Japan into a deflationary constellation.

2.5.2 Labour market institutions

Wage policy and wage development

A wage development is functional when it is in line with the trend of productivity development and the target inflation rate and does not allow significant deviations above or below this wage norm. Wage increases that are too high involve the risk of inflation and those that are too low threaten to incite a deflationary development. Both are dysfunctional.

We can clearly speak about monetary policy, simply because an agent, the central bank, exists which must take into account macroeconomic effects of its policy. Wage policy in a macroeconomic policy regime, in contrast, is only possible if agents exist which can act on a macroeconomic level. A straightforward case for this would be wage negotiations between a trade union federation and a federation of employers' associations conducting negotiations for all employees in a country. This type of negotiations was, and to a certain extent still is, typical for Scandinavian countries. On the other hand, wage negotiations on an industrial level can internalise macroeconomic effects of a wage development under certain conditions too. If the agents in such negotiations know that they have macroeconomic responsibilities and if the outcome of such negotiations has signalling effects for the whole economy, or at least for important segments of it, we can also speak of wage policy. Wages can be influenced by governments (including central banks) and/or wage coordination can be taken over by employers' associations alone. In these cases, too, we speak of a wage policy. However, if wage negotiations are conducted on a corporate level or even between individual employees and the management, wage policy is not possible.

Wages in such institutional frameworks are completely driven by microeconomic considerations. The resulting wage development does not reflect a macroeconomic wage policy.

Changing labour markets

Labour markets were always more intensively regulated than goods markets. Manpower cannot be de-linked from human beings. Like money and nature labour is an area which cannot be left to pure market forces (Polanyi 1944). In this respect the neoclassical ideal of a completely deregulated labour market with only individually stipulated working contracts is an illusion. In almost all historical periods of capitalism there was a surplus of labour. Such a constellation leads to an asymmetrical power relationship between companies and individual workers in the labour market, forcing workers to offer their manpower at any price. Workers do not have the physical means to start producing goods. Neither do they usually have sufficient wealth to decide to 'consume' leisure time and stay at home if wages become too low.[62] Workers in completely market-driven labour markets suffer from the extreme pressure to sell their working capacity at any price to survive. In a constellation of unemployment and a completely market-driven labour market, not only does the wage level decrease leading to deflationary processes, but also the wage structure most likely widens in such a way that the low paid workers are no longer able to survive. An example of such disastrous constellations is the industrial revolution when wages of the poor fell to such low levels that whole families including children had to work to survive. Today this phenomenon can be found in developing and also in some developed countries where the 'working-poor' need several jobs to survive. To guarantee that negotiations between capital and labour are on an acceptable and equal level, trade unions as workers' associations are needed. In this sense trade unions are the endogenous result of labour markets and the precondition for the stability of macroeconomic development and for the prevention of an extremely wide wage structure.

Trade unions can negotiate wages (and other elements of working contracts) on a company level. However, in many countries wage negotiations are stipulated on a more general level in the economy, for example on the industrial or even central level. For this purpose well-organised employers' associations are needed to negotiate with trade unions. In addition to trade unions and employers' associations governments deeply influence labour markets by labour market laws including regulations on minimum wages, on unemployment insurance and on social benefits. If workers are not covered by collective agreements, for example in industries or firms with no or weak unions, minimum wages and social benefits represent a so-called reservation wage as no one would like to work below this rate. The reservation wage constitutes the wage level of the lowest paid: when no minimum wages exist, their wages fall to the level of social benefits; if there are minimum wages, which only make sense if set sufficiently above the level of social transfers, the wages of the lowest paid fall to the minimum wage. Germany, which does not have statutory minimum wages, is an instructive example for the first case (see the case study on Germany).

Table 2.8 reveals that unemployment rates in almost all developed countries increased. For all OECD countries they have been rising from a particularly low level in the 1960s. In the group of the four case study countries, the increase in Germany was especially pronounced while in Japan, too, unemployment rates climbed continuously. In the UK and the US unemployment rates jumped in the 1980s to high levels, improved a bit in the decades that followed, but overall showed an increase as well.

At the same time union density in many countries decreased (OECD 2009d). In the US, the UK, Japan and Germany union membership in percentage of all employees dropped substantially. Most countries experienced a peak in union density in the 1970s or 1980s and then a dramatic decline. However, there are important exceptions, for example union membership remained high in Scandinavian countries. Yet, in most countries, and definitely in the four countries selected as case studies, we had the combined effect of increasing unemployment and falling union density. The result was that the bargaining power of individual workers and of trade unions substantially weakened. Together with this development deflation is becoming a real danger again. Simultaneously, the wage structure widened in all countries and the percentage of employees with low paid jobs increased. Also, in almost all countries the percentage of employees and persons in society who live under precarious conditions rose. In the following section we analyse the main factors which led to these developments.

The train of Neoliberal Globalisation, which gained pace in the decades after the neoliberal revolution in the 1970s/1980s, had a profound impact on the labour markets. Financial and goods markets, as well as labour markets, were all exposed to frequent and sometimes far-reaching shocks under Neoliberal Globalisation. The globalisation of international trade, the rise of multinational companies, exchange rate shocks and a new role of some big players in the international distribution of labour like China, India or Brazil put pressure on labour markets in developed countries. Developed countries were exposed to far-reaching changes in the distribution of labour. Labour-intensive and low-skilled

Table 2.8 Unemployment rates in selected OECD countries, 1960–2009 (annual average)

	1960–1969	*1970–1979*	*1980–1989*	*1990–1999*	*2000–2009*
Germany[1]	0.65	2.01	5.83	7.87	8.65
United Kingdom	1.61	3.49	9.45	8.00	5.41
Japan	1.29	1.66	2.47	3.05	4.74
USA	4.78	6.21	7.27	5.71	5.54
OECD	2.17	3.41	6.37	7.87	7.84

Source: AMECO (2010).

Note

1 Up until 1990 Federal Republic of Germany.

jobs were transferred to high growth countries like China and other Asian countries, but also Latin America or the countries of the former USSR and its satellites. Additionally, skilled jobs were lost in developed countries as multinational companies outsourced production to cheaper developing countries. Furthermore, the change in technologies throughout the past few decades reduced the number of unskilled jobs in the manufacturing sector (Brown *et al.* 2010). All of these developments hit the traditional industrial sectors in developed countries and reduced employment in these sectors. As they used to be the core sector of unions' representation, union membership shrunk. The expanding service sectors such as low-value-adding personal services like cleaning or deliveries or the financial sector usually have a low union density and for traditional unions were more difficult to organise. The quickly changing distribution of international labour brought industries in developed countries with comparative disadvantages (for example simple textile or electronic products) under pressure. The (in the end hopeless) fight to keep jobs in these industries in the country increased pressure to accept low wages and deteriorating labour conditions. Unskilled workers were especially hit by these developments.

It would be a mistake to argue that the factors explained above are the only ones responsible for the changes in the labour markets. A policy towards institutional change with the aim to influence the behaviour of agents and to create new rules has been equally important. In the early 1980s, starting in the US and the UK, policies to reduce the protection of workers including some policies extremely hostile to trade unions and collective wage bargaining were introduced. These policies spread to most other developed countries, but not to all. After her election in 1979, Margaret Thatcher followed a policy of blasting the British trade unions. Overall she succeeded in her efforts to weaken the unions with the result of restricting their sphere of influence to the corporate level and only a small part of the economy. A no less radical strategy was followed by Ronald Reagan. Shortly after his election in 1980 air traffic controllers went on strike. After refusing Reagan's ultimatum to return to work within 48 hours, the air traffic controllers' union – one of the few that supported Reagan's election – was destroyed and military air traffic controllers took over for some time. This had a symbolic effect in the US: a change from the Treaty of Detroit,[63] as Frank Levy and Peter Temin (2010) call it, to the market fundamentalism-based Washington Consensus was initiated.

Weaker labour market institutions and weaker union power in almost all western countries led to a sharp increase in precarious jobs like part-time work, fixed-term jobs and temporary employment. Domestic outsourcing of companies with good salaries and/or strong unions to low-wage sectors with precarious jobs and no unions became widespread. This regulation arbitrage covers transferring the production of assembly parts to supplies, the external purchase of cleaning, accounting and security services, call centres and much more.

Thus, changes in labour market institutions coincided with new economic forces that were triggered by the Neoliberal Globalisation chosen in the 1970s/1980s. As wage development is one of the key questions for the macroeconomic policy regime, in the following section we look more closely at wage bargaining systems.

Wage bargaining systems

There are many types of labour market institutions and different countries have different institutions according to their historical development. We concentrate on institutions which are important for the development of wages.

There is a long continuing debate concerning the relationships between specific wage-setting institutions and wage development on the one hand, and the economic development and unemployment levels on the other. In an influential study of wage-setting mechanisms in western industrial countries, Lars Calmfors and John Driffill (1988) suggested that both highly centralised as well as highly decentralised wage setting systems produce very low wage cost pressure, whereas wage setting at an intermediate level tends to produce higher wage settlements. According to them countries like Sweden, Norway and Austria had highly centralised bargaining systems, Japan and the US highly decentralised ones, and countries like Germany or the UK were somewhere in the middle. Adopting their argument, decentralised and centralised wage bargaining systems increase the likelihood of moderate wage developments and allow central banks a relative expansionary monetary policy. Countries with such labour market institutions have relatively low unemployment rates in the long run. On the other hand, intermediate wage bargaining systems permanently lead to too high wage increases and to overall restrictive monetary policy, low growth and high unemployment in the long run. In the Calmfors–Driffill model the main reason for the functionality of centralised wage bargaining systems can be found in wage coordination by trade unions. Unions in centralised bargaining systems take into account macroeconomic considerations and know that excessively high wage increases lead to inflation and restrictive monetary policy and consequently may trigger a stabilisation crisis with high unemployment. Wage bargaining at the corporate level takes into account the competitiveness of individual businesses. Excessively high wages for a single firm simply kick the firm out of the market and result in lay-offs of its employees. Firm unions know this and demand only moderate wage increases. However, when wage negotiations take place at an intermediate level neither business interests nor macroeconomic considerations are taken into consideration, which tends to lead to greater pressure for increased wages.

Yet, David Soskice (1990) argued correctly that the formal level of wage negotiations does not really reveal whether wage negotiations take into account macroeconomic repercussion of changes in the wage level or not. A high degree of macroeconomic wage coordination can also arise when wage negotiations are carried out at the industry or even individual business level if informal coordination mechanisms exist or other agents than unions take over the coordination function. This is especially the case if the role of employers' associations and of the government in wage bargaining processes is considered. For example, Japan is considered a country with a highly coordinated wage development despite formal wage negotiations on the corporate level. In the Japanese case the group of big, usually export-oriented companies, together with the government and the weak Japanese union federation, determines the broad wage development that is more or less adopted by the other firms. A similar informal signalling mechanism used to exist and is still partly in place in Germany. Wage negotiations are conducted on a regional industrial level, usually in the metal industry in a region with strong unions and employers' associations. The outcome of the bargaining has signalling functions for the whole industry and is of key importance for other industries as well. After the German unification in 1990 the signalling effect between the industries with strong unions and industries with weak unions broke down. However, for a part of the German economy, especially in the big export industries, the coordination still works. Governments can also play an important role in the wage bargaining process by cushioning negative employment effects of economic and institutional restructuring, for example through the offer of generous early retirement schemes. This was an instrument extensively used in Germany. Calmfors and Driffill classified the US as a country with decentralised bargaining structures. Indeed, the US until today is to a large extent characterised by corporate level wage negotiations with no macroeconomic coordination. According to the same study by Calmfors and Driffill, the UK was classified as a country with uncoordinated industry level bargaining. As noted above the government of Margaret Thatcher substantially weakened trade unions with the result that firm level negotiations became more important. Looking at the present situation, the US and the UK have clearly decentralised and uncoordinated wage bargaining systems. Japan still has a coordinated wage bargaining system but the coordination is mainly done by employers' associations, especially in export-oriented industries (Traxler 1999). In Germany the comprehensive wage coordination system, which was in place after the Second World War, fell apart in the 1990s. But among the key export industries the coordination is still functional.

Just like governments, the central bank can substantially influence the wage bargaining process. Approaches that use game theory to examine the interaction between the central bank and agents responsible for wage setting, particularly trade unions, became fashionable. The argument is that a central bank with a significant commitment to price level stability has the advantage of the first move, and this sets a hard constraint for wage bargaining agents and leads to wage moderation. For Germany this argument has some importance (Scharpf 1987). Before the start of the European Monetary Union (EMU), the German Bundesbank always threatened agents responsible for wage bargaining that it would not tolerate inflationary wage increases and would immediately react with restrictive monetary policy had they not complied with the central bank's recommendation. The Bundesbank did not only threaten, but in fact reacted when it thought necessary. The clearest example for prompt reaction can be found in the early 1970s. In 1973 wage increases became quite high by German standards. The Bundesbank reacted immediately and the recession that followed in 1975 was especially severe. After this episode the unions turned once again to moderate wage increases, as had been the case in the 1950s and 1960s. Other countries used the exchange rate to restrain domestic wage development. For example, many European counties within and outside the European Monetary System (EMS) pegged their currencies to the D-Mark. The central banks of these countries promised to defend the exchange rate peg. Wage bargaining agents predicted that too high wage increases would lead to an erosion of national competitiveness and to current account deficits and that the latter in turn would lead to appreciation pressure, restrictive monetary policy and unemployment.

The debate above focuses on how wage bargaining processes can internalise macroeconomic effects of wage changes and in this way lead to a functional wage development according to the wage norm. Calmfors and Driffill offer, as was mentioned above, some solution to the complicated macroeconomic wage coordination. They argue that firm level negotiations are as good as macroeconomic wage coordination as firm unions care for the competitiveness of the firm and moderate wage demands. Despite the fact that company unions may care for the competitiveness of their firm, the Calmfors–Driffill argument has some shortcomings (Soskice 1990). In a situation of low unemployment rates there is no guarantee that firm-based negotiations lead to wage moderation. Actually the opposite is likely to happen: if productivity levels of firms in an industry are different, firms with high productivity gains and high profits usually pay higher wages than those with lower productivity. However, employees in firms with poorer technology and lower productivity – working with the same effort as their colleagues in more productive firms – have an incentive to demand equally high wage increases. They can even refer to the law of one price, which is also valid in the labour market. Yet, a catch-up of wages in low productivity firms can trigger additional wage demand in high productivity firms, and so on. Another factor that may provoke such a wage–price spiral is the different strength of firm unions, the local pushiness, as Soskice calls it. Radical firm level unions probably push for higher wages. In general firm-based negotiations make it difficult to prevent a wage–price spiral if unemployment rates decrease as firms that follow a micrologic may push up wages by headhunting highly qualified personnel from other firms. Strong employers' associations and wage negotiations on a central level can prevent such inflationary competition for workers.[64]

Equally dangerous besides an inflationary wage development is the problem of too low wage increases or even reductions in nominal wages. The possibility of deflationary wage cuts has been neglected in the whole debate. This is understandable against the background of the inflation wave of the 1970s. However, limiting theoretical and empirical considerations on the question of wage moderation is not satisfactory. In Japan deflation came back and in other countries, for example Germany, inflation rates became very low. Future wage inflation does not seem to be a problem for many countries.

Both a coordinated wage bargaining process and a non-coordinated one can lead to deflationary wage developments. We start with coordinated bargaining. If the macroeconomic decision makers, including trade unions and employers' associations, are orientated towards a neoclassical model, and thus believe wage reductions lead to higher employment, then a coordinated macroeconomic wage-setting mechanism can lead to deflationary developments. Moreover, if the export sector of a country dominates the wage negotiations, it is conceivable that wage development will be subject to a mercantilist strategy, whereby the international competitiveness of the country is to be increased by wage restraint (Franzese 2001; Hein 2003). Japan is a very good example of this. Employers' associations, the unions and the government all follow a corporatist mercantile strategy in discussing wages and exchange rate movements. 'Although exports are a relatively small share of GDP, these discussions are based on the requirements of maintaining as far as possible cost competitiveness. They therefore involve working out with government likely exchange rate movements.' (Soskice 1990: 41). Similarly, Hiwatari (2002: 4) wrote about Japan more recently:

> By comparison, if unions are weak and decentralised, the employers, especially large export sector employers, may coordinate wages if they share concern over worsening terms of trade caused by currency appreciation and the increasing costs of domestic goods (due to labour costs). Fear of a recession originating from export stagnation should lead export-dependent employers to persuade their domestic counterparts to join wage coordination.

The situation in Germany is similar. However, in Germany it is the coordination between employers' associations and unions in the export sector which led to very low wage increases in this sector in the past. As this sector in almost every year has taken the lead in wage negotiation rounds, wage increases in Germany were too low compared with the wage norm, even in the sector where coordination still works.

Thus, the development of individual sectors can have a decisive influence on wage developments in the economy as a whole. The export sector is one example, the public sector another. For instance, the significant wage reductions in the public sector under the German Brüning government in the early 1930s opened the way for general wage reductions and deflation in Germany (Heine 2004).

Firm-based wage negotiations are susceptible to result in competitive wage cuts. When a certain unemployment level is reached, the danger of the unemployed competing for jobs and accepting lower wages as well as of employers cutting wages exists. This can easily bring the economy into a deflationary spiral.

When we look at wage development in the UK and the US, both of which have uncoordinated wage bargaining systems, the mercantilist wage coordination that has been a hallmark for Japan and Germany did not exist. In the early 1990s probably nobody expected that Japan and Germany with coordinated bargaining systems would violate the wage norm, while the UK and the US with firm-based bargaining systems would follow a much more functional wage development and develop much better on the whole than Japan and Germany. But the danger of deflationary wage cuts is also increasing in the US and the UK. If unemployment rates increase to high levels and prevail for a long time, the microeconomic logic of wage cuts can become overwhelming. Given the erosion of labour market institutions in recent decades deflation becomes a serious potential problem once again.

The NAIRU

There is an inherent conflict between very low and very high unemployment rates and the aim to have a relatively stable positive inflation rate in the medium term. In a situation of low unemployment, there is an inflationary threat, while in a situation of high unemployment deflationary developments are possible. The intensity of this conflict with regard to both inflation and deflation depends on labour market institutions, first of all on wage bargaining mechanisms. An attempt to analyse this conflict is the NAIRU approach (NAIRU as Non-Accelerating Inflation Rate of Unemployment). A typical NAIRU curve is given in Figure 2.21. If $\dot{P}$ is the inflation rate and u is the unemployment rate, then the NAIRU function is given by $\dot{P} = \dot{P}(u)$. With $\dot{P}_T$ as the target rate of inflation, the corresponding unemployment rate can be determined. The unemployment rate u_1 then is the NAIRU.

The NAIRU curve is based on Keynesian thinking since a relationship between nominal wage development and the price level is assumed, whereby the nominal wage depends on the unemployment rate. The NAIRU curve has increasingly gained approval, particularly within the context of New Keynesianism.[65] The shape and location of the NAIRU curve is country specific and depends on a number of factors, including labour market structural problems, such as the regional- and qualification-dependent mismatch in labour supply and labour demand, demographic developments and, of course, the wage bargaining process.

The NAIRU curve should not be confused with the short-term Phillips curve which looks similar but is based on neoclassical thinking. In the Phillips curve

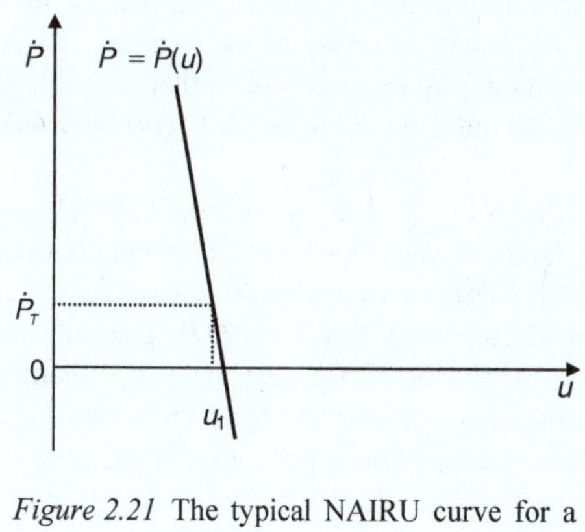

Figure 2.21 The typical NAIRU curve for a labour market with flexible nominal wages.

an inflationary process triggered by an excessively high exogenous money supply by the central bank leads to inflation. In contrast to company managers, workers are assumed to have money illusion: as they do not see a decline in real wages right away, they do not claim higher nominal wages, which leads to higher profits on the part of the firms. If this happens, according to the neoclassical labour market, unemployment decreases. New Keynesian thinking is similar. However, the money illusion argument to explain constant nominal wages is substituted by the idea that workers and managers prefer long-term labour contracts to reduce transaction costs and uncertainty (Mankiw and Romer 1991). In this case, workers simply cannot increase nominal wages in an inflationary situation and have to wait until new contracts are possible.

Neither has the NAIRU anything to do with the so-called natural rate of unemployment that was introduced by Milton Friedman (1968). Although Friedman partly includes those factors which are regarded as responsible for the NAIRU, irreconcilable theoretical differences remain. According to Friedman, rigidities and distortions in the labour market lead to too high real wages that are incompatible with full employment. In his view, the price level is determined by the money supply in the tradition of the quantity theory of money. The relationship between nominal wages and the price level is, however, the central theme of the NAIRU. Real wages do not play a role in this concept.

The logic of the NAIRU is given by the fact that from some point or other, nominal wages have the tendency to increase with falling unemployment rates. Typically this does not primarily result from strengthened market power of trade unions – which, however, can also be the case in specific situations – but from the high demand for labour that leads to wages above collective bargaining agreements. A certain unemployment rate is therefore necessary to retain price level stability. The level is country specific. In this respect, we essentially agree with the NAIRU concept. However, it should also be emphasised that rising unemployment can lead to deflationary wage developments should labour market institutions fail to prevent wage cuts. It is surprising that, until now, the deflationary part of the NAIRU function has hardly been noticed.

Yet, the NAIRU approach has its limitations. It would be completely misleading to argue that unemployment is always or even in most cases caused by restrictive monetary policy keeping unemployment at a level that prevents inflation. In many circumstances unemployment rates are much higher than needed to keep wage increases stable.

Empirically, the NAIRU is as difficult to calculate as potential output. Calculations of a NAIRU curve are usually based on past developments implicitly extrapolating a moving average. In the end a NAIRU curve that could be used for monetary policy cannot be calculated in a satisfactory way (Stiglitz 1997). The only reason for using the NAIRU is to show, as mentioned above, that there is a relationship between unemployment (employment) and price level changes, while very high and very low unemployment rates can lead to destabilising price level changes.

On purely theoretical grounds the NAIRU curve in Figure 2.21 is possible, albeit unrealistic. It would prevent any stable economic development. Every deviation from the NAIRU unemployment rate u_1 would produce big changes in the price level. As a central bank is not able to control unemployment rates in any direct way, volatile price level changes including deflation would be the result of a NAIRU curve shown in the Figure. Empirically, such volatile price level developments cannot be found.

More plausible is the NAIRU curve presented in Figure 2.22, which allows a whole range of unemployment rates, exactly the unemployment rates between u_1 and u_2, where unemployment can change without affecting the nominal wage development and the price level. The longer the horizontal branch of the NAIRU is, the more favourable the situation is for the economic regime. Thus, the significance of functional wage-setting systems can be clearly shown with the help of the NAIRU concept. Also, in the curve very high unemployment rates do not lead to nominal wage cuts and deflation. Theoretically, a completely horizontal NAIRU curve at the level of a moderate inflation rate would be the best constellation. However, such a curve is not plausible as very low unemployment rates normally lead to higher wages and in a situation of very high unemployment rates a nominal wage anchor becomes more and more difficult to defend. The NAIRU curve in Figure 2.22 makes clear that nominal wage development is the main argument of employment only in exceptional constellations. As mentioned above, usually unemployment rates are much higher than what would be needed to guarantee price level stability. This stresses the Keynesian argument that unemployment in most historical constellations is the outcome of insufficient aggregate demand which is independent of the nominal wage level.

2.6 Fiscal policy

2.6.1 Institutional changes

By definition monetary policy is macroeconomic policy. Wage policy, as macroeconomic policy, is more difficult to achieve. It is only possible under certain conditions (e.g. strong trade unions and employers' associations). Fiscal policy

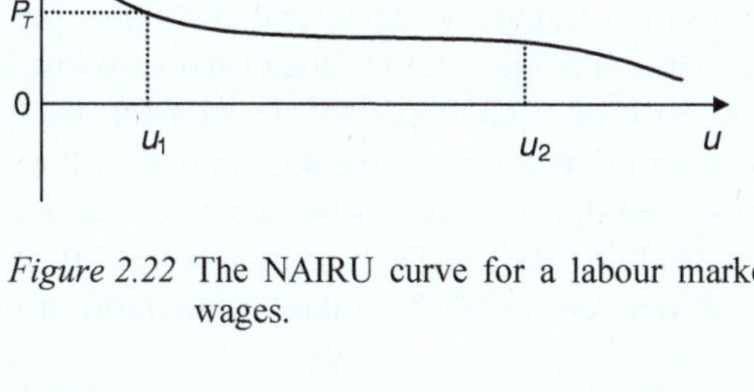

Figure 2.22 The NAIRU curve for a labour market with relatively rigid nominal wages.

is in between. Central governments usually follow macroeconomic-oriented fiscal policy, but for states, counties or local communities there is hardly any incentive to shape their expenditures and revenues according to macroeconomic needs. For example, an expansionary fiscal impulse of a local community will, to a large extent, stimulate the economy outside the community. For small open economic units it is rational to wait for fiscal impulses from other units and benefit from them. For this reason active fiscal policy is hardly a rational instrument for government units below the central state. Also, in many cases lower government levels only have limited or no room for manoeuvre to finance expenditures by credit according to fiscal policy needs. Due to the reasons given above, we concentrate on central governments when discussing fiscal policy decisions. Central governments can either carry out active fiscal policy or coordinate fiscal policy at lower government levels.

Last but not least, government expenditures and revenues reflect political struggles that do not always follow macroeconomic logic. Decisions by governments to increase public expenditures and/or cut taxes may be driven by political rather than macroeconomic reasons and may consequently lead to economically unwarranted and potentially harmful increases in budget deficits. Even for central governments anti-cyclical fiscal policy in line with macroeconomic needs is not guaranteed.

The environment for fiscal policy has been changing for some decades. Together with the increased independence of central banks, direct central bank credits to governments are now more or less forbidden in all developed countries. We agree that it makes sense to have such an institutional arrangement. It would be dangerous to subordinate monetary policy generally to the needs of fiscal policy as this would lead to a soft budget constraint for governments and the temptation to use central bank credits to finance expenditures which would be better financed by taxes. However, under certain constellations direct financing of budget deficits by the central bank can be useful. For example, this is the case when an economy suffers from deflationary developments. In such a situation, an 'unconventional' monetary policy in cooperation with fiscal policy can help to overcome deflation. The combination of some central bank independence with the option of giving central bank credits to governments under certain established circumstances seems to be the best institutional arrangement. We shall also bear in mind that theoretically high and unlimited government deficits can be indirectly financed by commercial banks: commercial banks finance governments and are in turn financed by central banks that buy government bonds.

Figure 2.23 shows the development of general government gross financial liabilities in percentage of GDP for the US, the UK, Japan and Germany. The most striking development is the increase in public debt in Japan from very low levels in the early 1970s to about 200 per cent of GDP in 2010. This reflects the period of low GDP growth after the asset price bubble in the second half of the 1980s (see case study). A less pronounced development in the same direction can be observed in Germany where the public debt to GDP rose from below 20 per cent in the early 1970s to around 80 per cent in 2010. In the US the ratio of public

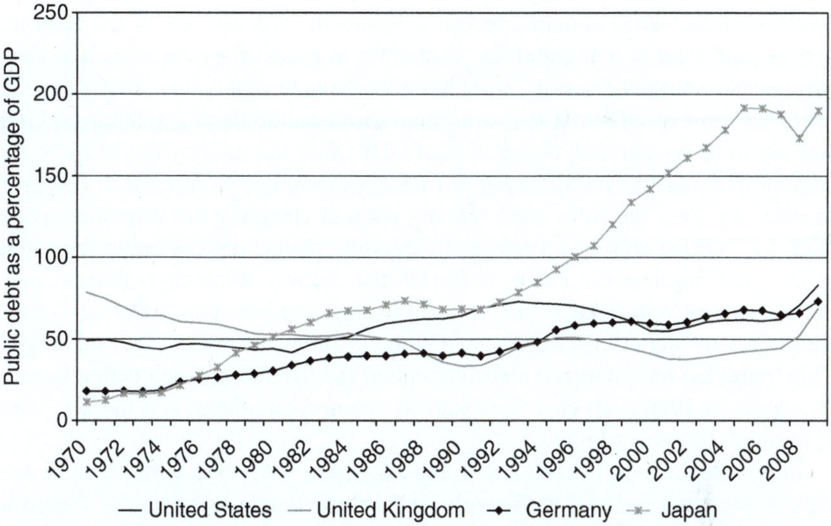

Figure 2.23 General government gross financial liabilities in percentage of GDP in the US, the UK, Japan and Germany, 1970–2009[1] (source: OECD 2009c).

Note
1 Figures for 2009 and 2010 are projections.

debt to GDP increased from 46 per cent in 1970 to around 90 per cent in 2010. The UK started with a debt ratio of about 75 per cent in the early 1970s, and after a period of reducing the debt quota increased it again during the subprime crisis. In the UK today's (2010) public debt quota is slightly higher than in the early 1970s. Overall, public debt ratios increased substantially in OECD countries.

Increasing public debt to GDP shows increasing demands for fiscal policy. The deregulation wave that began in the 1970s has led to a more unstable type of capitalism characterised by lower GDP growth and much higher unemployment rates compared with the decades before. Fiscal policy has been used to stabilise aggregate demand. A striking development related to fiscal policy throughout past decades has been the sharp increase in budget deficits and public debt in relation to GDP during periods of downturns and the very slow and insufficient reduction during periods of higher growth. The outcome is the above-described increase in public debt ratios over the business cycle in most OECD countries.

There were several institutional attempts to prevent budget deficits or increasing public debt ratios. The most ambitious and far-reaching regulations are the Maastricht Treaty of 1992 and even more the Stability and Growth Pact which was adopted in 1997 to prevent high budget deficits. Especially the Stability and Growth Pact became the cornerstone of fiscal policy regulation for the countries who are members of the European Monetary Union (EMU). It was thought that fiscal discipline was not only required to enter the EMU, but also to guarantee fiscal discipline after countries became members. The essence of the Stability and Growth Pact is that countries, excluding in exceptional cases such as deep recessions or natural disasters, were not allowed to have a budget deficit exceeding 3 per cent of GDP. At the same time gross public debt in relation to GDP was not to be greater than 60 per cent of GDP. Should a country not abide by the pact's rules, sanctions in the form of fines were imposed to force such countries to obey. In 2005 the rules were relaxed without changing the substance of the pact. In a similar spirit, as a result of exploding budget deficits under the ruling of Ronald Reagan in the 1980s, in the US the Gramm–Rudman–Hollings Emergency Deficit Control Act (1985) and the Budget and Emergency Deficit Control Reaffirmation Act (1987) were signed with the aim to achieve a balanced budget. They provided for automatic spending cuts if the deficit exceeded deficit targets. However, in 1986 such cuts were judged as unconstitutional and the acts were revised in 1987 accordingly.

In both regions, in Europe and in the US, these laws were violated as budget deficits were not reduced sufficiently to fulfil the regulations. One of the problems of these acts is that during economic booms governments are not forced to bring budget deficits to GDP, for example in the case of the Stability and Growth Pact, to levels sufficiently below 3 per cent. In a period of low growth, budget deficits then become greater than 3 per cent. The pacts have the shortcoming that governments have to realise a target they cannot easily control. To a large extent budget deficits are determined by economic development. During economic slowdowns tax revenues decrease as the tax base shrinks and at the same time expenditures for unemployment benefits and so on rise. Endogenously budget surpluses decline and, in typical cases, budget deficits increase. Theoretically, in such situations the budget deficit can be reduced by changing tax laws to increase government revenues and/or by changing government expenditures. However, such a policy is extremely costly and unwanted because policies to reduce the budget deficit reduce aggregate demand, make economic development even worse, reduce tax revenues and lead to new holes in the budget. Thus, consolidating public budgets in a constellation of economic crisis is not a very wise policy. Overall, budget deficit rules lead to the danger of dysfunctional procyclical fiscal policy. For good reasons, governments not forced by external pressure – like Greece and Ireland in 2010 by other EMU countries or countries following adjustment programmes enforced by the International Monetary Fund – have so far tended to prefer to break the fiscal act.

In spite of negative experiences with budget-deficit acts Germany undertook a new attempt in this direction. In 2009 a balanced-budget law was added to the German constitution. According to this law, in 2016 and thereafter it will be illegal for the federal government to run budget deficits over the business cycle of more than 0.35 per cent of GDP and, beginning with 2020, the federal budget will have to be completely balanced over the business cycle, i.e. with no deficit. This law is much stricter than the Stability and Growth Pact and seems to be closer to the US Gramm–Rudman–Hollings Act, which also aimed at reducing budget deficits to zero in the medium term. One does not need much imagination to predict that the German version of the balanced-budget law is likely to fail as well.

In the US in 1990 the Budget Enforcement Act replaced the failed fiscal acts of the 1980s. The new act was no longer aimed at limiting the budget deficit but at controlling public expenditure. Here, a distinction was made between legally binding and discretionary expenditures. The latter can be decided upon every financial year without changing laws. According to the pact, an increase in discretionary expenditures was only possible according to strict rules. Every increase in discretionary expenditure or the reduction of taxes had to be counter-financed.[66] The Budget Enforcement Act expired in 2002.

From an economic point of view the Budget Enforcement Act is much more useful than attempts to control budget deficits. The stabilisation of discretionary expenditures in the Budget Enforcement Act produces an anti-cyclical fiscal policy. Expenditures do not have to be cut during recessions to fulfil a budget target, as there is no limit set on the deficit. Thus, the government can incur high deficits in a recession, whereas in economic growth phases increased revenues do not lead to greater expenditures since there is an upper expenditure limit that has to be complied with. Thus, increased revenues during higher growth lead to a consolidation of public budgets. The period of high GDP growth in the second half of the 1990s led to budget surpluses in US, not least because of the Budget Enforcement Act (Blinder and Yellen 2001). However, in a situation of deep recession, when additional expenditures are needed to stabilise aggregate demand, rules like the Budget Enforcement Act have their limitations and require exceptions for cases like deep recessions and natural disasters.

Fiscal policy as well as monetary policy has to react in a discretionary way to stabilise aggregate demand and economic development. For central governments strict fiscal rules are not very useful. Especially rules to control budget deficits must be judged as negative institutionalisations which can prevent a functional fiscal policy, as explained in detail in the next section. If a country wants to give itself a fiscal rule, a certain time path of discretionary expenditures is the best basis, letting the budget deficit fluctuate endogenously. While for lower government levels expenditure rules seem preferable, for central governments even such measures can lead to not acceptable restrictions of fiscal policy and are not recommendable. In addition, history shows that fiscal laws can easily break down when the economy is under pressure.

2.6.2 Fiscal policy options

In economic thinking there is no consensus about fiscal policy and its effects on the economy. In a radical neoclassical tradition Barro (1974) points out that, on the basis of neoclassical rational expectations, budget deficits lead to higher expected future tax burdens. Higher expected taxes reduce current private demand exactly to the extent of government increases in demand, thus nullifying the effect on aggregate demand. The New Keynesians see a role for fiscal policy similar to the one for monetary policy. As menu costs, staggered prices, coordination failures or efficiency wages can lead to market failures, there is room for active fiscal policy. The New Consensus model also follows this mode of thinking (Mankiw 2008). Accordingly, fiscal policy only makes sense when the economy is below or above its supply side given equilibrium. This implies that demand management cannot influence the long-term growth trend.

Among Post-Keynesian thinkers there is a common belief that fiscal policy is unfairly ignored by the New Keynesian school of thought. The former find the fiscal policy to be an effective tool that stabilises demand and output in the short, as well as in the long run. Among them, some even discuss that fiscal policy should be the main macroeconomic instrument for the stabilisation of aggregate demand and output in the short and long run, whereas wage policy should aim at stable inflation and exchange rates, leaving the interest rate the role of influencing income distribution and the distribution between monetary wealth owners and firms.[67] Others propose that fiscal policy should be used along with monetary and wage policy, without giving it a specific position. Colander and Matthews (2006) argue that spending and taxation must be adjusted in an anti-cyclical fashion, recommending budget deficits in recessions and sound finance in expansions. By demanding functional finance Arestis and Sawyer (2004: 132) make the case for a fiscal policy that increases 'the level of aggregate demand, where it would otherwise be too low'.[68]

Fiscal policy is an important macroeconomic policy for stabilising economic development. We assume that a functional fiscal policy in our sense, together with other macroeconomic policies, does not only stabilise the business cycle but is also vital for the long-term development of an economy.

Let us start with a discussion of anti-cyclical fiscal policy over the business cycle. Fiscal policy can and should raise insufficient demand in economic recessions and thereby influence the business cycle positively, whereas it can also reduce demand in inflationary booms and thus avoid restrictive monetary policy. To follow this type of anti-cyclical fiscal policy governments should at least accept endogenous automatic stabilisers, which can be considered a passive anti-cyclical fiscal policy. In a recession value added tax, corporate tax, income tax and other government revenues fall because of a shrinking tax base, but at the same time certain expenditures increase, especially those in the social security system. To stabilise demand endogenously increasing budget deficits have to be accepted in such a cyclical phase. In an economic expansion the reverse process occurs. To let the automatic stabilisers fully work two conditions have to be fulfilled. First, governments should not change laws to influence revenues and expenditures. Second, governments should not change discretionary expenditures. If, for example, a government changes its tax laws to reduce budget deficits in a downturn, and/or if discretionary expenditures like public investment are reduced with the same aim, automatic stabilisers are prevented from working sufficiently. Automatic stabilisers have different strengths in different countries. This depends on the specific national tax system, the national expenditure structure and the share of government expenditures or revenues in GDP.

Especially in a deep or even deflationary recession passive fiscal policy is not enough. Active fiscal policy in addition to the automatic stabilisers is needed. That means that in a deep crisis discretionary expenditure and/or tax cuts have to be used to stabilise the economy. Public investment is a good indicator for discretionary fiscal expenditures. If automatic stabilisers are to work, public investment must be independent of the cyclical development and thus contribute to stabilising economic development. In situations of sharp recessions public investment has to be brought forward or even new and not planned public expenditures have to be used to stabilise goods market demand. Likewise, changes in the tax system also belong to active fiscal policy, for instance, in the form of cuts in tax rates in a recession. As a rule, public investment is more suitable for a discretionary fiscal policy than discretionary tax cuts or additional transfer payments. Public investment has the highest multiplier effects as 100 per cent of expenditures effectively increase aggregate demand. If taxes are cut or transfer payments increased the first round effect for demand is smaller because the private sector will save some of the additional disposable income. Nevertheless, in order to stimulate aggregate demand in a recession quickly to cut taxes and/or increase transfers to the poor can be an efficient policy. On the other hand, for expansionary fiscal policy it is obviously not a good idea to cut taxes and/or increase transfers for the rich as this income group has a high savings rate.

So far Keynesians of different persuasions including Neo-Keynesians and even not too stubborn neoclassical economists would agree with most that has been said about fiscal policy. For example, in the first phase of the subprime crisis almost all economists demanded fiscal stimulation. They all agree that expansionary fiscal policy is needed in a deep recession. However, the analysis of the long-term effects of fiscal policy and especially the question as to whether public debt quotas should be allowed to increase in the medium and long run are far more controversial.

Let us now turn to these more controversial dimensions of fiscal policy. The so-called Haavelmo theorem points out that government can stimulate aggregate demand by increasing taxes and spending additional revenues for additional expenditures. The expansive effect is based on the fact that taxpayers save some of their income and their consumption decreases only according to their marginal propensity to consume, whereas governments spend all additional revenue (Haavelmo 1945). The expansionary effect can be increased by taxing high income groups more extensively as these groups have a high marginal savings rate. Haavelmo's argument can be combined with Wagner's Law (Wagner 1893). Wagner argued that, on the basis of technological and societal reasons, the government share of GDP increases when industrial societies become richer. Regardless of whether Wagner's Law can be upheld or not, an increasing public sector measured in percentage of GDP will not only increase automatic stabilisers, but will also lead to a long-run expansionary fiscal effect.

This leads us to an argument that goes back to John Maynard Keynes. He argued that a higher propensity to consume increases demand and output, which influences the long-run performance of an economy. In a formal way the value of the goods market multiplier increases with increases of the marginal propensity to consume. Given the value of autonomous demand elements such as investment demand, the greater the propensity to consume is, the higher aggregate demand and output will become. Government policies are able to influence the propensity to consume by making income distribution more equal. 'If fiscal policy is used as a deliberate instrument for the more equal distribution of incomes, its effect in increasing the propensity to consume is, of course, all the greater.' (Keynes 1936: 95) A more equal income distribution will lead to a more stable and higher aggregate demand than a less equal income distribution and consequently to a higher probability of long-term prosperous growth.

The final and most controversial point to discuss here is the question of whether fiscal policy can and should be the key policy to guarantee long-term growth and full employment. Above we have pointed out that some Post-Keynesians argue in this direction. We do not adhere to this argument. Essentially, the state budget should be balanced in the medium term. The level of public goods and social standards a society would like to permit and which tax rates are necessary to finance this, is a political question. Therefore, we regard a permanently increasing level of state debt to GDP as a result of government consumption as unsustainable. The increase of public debt to GDP, for example in Japan throughout recent decades, has clearly negative effects, which will be discussed below. There is no argument against governments taking credit for investment purposes when a direct cash flow is created. The classical example would be public investment in a bridge where the government can charge a toll for passing over it. In general public investment is difficult to measure, and/or has no clear return, and/or the returns are very long term, for example in the case of government-run public schools. When government investment is difficult to evaluate, it should be financed from taxes too.

There is no clear limit as to when public debt to GDP becomes too high. Some countries can live with very high public debt quotas. Notwithstanding, high public debt has several negative effects. First, it can lead to a more unequal income distribution. Holders of public debt are the wealthy in society whereas taxes are paid by nearly everybody. If the tax system does not interfere substantially in market-based income distribution, high public debt can lead to redistribution from the poor to the rich.[69] Second, public interest payments can explode in a cumulative way. Let us take the example of Japan with over 200 per cent public debt to GDP. As long as interest rates are very low there is no cash flow problem for the government. But let us assume interest rates increase to 8 per cent. In such a case the public interest burden jumps to 16 per cent of GDP. A Ponzi scheme of constellation can easily develop where the government has to take credit to be able to pay interest. The governments' room for manoeuvre definitely shrinks when public debt to GDP permanently increases. Third, high public debt to GDP can erode confidence in whether a government can fulfil payments on interest and principle. This can lead to an explosion of risk premiums (then we are in the scenario mentioned above in the second point) or even a refusal to give new credit to the government. In 2010, Greece and other EMU countries suffered from the scenario mentioned here. Fourth, if private investment is stagnating, fiscal policy in the end will not be able to stimulate the economy in the long run. If gross capital formation is zero, to take an extreme case, and fiscal policy keeps demand high, full capacity utilisation is soon reached and output cannot increase. Fiscal policy will then lead to demand inflation. Keynes argued that it is not fiscal policy that is of key importance to overcome a long-run stagnation, but rather the control of private investment, which goes far beyond traditional fiscal policy.

> Furthermore, it seems unlikely that the influence of banking policy on the rate of interest will be sufficient by itself to determine an optimum rate of investment. I conceive, therefore, that a somewhat comprehensive socialisation of investment will prove the only means of securing an approximation to full employment; though this need not exclude all manners of compromises and of devices by which public authority will co-operate with private initiative.
>
> (Keynes 1936: 378)

Finally, we turn to the more political problems of high public debt. The third point above, a refusal to give credit to the government, is hardly acceptable by governments, as this would imply the collapse of vital government functions. It is very likely that under such a constellation governments will and indeed have to force central banks to give direct credits to governments (or force commercial banks which are financed by the central bank to do this). The independence of central banks in the above-mentioned constellation will quickly break down – at least if the central government is over-indebted. Such central bank credits to governments must not lead to inflation. Japan is an impressive example that high budget deficits and increasing public debt does not automatically lead to inflation. But there is the temptation that governments will try to free themselves from an unacceptable debt burden. Printing money and pumping it into the economy easily leads to a situation of domestic wealth-owners exchanging domestic wealth for foreign currency. A depreciation–wage–price spiral can be triggered which is fed by central bank credits to public households (Robinson 1938). Another political way to get rid of bone-crushing public debt is a currency reform or very high taxes on monetary wealth. We do not argue that such developments are unavoidable; the argument is that we cannot exclude such developments for political reasons if public debt is exploding.

2.7 Income distribution

Income distribution in countries worldwide has undergone significant changes. In this chapter we discuss its development and its effect on aggregate demand and growth. We start with the debate on how the distribution of income and its development can be explained.

2.7.1 Development of income distribution

Three dimensions with regard to income distribution are of special importance: the functional income distribution between wages and profits; wage dispersion or income distribution within the working class; and the distribution of disposable income which reflects government redistribution policies.

Financial system and functional income distribution

Functional income distribution is explained in different ways in different paradigms. In the neoclassical paradigm real wages as well as the remuneration of capital depend on the marginal productivity of labour and capital respectively. Each factor gets what its marginal input contributes to physical output and thus value creation. If P is the price level, w the nominal wage and $\frac{\partial Yr}{\partial H} = MP_L$ the marginal productivity of labour with Yr as real output and H as labour input, according to the neoclassical argument $P. \frac{\partial Yr}{\partial H} = w$ or $MP_L = \frac{w}{P}$. The marginal product of labour in equilibrium is identical with the real wage (w/P).[70] We can also write $P = \frac{w}{MP_L}$. All shows the profit maximising condition under pure competition. All firms maximise profits when marginal revenues equal marginal costs. Under pure competition marginal revenue is equal to the price P. Marginal costs are given by nominal wages divided by the marginal productivity of labour.[71] A similar argumentation is followed for capital. In equilibrium the marginal productivity of capital is equal to the real return of capital. The real interest rate (the inflation-adjusted money interest rate) must reflect the rate of return, which is determined in the so-called real sphere by the marginal productivity of capital. The real interest rate must then be equal with the marginal productivity of capital.

In the classical paradigm (Adam Smith, David Ricardo) and in Marxian economics including its modern versions, the distribution of income is determined by assuming a certain sum of real wages and defining the rest of the total income as profit. Or to put it differently: labour produces a certain total real income. If the real wage sum is given, the remaining part of income is profit. Real wages depend on the reproduction cost of labour or on a certain basket of goods. This basket is not possible to define in any objective way, as it very much depends on the class struggle. The state of unemployment and the strength of the organisation of the working class in the form of trade unions play a decisive role in the determination of the wage basket (Marx 1867).

It is obvious that the neoclassical and the classical paradigm are rejected at least by followers of original Keynesian thinking. In Section 2.5.1 it was argued that the ratio of nominal wages per hour and the hourly labour productivity determines nominal unit labour costs and the latter in turn defines the price level. However, if the price level is given by nominal wages together with productivity, nominal wages cannot explain distribution. Real wages are not determined by nominal wages, but are given by productivity, the capital coefficient and the profit rate. The result of the Keynesian analysis is: real wages cannot be negotiated and nominal wages only influence the price level and not the functional income distribution.

Before going deeper into this topic let us look at Post-Keynesian explanations of distribution. There are growth models in the tradition of Michael Kalecki which do not include a monetary sphere. They are usually built on the assumption that workers save less out of their income than profit receivers. A certain distribution then leads to a certain dynamic of aggregate demand.[72] These models point out the role of distribution for demand, but they are not able to explain equilibrium income distribution in a Keynesian tradition. In principle Kalecki (1971) follows the argument that higher nominal wages lead to higher prices and not to lower profits. However, he states that large increases in wages would intimidate firms into accepting lower profit mark-ups. Here he argues on the basis of a behavioural assumption, which is not convincing. In a closed economy, the proportional relationship between nominal wages and the price level only disappears when profit mark-ups change. However, there seems to be no good argument in favour of an impact of wages on profit mark-ups (Tarling and Wilkinson 1985). Many Keynesians are not very clear when they discuss the relationship between nominal wages and distribution.[73] In this book we follow Keynes' argument: in the medium term the nominal wage level determines the price level and not the functional income distribution.

If demand in product markets and capacity utilisation are high, firms can increase prices and profits. On the other hand, if demand is weak and capacity utilisation is low, firms may be forced to reduce prices. The interaction between demand and supply influences profits in the short term. In the medium term these factors cancel out and are not able to explain secular development of functional income distribution over decades. In the following we look for the factors that change distribution in the long term. We can also speak of the supply-side factors of functional income distribution.

It should be mentioned that Keynes followed the classical idea that all values are created by labour, and the market mechanism allows part of the value created by labour to be transferred to capital income.

> I sympathise, therefore, with the pre-classical doctrine that everything is *produced by labour*, aided by what used to be called art and is now called technique, by natural resources which are free or cost a rent according to their scarcity or abundance, and by the results of past labour, embodied in assets, which also command a price according to their scarcity or abundance. It is preferable to regard labour, including, of course, the personal services of the entrepreneur and his assistants, as the sole factor of production, operating in a given environment of technique, natural resources, capital equipment and effective demand.
>
> (Keynes 1936: 214)

If the (money) rate of interest were zero, Keynes argues, the profit rate would be zero, too. If, however, the rate of interest exceeds zero, a new cost element comes into play, which enforces a profit rate (Keynes 1936: 216). As long as a firm works with credit, interest payments are cash flows that have to be earned. If own capital is used, the opportunity cost argument makes it clear that in equilibrium own capital must earn a return at least equal to the interest rate.

In Chapter 17 of his 'General Theory of Employment, Interest and Money' Keynes (1936) develops his distribution model. It is the money rate of return, the (long-term) interest rate, which 'rules the roost' as it does not fall to zero, whereas the rates of return for productive capital, the marginal efficiencies of capital assets, fall to the interest rate.

> For it may be that it is the *greatest* of the own-rates of interest (as we may call them) which rules the roost (because it is the greatest of these rates that the marginal efficiency of a capital-asset must attain if it is to be newly produced); and that there are reasons why it is the money-rate of interest which is often the greatest (because, as we shall find, certain forces, which operate to reduce the own-rates of interest of other assets, do not operate in the case of money).
>
> (Keynes 1936: 223)

The money rate of interest usually rules the roost as money or more precisely liquidity earns a liquidity premium. The liquidity premium is a non-pecuniary rate of return, which expresses the advantage of keeping liquidity (money) in an uncertain world. In addition, money takes over other service functions like making transactions of goods easier. Of course nobody will part from liquidity if the interest rate is below the liquidity premium. The liquidity premium then sets a minimum for the interest rate and the interest rate enforces a profit rate.

There is a clear sequence from the (marginal) liquidity premium (l), which is always positive, to the interest rate (i), and from the interest rate to the profit rate (q). We get $l = i = q$. Wealth-owners are only willing to part from their liquidity and invest in productive capital if the rate of return of productive assets is identical with the liquidity premium.

If liquidity kept in official money does not satisfy the demands of wealth-owners, other scarce assets can take over the function of money and can earn a liquidity premium to rule the roost. Even scarce assets like real estate can take over the function of setting the minimum for the rate of return for productive capital. Thus, it would be an illusion to bring interest rates down by government policies and believe that profit rates would automatically fall.

We can use Sraffa (1960) to make the point even clearer. Piero Sraffa modelled the Ricardian production price model. In such a system relative prices (and also the value of GDP and of the capital stock) depend on the existing technology and on the distribution of income. The system itself has no solution for the distribution of income.[74] Following the classical paradigm real wages are given by the reproduction needs or class struggle (see above). Or, and Sraffa mentions this possibility, the profit rate is taken exogenously for the production price system. If the profit rate is given, real wages result. The Keynesian paradigm obviously follows this last option.

It could be argued that it is not, or at least not alone, the liquidity premium which enforces a positive long-term interest rate, but also the refinancing rate of the central bank, which is usually positive. If we assume that a central bank sets a minimum for the interest rate, Keynes' argument does not fundamentally change. Also, in such cases the interest rate enforces the profit rate.

Given the profit rate we can determine the functional income distribution. National accounting of a closed economy gives us $Y = W + Q$ with Y as nominal national income, W as the wage sum and Q as the sum of profits. The wage quota is defined as the wage sum divided by the nominal income (W/Y). Then we get $W/Y = 1 - Q/Y$. The value of the capital stock is $P{\cdot}K$, the price level multiplied by the real stock of capital. With q as the profit rate we get $Q = q{\cdot}P{\cdot}K$ and $W/Y = 1 - q{\cdot}P{\cdot}K/Y$. We define the capital coefficient (k) as the nominal capital stock divided by nominal income, $k = P{\cdot}K/Y$. It follows:

$$\frac{W}{Y} = 1 - q \cdot k$$

The wage quota depends on the profit rate, which is determined in the asset market and the capital coefficient.[75]

Throughout the past five decades functional income distribution has changed substantially (see Figure 2.24). Adjusted wage shares (adjusted for changes in the composition of employment in employees and self-employed) in almost all countries had relatively high levels in the early 1960s, reached their peaks in the 1970s/1980s and then dropped dramatically. In Japan, for example, the wage

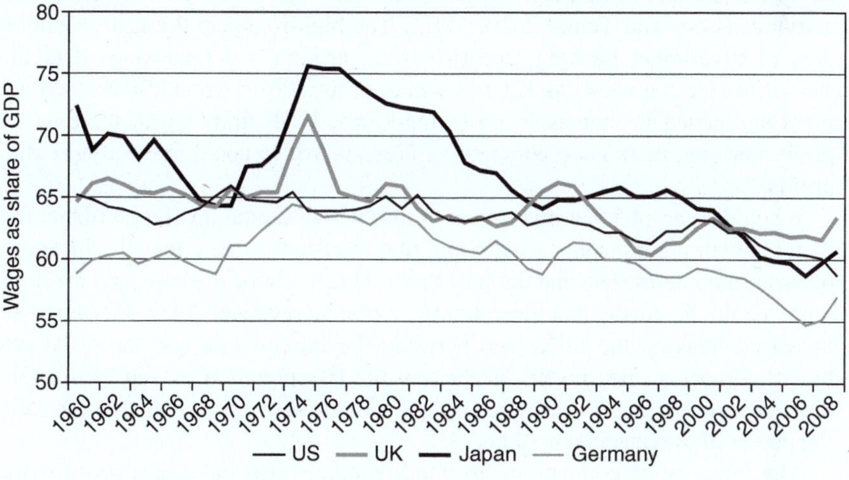

Figure 2.24 Adjusted wage shares in the US, the UK, Japan and Germany, 1960–2008 (source: AMECO 2010).

quota dropped dramatically, but also in Germany the wage quota decreased sharply after its peak in the 1970s. Even though we see a similar pattern in the US, the wage quota did not fall as much as in many other countries. In the UK wage quotas increased in the 1970s and fell back to levels below those of the 1960s.

How can falling wage quotas be explained? Theoretically, the explanation can be found in an increasing capital coefficient and/or in an increasing profit rate. We believe that the main effect can be found in an increasing profit rate. The explanation of the latter effect is given by the changing nature of the financial system (and not in the reduction of the bargaining power of workers which undoubtedly also took place). Following Keynes, in an equilibrium constellation and in the long run the lowest possible profit rate is equal to the interest rate. However, firms and the whole enterprise sector can achieve an equilibrium profit rate above the interest rate. We believe that the power of the agents and institutions in the financial system increased after the deregulation of financial markets in the 1970s and 1980s and that these agents and institutions pushed for a higher profit mark-up. This implies that a deregulated financial system will offer a higher profit rate than a strictly regulated one. A good expression of the pressure for higher profit rates coming from the financial system is the shareholder-value principle, which became popular after the mid-1980s (Rappaport 1986). The shareholder-value principle gears corporate governance to only one aim, the maximisation of profits. The regulated type of capitalism which was built-up during the New Deal in the 1930s and 1940s and was dominant until the 1970s was a stakeholder capitalism. Under this principle management was forced to look for a compromise amongst the different stakeholders, without increasing profits whenever possible. A substantial part of the financing of investment shifted during the deregulation period from own profits to financial intermediaries which started to earn very high returns, much higher than firms in productive activities (Levy and Temin 2010: 38ff.). The high return in the fast expanding area of investment banking, securitisation, packing and repacking of credits started to rule the roost, as Keynes would argue. Profit demand increased and firms succeeded in increasing profit mark-ups. If all firms try to increase the profit mark-up, there is no competitive pressure which could prevent increasing profits.[76]

It could be argued that investment in productive capital involves a higher risk than maintaining monetary wealth and that this leads to a systematic difference between the interest rate and the profit rate. This might be the case, and the argument could be made that uncertainty in the deregulated type of capitalism increased, making the difference between the interest rate and the profit rate bigger. However, the general increase in the risk premium, which can explain the higher profit rate, is very much in line with the above argument of an increasing power of the financial system.

The intensity of competition in goods markets also influences profit markups, an argument always pushed by Kalecki (see for example Kalecki 1971). Monopolies and oligopolies can permanently realise higher profit mark-ups than firms under pure and monopolistic competition. In many industries a small number of firms is dominant, which supports the argument. However, the globalisation in recent decades has also intensified goods market competition. The increasing power of the financial system after its deregulation starting in the 1970s/1980s remains the most plausible explanation for the OECD-wide decrease in wage shares in past decades.

Wage dispersion and distribution

Functional income distribution is an important factor when explaining income distribution in society. However, no less important is how wage income among the different groups of employees is distributed. For the latter question the wage differentials become important. Wage dispersion depends on the wage struggle among the different groups of employees. If one group of employees, let us say the workers in the steel industry, is in a position to push up its wages and the rest is not, real wages of the group with increasing nominal wages will increase. In our example the price level will rise slightly as the price of the product produced by employees with higher wages increases. Real wages of the rest of the workforce will slightly fall. Keynes is very clear on this point: In other words 'the struggle for nominal wages … is primarily (influenced) by the distribution of the sum of the real wages between the different worker groups and not the average amount per work unit, which … depends on a different series of forces' (Keynes 1936: 12). It is important to note that the dispersion of nominal wages regulates the distribution within the working class whereas the functional income distribution depends on different forces, like the profit mark-up which is independent of wages (see above).

The neoclassical paradigm explains wage differentials by different productivities of workers. Let us assume there are five groups of workers with five different productivities depending on their level of education. In this case there are five different demand functions for labour, which reflect the five specific marginal productivity functions. In each market segment there is also a specific supply function of labour. We get five equilibriums with five different real wage levels; each reflecting a certain marginal productivity of labour. If the real wage in the market with the lowest productivity of workers is too high, for example because of minimum wages, some of the lowest qualified workers or even all become unemployed. Any increase of real wages above the marginal productivities in equilibrium leads to unemployment and a loss in output, which is determined from the supply side. If, to add another example, as a result of technological changes demand for highly educated workers increases and decreases for low-skilled workers, the wage structure will change, increasing the equilibrium wages of educated workers and reducing the equilibrium wages of low-skilled workers.[77]

We reject this argument as an explanation of wage dispersion. Wage differentials depend on the struggle about the relative wage rate of different groups of workers, as Keynes argued above. Changes in the nominal wage level do not, as mentioned above, change the level of real wages in the whole economy; it is rather nominal wage differentials that determine the differentials in real wages and thus the distribution of wages within the working class. For a single group of workers, fighting for nominal wage increases is a rational strategy to increase real wages. If all groups act in such a way, of course no group will be able to increase real wages, but the economy will suffer from inflation. What we have here is a coordination problem in which individual logic leads to negative macroeconomic results.

The wage struggle depends on factors like labour market institutions, the strength of unions, the existence and level of minimum wages and the values in society concerning acceptable levels of wage and income differentials. A completely deregulated labour market would produce an unacceptable dispersion of wages. As unemployment is a normal state of affairs in capitalist societies, the resulting oversupply of labour in a completely market-driven system would reduce nominal wages for the groups of workers with low skills to unacceptably low levels, probably to levels which would not allow the reproduction of workers. Such falling wages have nothing to do with productivity; they are simply the result of excess supply in this segment of the labour market. Very low real wages usually lead to an increase in labour supply, as the poor workers need more than one job to survive. This phenomenon can be traced to the Industrial Revolution, and it still exists today in developing countries, and for the working-poor in developed countries.

Germany after 1995 is a good example for radically falling nominal and real wages for low-skilled workers. As traditionally unions were strong enough to guarantee sufficiently high wages for low-skilled workers Germany has no statutory minimum wage. In the old wage bargaining model industries and regions with weak unions and employers' federation took over the negotiated wages in industries and regions with strong unions and employers' federation. However, since the mid/late 1990s trade union power and also the organisational capacity of employers' federations have eroded and the signalling effect has broken down. As a result, wages of low-skilled workers in some industries and regions fell to around four euros in the 2000s. This is a level which does not guarantee a decent life in Germany and is far below the statutory minimum wage of many other member countries of the European Monetary Union (EMU) (see the German case study).

On the other hand, in deregulated labour markets some scarce professions may be able to earn extraordinary high wages, which can barely be explained by productivity differentials. Especially when unions organise certain professions – for example pilots or train drivers – there is the danger that, depending on the economic situation, such groups are able to push for extraordinarily high wages.

In the neoclassical model a firm maximises its profit when marginal revenues are equal to marginal costs. For pure competition this is given when the price of the produced and sold product of a firm is equal to marginal costs: $P = \frac{w}{MP_L}$ (see above). Differences in marginal productivities (MP_L) of workers explain different wages. If we assume the more realistic model of monopolistic competition where companies are able to change prices, the marginal revenue of a firm is $P(1+\frac{1}{\varepsilon_p})$ with ε_p as direct price elasticity of demand.[78] The direct price elasticity, which normally has a negative value, expresses that a 1 per cent increase in the price of a product of a firm will reduce the demand for the product by a certain percentage.[79] If we set the marginal revenues equal with marginal costs and rearrange the equation, the price a company will set is:

$$P = \frac{w}{MP_L(1+\frac{1}{\varepsilon_p})}$$

Here the logic of the neoclassical marginal productivity theory is turned around. The price of a product depends on the nominal wage, the marginal productivity and the price elasticity of demand. Wages are not determined by marginal productivity, but marginal productivity is one of the factors that influence the price. For different products prices are determined according to the formula above. Wage differentials and productivity (technology) are the basic factors that are behind the structure of prices.

Of course, a certain structure of wages and prices leads to a certain demand structure and structure of output. However, the level of output and level of employment does not depend on the structure of wages and prices. Aggregate demand determines the *level* of output whereas the *structure* of demand and output is set by the structure of wages and prices as well as by the technologies used.

Let us assume that a rise in minimum wages increases wages in labour-incentive industries, for example, in the labour-intensive chip assembly in the semi-conductor industry. Wages in other industries may not be affected. As a result of higher wage costs the semi-conductor industry reacts in two ways. It first searches for a new profit maximising technology and, if one is available, implement it. Second, it increases the prices of its products because even with the new technology prices are higher, otherwise the technology would have been used before. Part of the workforce in the semi-conductor industry becomes unemployed. How big this effect is depends on the degree of the change in technology and/or the price elasticity of demand for semi-conductors. So far we analysed only the semi-conductor industry. Whether there is a loss in employment in the economy as a whole is difficult to say because a higher capital input in the semi-conductor industry increases employment in the capital-goods producing industry. However, the story is not yet finished. Semi-conductors are inputs in many other industries, which, according to their technology, are affected differently by a price increase of the former. All of the affected industries also switch to new technologies because the price relation of their inputs has changed. Some industries probably shift to a more labour intensive production, as for them capital inputs became more costly. In the end the complete structure of prices, the technology, the composition of inputs and the structure of output have changed. When raising the minimum wage, it is simply not possible to find out whether the economy will employ less or more labour.[80]

Even in simpler cases the employment effects are difficult to figure out. Let us take the hairdressing industry and assume that a change in technology is not possible and the output of the industry is not an input of other industries. In this case a rise in minimum wages pushes up the price of hairdressing services according to the increase in wage costs. Given the price elasticity of demand of hairdressing services we can calculate how many hairdressers lose their jobs. However, in this case, too, the story is not over. The wage sum in the hairdressing industry may increase or decrease. This depends on the price elasticity of hairdressing services. If the wage sum increases the employed hairdressers create additional demand. Let us assume they go to fitness studios, which in this case experience a higher demand and probably employ unemployed hairdressers. However, we have to take into account that an increase in the wage sum in the hairdressing industry reduces the purchasing power of other consumers, which now have to pay more for hairdressing services. Demand in many different industries is affected. These industries themselves are linked to many other industries. If the wage sum in the hairdressing industry shrinks, consumers spend more of their income on other goods. Again, many other industries are also affected and have in turn an impact on further industries. To sum up: Which industries will be affected by changing wage dispersion and in which way is impossible to predict. Obviously, wage and price structures have no clear relationship to aggregate output, which in the Keynesian paradigm primarily depends on aggregate demand. The extensive empirical debate about minimum wages has shown that increasing minimum wages are unlikely to cause negative employment effects – a big surprise for neoclassical economists (Herr *et al.* 2009).

Let us look at the changes in wage dispersion in recent decades. Figure 2.25 shows that wage differentials in almost all countries widened substantially.[81] Comparing developments, three typical scenarios emerge (ILO 2008: 23ff.): in the case of a 'collapsing floor', lower wages break away and a rising low wage sector emerges. In the 1990s and 2000s Germany has been the most extreme case of the exceedingly rapid development of a low wage sector. In the case of a 'rising ceiling', the wages of high earners have escalated. Canada, Germany, the UK, Ireland and the US, all fit this scenario from the 1990s. It must also be emphasised, however, that in Anglo-Saxon countries the low-wage sector grew strongly in the 1980s and that this development was at least partially combated in the 1990s by a policy of increasing state minimum wages. Countries that experienced both, wage dispersion downwards and upwards, are characterised by the third scenario, wage 'polarisation'. If one looks at the whole period from the 1980s there was a high polarisation particularly in Germany, the UK and the US. Looking at wage development, in nearly all OECD countries some polarisation of the wage distribution can be observed.[82] The problem is not only that in most developed countries wages in the low-wage sector dropped for decades relatively (and in many cases absolutely), but also that these low-wage jobs are usually precarious jobs with a very low or no level of social protection.

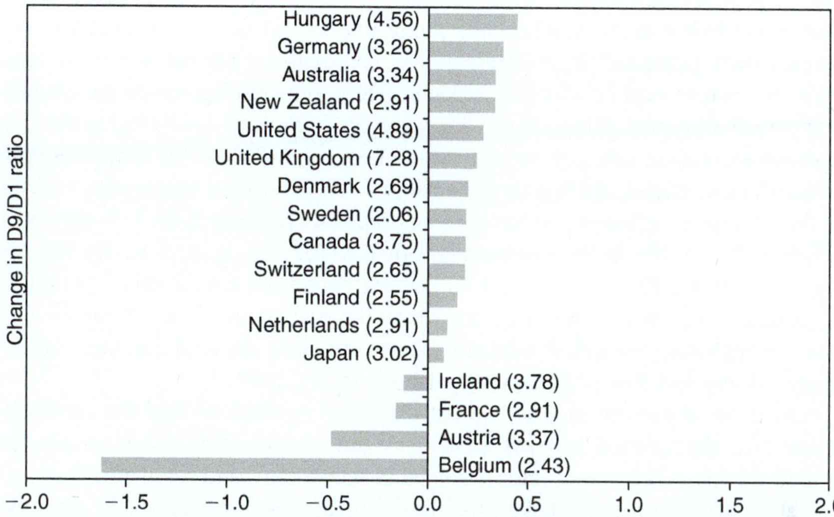

Figure 2.25 Wage inequality, D9/D1 ratio: Differences between the periods 1995–97 and 2004–6 (latest ratio shown in brackets) (source: ILO Global Wage database 2009).

The traditional explanation for the relative decline of wages of low-skilled workers is fourfold. First it is argued that new technologies reduced the number of simple jobs as they were taken over by machines. For example, the robots in motor-vehicle assembly lines substituted relatively simple jobs and increased jobs for those highly skilled workers who designed and programmed the robots. Second, globalisation has shifted low-skilled jobs to countries like China that have a comparative advantage in producing low-tech simple products. A radical decrease in transportation costs and liberalisation of trade supported this development. Third, the western world had to accept immigration from poorer countries. Most immigrants were low skilled and increased the pressure for falling wages in the market segment of the low skilled. And fourth, education efforts in developed countries were not sufficient to compensate for this development. It would have been necessary to increase the supply of highly skilled workers and academics and to reduce the supply of low-skilled workers to limit the widening of the wage gap. Better education is seen as the key factor to reduce the wage gap again. Overall it is argued that the widening of wage dispersion is the result of market forces; government interventions to increase low wages are assumed to cause unemployment (for a critical overview see Brown *et al.* 2010; Levy and Temin 2010; Palley 1998: chapters 4 and 5).

We do not deny that the above factors can play and have partially played a role for the changing wage dispersion. The factors mentioned changed the power relationship within the working class. Some groups were probably able to fight more successfully for their interest than others. However, even when we restrict ourselves to these traditional arguments some caution is needed. In developed countries most of the low-wage jobs cannot be found in the tradable goods sector, but rather in the non-tradable sector like the service sector, which is to a large extent protected from international competition. Globalisation, at least directly, cannot explain this phenomenon. Here, outsourcing inside the country has played a big role. Companies with relatively high wage levels and protection outsource cleaning services, security, book-keeping and so on to companies with relatively low wages and low or no social protection for their employees. Neither is the education argument, which became especially popular in the US, very convincing. Wages for male employees with BA degrees went down in the US beginning in the 1970s, very much in line with male and female employees with high school diplomas. Generally, more than three-quarters of the labour force in the US including educated workers face insufficient demand for their labour supply (Levy and Temin 2010: 24ff., also see Palley 1998).[83]

Our main argument is that without changing institutions and the establishment of a deregulated type of capitalism and globalisation, wage dispersion would not have become so big. Changes in technology and intensified international competition would have most likely created some pressure in the low-wage sector, also under a system of regulated capitalism and globalisation, but this pressure would have been compensated by institutions and regulations. For example, a changing international distribution of labour that creates pressure on low-skilled jobs in developed countries could have been handled in such a way as to let all low-paid jobs move to foreign countries. At least in the long run the exchange rate is a sufficient instrument to guarantee a balanced current account (when net capital flows do not create imbalances) even if a country has a very equal wage structure. In the end, the problem is to manage structural changes if international distribution of labour changes quickly. However, beginning with the conservative revolution, policies did not moderate market forces, but rather the opposite was done. In almost all developed countries governments changed labour market laws, which weakened workers' protection, trade unions and employers' federations, union density, the coverage of employees by collective bargaining and so on (see Section 2.5 for more details). Overall, unions were no longer able to protect the poorer groups of workers, especially as the signalling effect from industries with collective bargaining to the rest of the economy broke down. Minimum wages were not sufficiently used to fight against the trend of a growing low-wage sector. Governments in many cases cut social security and unemployment benefits and let real minimum wages fall. This brought down the so-called reservation wage and it is no surprise that wages of unskilled workers fell to this level. We agree with Levy and Temin (2010: 19): 'The Golden Age reflected market outcomes strongly moderated by institutions and norm. In our interpretations, the recent impacts of technology and trade have been amplified by a collapse of these institutions that occurred in the 1970s and 1980s.'

So far we have discussed the 'collapsing floor' of wages. Let us now come to the 'rising ceiling', which was even more spectacular in some countries. Income distribution, including wage dispersion, during the Great Depression and the New Deal policies was compressed in all western countries and more or less remained stable until the deregulation that started in the 1970s. Looking at income distribution and especially at the position of the super-rich, the US is back in the world before the Great Depression, or even back in the world of the harsh capitalism of the nineteenth century (Krugman 2002). A contemporary document of the institutions and norms of the regulated type of capitalism after the Second World War is Kenneth Galbraith's book *The New Industrial State* published in 1967. About the US, he wrote:

> Management does not go out ruthlessly to reward itself – a sound management is expected to exercise restraint. ... With the power of decision goes opportunity for making money. ... Were everyone to seek to do so ... the corporation would be a chaos of competitive avarice. But these are not the sort of things a good company man does; a remarkably effective code bans such behaviour. Group decision-making insures, moreover, that almost everyone's action and even thoughts are known to others. This acts to enforce the code, and, more than incidentally, a high standard of personal honesty as well.
>
> (Galbraith 1967: 1461)

Galbraith describes a stakeholder capitalism that searches for a compromise between the different stakeholders – a compromise that includes, compared with today, modest differences in salaries. This way of thinking summarised by Galbraith was universally valid after the Second World War. In continental Europe and in Japan the logic of stakeholder capitalism was even more pronounced.

The situation changed with the conservative revolution in the late 1970s. The deregulation of labour markets was the most important factor that led to the 'collapsing floor' of wages, while the deregulation of the financial system was the most important factor for the 'rising ceiling' of wages (if we assume that the top management's remuneration is part of the wage sum). In the years 1913 and 1929 the top 1 per cent of income earners received nearly 20 per cent of the total income in the US and the UK, in Europe and Japan slightly less. This share decreased substantially after the Great Depression and was below 10 per cent in 1970 and 1980 in almost all countries – still revealing substantial inequalities in income distribution. In 1999 in the US and the UK the share of the top 1 per cent of income earners spectacularly doubled and went back to levels which had existed before the Great Depression. In continental Europe and Japan the increase of the income of the top income earners remained comparatively modest (Piketty and Saez 2006, Atkinson *et al.* 2009).

The development of the income share of the top 0.1 per cent of income share for the US is shown in Figure 2.26. Before and after the period of the regulated type of capitalism, from the 1930s to the 1970s, the relative income position of this group of the very rich was substantially higher, supporting Krugman's argument that the US is back to old times. However, there is one significant difference. It is noteworthy that especially business income and salaries of the super-rich after 1980 played a much bigger role than before the Great

Depression where capital income (dividends, interest, capital gains and rents) was the main source of high incomes. In the 2000s the trend of extreme increases in income of the super-rich in the US has continued unhindered. From 2002 to 2007, the average inflation-adjusted income in the US for the bottom 90 per cent of income receivers increased by 0.8 per cent, for the next 9 per cent by 13.0 per cent, for the top one per cent by 61.8 per cent and for the top 0.1 per cent by 94.1 per cent (Feller and Stone 2009).[84] The salaries of the top earners are dominated by earnings of CEOs and other executives. Individuals in finance-dependent occupations account for about 40 per cent of salaries in the high income brackets (Jacoby 2010: 100f.).

One possibility to explain the extremely high salary increases of the top income group is the 'superstar' argument (Rosen 1981). Markets with superstars function in ways that winners take 'everything', like film stars and football stars. It could be argued that there is such a shortage of talent that the few with talent become superstars and earn fantastic incomes. However, this argument is not very convincing. Superstars in many cases are artificially produced (like boy-groups by record companies). People who have substantially contributed to the development of society, the real superstars, let's say scientists like Albert Einstein, were not able to earn superstar salaries. It has already been mentioned that about 40 per cent of the top earners in the US work in the financial sector. There was probably a shortage of financial managers when the deregulation of the financial system started in the 1970s. This can explain some of the early increases in incomes in this sector. But we believe that the main argument is that agents in the financial sector and in business in general were able to shape institutions according to their interest. Backed by the conservative revolution in the

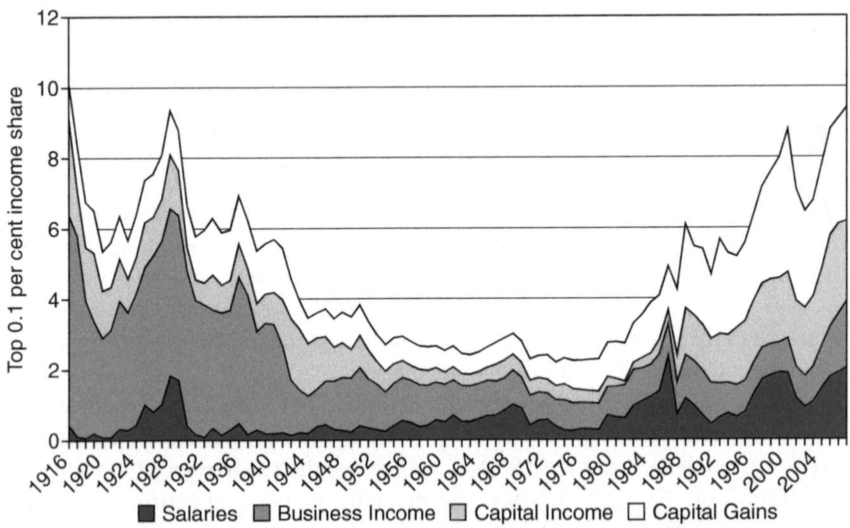

Figure 2.26 Income share of the top 0.1 per cent income earners share and its sources in the US, 1916–2007 (source: Piketty and Saez 2009).

1980s the stakeholder model of corporate governance was actively dismantled and substituted by shareholder capitalism. Executives, managers, staff in investment banks and hedge funds, and so on managed to change their remuneration system, being supported by the shareholder value system or corporate governance, which was new at that time. For example stock options as part of salaries were almost unknown until the 1980s. Then they quickly became the general way of handling management remuneration. In contradiction to Rappaport's original idea, stock options and other bonuses were not paid according to relative performance. Increasing asset prices benefited all executives, even when their company underperformed in comparison with the market average. In substance, shareholder capitalism led partly to the appropriation of shareholders because the management was also able to increase its income at the cost of shareholders. Figure 2.26 supports this idea showing the enormous increase in salaries of top income earners. These developments in the US were also very much followed by the UK and to a lesser extent by the rest of the world.

Personal income distribution

Households can have wage income and at the same time income coming from profits. Functional income distribution and wage dispersion is reflected in the market-determined personal income distribution. There can be no doubt that in most industrial countries market-determined income distribution became more unequal. However, government policies, especially tax policy and social transfers including the financing of the social safety net, modify income given by market forces. In all western countries government policies reduce income inequality. Theoretically, it would have been possible for government policies to have compensated the changes in the market-given income distribution, but the opposite was done. The conservative revolution privileged high income earners. High and super-high incomes were no longer considered condemnable. The slogan 'effort has to pay off' dominated the political arena. Marginal income tax rates were cut in almost all countries. Tax competition between countries led to a reduction in enterprise taxes. Multinational companies could use international trade and other transactions within the corporation to shift profits to the places they wanted. Open capital accounts made it easier to invest monetary wealth in offshore centres and to shift income to countries with low tax rates and to tax havens.

Due to the space limitation, we are unable to analyse the direct redistribution policies by governments or the complex policies which indirectly influence personal income distribution. However, we take a look at how personal income distribution developed. Using the Gini-coefficient the distribution of disposable income, the income after government redistribution policies, in selected OECD countries is shown in Table 2.9.[85]

In 2005, the Scandinavian countries, Austria, Belgium, the Netherlands and France exhibited a comparatively equal income distribution. For the countries shown the US has the most unequal distribution as far as disposable income of

Table 2.9 Development of the Gini coefficient in selected OECD countries (disposable household income),[1] 1975–2005

	1975	*1985*	*1990*	*1995*	*2000*	*2005*
Belgium	–	0.274	–	0.287	0.289	0.271
Canada	0.295	0.287	–	0.283	0.301	0.317
Denmark	–	0.221	–	0.215	0.226	0.232
Finland	0.235	0.207	–	0.228	0.261	0.269
France	–	0.300	0.290	0.270	0.270	0.270
Germany	–	0.257	0.258	0.272	0.270	0.298
Greece	0.413	0.336	–	0.336	0.345	0.321
Ireland	–	0.331	–	0.324	0.304	0.328
Italy	–	0.309	0.297	0.348	0.343	0.352
Japan	–	0.304	–	0.323	0.337	0.321
Netherlands	0.251	0.259	0.278	0.282	0.278	0.271
Portugal	0.354	0.329	0.329	0.359	0.385	0.385
Spain	–	0.371	0.337	0.343	0.342	0.319
Sweden	0.212	0.198	0.209	0.211	0.243	0.234
UK	0.282	0.325	0.373	0.354	0.370	0.335
US	0.316	0.338	0.349	0.361	0.357	0.381

Source: OECD (2009b).

Note

1 Adjusted for different household sizes.

the households is concerned. But countries such as Canada, the UK, Greece, Ireland, Italy, Portugal and Spain are also characterised by sharp inequality. Germany lies in the middle, near the OECD average. Comparing 1975 or 1985 with 2005, distribution of disposable income became less equal in the US, the UK, Japan, Germany and Italy, among others. Some countries were able to reduce inequalities with regard to disposable income, including France, Greece, Ireland and Spain. Yet, the latter three countries have traditionally been characterised by very high inequalities with regard to personal income distribution and still have a relatively unequal income distribution. To sum up, the average of the OECD countries and especially the four biggest OECD countries we focus on in our case studies moved to a more unequal income distribution.

2.7.2 Income distribution and growth

In the Keynesian paradigm the link between distribution and growth is aggregate demand, which depends on distribution. We have to distinguish between a short-term and long-term analyses. In a constellation of a cyclical downturn with unused capacities in all industries, all elements of demand are able to increase output. Anti-cyclical fiscal policy is warranted in such a constellation to increase aggregate demand and output. But if an increase in investment demand, consumption demand or export demand can be achieved, the output is raised too. Contrary to the Neoclassical Synthesis and the New Keynesians, in the original Keynesian approach aggregate demand does not only play a role in smoothing the business cycle around a long-term supply-side given growth path, but also becomes the decisive factor for long-term development. In the long-term perspective also the structure of demand starts to play a role.

Investment in productive capital has a double effect. Investment is an element of aggregate demand and at the same time creates a capacity effect. Net investment increases the stock of capital in society and the ability to produce. Also, gross investment is of vital importance as, at least potentially, all investment embodies the newest available technology. It was Marx (1867) with his argument of relative value creation and Schumpeter (1926, 1976) with his model of economic development and creative destruction who most strongly pointed out that the chase for extra profit or technological rents permanently revolutionises technology and creates innovations, and in this way leads to increasing productivity and living standards of societies which, however, do not automatically bring benefit to all members. Without gross investment economies would stagnate. Other demand elements cannot trigger long-term growth without investment.

Too high investment demand is not sustainable. Building up capacities for production without additional demand will lead to crises sooner or later. Of course one could imagine that investment demand increases on the basis of high animal spirits and available credit in an exponential way and that it keeps capacities fully utilised. But in the end, capacities are built up to satisfy demand elements other than investment. To allow a sustainable, sufficient growth process there must be a proportional relationship between investment demand (increase in production capacities) and other demand elements.

Consumption demand, which is usually the biggest part of demand, plays a vital role in keeping capacities utilised. In this sense sufficient consumption demand is the backbone of sufficient growth whereas investment demand is the backbone for productivity increases and innovation. The more equal the income distribution is, the higher the likelihood of high and sustainable consumption demand will be. High-income households usually have a lower marginal (and average) propensity to consume than low-income householders. The argument given above is not a law, but is drawn on the basis of historical developments. At least theoretically high-income households could live such a luxurious life that their propensity to consume is equally high as that of low-income households. However, empirical investigations show that high-income households on average tend to spend less of their income on consumption than low-income households. If the rich and super-rich are able to attract a higher and higher income share, as for example in the US, the average propensity to consume in a society is likely to suffer.

The regulated capitalism, which was established after the Great Depression, was characterised by a relatively equal income distribution. For almost all income groups income increased according to productivity and almost all were able to participate in the benefits created by the capitalist productivity and innovation machine. This outcome was guaranteed by a stable and relatively high wage quota and relatively low wage dispersion. 'Fordism' is one of the catch-words expressing this economic model. It means that a broad middle class was created which was able to consume sufficiently out of their income. Henry Ford could, so to speak, produce automobiles on a mass scale and sell all of his cars as his workers were paid enough to afford them. One of the secrets of the economic miracles in so many countries in the decades after the Second World War can be found in the relatively equal income distribution that allowed the above-described proportional relationship between investment demand and the other demand elements.

It was shown that in most OECD countries income distribution has been becoming more unequal in recent decades. From the above argument we can expect that GDP growth rates went down. Indeed, in the average OECD country GDP growth rates decreased and unemployment rates increased. Tables 2.10 and 2.11 support these arguments. Growth rates in the 1960s were higher than in the decades that followed; unemployment in the 1960s was lower than in the following decades.[86]

We do not however go so far as to argue that income distribution is the only factor which explains the growth differences after the decades immediately following the Second World War. Other demand elements are also important. Investment demand became much more unstable after the breakdown of regulated capitalism and showed frequent collapses and negative growth rates of GDP became frequent. However, this is not related to a lack of consumption

Table 2.10 Growth rates in selected OECD countries (real GDP; annual average), 1960–2008

	1960–1969	*1970–1979*	*1980–1989*	*1990–1999*	*2000–2008*
Australia	5.53	3.09	3.38	3.34	3.13
Austria	4.45	4.18	1.93	2.58	2.25
Denmark	5.23	2.47	1.90	2.40	1.52
Finland	4.54	4.13	3.51	1.57	3.07
France	5.71	4.15	2.32	1.86	1.92
Germany[1]	4.39	3.27	1.96	2.32	1.44
Great Britain	2.90	2.42	2.45	2.23	2.52
Italy	5.77	4.02	2.55	1.43	1.19
Japan	10.14	5.21	3.71	1.50	1.47
Netherlands	5.01	3.42	2.15	3.20	2.17
Norway	4.44	4.43	2.79	3.58	2.42
Portugal	6.33	5.11	3.35	2.91	1.20
Spain	7.71	3.86	2.70	2.69	3.34
Sweden	4.45	2.45	2.27	1.69	2.64
Switzerland	4.58	1.48	2.30	1.10	2.04
US	4.69	2.42	3.06	3.13	2.34
OECD	5.23	3.77	2.99	2.51	2.36

Source: AMECO (2010).

Note
1 Up until 1990 Federal Republic of Germany.

Table 2.11 Unemployment rates in OECD countries (annual average), 1960–2008

	1960–1969	*1970–1979*	*1980–1989*	*1990–1999*	*2000–2008*
Australia	1.74	3.85	7.62	8.81	5.52
Austria	2.13	1.43	2.70	3.87	4.31
Denmark	1.11	3.19	6.67	6.93	4.46
Finland	2.20	3.78	4.79	11.87	8.36
France	1.72	3.76	8.50	10.51	8.74
Germany[1]	0.65	2.01	5.83	7.87	8.76
Great Britain	1.61	3.49	9.45	8.00	5.14
Italy	4.86	5.94	8.39	10.27	7.98
Japan	1.29	1.66	2.47	3.05	4.61
Netherlands	0.84	3.80	8.16	5.41	3.41
Norway	–	1.79	2.81	4.80	3.68
Portugal	2.37	4.56	7.53	5.60	6.40
Spain	2.39	4.52	15.44	15.90	10.17
Sweden	1.70	2.05	2.59	7.21	6.00
Switzerland	0.01	0.19	0.55	2.88	3.36
US	4.78	6.21	7.27	5.71	5.13
OECD	2.17	3.41	6.37	7.87	7.88

Source: AMECO (2010).

Note

1 Up until 1990, Federal Republic of Germany.

demand. Volatility in investment demand depends on the rhythms of mostly endogenous shocks, which have hindered economic development since the early 1970s. Shocks were caused by imploding asset market bubbles, domestic financial crises, international financial crises resulting from volatile international capital flows, and periods of harsh monetary policies to fight against inflation and depreciations.

When we look at the four biggest OECD countries (Table 2.10) we find that the US and the UK realised much higher GDP growth rates than Germany and Japan in the period 2000–2008 (the US realised an average annual growth of 2.34 per cent, the UK 2.53 per cent, Germany 1.44 per cent and Japan 1.47 per cent). Also, in the period 1990–1999 the US realised much higher average annual GDP growth than Germany and Japan. An explanation for this is that the US and the UK started earlier and went further in deregulating their financial systems than Germany and Japan did.

In the US and the UK especially, the period 2000–2008 was driven by private household demand, partly in the form of real estate investments, partly in the form of direct consumption. However, the basis for this consumption boom was not earned income, but the households' credit-financed demand (see Section 2.2.2) and demand stimulated by increasing asset prices, whereas asset price hikes and increasing household debt interacted positively (e.g. credit card credits, using collateral from increasing real estate assets for consumption). Thus, consumption demand in the US and UK was high and savings rates were low in spite of a highly and increasingly unequal income distribution in these countries. The contrast with the 1950s and 1960s could not have been more profound. A credit-financed consumption and real estate boom is not sustainable in the long run. It was only a question of time before such a development had to come to an end. Thus, the subprime crisis, which started to develop in 2007 and hit world GDP growth in 2008 and 2009, was no surprise.[87]

Government demand is able to effectively stabilise demand in a constellation of unequal income distribution not only during recessions but also in the long run. The condition for this is an increasing share of public expenditures in GDP financed by government revenues. Such policies did not adhere to the philosophy of the conservative revolution that aimed to make government smaller and to cut taxes especially for the rich, the group which was believed to deserve high income. The enforcement of this view is shown by the development of the wage quota and wage dispersion. In the 1970s and thereafter, governments stabilised demand, reflected in increasing government debt quotas. However, using high public debt to stabilise demand was not considered a long-run strategy. Indeed, high and long-lasting public debt is inappropriate and potentially harmful (see Section 2.6).

The last demand element that needs to be discussed is export demand. It should be clear that for the world as a whole increasing current account surpluses are not a feasible strategy. This also implies that mercantile strategies of countries and currency areas in order to push domestic demand will not lead to such prosperous development of the major parts of the world economy as were experienced in the 1950s and 1960s. The opposite is the case. If some countries successfully push for higher current account surpluses, the danger of deficit countries becoming over-indebted and falling into currency and financial crises and/or long-run stagnation increases. Japan and Germany, the two OECD countries with distinctly aggressive export-oriented strategies in recent decades, have become disturbing factors for the world economy (together with some developing countries like China). As current account surpluses compared with domestic demand elements are always relatively small, even high external surpluses are not sufficient for a prosperous domestic development. Japan and Germany in the 2000s are excellent examples of this. In the 1950s and 1960s export demand added to high domestic demand in these two countries and led to especially pronounced miracles. In the 2000s, however, export surpluses were combined with stagnant domestic demand. The outcome was low growth in spite of the high current account and export surpluses.

2.8 Macroeconomic policy regimes – a summary

Now that each dimension of macroeconomic policy has been described in detail, it is time to combine them in an integrated approach. In this section an ideal macroeconomic policy regime is sketched. According to our approach it encompasses the institutional structures of an economy and its changes (Ordnungspolitik) plus the conduct of the key macroeconomic policies, especially monetary policy, fiscal policy, wage policy and foreign economic policy. Of course, institutions and policies of a macroeconomic regime are interrelated.

Macroeconomic policy regimes cannot be established or changed easily. Deeply embedded traditions, norms and informal institutions make it difficult or even impossible to shape societal structures. However, the 1930/1940s as well the 1970/1980s prove that Ordnungspolitik or fundamental changes of institutions as well as rules and changes in the key macroeconomic policies are able to deeply change economies and societies. The purpose of delineating an ideal macroeconomic regime is not only to give an idea in which direction the present neoliberal type of macroeconomic policy regime that is prevalent in most countries could be reformed, but also to provide a benchmark to compare historically existing macroeconomic policy regimes and to understand their strengths and shortcomings. The case studies below elaborate on this point.

We have learned from Vilfredo Pareto who, on the basis of the General Equilibrium Model developed in the 1870s by Léon Walras, built the argument that interpersonal comparisons of satisfaction (or if we want happiness) are not possible. Who knows whether a rich man who has to give up his Porsche car to help 100 poor people to increase their consumption does not suffer more than what the 100 gained in satisfaction? We do not even know how to calculate the increase in satisfaction of the 100 persons who gained. Let us look at the General Equilibrium Model, the core of neoclassical thinking. The endowment of individuals in this model is given exogenously, like manna from heaven. If the endowment is allocated to individuals, extremely unequal market equilibriums can result which allow one part of society to live in luxury whereas the other part hardly manages to survive. Such equilibriums are Pareto-efficient as not even one person can increase his or her satisfaction without decreasing the satisfaction of somebody else. Each exogenously given allocation of the endowment will produce a set of relative prices, a specific distribution of income and specific consumption and production patterns which are all market efficient in Pareto's definition. There is no good economic model to tell which one of the efficient equilibriums is the best one or even which one should be excluded (Hahn 1981). Only a political process including value judgements can decide which of the market outcomes is acceptable and which one not.

This abstract debate can be transferred to macroeconomic policy regimes. Any macroeconomic policy regime privileges some groups and has disadvantages for others. Whether a regime is acceptable or not has to be decided politically. For the foreseeable future our recommendation of a regulated capitalism seems to be the best option to organise economies and with that an important part of societies. However, it involves value judgements.

In the course of this book we made clear that we are convinced that a deregulated type of capitalism is unacceptably unstable and is only preferable for a small group of the society as it produces a very unequal income distribution. In such a regime most people are pushed around by markets and live in high uncertainty, even if their income situation is acceptable. Unemployment is high and volatile. Last, but not least, firms also are exposed to high uncertainty as well as to shocks in financial markets and goods markets. However, as just mentioned, even such a radical market-based macroeconomic policy regime privileges some groups in society, for example agents in the financial sector or top income earners. It would also be a misunderstanding to assume that such a regime automatically breaks down. It can be accompanied by government actions that prevent extreme instabilities without changing the basic rules of the system. The subprime crisis and the Great Depression, for example, were such phases of extreme instability. Whether new regulations following such deep crises are more than cosmetic and will take effect at all is an open question. After the Great Depression deep changes happened. What will happen after the subprime crisis remains to be seen.

Moreover, we are convinced that in the foreseeable future there is no realistic alternative to a regulated type of capitalism. Even radical ecological reforms based on completely different production and consumption patterns must be kept together by a macroeconomic policy regime. Of course, a regulated type of capitalism may transform itself into a system that might no longer be called capitalism. But this is speculation and not the topic of the book.

In the following we discuss the different elements of a regulated capitalism. Regulations and institutions are complementary to each other and create a coherent system.[88] Some of the details discussed below are only examples of how institutions and regulations could look. In many cases different options to achieve the same goal depending on traditions, values and cultures in societies are possible. A macroeconomic policy regime does not cover all dimensions of economic policy making. For example institutions and policies to stimulate innovation or to solve ecological problems are beyond the debate below.

Figure 2.27 gives an overview of the different dimensions of a macroeconomic policy regime of a regulated capitalism.

2.8.1 Regulated financial systems

Financial systems are inherently unstable and driven by expectations which have no intrinsic anchor. They tend to create cumulative asset price inflations with unsustainable credit expansions and over-indebtedness of economic agents and sectors. Asset price deflations and credit crunches are likely to follow. Financial systems can also become dominated by speculation and fraud. In short: there is a great need to intensively regulate financial systems. The basic function of a financial system is to finance productive investment and in this way to contribute to the positive dynamic of capitalist systems. Regulations should be made in a way that the positive functions of financial systems are not depressed but the instability potentials of financial systems are contained. We distinguish between the regulation of the domestic financial system and the international regulation of the financial system.

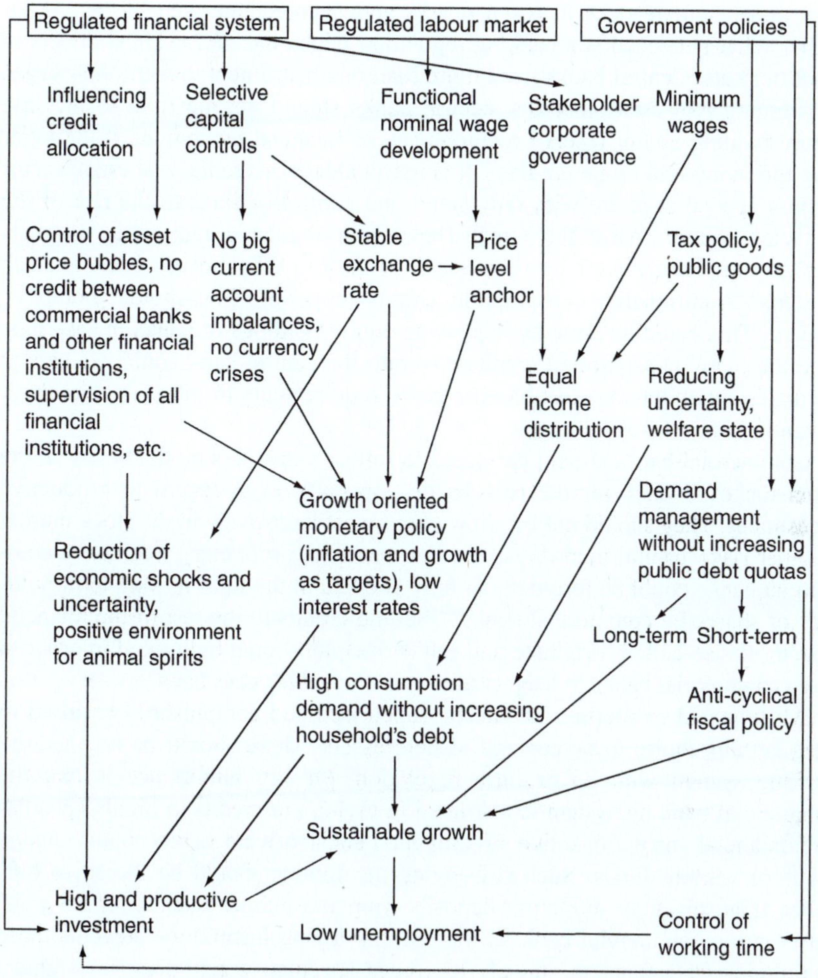

Figure 2.27 An ideal macroeconomic policy regime (source: authors' illustration).

Domestic financial system

A domestic financial system should have highly regulated commercial banks and insurance companies. The stability of these institutions is a public good as the functioning of the whole economy depends on it and the general public keeps its wealth in these institutions. In the first case especially the stability of commercial banks is of paramount importance. If a capital-based pension system exists, pension funds also have to be intensively regulated.

Commercial banks should be forced, as generally done, to keep a certain percentage of their assets as equity. Basel II has the main shortcoming that equity holding is based on banks' own risk models. Such models are pro-cyclical as they underestimate risks in boom phases and overestimate them in periods of crisis. What is needed is a banking regulation which has anti-cyclical effects in asset markets. Central banks need more than one instrument to fulfil their tasks. Concerning real estate markets, central banks should get the right to increase equity holding and/or reserve requirements of financial institutions if the latter give too many real estate credits.[89] It is reasonable to make the real estate sector again a special segment with only small and controlled links to the rest of the financial system. After the Great Depression regulated real estate markets worked sufficiently well in all western countries. Why not go back to such systems? Additionally, consumption credits to private households should be limited. This could be done by increasing equity holdings of banks in case they give too many consumption credits. Overall, the central bank could use capital adequacy requirements/asset-based reserve requirements to influence the credit allocation of commercial banks.

Commercial banks should be forced to follow a business model based on the provision of finance for the real sector, especially with regard to productive investment. They should not be allowed to invest intensively in the stock market or other risky capital market papers. For example, proprietary trading by commercial banks could be forbidden or only allowed in the form of long-term holdings of shares by commercial banks.[90] Selling credits to the rest of the financial system, the so-called 'originate and sell' principle, should be limited in order to force commercial banks to keep credits until the debtor pays back.

All financial institutions should be supervised and compulsorily required to keep certain equity in percentage of held assets. There should be no shadow-banking system with no or little regulation. Of key importance is that the commercial banking system is restricted in giving out credits to highly speculative financial institutions like investment banks, private equity funds, hedge funds or venture funds. Such risk-loving institutions should be forced to refinance themselves by attracting deposits from the public. Such a 'credit-wall' between the commercial bank sector and risk-loving institutions prevents these institutions from financing hugely leveraged speculative activities by commercial bank credit and indirectly by central bank credit via the refinancing of the commercial banking system. While under such regulations huge leverages of non-bank financial institutions like hedge funds or private equity funds are no longer possible, venture capital to finance risky start-ups and so on is still sufficiently available. However, risky and speculative activities would be financed directly or indirectly by the public and not by commercial banks and in the end the central bank.

Generally, future markets serve a positive purpose as they allow hedging of individual risks for certain activities. All the positive functions of such markets also remain in the absence of opaque OTC derivative markets; all derivatives should be bought and sold in organised exchanges. Financial products should be checked and standardised by supervision agencies before they are allowed to be used. While a tax on all transactions in asset markets is not sufficient to stabilise markets, it is a useful source of tax revenues. In future markets of commodities only agents really selling and buying commodities should be allowed to take part. All these types of regulations have the aim of restricting the financial sector to its actual purpose: by cutting down and/or simplifying activities excessive speculation is limited while the basic functions of financial systems, such as the reduction of individual risk by making future contracts, are preserved.

The role of rating agencies should be curtailed, for example by reducing the role of risk models and by standardising derivatives. Public rating agencies financed by the buyers of financial products seem to be more suitable for evaluating assets than an oligopoly of three dominating private rating agencies financed by the sellers of financial products.[91]

Finally, the payment of agents in the financial system should not be related to short-term developments. The best solution is to go back to fixed salaries that are independent of performance, at least for the lion's share of income. If small bonuses in the form of stock-options and so on are paid, this should be the case only according to relative performance in the market and only after a long-term positive performance covering a business cycle. Generally, salaries including bonuses for agents in the financial system should be cut back.

Restrictions on the investment decisions of insurance companies and pension funds should remain. Additionally, to stabilise international capital flows, foreign investment of such institutions needs to be highly regulated too.

A regulated financial system is not compatible with a shareholder value strategy in corporate governance. To guarantee a long-term strategy of firms, to achieve a more equal income distribution and have a more democratic structure a stakeholder corporate governance system is much more suitable. In such a system owners are only one of the important stakeholders and short-term stock price development is relatively unimportant for management decisions. In a regulated financial system profit mark-ups are reduced, which helps to increase wage quotas. Together with the elimination of the important role of bonuses, managers' salaries go down and income distribution becomes more equal.

The overall objective of a financial system shaped in the described way is threefold: to focus credit expansion to the real sector, to force agents to have a long-term horizon and to cut down speculative activities. Many of the present activities in the financial sector serve no purpose for the development of the real economy or are even negative as they increase volatility and shocks. In many cases the important functions of the financial system can be fulfilled in a more simple way. Then, shocks coming from the financial system become weaker and much less frequent as asset price bubbles, over-indebtedness and volatility are reduced. All this creates a better environment for entrepreneurship and animal spirits and focuses activities towards long-term productive investment.

International financial system

While a new order for global governance is certainly urgently needed, to sketch a blueprint of it exceeds the scope of this book. Nevertheless, we like to stress the need for selective international capital controls. Such controls serve three purposes.

First, they can reduce the volatility of exchange rate movements. The obvious problem is that international capital flows are driven by expectations that have no anchor in fundamentals. Exchange rate movements then become driven by potentially big shifts in expectations and by the logic of asset markets with all the short-term and long-term instabilities involved in them. Thus, selective capital controls help to stabilise exchange rates. For big currency areas like the US, the EMU or Japan even isolated capital controls are possible, although it would be more recommendable to achieve a global solution in the tradition of Keynes proposal (1942) regarding the Bretton Woods system.

Second, capital controls help to prevent external imbalances which are only possible if corresponding net capital flows exist. Similarly, like asset market bubbles, international imbalances can lead to over-indebtedness and to financial crises – in this case of countries. Long-term stagnation in the countries affected by such crises cannot be excluded. It is also not justifiable that some countries use capital flows strategically to follow export-led growth strategies that harm growth in other countries. Keynes (1942) argued for symmetric adjustment processes in both current account surplus and current account deficit countries and not, as usually done by the market, for a painful adjustment process in the deficit countries only. Keynes called for demand stimulation in the surplus country and demand contraction in the current account deficit countries. If imbalances are too big, for example because of an inflationary development in one country, controlled exchange rate adjustments are recommendable.[92]

Third, besides the interest rate and administrative instruments to fight asset price bubbles, selective capital controls are the third instrument that central banks should have to influence the exchange rate and the current account constellation. Capital controls and administrative controls of asset price bubbles give room for the central bank to use the interest rate more for domestic purposes.

A regulated external regime reduces the potential of the exchange rate to be a shock machine and makes it an external nominal anchor of the price level. The stability of the exchange rate is the key point; yet, it is not necessarily required to have a fixed exchange rate regime. In a constellation of big current account imbalances controlled exchange rate movements are useful to reduce the imbalances. The avoidance of exchange rate volatility and of currency crises that can quickly transform into domestic financial crises reduces shocks in the economy and improves the conditions for high investment in the real sector.

Currency areas can combine capital controls, central bank interventions and interest rate policy to keep the exchange rate relatively stable and the current account more or less in balance. Such a policy is possible even without interfering in free trade and without isolating a country from international capital markets. But it should be kept in mind that free trade and free capital flows are no ends in themselves (Stiglitz 2004). They have to be integrated into an overall macroeconomic policy regime.

2.8.2 Regulated labour markets

Labour is a very specific good and labour markets have very distinctive characteristics. Working power is a part of a human being and many workers lack assets to make a living without working. They are forced to rent their working power to employers to get an income. This imbalance of power alone makes it necessary that government interventions and/or institutions ensure decent working conditions and protect labour from the imponderability of markets.

A surplus of labour does not disappear like, for example, an oversupply of tomatoes. If too many tomatoes are produced, production is reduced until supply meets demand. In the case of labour such a mechanism does not exist. Falling wages make the situation worse and do not lead to equilibrium; quite the contrary, they lead to deflation and an escalation of a crisis. Macroeconomic policy has to try to keep unemployment rates low. This is one of the preconditions to guarantee an equal power balance between labour and capital. Additionally, since workers are at the same time consumers, they play an equally important role in the goods markets.

From a macroeconomic point of view regulated labour markets have two main functions: first, to guarantee a functional development of the nominal wage level and second, to control wage dispersion.

Functional development of the nominal wage level

Nominal unit labour costs are the most important factor determining the price level in a domestic economy. A stable development of nominal unit labour costs serves as a domestic anchor for the price level or more precisely for the target inflation rate. As mentioned above, the external anchor for the price level is the exchange rate. For a country it is much more preferable to rely on wages as a nominal anchor than on the exchange rate, which then can be much more easily used as an instrument to balance the current account. For monetary policy a stable nominal wage anchor is of paramount importance. Restrictive monetary policy, which is costly in respect to growth and employment, is not needed if wage development prevents inflationary wage–price spirals. Even more important than preventing an inflationary development is the prevention of deflation. Deflationary processes leave central banks in a weak position as the nominal interest rate cannot become negative.

According to the wage norm nominal wages should increase proportionally to medium-term productivity plus the target inflation rate. In this case wage inflation is equal to the warranted inflation rate and wage policy is functional. The best institutionalisation to achieve a wage development in line with the wage norm is the existence of strong trade unions and strong employers' associations that take into account the macroeconomic effects of wage development.[93] Strong federal union organisations help to control competition between different unions which may have the incentive to push up wages in a situation of low unemployment. Strong employers' associations help to prevent firms from competing for workers by inter alia paying wages above collectively negotiated ones. In the ideal case all employees are covered by collective bargaining. This can be achieved in different ways: for example by forced membership of all firms of employers' associations as in Austria, by declaring all wage bargaining outcomes as generally binding as in France, or by informal signalling effects as in many countries after the Second World War. It should be mentioned that in the years after the Second World War until the 1970s, even in liberal market economies such as the US (Hall and Soskice 2001), wages in industries with strong unions and employers' associations were determined by collective bargaining and that the result of the bargaining had a signalling effect for the whole economy (Levy and Temin 2010).

In a macroeconomic perspective employers' associations should have an interest in establishing the law of one price also on the industry level.[94] Equal wages for equal work in all firms in one industry creates equal conditions and is an engine for productivity development. Moreover, it reduces transaction costs for firms that are otherwise forced to negotiate each individual contract and to observe the wage development in competing firms. It is unreasonable to subsidise firms with relatively low productivity by relatively low wages.

Economic shocks make the compliance with a wage norm more difficult. Real wage might be suddenly reduced, for example by strong real depreciations or by sharply increasing prices of natural resources and food as in the years after 2006 or in the 1970s. Such real wage decreases make it politically difficult to keep the nominal wage development in line with the wage norm. As far as a regulated capitalism reduces economic shocks it also increases the likelihood that the wage norm can be followed even in a constellation of high employment.

An active minimum wage policy by the government can help to prevent deflationary tendencies. If minimum wages increase at least according to the wage norm, it is not likely that the nominal wage level decreases. However, minimum wage policy against deflation is actually more important in the deregulated type of capitalism which exists today; in a regulated type of capitalism it is definitely possible that high employment and the established wage bargaining system are sufficient to prevent a deflationary wage development.

Low wage dispersion

Strong unions and strong employers' associations and a broad wage bargaining process usually guarantee relatively small wage dispersions. Unacceptable wage differentials, especially relatively low wages, in most cases are the result of an incomprehensive wage bargaining process, which increases the wage differentials between workers protected by unions and the unprotected.

Statutory minimum wages can play an important role in preventing the creation of a big low-wage sector. Theoretically and empirically the main function of statutory minimum wages is to compress the wage structure from below, thus to reduce the wage dispersion by an increase of the lowest wages. To be effective statutory minimum wages should be equal to the lowest paid wages and they should be able to affect the living standards of a certain percentage of the workforce, let us say 10 per cent. At the same time minimum wages should be kept at a certain percentage of average wages – let us say 60 per cent of average wages. Of course, the degree of wage dispersion in the end is a question of norms and values and has to be decided politically.

In the UK the government of Tony Blair established the Low-Wage Commission. With one-third of its members appointed by unions, one-third appointed by employers' associations and one-third independent experts (scientists), it seems to be a good institutionalisation to determine minimum wage development. The Low-Wage Commission every year gives a recommendation how minimum wages should be changed. This recommendation is not legally binding; however, it is politically difficult for the government not to follow it.

Low wage dispersion is an important element for an equal income distribution and indirectly for sufficient consumption demand based on income and not on credit. Thus, a relatively equal income distribution within the working class involves not only the question of justice; it is also of vital importance for creating a sufficient consumption demand, which is not based on households' debt. This is one of the messages learned from the regulated capitalism established as a consequence of the Great Depression.

2.8.3 Government policies

Government policies (excluding monetary policy, which is of course also a government policy but will be discussed separately) have two dimensions. The first one is Ordnungspolitik, the second one is policies related to demand management.

Ordnungspolitik

The government is the key player in setting the institutions and the general framework for economic activities. The structure of taxes and expenditures together with the organisation of the social safety net is one important area. The other one is the legal system, which regulates all markets, but especially financial and labour markets.

We start with the function of governments in providing certainty. Capitalist economies endogenously create uncertainties not known by other modes of productions. All societies in history were affected by natural disasters, illness and so on. But the uncertainty of a capitalist society, where most individuals have lost their own means of production and are not necessarily integrated in family ties, tribes or the like, goes further. Examples of system-specific uncertainties are the risk of becoming unemployed, the risk of going bankrupt or the risk of losing wealth that can be kept as a protection against uncertainty (monetary wealth, shares, etc.). Economic agents suffer from such uncertainties and can find themselves in precarious situations without personal misbehaviour. Especially in deregulated types of capitalism, individuals suffer from uncontrollable and destructive market processes. The provision of certainty is vital for a regulated market economy and has many dimensions. We discuss only a few of them.

Governments can decide to join, or together with other countries create, an exchange rate system with relatively stable exchange rates. The Bretton Woods System is such an example or the EMS. The breakdown of the Bretton Woods System in the 1970s was a political decision. To defend it would have meant not to follow the Neoliberal Globalisation strategy with its completely free capital flows and deregulated financial domestic systems.

Another area of key importance to reduce uncertainty is the establishment of a comprehensive welfare state. Unemployment insurance or basic healthcare and a pension system for all citizens are elements of it.[95] There are other public goods that should be delivered by the state, for example a free and good education system, at least from the kindergarten to high school and preferably also universities, or affordable public transport. A comprehensive production of public goods and policies to reduce uncertainties lessen the need and incentive to save and increase consumption demand. Such policies add to long-term economic dynamics.

However, contrary to the principle of uncertainty reduction, in almost all developed countries over the last decades precarious jobs (temporary and fixed-term employment, part-time employment without contributions to the social safety net, etc.) were created. These jobs are usually not new jobs but substitute the already existing full-time work places. In many cases this is achieved by outsourcing production in less regulated areas. If more employees are needed to satisfy rising demand, employment increases, regardless of whether the created jobs are precarious or normal full-time jobs. This was the case in the 1950s and 1960s, and it would also be the case today. On the other hand, if demand stagnates or declines, a shift to more precarious work is hardly able to prevent or even reduce unemployment. With regard to employment all the deregulation measures were strictly for the birds – they were implemented without reducing the unemployment problem which is not based on insufficient wage dispersion and too rigid labour market institutions. This is a tragedy especially for the many social democratic parties which followed the neoclassical paradigm in deregulating labour markets. The Hartz IV reform and the Agenda 2010 in Germany are instructive examples for labour market deregulations without employment effects. Rather, the effect of these reforms was that people felt a higher level of uncertainty and saved more. Consequently, over a long period of time Germany suffered from a lack of consumption demand (see the case study about Germany).

On the other hand, there is a range of policies that is well able to strengthen the spending capacity of households and to add to an economic model with sufficient consumption demand based on earnings.

Governments can support a functional wage development by strengthening trade unions and employers' associations in many different ways – from compulsory membership to declaring wage negotiations in an industry as generally binding to organising a tripartite macroeconomic dialogue about topics relevant for trade unions and employers' associations. Similarly, statutory minimum wages can be an effective way to reduce wage dispersion provided they are set sufficiently above the level of social transfers. Social transfers can be interpreted as reservation wages as nobody would like to enter gainful employment being paid an amount below them. Statutory minimum wages should sufficiently exceed the reservation wage to prevent the unsatisfying situation that wages of full-time employees fall to the level of social transfers. The latter case can be observed in Germany which lacks a statutory minimum wage.

Nevertheless, even in a regulated market economy with a relatively high wage quota and limited wage dispersion, market-determined income distribution is likely to be unacceptably unequal. Thus, governments have the important function to modify the market-given income distribution by tax policy and expenditures. A broad income tax base with low exceptions and high marginal tax rates as well as a broad supply of public goods are the key instruments to increase equality in income distribution. A good example is inheritance tax: high inheritances are alien even to the conservative ideology of a performance-based society; high taxes on them can make the 'endowment' of all market participants more equal.

Demand management

Governments have to follow an anti-cyclical fiscal policy to stabilise the business cycle and in such a way increase the long-term performance of an economy. Anti-cyclical fiscal policy first implies the acceptance of automatic fiscal stabilisers, which endogenously increase the budget deficit (reduce the budget surplus) in an economic slowdown and reduce the budget deficit (increase the budget surplus) in a period of an economic boom. We recommend a constellation in which over the business cycle the public budget, at least for consumption spending, is balanced.

In deep recessions additional discretionary public measures to stabilise aggregate demand are needed. Only public investment, preferably which directly creates future cash-flows, should be financed by public debt.

However, in the case of long-term demand weaknesses government spending is not sufficient to compensate the lack of aggregate demand. For this reason we reject the idea of functional finance that goes back to Lerner (1943) and advocates fiscal policy without limits that guarantees full employment by compensating insufficient personal demand.[96]

For demand management in the long-term, three government policies are of importance. First, as described above, governments with a variety of measures can add to an equal income distribution and a reduction of uncertainty and via these measures stimulate consumption demand. Second, investment demand also can be strengthened by a reduction of uncertainty for firms and other 'supply-side' measures, for example to strengthen the equity base of firms or to stimulate reinvestment of profits. Last but not least, publicly owned enterprises or private firms that are indirectly controlled by the government can stabilise investment in the productive sector. There are no good arguments why the government should not own companies that produce public utilities and public infrastructure. Also public banks can play an important role for the investment dynamics. The German public banking sector (the Sparkassen) has been financing small- and medium-sized firms on a local level for decades and does nothing else as the celebrated micro-finance sector is doing in many developing countries.

2.8.4 Growth-oriented monetary policy

A central bank in a regulated type of capitalism can be institutionally independent or not. This is not the key point. However, some independence of central banks makes sense. For example, central banks should not be allowed to directly finance budget deficits – probably with the exception of very special constellations like a deflation – and monetary policy should not be subordinated to fiscal policy. More important is that the central bank is a part of an overall growth-oriented structure and itself follows a growth-oriented monetary policy. A central bank should be forced to justify its policies openly and should have a transparent structure that includes the mandatory publishing of the debates within the policy- making body. Moreover, the bank should take part in tripartite cooperation and in coordinating institutions.

In our approach to capitalism, the central bank has a comparatively high control over credit allocation. The dilemma of central banks in deregulated financial systems that credit expansion spurs asset price inflation and speculation and not real sector activities is very much reduced in regulated financial systems. The limitation or even ban on proprietary trading of commercial banks and the cut of credit relations between commercial banks and non-bank financial institutions stop central bank financed credit expansion that stimulates speculation and asset price bubbles as well as too high indebtedness of agents in the economy. In addition, the central bank has more than the refinancing rate as a monetary policy instrument. For example, commercial banks can be forced by discretionary interventions to keep higher equity and/or higher reserves in case they expand credits to real estate markets, give more consumption credits than wanted by the central bank and so on.

In deregulated financial systems monetary policy in many circumstances has to be subordinated to the need to prevent exchange rate volatility, currency crises and all endogenous market shocks. Selective international capital controls help to reduce such shocks and at the same time give more leeway for domestic-oriented monetary policy. Central bank interventions in the foreign exchange market to control the exchange rate can be added to capital controls. A global governance structure including the establishment of a stable international currency and a stable financial system is preferable to isolated policies of currency areas. But the recommended policies can also be carried out by single currency areas, especially if they are big enough.[97]

If labour market institutions work well, nominal wage development follows the wage norm. This prevents, on the one hand, deflationary developments and supports and even guarantees the stability of the economy as central banks are too weak to fight against deflation. Wage development according to the wage norm, on the other hand, relieves the central banks from using the interest rate to fight against inflationary wage increases and to use unemployment to bring down inflation or keep inflation low. But there is no guarantee that even in a regulated type of capitalism, inflation never becomes a problem. In such situations central banks have to use restrictive monetary policy to stop the inflationary process. Otherwise the monetary system will erode.

The target inflation rate of the central bank should not be too close to zero to give monetary policy the room to cut real interest rates substantially in case the stabilisation of the economy makes this necessary. Moreover, central banks should not be too sensitive about demand inflation and should allow some volatility of the inflation rate over the business cycle. During economic booms, when aggregate demand is driven by high investment, demand inflation is not dangerous as long as a wage–price spiral is not triggered. In such a case high investment demand soon increases capacities and goods supply and this potentially solves the problem of excess demand.

Monetary policy should have more than one target. Thus, monetary targeting and inflation targeting are not recommended strategies. Also the NAIRU curve cannot be a satisfactory guideline for monetary policy. The Federal Reserve (Fed) at this point can serve as a positive example as it has to search for a compromise between three targets: price level stability (low inflation rate), high GDP growth and low long-term interest rates. Looking at interest rate policy Alan Greenspan, Chairman of the Fed from 1987 until 2006, followed an interest rate policy very much in line with our ideas. He did not follow any rule and stood for a policy 'on-sight', i.e. he started to fight against inflation when actual inflationary pressures were observable, and he cut interest rates quickly and substantially when there were signs of an economic slowdown. But his interest rate policy does not excuse that his ideological belief in efficient and stable financial markets made him partly responsible for the subprime disaster and the deep worldwide recession it triggered. He persistently rejected the idea of controlling financial markets – from the Internet bubble in the 1990s to the real estate bubble one decade later.[98]

An ideal monetary policy keeps interest rates low whenever possible without creating inflation. As long as labour market institutions control inflation low (real) interest rates are possible and support the aim of a low profit mark-up and a high wage quota. If there is the danger of an economic slowdown, monetary policy should act quickly and not as hesitantly as, for example, the European Central Bank in the past. In case of a wage–price spiral, which violates the inflation target, increasing interest rates are unavoidable. A central bank should, however, test out how high interest rates must be pushed up to reduce the inflation rate. Overall, a discretionary monetary policy which reacts to historical circumstances is recommended. Monetary policy, the policy which out of all macroeconomic policies can act in the quickest and most uniform way, then becomes an important element to stabilise a capitalist economy.

2.8.5 Stakeholder corporate governance

In a regulated capitalism, shareholder corporate governance has to come to an end. Management should be forced again to organise a compromise among all stakeholders. Also democracy should not end in factories. Especially employees and their representatives should be given the right to take part in firms' decision-making. Such firm structures existed in the 1950s and 1960s and it is only a political matter to go back to structures in the tradition of stakeholder capitalism. Such a step involves several elements.

The role of the financial system in the form of anonymous owners or short-term oriented investment funds, private equity funds and so on should become less important for management decision-making. Firms should try to increase their equity base and finance a substantial part of their investment out of profit. Tax policy could support such a development, for example by taxing profits that are paid out to owners higher than those that kept in a firm. It should be forbidden to pay dividends or pay income to owners if firms make no profit.[99] Also the possibilities to buy back own shares should be limited to very special cases. And last but not least, hostile takeovers should be made very difficult. Such policies take away the pressure of the management to care for the short-term development of share prices and to orient corporate governance towards short-term targets, which can destabilise long-term development and reduce productivity. Bonus systems (share-options, etc.) for management (also for management in non-finance enterprises) have to be cut down.

2.8.6 Dynamic investment, dynamic consumption and full employment

In the model sketched above investment demand as well as consumption demand are dynamic and develop in a proportional way. Investment in productive capital is dynamic as an economic system with few endogenous shocks and a high level of certainty gives the best conditions for animal spirits or entrepreneurship. Cheap and sufficient finance and a government's role in the investment process support sustainable high investment. Consumption demand is high on the basis of an equal income distribution. It is sustainable as it is not financed out of credit. Anti-cyclical fiscal policy can add to the stability of demand. In the macroeconomic policy regime described throughout this book export surpluses should not play a role as demand engine. Current account surpluses in some countries are tantamount to current account deficits in others. Thus, mercantilist policies to increase current account surpluses can never be a solution for all countries in the world. For a macroeconomic policy regime that takes into account the international dimension, current account balances should be small.

Mature industrial societies have to decide how to use productivity increases. GDP growth, productivity development and population growth have to be combined in a way that, in the medium term, full employment can be achieved.[100] Population growth and productivity development cannot be controlled in a direct way. If necessary, and if part of the productivity increase is not used for GDP growth, reduction of working time is a suitable instrument to guarantee full employment. At least Keynes (1930a) argued for this possibility. Of course change in working time cannot be used as a short-term policy. But as a medium- and long-term policy it is an important part of a regulated type of capitalism which does not accept that part of the population works long hours and more and more intensively while the other part suffers from unemployment.

3 Case studies

The case studies covers the period from the 1970s to the subprime crisis which broke out in 2007 and led to a worldwide recession in 2009. The case studies in the selected countries show how the regulated type of capitalism which had developed after the Great Depression in the 1930s and dominated western countries in the 1950s and 1960s broke down and paved the way for the Neoliberal Globalisation model which has been developing ever since.

As cases we have selected the four largest capitalist countries with respect to GDP: the United States, Japan, Germany and United Kingdom. But the size of the countries was not the only criteria. The countries apply different versions of the Neoliberal Globalisation model which developed in different and distinctive ways. In the United States and Great Britain it is fair to speak of a conservative revolution. Conservative governments with a vision of a radical liberal type of capitalism came into power and changed the structures of the economy. Of course there was an interaction between Ordungspolitik, macroeconomic policies and economic development. Structural changes led to a certain economic development which by itself triggered structural changes. Germany and Japan were latecomers, establishing the deregulated type of capitalism relatively reluctantly at first and also quite late.

Within this deregulated type of capitalism, which has been developing since the 1970s, there are different versions. For example, the United States and United Kingdom followed a much more finance-driven development than Germany and Japan. The latter two deregulated their financial systems but, in contrast to the United States and UK, without triggering a domestic expansion. Japan and Germany followed aggressive export-led growth strategies and continued the tradition which brought them spectacular economic miracles in the decades immediately after the Second World War. However, this export orientation produced lower GDP-growth rates than in the US and UK. Germany also gives the chance to analyse problems within the EMU. In short, the four countries (US, UK, Japan and Germany) stand for four unique versions of the deregulated type of capitalism and are characterised by different macroeconomic policy regimes.

In each of the case studies below we first give a short overview of the country's economic and political development. Then, in much more detail we shall discuss developments in the financial sector, the country's embeddedness in the global market, its wage policy and wage development, monetary policy and finally we offer an overall interpretation of each macroeconomic policy regime and its dynamics.

3.1 The finance-led growth model of the United States

3.1.1 Overview of the political and economic development

The United States occupies a special position in the world community. After the Second World War it became the unchallenged hegemonic power of the western world. Throughout the past decades this position has been eroding somewhat, but the US has remained thus far the most powerful country in the world, both economically and militarily. In terms of real gross domestic product, it is the world's largest economy and at present with respect to GDP it compares with the European Union. After the Second World War the US dollar became the leading currency worldwide. The international role of the US dollar gave the US several privileges. But the international role of the US dollar also led to very high US capital imports which pushed the country into a constellation of huge current account deficits (see below).

After the Second World War, the US experienced a relatively gradual decline in GDP compared with the world's GDP and other economic indicators, since especially Japan and the western European countries managed to start an economic catching-up process. The international role of the US dollar has been reduced, but it is still number one in the currency hierarchy (see Section 2.3). In the late 1960s and thereafter the US slipped into a decade of an overall weak US dollar. Increased inflation rates towards the end of the 1960s and early 1970s as the Vietnam War progressed led to high public spending and an overheating of the economy. International competitiveness eroded and due to the fixed exchange rates under the Bretton Woods system there was a danger of a US current account deficit which at that time was considered a problem. International capital flows were already liberalised to such an extent that the potential danger of a depreciation of the US dollar (also in the form of a realignment within the Bretton Woods System) caused capital outflows from the US and forced other countries in the Bretton Woods System to intervene heavily in the foreign exchange market to defend the US exchange rate. To stabilise the exchange rate, restrictive macroeconomic policies to reduce inflation and the imposition of controls on international capital flows would have been the best policies, since instruments to control capital flows were still being used by many other countries and would also have been available for the US. However, the Republican President Richard Nixon was not interested in such polices. In 1971 he announced that the US would no longer exchange gold against central bank US dollar reserves. The US dollar was allowed to float. Attempts to save the Bretton Woods System failed on the basis of a lack of political will to defend it. In 1973 the world economy switched to a system of flexible exchange rates. In 1974

Nixon had to step down because of the Watergate affair and Gerald Ford became President until 1976 when Jimmy Carter was elected President.

Carter was confronted with a complex and unstable political and economic development. In 1975, the United States, together with most other industrial countries, had to accept the first great recession of the post-war period. Indicators such as productivity development also received poor marks in this phase. The US was also forced to accept political defeats. They had to disengage from Vietnam at the beginning of the 1970s and were unable politically to prevent the oil price shocks in 1973 and 1979, initiated not least by the decline in value of the US dollar. In 1979 there was the Islamic revolution in Iran, followed by the Soviet invasion of Afghanistan the same year. The Iran hostage crisis also distracted Carter for well over a year, from November 1979 to January 1981. By the end of the 1970s, monetary instability had become critical. The inflation rate in the US rose considerably at the end of the 1970s, not least because of the collapse of the US dollar at the same time. The inflation rate rose further, reaching double digit figures by the beginning of the 1980s. The US dollar came under further pressure to devalue, which made OPEC consider switching to a basket of currencies as a denominator for the oil price. The US found itself in a devaluation–inflation spiral with pressure towards increased domestic wage costs and the threat of more and even cumulative capital flight. Carter used price and wage controls and tried to get the support from the unions to demand nominal wage constraint. All of these policies failed and the inflation and exchange rate problem escalated even further (Ruckstad 1985).

Before the end of the Carter administration, Paul Volcker, then a representative of neoclassical monetarism, was appointed President of the US central bank in 1979. Even under Volcker the Fed tried to get support from the German Bundesbank and other central banks to stabilise the US dollar, but this was rejected (Emminger 1986). A firm strategy change was carried out in monetary policy. Volcker tried to intensify the control of the money supply, a policy which led to extremely high and volatile interest rates. The monetarist experiment of strict control of the money supply was soon abandoned again, at the beginning of the 1980s. However, this radical attempt to control the money supply and the extremely high interest rates which were used to put a halt to the increases in the money supply led to the biggest ever, at that time, downturn in the US and the world economy since the Second World War. Especially Latin America was pushed into the 'lost decade' as its export market broke down and interest payments increased, resulting in exchange rate collapses and distortions in domestic financial systems. Without a doubt the US was forced to fight against the inflationary development which was on the verge of spinning out of control, but its monetary targeting, used as monetary policy strategy by the Fed, maximised costs to bring inflation down (see Table 3.1).

President Carter had no real chance of being elected for a second term. The economic crises with sharply increasing unemployment rates and also the obvious erosion of the hegemonic position of the US created a favourable climate for the election of Ronald Reagan as the next US president in 1980.

Table 3.1 Macroeconomic indicators in the US, 1971–2009 (average values over the business cycle)

	Business cycles					
	1971–1975	*1976–1982*	*1983–1991*	*1992–2001*	*2002–2009*	
Real GDP growth rate	2.83	2.73	3.52	3.58	1.71	
Unemployment rate	6.10	7.30	6.72	5.37	5.83	
Inflation rate	6.80	8.74	3.91	2.67	2.42	
Change in nominal unit labour costs (%)	6.05	7.75	3.06	1.87	1.51	
Change in real wage per employee (%)	1.05	0.98	1.14	1.73	0.78	
Budget balance (% of GDP)	–2.10	–2.48	–4.54	–1.79	–4.69	
Current account balance (% of GDP)	0.39	–0.06	–1.97	–2.15	–4.89	
	Mid-1970s	*Mid-1980s*	*1990*	*Mid-1990s*	*2000*	*Mid-2000s*
Gini coefficient	0.316	0.338	0.349	0.361	0.357	0.381

Source: AMECO (2010), OECD (2009c), authors' calculations.

President Reagan immediately began to implement his neoliberal reform agenda. The key elements were the full-fledged deregulation of domestic financial markets and international financial transactions, a policy already partly followed by Jimmy Carter, and a policy to increase flexibility in the labour market, including an anti-union policy. Tax cuts were planned for the higher income group as well as welfare expenditure cuts. Military expenditures increased with the purpose of reversing the erosion of the political, military and economic power of the US. Another important element of the development was the introduction of a new corporate governance system geared only towards the interest of shareholders (Rappaport 1986).

Growth performance in the 1980s was better than in the period of crisis in the 1970s. The inflation rate was also brought down quickly and has never become a serious problem again. Confidence in the US dollar increased and even when interest rates were cut, capital imports grew and pushed the US current account into a deep deficit for most of the 1980s. However, the dominant feature of the 1980s was the advent of a huge wave of mergers and acquisitions, many in the form of unfriendly takeovers without leading to overall dynamic private investment. The government supported these restructuring steps which were stimulated by the changes in the financial system. Unions or other groups in society were not able to prevent restructuring, which in many cases was harmful for workers and led to 'traumatized workers' (Blinder and Yellen 2001: 39). The restructuring phase led to a permanently high 'flux' of workers in the labour market with a high number of dismissals and new appointments. Wage dispersion increased radically in the 1980s and led to a large low-wage sector in the US and a change towards a more unequal income distribution. The wage quota also dropped from 65 per cent in 1980 to 61 per cent in 2008 (see Figure 2.24). One of the reasons for the faster increase in productivity compared with the 1970s can be found in this period of restructuring (Blinder and Yellen 2001). In the 1980s consumption demand and government demand contributed substantially to GDP growth. In the first half of the 1980s increasing current account deficits reduced growth, but in the second half of the 1980s they were reduced and the external sector stabilised demand (see Figure 3.1).

A key element to understanding US development in the 1980s and also in the periods that followed is the combination of radical neoliberal reforms and pronounced discretionary monetary and fiscal policy which usually followed a Keynesian logic. In the early 1980s, for example, monetary and fiscal policy became very expansionary. Together with a positive expectation shock for business brought about by the election of Ronald Reagan, this led to relatively high GDP growth. Wage policy in the US was not possible and also unwanted. It was not possible because trade unions were too weak to play a role on a macroeconomic

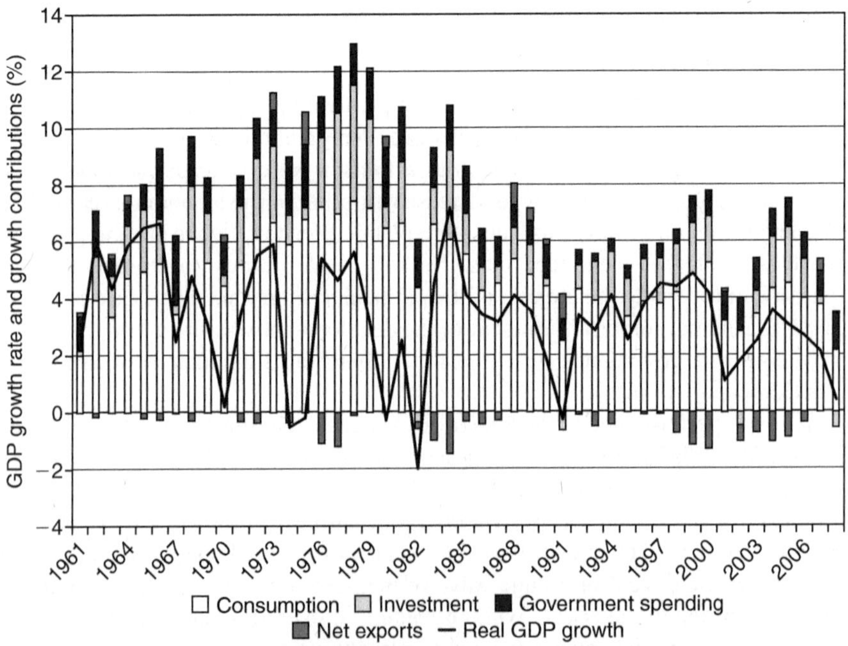

Figure 3. 1 GDP growth rate and growth contributions of its components in the US in per cent, 1961–2009 (source: AMECO 2010, authors' calculations).

level; it was unwanted because the conservative government rallied against unions wherever possible.

Ronald Reagan served for two terms. In 1988 his vice-president George H. W. Bush was the candidate for the conservatives and became President. Thus, the conservative revolution which was already more or less established could be developed even further without interruption. Under George H. W. Bush Panama was invaded and Bush led the coalition during the Gulf War after Iraq had invaded Kuwait in 1990. But he lost the next election because of a number of domestic and foreign issues such as tax increases and in 1993 the Democrat Bill Clinton became the next US President until 2001. Bill Clinton did not turn back the conservative revolution. However, minimum wages and taxes for the middle classes and the rich were increased. The 1990s was a fabulous decade of growth. The dominant economic development of the 1990s was the Internet bubble with exploding share prices and high investment which added substantially to GDP growth. Consumption demand also added to growth compensating for the overall negative demand effect of the again exploding current account deficit, especially in the second half of the 1990s. The Internet bubble came to an end in the early 2000s leading to a sharp downturn in 2001. Republican George W. Bush became the next US president in the middle of the economic crisis in 2001. He served two terms until the Democrat Barack Obama was elected in 2008. Bush Junior followed a very conservative agenda; his tax policy is exemplary. Terrorists attacked on 11 September, 2001, the World Trade Center just six months into his first term of office, and the following wars against terror in Afghanistan and Iraq pursued by the Bush administration were to affect public budgets profoundly.

After the crisis in 2001 economic growth in the US was driven mainly by private household demand. The main feature of the expansion in the 2000s was the real estate bubble which stimulated construction and via increasing real estate prices credit, demand and consumption. Without the deep changes in the financial system including the integration of real estate financing into national and even international financial markets such a development would not have been possible. Credit-driven private household demand was so dynamic that in spite of only moderate investment demand and further increasing current account deficits, which reduced aggregate demand, a relatively high GDP growth rate was possible. The end of the expansion came in 2007 when the subprime crisis broke out and later, in 2009, ushered in the global recession.

3.1.2 Financial system

The financial system in the US after the Second World War was institutionally based on the Glass–Steagall Act from 1932/1933. According to this act commercial banking and investment banking were separated, which basically meant that commercial banks were not allowed to engage in investment banking (for example in keeping or speculating with shares, organising mergers and acquisitions, underwriting securities issues or selling them to the public, etc.).

The Glass–Steagall Act also included interest rate ceilings for savings accounts and prohibited interest payments for demand deposits – the so-called Regulation Q (Tobin 1998: chapter 8).[1] One consequence of Regulation Q was that competition between banks was limited as they could not compete for bank deposits by high interest rates. Yet, inflationary pressure starting in the late 1960s and reaching unprecedented highs in the 1970s undermined the regulation. With higher inflation rates and accompanying pressure to increase nominal interest rates banks and other institutions found ways to circumvent Regulation Q by encouraging depositors to switch to alternative financial assets. Such financial innovations included the creation of money market mutual funds, negotiable orders of withdrawal or automatic transfer services. All these innovations meant a securitisation of liquidity holdings and allowed financial institutions to compete for funds by offering higher interest rates. Instead of raising the interest rate ceiling, for instance by setting it in terms of a real interest rate,[2] the penetration of this part of the Glass–Steagall Act was politically tolerated and later the law was adjusted. The Depository Institutions Deregulation and Monetary Control Act (DIDMCA) of 1980 can be considered one of the first fundamental changes in the US financial system. According to this act interest regulation was phased out over a period of six years and all depository institutions were free to offer the new financial products (Ruckstad 1985).[3] The DIDMCA and the following Garn–St. Germain Depository Institutions Act of 1982 substantially increased competition within the US financial system. For example, statutory restrictions on real estate lending by national banks were removed. As has been pointed out, competition in financial systems is not always desirable as it increases the likelihood of risky behaviour.

One aim of these deregulatory actions was to solve liquidity problems of the savings and loan associations. Supported by the government with interest rate advantages within the scope of Regulation Q and the provision of a secondary market for mortgage loans (see below), the thrifts' mandate used to be the attraction of saving deposits with relatively low interest rates to provide cheap long term and fixed rate loans for home purchasers. However, facing withdrawals of funds during the 1970s and rapidly rising deposit rates following the passage of the DIDMCA, the profitability of these institutions was seriously squeezed and many of them became technically insolvent. Further changes established by the DIDMCA and even more resolutely by the Garn–St. Germain Depository Institutions Act, including the loosening of capital requirements, failed to serve their purpose of restoring the stability of thrifts. Rather, deregulation led to soaring growth of the thrift industry with a large number of new financial institutions, some entering the market with little own capital. Savings and loan associations were granted many rights that had been available only to commercial banks before (for example, they could enter consumer loan and credit card businesses). They started to engage in risky investments such as junk bonds and derivative instruments, and also commercial real estate lending. 'The rush of new competitors, all eager to lend to developers, had a negative effect on existing commercial banks, on their underwriting standards, and on the quality of their loans.' (FDIC

1997: 185). Due to the low quality of the loans and collapsing real estate prices the number of technically insolvent savings and loan associations rose rapidly during the second half of the 1980s. Insured by the Federal Savings and Loan Insurance Corporation but lacking effective supervision, heavily insolvent thrifts remained open, in some cases for a few years. The costs for resolution of the latter are estimated at having amounted to about $150 billion by 1995 (Curry and Shibut 2000). Efforts for re-regulation after the savings and loan crisis remained limited. In fact, a new wave of deregulation started in 1994.

The wave of friendly and unfriendly takeovers and the large-scale change and restructuring of ownership in the US in the 1980s led to a boom in investment banking. Of course, it is also true that without investment banking such enormous restructuring steps would not have been possible. Investment banks, private property funds and so on started to expand their business as these institutions were the ones that carried out the financial side of the restructuring. The increasing role of investment banking was intermingled with the shareholder value principle which started to dominate corporate governance in the 1980s. For example, takeovers became one way to increase asset prices in the short term. Investment banking started to generate high returns. Financial corporations earned profits of around 1 per cent of GDP at the beginning of the reform in the early 1980s. At the end of the 2000s before the outbreak of the subprime crisis, financial corporations earned about 5 per cent of GDP (US Bureau of Economic Affairs (2010: Table 1.14).

Especially for private housing real estate markets used to be a special and sheltered segment of the financial market. Fannie Mae, a government-owned corporation created by the Roosevelt Administration in 1938, bought prime mortgage loans from savings and loan associations and in this way established a secondary market for mortgage credit. In 1968 Fannie Mae was privatised and in 1970 Freddy Mac was founded as a private institution to create some competition. However, both institutions received guarantees by government, issued debt securities to finance themselves and remained subject to strict regulatory oversight. Fannie Mae, later together with Freddy Mac, was able to indirectly influence the credit volume for real estate credits by regulating the volume and quality of mortgage credits they bought. This securitisation transaction was the American way of boosting house building, since it led to the availability of credit on reasonable terms for the purchase of real estate. Fannie Mae regulated the quantity and quality of real estate loans centrally, thereby contributing to the stability of the real estate market. As early as the 1970s, the first mortgage-backed securities were issued. This involved the packaging together of a number of real estate loans, whose cash flows served as the basis of the mortgage-backed securities. In principle, there is nothing disreputable about these securities, which are only a special type of debt securities. The situation changed fundamentally only after the economic downturn in 2001/2002. In 2003, 57.6 per cent (52 billion US dollars) of mortgage-backed securities were traded as prime loans, 37.4 per cent (34 billion US dollars) were subprime loans and 15.8 per cent (14 billion US dollars) were somewhere in between and counted as so-called Alt-A loans. In contrast, in the first half of 2006, only 26 per cent (67.2 billion US dollars) of mortgage-backed securities were issued as prime loans, while 44 per cent (114.3 billion US dollars) counted as subprime loans, the other 30 per cent (76.5 US dollars) being Alt-A loans (Dodd 2007). The central innovation which made the mass sale of subprime and Alt-A credits possible was the so-called 'waterfall principle'. Asset-backed securities and other collateralised debt obligations were subdivided into separate tranches, typically known as the equity tranche, the mezzanine tranche and the senior tranche. If borrowers in the package could not service their debt at first only the so-called equity tranche (the first loss piece) was affected, which had to bear the entire loss. Then came the mezzanine tranche and only when the equity and the mezzanine tranches were completely exhausted due to losses did the purchasers of senior tranches have to take a hit. Senior tranches, therefore, seemed secure, and received the highest valuations from rating agencies. The equity tranche, because of its high yield, was bought by hedge funds and other aggressively speculative investors. The quality of real estate loans diminished increasingly in the course of the US real estate bubble in the 2000s. Among other things, this was due to increasing competition in real estate financing, which manifested itself in the establishment of a multitude of mortgage financiers, which were not subject to standard banking regulation. At the same time Wall Street investment banks ensured the refinancing of these companies through the placement of mortgage-backed securities and collateralised debt obligations. There was a clear problem of moral hazard, since the originators of the real estate loans paid no attention to the quality of the loans, which they had no difficulty selling. The whole process only became possible because real estate financing became integrated into the general US and even the world financial market.

Partly resulting from the growing need for hedging risk, but also reflecting increasing speculative activities, the boom in investment banking was accompanied by a rapid growth of derivative markets. The Commodity Exchange Act of 1936 (CEA) granted the Commodity Exchange Commission and its successor, the Commodity Futures Trading Commission (CFTC), the authority to regulate derivative contracts. However, in the 1980s with the emergence of over-the-counter (OTC) derivatives that are traded off the regulated future exchanges, legal uncertainty arose about possible conflicts with the exclusive CFTC jurisdiction (Jickling 2003: 6). The Commodity Futures Modernization Act of 2000 (CFMA) addressed this issue.[4] Provided that no small investors were involved, financial OTC derivatives were excluded from CFTC regulation. This meant that by far the biggest part of the derivative market became completely uncontrolled. The size of the OTC derivative market skyrocketed in the subsequent years, the total national value of the market for example almost quintupled from June 2002 to June 2008 – an increase that was associated with increasing opacity and hence especially increasing counterparty risk in the overall financial system (BIS 2009a). The CFMA further relaxed derivative trading in commodities. Derivative transactions not accessible to small investors and based on commodities other than of agricultural or financial nature were exempted from most provisions of the CEA if trade is not done on a trading facility or if transactions are executed on an electronic trading facility. Since these exemptions were made especially available to the trading of energy contracts, they became known as the 'Enron loophole'.[5] Contrary to the CFTC's original aim of preventing price distorting speculation, it is frequently emphasised that in the years following the deregulation of commodity derivatives commodity prices were also driven by excessive speculation (see, among others UNCTAD 2009). Aiming to close the 'loophole', provisions included in the 2008 Farm Bill[6] made exempt commodities transactions executed on electronic trading facilities subject to regulation (Jickling 2008). Yet, derivative commodity contracts not traded on a trading facility have remained largely deregulated.

The Glass–Steagall Act, the heart of the financial system of the New Deal, was finally abolished in 1999. The Financial Services Modernization Act[7] of 1999 allowed commercial banks, investment banks, securities firms and insurance companies to consolidate. Also, prior to the passage of the Act, there were many relaxations to the Glass–Steagall Act. For example, even before the complete abolishment of the act, commercial banks were allowed to engage in investment banking. Even earlier, banks had obtained the right to go into stock and insurance brokerage. Stiglitz (2008) argued about the end of the act: 'As a result, the culture of investment banks was conveyed to commercial banks and everyone got involved in the high-risk gambling mentality. That mentality was core to the problem that we're facing now.' Parallel to these institutional developments a shadow financial system outside the traditional banking system developed, which grew dramatically in size and at the same time institutions in this sector based their business model to a large extent on speculative risky short-term transactions (see Section 2.2.2).[8]

The overwhelming feature of the credit expansion in the USA since the early 1970s is the explosion of indebtedness in percentage of GDP of non-financial sectors (Figure 3.2) signalling an increasing fragility of the financial system and the total economy. Indebtedness of firms was around 70 per cent of GDP in the 1970s and almost doubled until 2009. In the IMF's Financial Soundness Indicators debt to net worth (to historical costs) of non-farm non-financial corporate business increased from 59 per cent in 1970 to around 70 per cent in 2009. However, in the late 1980s it was around 90 per cent. Total debt to equity for non-financial corporations was around 70 per cent in 1990. Compared with other industrial countries this is relatively low. This indicator towards the late 2000s was nearly twice as high in Germany, and in the United Kingdom three times as high (IMF 2010c).

Starting below 50 per cent of GDP private households debt increased to over 100 per cent in 2008. Especially during the 2000s private household debt exploded, mirroring the bubble in the real estate market. Private households create no market income. High debt in this sector makes the economy even more fragile than high corporate debt. Public debt increased from around 50 per cent in the early 1970s to over 80 percent in 2010. During the second half of the 1990s this rate was reduced, but began to explode when the subprime crisis hit the US.

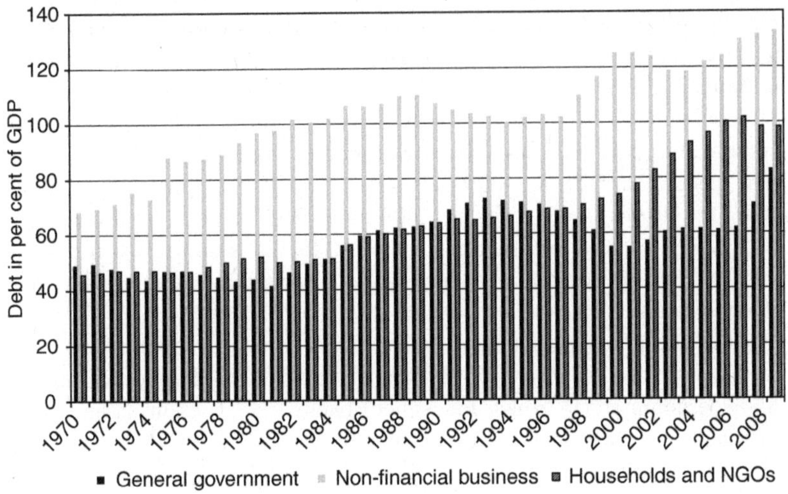

Figure 3.2 Debt in percentage of GDP in the US, 1970–2009 (source: AMECO 2010, Fed 2010).

3.1.3 Foreign economic policy

One of the key features of the US development and of the development of the world economy as a whole is the huge current account deficits of the US that surfaced after the deregulation of financial markets. The first wave of current account deficits started in the early 1980s. After the election of Ronald Reagan confidence in the economic and political development in the US increased and the reputation of the US dollar was restored. High net capital inflows pushed up the nominal and real external value of the US dollar and led to high current account surpluses. The revaluation phase up to the middle of the 1980s helped the US to pull back the rate of inflation quickly despite an economic recovery (see Sachs 1985). The sharp devaluation of the US dollar began in 1985 and reduced the current account deficit to near zero by the beginning of the 1990s. In comparison with the late 1970s the depreciation of the US dollar did not lead to an inflationary problem. This time nominal wages did not respond to increasing import prices. The US was also lucky. After 1985 the falling oil and natural resource prices reduced the cost pressure caused by the depreciation.

Capital imports started to increase again in the 1990s and again financed an increasing current account deficit of around 4 per cent of GDP. Capital imports also led to a stronger US currency in the second half of the 1990s. The slowdown in the early 2000s could not reduce the current account deficit. The continuous swelling of capital imports led to the enormous US current account deficit of 6 per cent of GDP before the subprime crisis in 2007, which then slightly reduced the deficit. Not all capital flows came from private sources. Central bank interventions financed a relevant part of the current account deficit and were also responsible for the overvalued US dollar. Given the absolute size of the US economy the high current account deficits in percentage of GDP stimulated demand in the rest of the world. And they offered a 'solution' for the mercantile strategies of some important countries in the world (see the explanations and figures in Section 2.3).

High US net capital inflows were definitely not caused by economic fundamentals like a substantial increase in productivity, higher growth or a lower inflation rate. Despite the exploding current account deficits capital inflows in the 1990s and 2000s did not fall to reduce the deficit. Apart from central bank interventions the explanation for this has to be found in political factors. Investors considered the US dollar a 'safe haven'. In addition, a long list of currency crises, for example Mexico 1994, the Asian crisis in 1997, the crisis in Russia in 1998 and the Argentinean crisis in 2001, promoted the US dollar as a an internationally preferred currency for wealth holders.

For the US the huge current account deficits are a doubled-edged sword. On the one hand they created a welfare import as the high value of the US dollar leads to positive terms of trade and cheap imported goods. US citizens can buy with their income a lot of comparatively cheap Chinese products. On the other hand, the current account deficit leads to a permanent leakage of aggregate demand as part of domestic purchasing power is used to buy foreign products. As long as there is domestic unemployment, current account deficits prevent the reduction of unemployment rates. In addition there is the tendency that fiscal and monetary policy has to be permanently expansionary-oriented to compensate for demand leakage. In the US the burden of big current account deficits were partly compensated by the investment boom of the new economy in the 1990s and the real estate bubble in the 2000s. Both booms were financed by credit and made the US financial system more fragile. Today, it looks as if the credit-driven consumption model in the US came to an end with the subprime crisis and the burden of a current account deficit in the form of higher unemployment will become greater for Americans in the future.

3.1.4 Wage policy

As already explained, in terms of the overall economy, a stability-oriented wage policy should be in line with medium-term productivity developments plus the target rate of inflation. This would ensure wage inflation in line with the target inflation rate of the central bank. Figure 3.3 shows clearly the wave of increasing nominal unit labour costs and price level increases in the second half of the 1960s and the escalation of the inflationary development in the USA in the 1970s. The oil price shocks in 1973 and 1979 as well as the weak US dollar in this period triggered nominal wage increases far above productivity increases and an inflationary development. It is no surprise that nominal wage increases were too high in the 1970s. In the early 1980s, after the extremely restrictive economic policy at the end of the 1970s, unit labour costs dropped very quickly. The reduction of the inflation rate was supported by the strong US dollar and the increase in real wages caused by it. The development of the nominal wage level in the 1980s and 1990s was very much in line with the desired wage norm, overall showing a functional development of the wage level.[9] During the sub-prime crisis increases in unit labour costs became dangerously low.

The overall functional development of the *level* of unit labour – we do not speak here about wage dispersion – from the 1980s until the end of the 2000s is one of the explanations why, compared with other OECD countries, growth and employment performance in the US especially in the 1990s and 2000s was relatively good. The Fed did not have to fight against inflationary developments as for example in the 1970s, and also was not confronted with deflationary wage developments, as for example in Japan (see the case study about Japan).

Hidden behind the functional development of the level of nominal unit labour costs are deep changes in the labour market. In Figure 3.4 the development of the wage structure is shown. The poorest 10 per cent of employees (the 10th percentile) had to accept harsh real wage reductions in the early 1980s. Only the boom in the 1990s allowed them to regain the same real hourly wages in the early 2000s. Then, in the 2000s wages stagnated at the level of the late 1970s. The 50th percentile covering 50 per cent of all employees had to accept stagnating real wages from the late 1970s until the mid-1990s. Then real hourly wages of this group increased around 10 per cent and stagnated again. Employees with high incomes were the clear winners of this development, especially the top earners. Overall, a fundamental change of income distribution within the working class developed in the US. This fits with the general change in income distribution where the top 1 per cent of national income receivers drew about 10 per cent of national income between the late 1930s and the late 1970s. Their

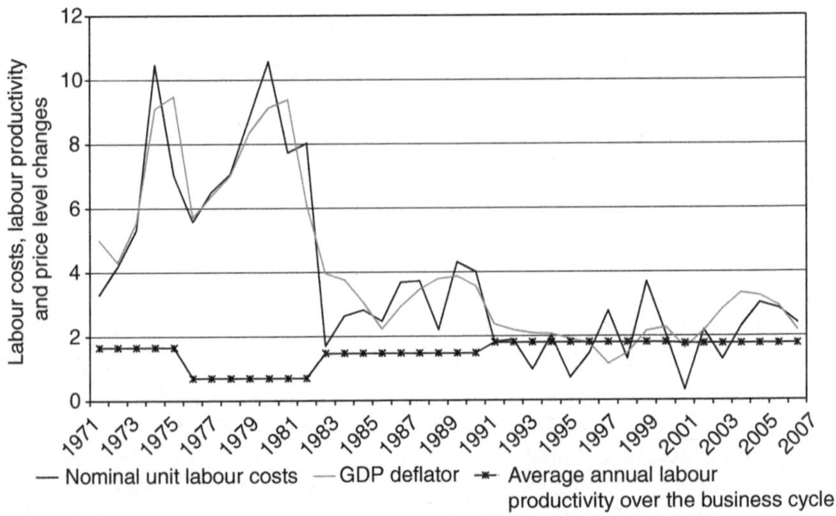

Figure 3.3 Productivity, unit labour costs and price level changes in the US, 1961–2009 (percentage change to the previous year) (source: AMECO 2010).

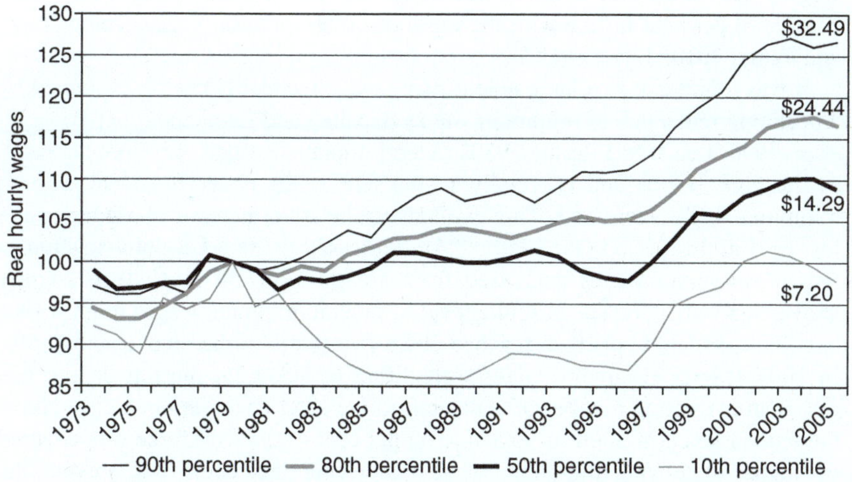

Figure 3.4 Changes in US real hourly wages at percentile points, all workers 1979–2007 (1979 = 100) (source: Mishel *et al.* 2006).

share increased to around 18 per cent in 2005 without capital gains and to 23 per cent with capital gains (Picketty and Saez 2009; see Section 2.7).

How could such fundamental changes in income distribution materialise? There had been no fundamental legal changes needed in the US to deregulate labour markets. Labour markets were never regulated as tightly as, for example, in continental Europe. In the US protection for workers in the 1950s and 1960s came from relatively strong unions, signalling effects of wage developments in key industries to the whole economy and minimum wage policy. The late 1970s and the 1980s brought big changes which are reflected in a sharply increasing wage dispersion. One of the key factors that explains increasing wage inequality is the weakening of the union movement, which was not able to protect low wage earners. Union density decreased from 22.3 per cent in 1980 to 11.6 per cent in 2007 (OECD 2009b). Union membership rates are decreasing in the private sector especially, while increasing in the public sector. In 2009 union density in the private sector was 7.2 per cent, whereas it was 37.4 per cent in the public sector (BLS 2010). Studies show a clear correlation between de-unionisation and rising wage inequality (Card 1992; DiNardo *et al.* 1996; Schmitt 2008).

Although unemployment rates over the cycle did not increase dramatically in the 1980s, the high unemployment rate of around 10 per cent in the years 1981/82 after the very tight monetary policy in 1979 and 1980 weakened unions and workers. At the same time President Ronald Reagan followed a fundamental and ideological policy against unions as an important element of the conservative revolution. One symbol of Reagan's policy was the demise of the air traffic controller's union in 1980. Part of Reagan's 'supply-side policy' was also to cut wages. Also in his first year in office he cut the top income tax rate from 70 per cent to 50 per cent in line with the top income tax rate for wage income (Levy and Temin 2010: 36ff.).

It was found that to a large extent rising wage inequality can be explained by a declining real value of minimum wages (Gosling and Lemieux 2001; DiNardo *et al.* 1996; Lee 1999). In the 1980s federal minimum wages were not adjusted. In the early 1990s and especially in the late 1990s under President Clinton minimum wages increased. This explains the relative increase of wages of the low paid in this period (see Figure 3.4). Expressed in 2006 US dollars statutory federal minimum wages decreased from around US$7.50 in 1979 to slightly above US$5 in 2006. The absolute level of federal minimum wages in the 1990s and 2000s in real terms then reached about two-thirds of the level in the 1960s. In 2007 federal minimum wages were lifted to US$7.25. Starting in the late 1980s an increasing number of states raised the level of minimum wages above the federal level (in 2006 for example 60 per cent of the workforce was covered by higher state-wide minimum wages), however this could not prevent the general nationwide drop in average real minimum wages (Reich 2010).

Immigration also created pressure on wages of low-skilled workers. In 1970, 700,000 Mexicans lived in the US, in the year 2000 it was eight million. Two-thirds of the adult Mexican inhabitants do not hold a high school diploma.[10]

As a result of relatively high GDP growth unemployment rates in the 1990s and 2000s became relatively low in the US. The question is why this did not lead to an inflationary wage–price spiral. Actually, only at the end of the boom phases in the 1990s and 2000s did unit labour costs increase slightly above the wage norm. Blinder and Yellen (2001: 35) reported that the NAIRU was estimated to be between 5.5 and 6 per cent at the beginning of the 1990s. However, unemployment rates fell well below that level. According to the NAIRU concept these unemployment rates should have led to significant pay rises and price increases. Blinder and Yellen (2001: 39) explain the wage restraint with fear of job loss and the fact that workers were traumatised from the extensive business restructuring throughout the 1980s. Farber (2003) supports this by pointing out that the job loss rate was astonishingly high despite a low and decreasing unemployment rate, which signifies that dismissals did not decrease at the same rate as unemployment during economic expansion. In many cases the unemployed were not covered by health insurance and sought re-employment as quickly as possible, often at lower pay. The Council of Economic Advisors sees a reason for the unexpected low wage increases mainly in the falling union membership.[11] Finally, the argument has been put forward that employees suffered a productivity illusion, in that they expected lower productivity increases than actually materialised (Stiglitz 1997; Mankiw 2001).

Whatever caused the comparatively functional development of the nominal wage level in the US after the start of the neoliberal revolution in the early 1980s, it was not based on macroeconomic formal or informal wage coordination. It was the result of various developments in the different labour market sectors – for example the high wage increases of already highly paid workers were compensated by a relative and even absolute loss in wage income of the already low paid workers. Thus, it can in no way be excluded that the nominal wage anchor will snap in times of economic crisis and a deflationary development will be triggered.

3.1.5 Monetary policy

The brief time interval between 1979 and 1982 represents a sharp break in the monetary policy practised until then. Before this phase, during the 1970s, monetary policy had reacted without much success to inflationary pressures and the loss of the external value of the US dollar. Escalating inflation, the collapse of the external value of the US dollar in 1979 and the resistance by other central banks and especially the German Bundesbank to help stabilise the US dollar exchange rate led to the 'Volcker shock'. Paul Volcker tried to follow monetary targeting to combat high inflation. The results of this policy were extremely high and volatile money market interest rates (see Figure 3.5). The inflation rate was reduced quicker than expected, but the USA suffered until then the deepest recession since the Second World War and the world economy was also drawn into a deep crisis leading among other things to the Latin American crisis of the 1980s. Paul Volcker maximised the costs in respect of growth and employment losses to bring inflation down. It is not clear whether the Fed's policy was so extremely restrictive because he believed in monetary targeting and wanted to realise monetary targets or whether he wanted to trigger a structural break in the US economic and political system.[12] In any case monetary targeting could not be

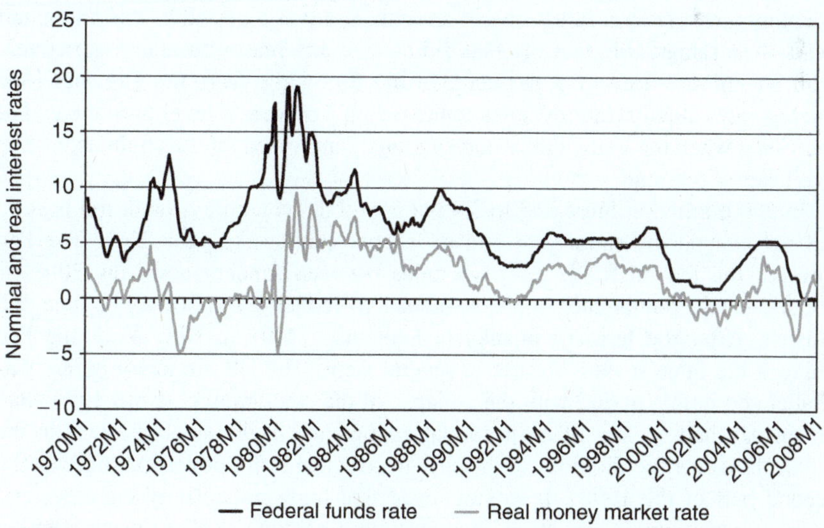

Figure 3.5 Nominal and real money market interest rates in the US, 1970–2009 (real rate: nominal minus change in CPI), (source: IMF 2010d).

successfully realised as the relationship between monetary aggregates and price level changes became increasingly unstable and the Fed had no option but to give it up in 1982. Interest rates were drastically lowered in that year when Mexico defaulted on its payments (and payment problems also occurred with other Latin American countries) and there were difficulties with the US banking system. On the basis of regained confidence, the US dollar remained stable and increased strongly in value up to 1985. The Fed interest rates increased moderately until 1984 along with the economic recovery. Then interest rates were significantly reduced to ease the appreciation pressure on the US dollar which had destroyed competitiveness in large parts of US manufacturing industry. The Fed, supported by government, pursued a weak dollar policy in the second half of the 1980s. This was possible without serious loss of reputation on the part of the US dollar, not least because it occurred when oil prices were falling and the depreciation did not lead to a rise in inflation as had been the case in the 1970s (Herr and Spahn 1989). At the end of the 1980s interest rates increased slightly as the US dollar had depreciated considerably. When the economy fell into recession in the early 1990s interest rates became considerably lower.

Since 1982 monetary policy has become strongly discretionary, especially after 1987 when Alan Greenspan became Chairman of the Fed. The Greenspan era lasted until 2006 when Ben Bernanke became President of the Fed. He followed in Greenspan's footsteps. Historically, the readiness of the Federal Open Market Committee (FOMC) to react strongly to recession risks with immediate and significant interest rate cuts can clearly be seen between 1991 and 1993. When recession set in, the Fed reduced the federal funds rate to low levels which corresponded to a real interest rate of around zero. With increasing growth and a falling unemployment rate in the first half of the 1990s, the Fed managed to maintain a real federal funds rate of around zero over a period of one and a half years. It is remarkable that the Fed did not see any reason to react restrictively with an inflation rate of 3 per cent. In the following years the Fed increased interest rates slowly. Interest rates remained on a moderate level until the end of the 1990s when the Fed slightly and cautiously increased rates to fight against an overheating economy.

In 2000, inflation increased to 3.4 per cent, but economic growth fell back to 3.8 per cent in the same year and to 0.3 per cent in the year 2001. The Fed lowered the federal funds rate five times between January and May 2001 by about 50 base points each time. Another two reductions followed in June and August. After the terrorist attacks in September 2001 in New York the Fed reduced the interest rates further in several steps. The US monetary policy was challenged in this period with the collapse of the stock market. Until 1996 Alan Greenspan had spoken of an irrational exuberance in the stock markets in the 1990s, however, he did not use this argument when share prices exploded in the second half of the 1990s. It was believed that high productivity increases and profit expectations in the New Economy were behind the share price inflation (Shiller 2001; Stiglitz 2003). The Fed, as mentioned above, reacted very rapidly and massively with interest rate cuts after the share bubble burst. The Fed justified the first interest rate reduction in January 2001 by declaring the financial system as strained because large loans had been taken out to buy now falling shares. The Fed did not want to make the Japanese mistake of lowering interest rates too slowly during an asset price deflation (Ferguson 2003, see the case study about Japan). The rapid interest rate reductions with the creation of distinctly negative short-term real interest rates during the 2001 depression must be seen as one of the important factors in stabilising the US economy. In any case, the feared collapse in consumer demand expected from falling asset prices did not materialise. Obviously, the positive cash-flow effect of cutting interest rates within the context of already high private debt was so great that consumer demand remained stable. An important fact was the possibility of transferring high interest rate long-term mortgage loans to low interest loans without penalties when interest rates fell. All in all for the US economy, monetary policy eased the liquidity and solvency problem in this phase considerably. In this respect, monetary policy in the US was functional even if a brief recession could not be prevented. However, the Fed was not cautious or concerned about the stock market boom in the 1990s and in this sense was responsible for the financial problems that ensued after the bubble burst.

Real money market interest rates became negative in the early 2000s, were then kept at low positive levels and were only substantially increased in the years 2006 and 2007 when the economy showed relatively high GDP growth. The low interest rates of the early 2000s planted the seeds for the next even stronger asset price bubble in the real estate market and the share market which started to gain momentum around 2003. There is no doubt that the deregulation in the financial markets is the main factor that explains the real estate bubble in the US in particular. And it is also clear that Alan Greenspan and vast numbers of the US financial elite closed their eyes to the dangers developing in the financial system in the 2000s, but the expansionary monetary policy also stimulated the bubbles. US monetary policy is understandable. The investment dynamic in the 2000s compared with the 1990s was weak and the economic expansion depended mainly on household demand which directly depended on the real estate demand and indirectly on increases in asset prices.

The late 2000s are characterised by the same constellation as in the late 1990s – however, the bubble in the 2000s was much bigger than in the 1990s and included the real estate market, which always involves much more credit than share markets. The Fed again cut interest rates quickly and radically. However, monetary policy was not able to prevent the subprime financial crisis which first affected the fragile financial system and later the real economy. Under Ben Bernanke the Fed was forced to fulfil its function as lender of last resort in extreme cases and followed unorthodox policies to try to stabilise the financial system and the real economy.

Overall we can follow James Tobin (1998: 231) in his judgement of Greenspan's monetary policy when he writes: 'Macroeconomic performance, some pragmatic amalgam of price inflation, unemployment, and real GDP growth, became the Fed's policy goal, and the FOMC fine-tuned its instruments – the federal funds rate – to aim directly at its desired macroeconomic path.' Monetary policy under Greenspan and Bernanke increased interest rates cautiously to fight against inflation, cut interest rates quickly and sharply when there was a danger of a slowdown in growth, and looked for a compromise between price level stability and growth. Of course, US monetary policy has had more freedom to follow domestically oriented policies and has not been restricted very much by external factors. Looking at monetary policy in the narrow sense it was functional and growth supporting. But paying little attention to asset price inflations during unavoidable periods of substantial asset price deflations the central bank was forced to use very expansionary policies. It would have been necessary that the Fed had warned the public and the political elites about the fragility and the danger which developed within the financial system over the last decades.

3.1.6 Fiscal policy

Looking at budget deficits, public expenditures and public revenues in the US, it can be seen that a period of relatively restrictive fiscal policy over the business cycle in the 1970s was followed by rather expansionary measures in the 1980s. While budget deficits returned to lower levels in the second half of the 1990s – in some years even budget surpluses were realised – the 2000s experienced another wave of expansionary fiscal policy (see Table 3.2, Figure 3.6). During the 1980s and the beginning of the 1990s public debt to GDP increased from around 45 to more than 70 per cent. In the following years the US government managed to scale down debt to less than 55 per cent of GDP in 2001. However, public debt then started to increase again and reached over 80 per cent in 2010.

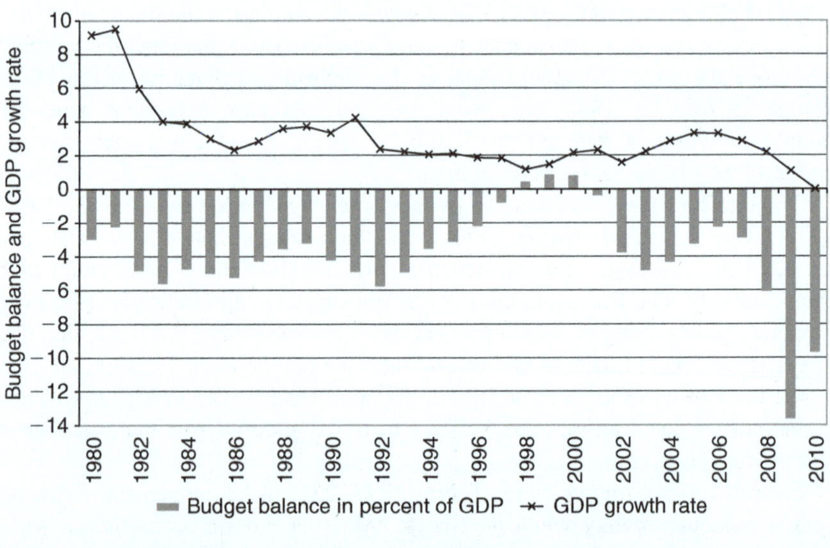

Figure 3.6 Budget balance in percentage of GDP and GDP growth rate in the US, 1970–2009 (source: OECD 2009c).

Table 3.2 Fiscal policy indicators for the US (average growth rate over the business cycle, unless mentioned otherwise), 1971–2008

Business cycles	*1971–1975*	*1976–1982*	*1983–1991*	*1992–2001*	*2002–2008*
Nominal GDP growth	9.64	10.35	7.04	5.59	4.98
Total expenditures	11.39	11.15	7.35	4.66	6.53
Discretionary expenditure indicator[1]	8.73	9.96	6.95	4.07	6.57
Government consumption	9.14	10.08	6.77	4.00	6.86
Government investment	8.00	8.69	7.86	3.98	6.28
Subsidies	3.90	19.32	7.83	7.97	0.88
Social benefits	17.94	11.23	7.39	5.87	6.98
Total revenues	9.31	11.49	7.38	6.02	4.33
Social security contributions	14.26	12.96	8.39	5.45	4.52
Direct taxes	7.88	11.40	6.35	7.21	3.89
Direct taxes, cyclically adjusted	8.73	11.51	5.80	6.98	3.75
Indirect taxes	8.17	8.69	7.37	4.78	5.14
Indirect taxes, cyclically adjusted	8.86	9.01	6.89	4.62	5.08
Budget balance (% of GDP)[2]	–2.10	–2.48	–4.54	–1.79	–3.90
Budget balance, cyclically adjusted (% of GDP)[2]	–1.83	–2.17	–4.38	–1.70	–3.84

Source: OECD (2009c), AMECO (2010) authors' calculations.

Note

1 Government consumption, government investment and subsidies.

2 Average size over the business cycle.

Budget deficits also reflect tax cuts. At the beginning of his first term in office, President Reagan pushed through massive tax reductions. This step had a theoretical foundation in the Laffer curve (Laffer 2004). The argument was that tax cuts via supply-side effects (for example the stimulation of economic activity by higher motivation of individuals) would increase GDP growth in such a way that the additional tax revenues would over-compensate the loss of tax revenues as the outcome of cuts in the tax rate and reduce the budget deficit. Not surprisingly, a Laffer effect did not materialise. Congress could not prevent tax cuts but prevented planned expenditure cuts in the social sphere. In addition, Reagan increased military expenditures as part of his so-called Star War programme. The conflict between the President and Congress was 'solved' in that the budget deficits remained high even during the economic expansion of the 1980s. The Gramm–Rudman–Hollings Emergency Deficit Control Act (1985) and the Budget and Emergency Deficit Control Reaffirmation Act (1987) were signed with the aim of achieving a balanced budget (for a debate about fiscal acts in the US see Auerbach 2008). They provided for automatic spending cuts in cases when the deficit exceeded deficit targets. However, in 1986 automatic spending cuts were judged as unconstitutional and in 1987 the acts were revised accordingly. All attempts to reduce budget deficits by directly controlling the budget balance failed and public debt to GDP increased in the 1980s.

The turn-around in fiscal policy came in 1990 with what is called the Budget Enforcement Act. The new act aimed at controlling public expenditure. Here, a distinction was made between legally binding and discretionary expenditures. Legally fixed expenditures are primarily expenditures for social security as the government has no short-term influence on these expenditures. Discretionary expenditures on the other hand comprise, among other things, defence spending and are fixed each year. Each of the discretionary titles was brought together with certain types of taxes into what was called PAYGO pools. When a fixed upper expenditure limit was exceeded, it had to be financed by tax increases and/or expenditure reductions in another position in the corresponding pool (Blinder and Yellen 2001).[13]

Gross public investment can serve as a good indicator of discretionary state expenditure. Public investment was exceptionally stable in the 1990s indicating that fiscal policy was strongly anti-cyclical during this period. Under the expenditure rule expenditures do not have to be cut during economic downturns, as there is no limit on the public deficit. Thus, in a recession the government can allow the automatic fiscal stabilisers to take effect completely. If during a boom increases in revenues do not lead to higher expenditures, the budget deficit decreases or a surplus is created. This happened in the US in the second half of the 1990s (Horn and Scheremet 1999: 4). Discretionary tax increases by the Clinton administration in 1993, which mainly increased the tax burden for higher incomes and reduced it for low income households, supported this development too (Blinder and Yellen 2001).

Budget deficits rose rapidly during the 2001 crisis due to falling tax revenues and increasing expenditures that were partly caused by the wars in Afghanistan and Iraq. Between 2001 and 2003, the Bush administration instituted a federal tax cut, again with reference to the Laffer curve.[14] The changes in the tax structure and also in the structure of expenditure that took place under the Bush administration were a matter of angry disputes not least because they benefited the richest in the US. The Bush tax cuts certainly helped stabilise demand and to overcome the recession in the early 2000s, but the effectiveness of the fiscal measures could have been higher had poor households and not primarily the rich been beneficiaries of the tax reforms. In 2003 around 450 economists including 24 American Nobel Price Laureates signed a statement opposing the Bush tax cuts. They argued that the cuts would lead to chronic fiscal deficits which would reduce the capacity of the government to finance social security and medicare benefits as well as investments in schools, health, infrastructure and basic research and in addition would lead to further inequalities in after-tax income (*Economists' statement opposing the Bush tax cuts*, 2003). Budget deficits became increasingly high after the outbreak of the subprime crisis which led to high reductions in tax revenues. Since 2008, also due to the stimulus packages, budget deficits in percentage of GDP have been double digit.

In the period analysed, the US used fiscal policy to stimulate the economy during economic slowdowns and in this way reduced recessions and stabilised the economy. The tax cuts under the conservative presidents Reagan and George W. Bush that favoured especially the rich led to higher public debt quotas. Moreover, since fiscal multiplier effects of tax cuts for the rich are small compared with other measures for fiscal expansion, these policies were not optimal to stimulate the economy. The described tax policy also added to the more unequal distribution of disposable income which had a negative effect on consumption demand and on indebtedness of private households. While policy rules in the 1980s to control budget balances failed, the Budget Enforcement Act which dominated fiscal policy in the 1990s can be judged as a preferable rule for fiscal policy. Obviously, it is much better to have fiscal rules which regulate variables such as discretionary expenditures that governments can control. Under the Budget Enforcement Act the US was well able to follow an anti-cyclical fiscal policy. Thus, it had no problem accepting deficits which were by far higher than 4 per cent of GDP as at other times, such as at the end of the 1990s, budget surpluses could be realised. Overall, fiscal policy in the US was anti-cyclical, however, the changes in the expenditure and revenue structure were not supporting a stable and sustainable development of the US economy.

3.1.7 Conclusion

The core of the present macroeconomic policy regime in the US was established at the end of the 1970s/the beginning of the 1980s when the economic instabilities of the 1970s, the extremely restrictive monetary policy and a deep crisis, paved the way for the conservative neoliberal revolution. The macroeconomic policy regime that developed in the subsequent years combined functional macroeconomic process policies with destabilising structural policies (Ordnungspolitik). Whether policies under President Obama will again bring a fundamental change in structural policies remains an open question which goes beyond this case study.

Monetary and fiscal policies in the US from the 1980s were growth oriented and came close to the process policies we recommend. In the early 1980s and thereafter low inflation rates allowed the Fed to follow an overall expansionary, growth-promoting interest rate policy. The explicit legal mandate of the Fed to find a compromise between price level stability and growth was not only on paper, but was actually followed. The Fed's monetary policy was far more discretionary than that of the European Central Bank or prior to that the Bundesbank. Opportunities to cut interest rates were taken and increases in the interest rate were carried out cautiously yet decisively to fight against goods market inflation when necessary. US monetary policy after the 'Volcker shock' shows that neither monetary targeting in the tradition of Milton Friedman nor the rigid adherence to a concept such as the NAIRU promises success. Monetary policy must be carried out according to the specific historical situation. 'Driving by sight' is thus inevitable in the case of stability and growth-oriented monetary policy.[15] Alan Greenspan, as no other president of a central bank to date, stands for such a philosophy.

Looking at public budget balances, fiscal policy was anti-cyclically oriented. During periods of low growth public households accepted high budget deficits and did not reduce them too early. However, in several cases expansionary fiscal policy was not carried out in an optimal way. Budget deficits exploded in the 1980s under Reagan as well as under Bush in the 2000s as a result of heavy tax cuts that privileged the rich, but did not stimulate aggregate demand as much as expenditure increases or tax cuts for the poor would have done.

Overall, after the inflationary period of the 1970s development of the wage level followed the wage norm described earlier. However, this was the outcome of different effects and in no way the result of a rational wage bargaining process and effective labour market institutions. Highly increasing nominal and real wages of high wage earners were compensated by relatively low nominal wage increases of low wage earners who were forced to accept real wage cuts. Looking at wage dispersion, wage development was dysfunctional and destabilising as it aggravated income inequality.

The external conditions for the US were double-edged. On one hand, after the 'Volcker shock' and the revitalisation of the US dollar, monetary and fiscal policies were not restricted by external constraints. The US did not much care about the exchange rate and accepted even strong depreciations of the US dollar when the market allowed. It was up to other countries' central banks to stabilise the exchange rate. Such a policy of course was only possible because the US was indebted against foreign countries mainly in its own currency and depreciations did not lead to wage–price spirals. On the other hand, capital inflows pushed the US into huge demand-reducing current account deficits and increased the need to stimulate domestic demand more than would have been necessary otherwise.

Reflecting on process policy, the four macroeconomic policy sectors in the US after the 1970s interacted in an overall functional way. However, the US regime did not result from a conscious coordination of the policies of all sectors. It can be partially explained by lucky circumstances. This applies particularly to wage developments and external developments which allowed monetary policy to become growth oriented. However, to understand the development in the US it is most important to see that macroeconomic policies were conducted on the basis of deep structural neoliberal changes. The neoliberal orientation of the US Ordnungspolitik after the late 1970s was inappropriate for a stable and social economic development. This was already noticeable before the breakdown of the Bretton Woods System that gave the capitalist world economy a stable framework after the Second World War. Of key importance was the fundamental deregulation of domestic and international financial markets that led to permanent asset price bubbles, to unsustainable credit expansions, asset price deflations and recessions and huge international imbalances. Monetary policy lacked instruments to guide credit expansions into productive sectors and did not care about instabilities in the financial sector. After the 1970s we can speak about a bubble-driven and to a large extent private household's credit-driven economic growth model which led the economy into an ever more unstable and fragile constellation. Thus, the subprime crisis was not a surprise; it was the consequence of the reforms that started in the 1970s and were especially carried out in the 1980s. The labour market in the US increased its potential for fragility too. Wage dispersion increased sharply during the neoliberal era, which was partly caused by non-adjusting statutory federal minimum wages. Weak unions and weak collective wage bargaining mechanisms in a situation of high unemployment make deflation a real danger.

When the US economy became fragile, the heart of capitalism became unstable, which means that the entire world became affected. It looks like the bubble and consumption model of the US in the past decades produced at least some growth in GDP on the basis of bubbles and unsustainable credit expansion. However, even if this were possible also in the future the next deep financial crisis with disastrous effects would be unavoidable.

3.2 The 'popular' finance-led growth model of the United Kingdom[16]

3.2.1 Overview of the political and economic development

In the 1970s the UK had proved ill equipped to cope with the oil price shocks and suffered from explosive inflation rates of up to 16 per cent in 1974 and 24 per cent in 1975 (AMECO 2010). Compared with the other three countries we have chosen as case studies the inflation rate in the 1970s in the UK was the highest. In addition, the 1970s were characterised by mass strikes by coalminers, petrol and railroad workers, and others. Moreover, the government was struggling with increasing current account deficits and the fall in value of the pound sterling after the collapse of the Bretton Woods System. A currency crisis in 1976 led to the escalation of the external problems of the UK.

The UK after the Second World War conducted a stop-and-go policy with the 'stop' as restrictive monetary policy when current account deficits increased and the pound became weak, and the 'go' with expansionary monetary policy as soon as current account deficits were corrected and the stability of the pound was restored. Especially in the 1960s and 1970s, overall economic performance in the UK was unsatisfactory.[17] In 1974 and 1975 economic growth turned negative. Out of the four countries used here as case studies; the UK had on average the lowest growth rate in the 1970s. In 1973 the UK also experienced a stock market crash, whereby stock prices fell by 32 per cent in that year alone (Stevenson 2008). A further difficulty was the sharp increase in unemployment in the second half of the 1970s and throughout the 1980s. During the 1970s and 1980s it also can be clearly seen that the UK export sector performed poorly, contributing negatively to growth.

Defeating the Labour Party in 1979, the Conservatives pushed for a monetarist and supply-side oriented macroeconomic policy. The changes that occurred in the process of liberalisation affected the financial market, the labour market, foreign economic policy, and also monetary and fiscal policy. On the agenda were deregulations in the financial market, privatisations, big public spending cuts, tax increases and the weakening of trade unions. This liberalisation process caused changes in the institutional setting and the overall macroeconomic regime of the UK.

During the rule of the Conservatives in the 1980s the unemployment rate amounted to 9.56 per cent on average (see Table 3.3). Private investment in the 1980s was also poor. Recovery was mainly brought about by consumption demand (see Figure 3.7). GDP growth revived and unemployment was reduced

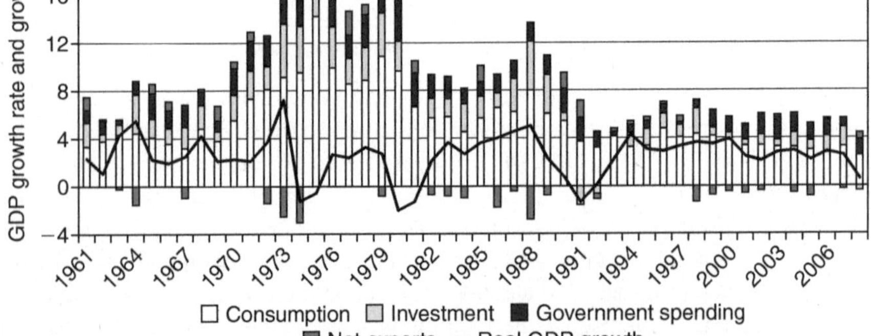

Figure 3.7 GDP growth rate and growth contributions of its components in the UK in per cent, 1961–2009 (source: AMECO 2010, authors' calculation).

Table 3.3 Macroeconomic indicators in the UK, 1971–2009 (average values over the business cycle)

Business cycles		*1971–1975*	*1976–1981*	*1982–1991*	*1992–2002*	*2003–2009*
Real GDP growth rate		2.20	1.25	2.73	2.86	1.33
Unemployment rate		2.64	5.65	9.56	7.27	5.51
Inflation rate		13.19	13.99	5.64	2.00	1.57
Percentage change in nominal unit labour costs		15.53	12.84	6.05	2.02	2.67
Percentage change in real wage per employee		3.66	0.23	2.02	1.68	1.02
Budget balance as a percentage of GDP		–2.72	–4.48	–2.46	–2.76	–4.92
Current account balance as a percentage of GDP		–0.97	0.28	–1.65	–1.48	–2.34
	Mid-1970s	*Mid-1980s*	*1990*	*Mid-1990s*	*2000*	*Mid-2000s*
Gini coefficient[1]	0.282	0.325	0.373	0.354	0.370	0.335

Source: AMECO 2010, OECD (2009c), authors' calculations.

Note

1 Based on disposable household income in cash, adjusted for household size with an elasticity of 0.5.

to 7 per cent in 1989. The inflation rate was brought down from very high levels, albeit remaining comparatively high and increasing again at the end 1980s.

The early 1990s were characterised by the entry of the UK into the European Monetary System (EMS), ultimately to use the nominal exchange rate anchor for keeping inflation under control. This was again a period of economic crisis for the UK. Increases in unit labour costs were inflationary and added to the erosion of the international competitiveness of the UK, especially compared with the other members of the EMS. As investment performed very poorly and GDP growth was low, EMS membership became a problem. The conservative government led by John Major, who became Prime Minister in 1990, chose to switch back to a flexible exchange rate regime in 1992, especially after the German Bundesbank as the leading central bank in the system showed no cooperation whatsoever.

Since the mid-1990s and up to 2008 (the outbreak of the financial crisis in the UK) growth in the UK was relatively stable, and compared with Germany or Japan relatively high. Especially consumption continued to relatively create high aggregate demand and income. These domestic demand elements overcompensated for the sharp increases in the UK current account deficits, particularly after 2000. It is noteworthy that the UK managed to keep its economy stable during the outbreak of the worldwide recession in 2001/2002. All in all, the late 1990s and 2000s were a period of relatively high and stable growth for the UK. However, although unemployment rates were reduced towards the end of the 2000s, they have never returned to the low levels of the 1960s.

In 1997 Labour Party leader Tony Blair became Prime Minister and served until 2007 when Gordon Brown (Labour Party) took over until 2010. In essence both Blair and Brown did not turn back the neoliberal revolution triggered by Margaret Thatcher in the early 1980s. However, under these labour governments some social measures like minimum wages were reintroduced.

Unlike the economies of Japan and Germany it is interesting to note that the growth pattern in the UK was largely driven by domestic demand. In this respect the UK can be considered the little brother of the US economy, especially in the 1990s and 2000s.

3.2.2 Financial system

Until 1971 the banking system in the UK was by and large of an oligopolistic nature whereby the 'Big Five' (Barclays, Lloyds, Midland, National Provincial and Westminster) dominated. In spite of the fact that there was no legal separation between commercial and investment banks in the fashion of the Glass–Steagall Act in the US after the early 1930s, the financial system in the UK functioned in an orderly way. Deposit banks were the main providers of short-term credit to the household sector and to firms and, together with the discount houses (which served as intermediaries between the deposit banks and the Bank of England), owned approximately 52 per cent of the total assets in the financial system. Long-term lending was in the hands of specialist financial institutions like building societies (Gola and Roselli 2009: 8). Long-term funding for firms was raised on the capital market, as the banking system did not provide sufficient long-term credit.

Secondary banks[18] were involved in the wholesale market and did not have the right to participate in the payment system and the clearing arrangements, a position, which was exclusively given to the commercial banking system (Gola and Roselli 2009: 6–8). This separation existed mainly because of the involvement of secondary banks in foreign markets and the concern of the central bank to keep the foreign sector from interfering in the domestic economy and the problems it might cause to monetary policy. It is no surprise that competition was strongly constrained through this division. Furthermore, the Bank of England set the interest rates of banks, applied quantitative limits on bank lending and determined, for example, the conditions for hire purchase loans with the goal of maintaining control over credit allocation.

The institutional setting of the financial system, which characterised the period from the Second World War until the 1970s, was rather of an informal and erratic nature. The Bank of England informally supervised deposit banks, discount houses and accepting houses, being more concerned about the implementation of the Bank's credit policy. The building societies were under the supervision of the Chief Registrar of Friendly Societies. However, secondary banks were left unsupervised even though they were formally registered as banks (Collins 1988: 367, 380). These loopholes in the regulatory framework later turned London into an ideal place to introduce new financial instruments.

With the crisis of the Bretton Woods System in 1971 the Labour government sought to reduce speculative attacks on the pound by using capital controls, which remained in place until 1979. In 1971 the government also decided to abolish interest rate controls and the quantitative limits on bank lending with the Competition and Credit Control Act, with the intention to increase competition in the banking sector (Revell 1973: 128). In the 1970s and thereafter competition in the UK banking system substantially increased and there were also cases of bank failures.

Left unsupervised, the secondary banks started to attract large amounts of funds, whereby a big portion was directed towards the fast-growing housing market. Together with the expansionary stance of monetary policy, a bubble in the real estate sector was created in the early 1970s (Buckle and Thompson 2004: 334). The importance of the commercial banks declined during this same period as households shifted from keeping their wealth in the form of bank deposits towards non-bank financial assets (largely in the hands of insurance companies, trusts and pension funds).

Due to the growth of the Eurodollar market in the 1960s and the higher number of new branches of foreign, especially American banks, London developed into an important financial hub. The presence of US banks in the UK significantly grew because of the fact that UK regulation in the financial market was less strict than the one in the US and because of the early reduction of foreign exchange controls. Furthermore, London was seen as a centre through which the US financial institutions could more easily have access to the markets of the EU. Also some governments, for example the Soviet Union, did not want to keep monetary wealth in US dollars in the US. As secondary banks were the main attractors of foreign finance, with the decision of the government to completely lift foreign capital flow restrictions in 1979, the growth and power of these financial institutions grew rapidly.[19] In addition, building societies (so-called 'near banks'), which had originally been given the exclusivity to deal with real estate credits, gained importance in the late 1960s and early 1970s (Gola and Roselli 2009: 8).

With the new freedom given by the Credit and Competition Act secondary banks and the near banks accumulated a huge number of funds and supplied vast amounts of credit (including long-term public loans). In 1973 when the discount rate was raised and prices of stocks and real estate fell, financial crisis was the outcome. With the fall in property prices secondary banks found themselves in the middle of serious liquidity and solvency problems. Twenty-five secondary banks were on the brink of collapse and a secondary bank crisis developed. The government and the Bank of England intervened by buying 16 troubled banks (Clarke 1986: 36).

In 1973 the Supplementary Special Deposits Scheme (the so-called 'corset operation') was implemented to regulate the financial chaos. This gave the Bank of England the ability to control the volume of funds that banks had available for loans and to control and restrict credit expansion (Dow and Saville 1990: 154). It penalised the financial institutions that had higher interest-bearing deposits than originally prescribed (Artis and Lewis 1981: 1–10). This measure was only intended for banks, and not for other financial institutions (like building societies). Even though it was not originally designed to be a general financial regulation, in the end all banks more or less adhered to it. The corset ended in 1975, but was reapplied again in 1976 and 1978 when the central bank was concerned about the increase in money supply. In the mid-1980s the corset was abolished.

The result of the bank failures in the early 1970s, the rapid entry of foreign banks and the impetus for financial innovation made it clear that there was a need for widening the scope of institutionalised supervision. The Banking Act of 1979 was then passed to extend supervision to secondary banks and formalise the supervision for commercial banks (Morrison *et al.* 1979: 17).

However, as one of the first actions of the Thatcher government, in the same year all restrictions on foreign exchange markets were lifted, a measure which understandably attracted great amounts of cross-border capital flows giving up an important monetary policy instrument. The growth of the secondary bank sector continued with increasing inflows of foreign capital. The share of secondary banks' assets to total assets in the banking sector was 73 per cent in 1975, rising to 79 per cent in 1984. The share of foreign banks' assets to total assets of secondary banks increased from 74 per cent in 1975 to 80 per cent in 1984. With the development it becomes clear that foreign banks gained a central position in the financial system in the UK (Grady and Weale 1986: 140). After the changes in the financial system in the 1980s, households turned increasingly to pension funds, investment funds, trusts for share purchase and other non-bank financial institutions with the aim of achieving higher returns.[20]

In the 1980s, pushed by the conservative government, a clear change in the financial environment became visible. Along with deregulations in the 1980s the London Stock Exchange was reformed, whereby the separation between jobbers and dealers was eliminated, fixed commissions were abolished and a switch from open outcry trading to a computerised screen-based system was made (Yarrow 2006). Privatisation was one of the key projects of the Thatcher government: British Telecom was privatised in 1984, British Gas in 1986, British Airways in 1987. The aim was to create a 'people's or popular capitalism' with widespread shareholding in the society. To illustrate this: within only one decade (1979–1989) the number of individual shareholders in Britain had increased from three million to nine million (Reitan 2002: 59).

The Financial Services Act of 1986 was the next significant regulatory change when the decision was made to put all regulatory power for financial services into the hands of the Securities and Investment Board, a private company funded and managed by investors themselves. The Securities and Investment Board in charge of supervision became the Financial Services Authority in 1997, and the entire supervision of banks, building societies, insurance companies and non-bank intermediaries was transferred to it. The Financial Services Act passed in 2000 strengthened even further the power of the Financial Services Agency as a sole supervisor of the financial system.

A highly influential institutional change was the revision of the Banking Act in 1987, whereby the separation between commercial banks and other depository institutions was abandoned. This meant for example that commercial banks were allowed to lend in the mortgage market, and building societies to act like commercial banks. However, only under Tony Blair in 1998 did the Bank of England become operationally independent, although the government kept the power to define the inflation target.

Throughout the 1980s and until the end of the 1990s, with the removal of the barriers in the UK financial system and with the switch to the shareholder value corporate governance systems, banks extended large amounts of loans to the non-banking enterprise sector. Companies increased their debts to an amazing level of 200 per cent of GDP in 1989 and 300 per cent ten years later (see Figure 3.8). This huge leverage of UK companies, also compared with other countries, is a way of increasing return on equity, but it makes the enterprise sector all the more fragile in times of crisis.

Also, measured in percentage of GDP, credit to private households rose in the 1980s, along with a sharp increase in real estate prices (see Figure 2.7). In the early 1990s the real estate bubble burst when the Bank of England sharply increased interest rates and the country fell into a period of low growth. As a result of the crash a sizeable number of small banks ran into problems between 1991 and 1994. The scope of this crisis was purely domestic as it was related to falling property prices and high interest rates. Funds from the Deposit Protection Scheme (formed in 1982 to protect depositors) were used for rescue operations.

Independent of the problems in the real estate market, in 1991 and 1995 two big banks failed: the Bank of Credit and Commerce International and Barrings. In both cases problems were mainly caused by fraud. The government did not get involved here, but losses were borne by the Deposit Protection Scheme; Barrings was sold to a Dutch bank (Latter 1997: 34).

After the digestion of the real estate bubble in the early 1990s, in the late 1990s a new and even more extensive credit expansion in the real estate sector developed. In the early 1990s household indebtedness had become as high as 75 per cent of GDP, but then catapulted to a level of more than 100 per cent of GDP by 2009 (see Figure 3.8). This third real estate bubble in the UK came to an abrupt end with the outbreak of the subprime crisis at the end of the decade. This crisis was bigger than any of the others before. The first institution that found itself in critical condition was the medium-sized bank Northern Rock that suffered a bank run in September 2007 (House of Commons Treasury Committee 2008: 13). It was nationalised in 2008. The crisis created liquidity and solvency problems for many other financial institutions and forced the Bank of England to fulfil extensively its role as lender of last resort and the government to bail out financial institutions.

In the 1980s and 1990s government debt averaged a stable level of around 50 per cent of GDP and was relatively low by international comparison. Yet, during the subprime crisis the debt quota increased sharply.

3.2.3 Foreign economic policy

When the Bretton Woods System broke down in 1973 the UK switched to a flexible exchange rate mechanism.[21] This meant that the UK no longer formally had

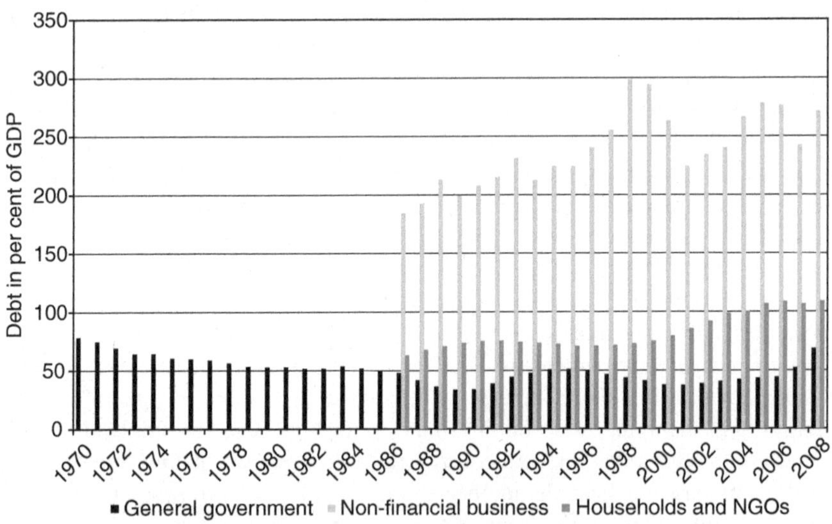

Figure 3.8 Debt in percentage of GDP in the UK, 1970–2009 (source: AMECO 2010, UK Office for National Statistics 2010).

to defend the exchange rate and the central bank was potentially able to focus on the needs of the domestic economy. In 1971, as mentioned above, foreign exchange controls were tightened to prevent speculative attacks on the pound sterling and were abolished in 1979 as one of the first actions of the new government. Exchange rate turbulences added to the eroding stability of the UK economy in the 1970s; the currency crisis in 1976 and the subsequent help from the International Monetary Fund, which granted a 3.9 billion pound rescue loan, forced the government to change its economic policy.

After a short appreciation phase at the end of the 1970s the pound sterling depreciated in nominal and real terms in the early 1980s against the major currencies, especially the D-Mark and the yen (see Figures 2.10 and 2.11). The current account balance improved and added to the recovery of the UK economy in that same period. It is noteworthy that the Conservative government in the UK, compared with the conservative administration of the US during the same period, was not immediately able to enhance the reputation of the pound sterling and trigger an appreciation of the domestic currency. This made it more difficult for the UK to bring down inflation quickly. However, this weakness of the pound sterling came to an end during the mid-1980s when the US dollar depreciated sharply. Two years later the pound sterling also stabilised vis-à-vis the D-Mark. Throughout the second half of the 1980s the pound sterling continued to appreciate, posing problems for the export sector and subsequently leading to a current account deficit (see Figure 2.12). The latter increased sharply until the end of the 1980s. Almost exclusively, since the 1980s the UK has continued to realise current account deficits. On average the deficit was around 1.6 per cent of GDP in the 1980s, around 1.5 per cent in the 1990s and 2.3 per cent on average in the first ten years of this century.

In 1990 the UK entered the EMS. Under the new exchange rate regime for the UK the Bank of England had to defend the exchange rate. The UK entered the EMS with an overvalued currency.[22] The relatively high inflation rates added to the external problems. A highly restrictive monetary policy was conducted in the UK to stop the inflationary development and to maintain the agreed exchange rate parity within the EMS. Because of the high economic and political costs of the restrictive monetary policy and the doubts as to whether the UK government would be prepared to bear the costs, massive speculation against the pound was instigated. The overly restrictive monetary policy of the German Bundesbank, particularly in 1992, put additional pressure on the Bank of England (see the German case study; Herr and Hübner 2005). In 1992 the UK left the EMS, the pound depreciated in nominal and in real terms. Control over inflation was achieved, allowing the UK a successful depreciation, which helped to reduce the current account deficit and stimulate growth. Monetary policy was now oriented more towards domestic needs. Compared with Germany and Japan, a long period of relatively high economic growth started.

In the second half of the 1990s the pound sterling appreciated, leading to a current account deficit of 2.3 per cent of GDP in 1999. After a period of stabilisation, the pound sterling appreciated again from 2002 until the end of 2007.

Between 2003 and 2009 average annual current account deficits remained at 2.3 per cent of GDP (see Table 3.3). During the subprime crisis the pound sterling then depreciated sharply.

In respect to current account deficits since the mid-1980s the UK has been in a similar constellation as the US. Except for the short period when it was a member of the EMS, the UK could combine current account deficits with relatively expansionary monetary policy. Growth was driven by domestic demand factors and could be achieved in spite of external deficits. Current account deficits in percentage of GDP in the UK were not as high as in the US. However, as in the US, the radical market policies and especially the liberal financial system in the UK, as well as the political role of the UK as the junior partner of the US in Europe, triggered permanent capital inflows, which led to the situation of permanent current account deficits.

3.2.4 Wage policy

In the UK after the Second World War a multiple-employer wage bargaining process existed which was executed by employers' associations and groups of trade unions for a particular sector (Richardson 1991). In contrast to Germany, for example, in many cases several unions organised according to professions existed in one industry and usually also in one firm. In the 1950s and 1960s there was a shift towards more plant-level wage negotiation. This change occurred at a time of low unemployment, whereby employers in certain sectors were paying a higher-than-collectively-agreed wage to attract workers. Plant-level collective bargaining agreements became particularly significant in the late 1960s and the 1970s. By 1980 single-plant wage agreements covered 30 per cent of all employees (Daniel and Millward 1983). As a result, the informal economy-wide wage coordination existing in the period after the Second World War eroded and competition between unions was enhanced.

These changes are going to be an important factor in explaining developments in the 1970s and 1980s. In the UK nominal wage increases were extremely high in the 1970s and substantially exceeded the increase in medium-term productivity and the inflation target by the central bank. Average annual nominal wage increases stood at around 17.5 per cent over the 1971–1975 cycle and at 14.6 per cent over the 1976–1981 cycle (see Table 2.7). High wage demands were triggered by the oil price shocks in the 1970s and the depreciation of the pound sterling, both of which led to the first round of price increases (Figure 3.9). As in many other countries at that time, parts of the labour movement in the UK also became more radical.

Up to the 1970s the labour market in the UK was regulated by the Trade Disputes Act of 1906 (Ewing 2006). In 1971 the Conservative government led by Edward Heath passed the Industrial Relations Act which created a new framework for industrial relations, made collective agreements legally binding, but also enacted individual rights of workers designed to weaken the closed shop principle (i.e. when firms agree to employ only union members) and discipline

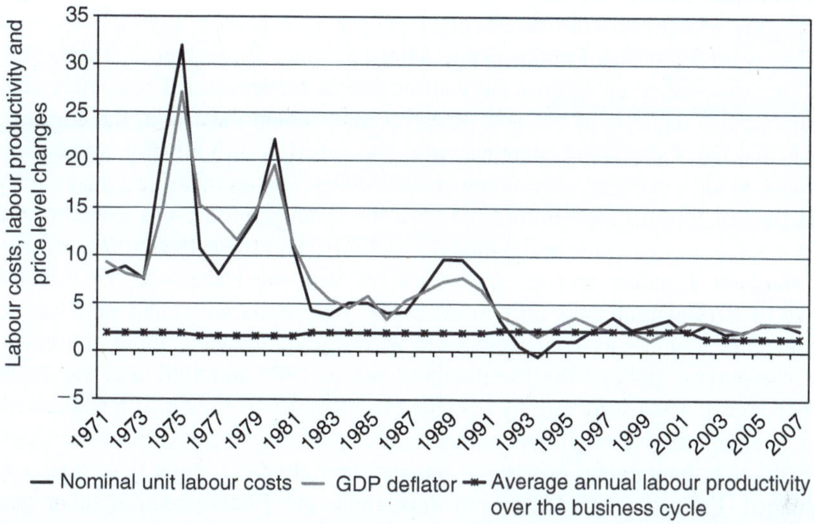

Figure 3.9 Productivity, unit labour costs and price level changes in the UK, 1961–2009 (percentage change to the previous year) (source: AMECO 2010).

the unions. Concerned about the inflationary development at that time Heath imposed price and wage controls in 1972 (The National Archives 2010). However, disregarding wage controls and thus winning sympathy from the public, unions pushed for higher wages (Kastendiek and Stinshoff 2006: 101). After the oil price shock of 1973 the miners' unions organised a massive strike, which further shook the confidence of the government. Elections in 1974 were won by the Labour Party, led by Harold Wilson, whose priority was to establish a 'social contract' between capital, labour and the state (The National Archives 2010). During the rule of the Labour Party (1974–1979) the role of the unions was strengthened through the Trade Union and Labour Relations Act of 1974 keeping the passage of protection against an unfair dismissal from the previous act of 1971. The Employment Protection Act of 1975

> provided positive rights to associations, guaranteed rights to time off for union activity, strengthened the position of unions against employers in information disclosure, terms of employment, and redundancies, created the Advisory, Conciliation and Arbitration Service and an arbitration mechanism for the failure to comply with its recommendations.
>
> (Freeman and Pelletier 1989: 11)

Particularly in the 1970s, union density increased steadily.[23] With many strike threats nominal wage increases became high. The government tried to bargain pension increases and higher public spending in return for wage moderation. However, wage development and inflation could not be brought under control.

Social tensions increased and wage demands could not be constrained any longer during the winter of 1978 (the so-called 'winter of discontent') when a series of strikes were organised. Labour Prime Minister James Callaghan, Wilson's successor, was pushed up against the wall by the social unrest and restrictive economic policy requests of the IMF, which came to help the UK in the currency crisis of 1976. Especially Callaghan, who was asked to curb inflation and budget deficits, made a stand to resist union attacks. After a series of strikes, the country was pushed into a deep conflict between the unions and the government, and thus a period of economic and political instability (Dimsdale 1991: 126).

Margaret Thatcher and the Conservatives won the election in 1979 and a wave of deregulation was introduced to the labour market. Their aim was to weaken the unions, as they were seen as the main obstacle for a successful macroeconomic policy. The Employment Act of 1980 and 1982 and the Trade Union Act of 1984 were strictly designed to increase the power of management and weaken union strength and authority.[24] Together with a loss of union membership, the bargaining power of unions through these laws was seriously damaged. From the late 1970s and throughout the 1980s unemployment was high (5.6 per cent on average in the 1976–1981 cycle, and 9.6 per cent throughout the 1982–1991 cycle). The high level of unemployment contributed to further weakening of the unions. Of symbolic importance was the one-year strike by the National Union of Mineworkers, which started in 1984 with the aim of preventing the closure and privatisation of mines. The miners' strike was utterly unsuccessful and allowed Thatcher to carry out her plans.

Unit labour cost increases in the 1980s were significantly lower than in the 1970s, but in spite of the changes in the labour market, still relatively high (see Figure 3.9). Obviously, in the 1970s and in the 1980s a coordinated wage bargaining process that could bring nominal wage development in line with the wage norm did not exist. In the 1990s wage development was relatively close to the wage norm. This wage development enabled the Bank of England to undertake expansionary monetary policy to support the declining economy at the beginning of the 1990s.

Margaret Thatcher dismantled minimum wages, which had a long tradition in the UK, in 1979. Together with the weakness of the unions this policy led to a substantial increase in wage dispersion. A large low-wage sector developed with substantial real wage losses of this group of workers. During the Thatcher government (1979–1990) real annual income of the poorest 20 per cent of the population increased by 0.4 per cent, whereas the income of the next four groups increased during the same period of time by 1.2 per cent, 1.9 per cent, 2.6 per cent and for the richest 3.7 per cent (Goodman and Shephard 2002; see also Machin 1996). The National Minimum Wage Act in 1998 again introduced statutory national minimum wages shortly after Tony Blair became Prime Minister.[25] The minimum wage is set according to a recommendation given by the Low Pay Commission, a tripartite body and is binding for all employees. The introduction of the minimum wage was successful as it improved the income of the lowest paid workers and contributed in compressing the wage structure and reducing income inequality in the country.[26] From the UK case we can conclude that under the conditions of a deregulated labour market and weak unions, a statutory minimum wage can be an effective instrument to control wage dispersion and prevent a race-to-the-bottom in terms of wages. In a situation of high unemployment deflationary tendencies can be reduced.

Overall, we can conclude that wage development in the UK was a disaster in the 1970s, was not coordinated on a macroeconomic level and led to the erosion of the economic and political system. Under Margaret Thatcher unions became much weaker and until today have not recovered their full strength. The fact that the development of the wage level in the last two decades has become stability oriented is to a large extent the result of luck. There was no macroeconomic coordination, wage dispersion developed in a way that low wage increases in the growing low-wage sector were compensated by the high wage increases in the high-wage sector. A positive development was the introduction of minimum wages which since 1998 have been a stabilising factor for wage development by compressing the wage structure from below.

3.2.5 Monetary policy

The first institutional change that was significant for the direction of monetary policy was the switch to flexible exchange rates when the Bretton Woods System ceased to exist. As a result, the Bank of England lost its monetary policy anchor – keeping a certain exchange rate parity – and with that the search for a new monetary policy strategy started. Following the strategies of the other big central banks (the US Federal Reserve, the Bundesbank) the Bank of England tried the then fashionable monetary targeting. At first the central bank used monetary targets only informally, but in 1977 the bank started officially announcing targets for the money supply, even though it still had a certain discretionary freedom to act.

With the electoral victory of Margaret Thatcher monetarism was put forward as the official strategy the Bank of England was going to follow. In 1980 the monetary aggregate M3 was chosen as a target and there was an attempt to control its growth rate (Cobham 2001: 11; Safford 1998: 105: Dimsdale 1991: 131). In 1980 the Bank of England introduced the Medium Term Financing Strategy, setting up a plan for a medium-term reduction of money supply growth rates. Concerned about the fact that money supply was growing faster than desired, the Bank of England turned to restrictive monetary policy and high interest rates (see Figure 3.10). Actually, M3 overshot its targeted level by 12.8 per cent in 1981/1982. In spite of very high interest rates the central bank was not successful in meeting the targets for M3. High economic and political uncertainty obviously led to the desire of the public to hold wealth in liquid form. The circular velocity of money became very unstable and extremely unpredictable (Cobham 2001). Hence, the Bank of England in 1982 decided to experiment with another intermediate target – the monetary base M0 (currency in circulation plus bank reserves kept with the central bank). Inflation was still not reduced to levels preferred by the Bank of England. In 1986/1987 the Bank of England prioritised the exchange rate as a target for monetary policy. It tried to prevent an even sharper appreciation of the pound sterling, purchased large amounts of US dollars in the foreign exchange markets and kept interest rates low.

In 1990, following the strategy to stabilise the exchange rate, the Bank of England (i.e. the government, as the central bank was not independent) made the decision to switch towards a hard nominal exchange rate peg within the framework of the EMS. The membership in the EMS was problematic for the UK economy as GDP growth dropped to 0 per cent in 1992 and unemployment was as high as 10 per cent, a time when a low interest rate policy would be most appropriate. Despite the needs of the domestic economy, the Bank of England had to maintain high interest rates because of the high interest policy conducted by the German Bundesbank, which was fighting against a unification boom with an overly restrictive monetary policy (see the German case study). The policy to keep the pound stable within the EMS became increasingly costly, especially when speculation against the pound started. In summer 1992 the UK left the EMS, immediately lowered interest rates by 5 per cent (see Figure 3.10) and depreciated substantially, albeit without pushing up the inflation rate.

From 1992 on, the official strategy of the Bank of England has been inflation targeting with an official target of 2.5 per cent, whereas in 2003 the target inflation rate changed to 2 per cent, similar to the ECB (Balls and O'Donnel 2002). Since 1993 the UK economy has experienced an undisturbed growth until the financial crisis of 2007. Monetary policy could remain expansion oriented, as there was no hard conflict between wage development and inflation.

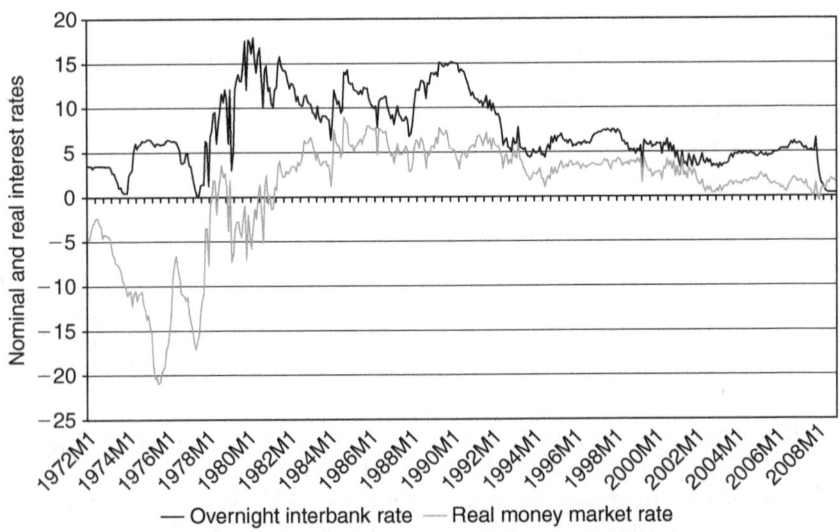

Figure 3.10 Nominal and real money market interest rates in the UK, 1972–2009 (real rate: nominal minus change in CPI), (source: IMF 2010d).

In 1997 a sharp increase in real estate prices developed and continued at a very strong pace until the last quarter of 2007 (see Figure 2.7). As with the Fed, the Bank of England had no instrument to curb the bubble except the economically harmful increase in interest rate. In 1997 the Bank of England increased interest rates for a short period of time, but soon decided to go back to lower interest rates, as inflation rates in 1997 and 1998 were 1.8 per cent and 1.6 per cent, respectively. Real interest rates increased slightly at the end of the 1990s but also fell back quickly. There was only a small increase in the nominal interest rate between 2003 and 2004. Then, interest rates were kept stable until the second half of 2006 when they were increased slightly. At this time a big real estate and stock market bubble was already building up which was not challenged by monetary policy. The Bank of England obviously did not see an inflationary threat and did not want to disturb economic growth by inflicting high interest rates to stop an asset price bubble.

After the breakdown of the Bretton Woods System and until the early 1990s both the government and the Bank of England struggled for a long time to find the right monetary policy strategy. Monetary targeting proved an unsuccessful choice as it was made clear that there was no stable connection between money supply and inflation, velocity was ever-changing and unpredictable, there were portfolio shifts from long- to short-term financial assets, and the definition of a monetary aggregate became almost unsolvable because of financial innovations. In addition, a nominal exchange rate anchor did not work smoothly for the UK. After 1992 inflation targeting worked better in the UK, and ultimately the Bank of England was able to keep interest rates low, as there were no relevant inflationary dangers.

3.2.6 Fiscal policy

In the UK the seventies were not only problematic because of the high inflation rates, but also because of fairly high budget deficits. As can be seen from Table 3.4 and Figure 3.11 budget deficits were on average around 2.7 per cent during the 1971–1975 cycle and 4.5 per cent in the 1976–1981 cycle. If we take a closer look, we can see that the deficits were particularly big between 1973 and 1976 (on average 5.3 per cent) and in 1978–1979 (on average 5.4 per cent). During these periods, the government took a strongly expansionary stance for fiscal policy.[27] At this time there seemed to be no coordination between monetary and fiscal policy (Hatton and Chrystal 1991: 71). Being under pressure to curb inflation after the currency crisis in 1976 and forced by IMF conditionality, Callaghan's government tried to reduce budget deficits, especially via contraction in public spending.

The Conservative government, which came into power in 1979, immediately dedicated itself to consolidating the budget, and this at a time when the UK economy had already dived into deep recession. The government adopted a so-called Medium Term Financial Strategy for the reduction of public debt and a control over money-supply growth in order to control inflation (Hatton and Chrystal

Table 3.4 Fiscal policy indicators for the UK 1971–2008 (average growth rates over the business cycle, unless mentioned otherwise)

Business cycles	*1971–1975*	*1976–1981*	*1982–1991*	*1992–2002*	*2003–2008*
Nominal GDP growth	15.72	15.76	8.87	5.47	5.08
Total expenditures[1]	19.72	15.80	7.43	5.02	7.90
Discretionary expenditure indicator	20.52	13.42	7.73	4.77	7.09
Government consumption	20.83	15.75	8.04	5.07	6.69
Government investment	15.85	1.42	10.39	2.85	28.85
Subsidies	34.76	8.76	–1.74	3.59	3.19
Social benefits	19.04	21.07	9.55	4.70	5.65
Total revenues	15.66	15.90	7.70	5.30	6.58
Social security contributions	21.79	15.68	8.32	5.31	7.54
Direct taxes	17.93	14.25	8.07	5.52	6.35
Direct taxes, cyclically adjusted	25.85	15.09	7.66	5.50	6.09
Indirect taxes	9.85	19.60	8.54	5.49	3.70
Indirect taxes, cyclically adjusted	11.78	20.31	8.28	5.37	3.56
Budget balance (% of GDP)[2]	–2.72	–4.48	–2.46	–2.76	–3.61
Budget balance, cyclically adjusted (% of GDP)[2]	–4.45	–4.49	–2.44	–2.73	–3.96

Source: OECD (2009c), AMECO (2010), authors' calculations.

Note
1 Government consumption, government investment and subsidies.
2 Average size over the business cycle.

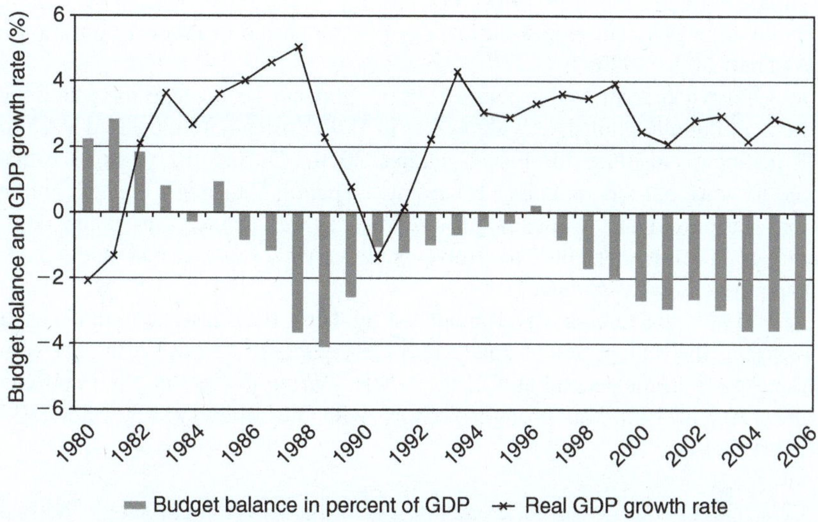

Figure 3.11 Budget Balance in percentage of GDP and GDP growth rates in the UK, 1980–2008 (source: OECD, authors' calculations 2009c).

1991: 73). The government turned towards supply-side economics. An important part of this policy was to cut top income tax rates and reduce the tax burden of companies. The top rate on earnings was cut to 60 per cent in 1979 and to 40 per cent in 1988 (Clark and Dilnot 2002). Privatisations, besides facilitating an increase in the sphere of private capital and with the aim to increase efficiency, were also meant to reduce public debt. There was a switch from direct taxes to indirect taxes for revenue creation. Value Added Tax (VAT) was introduced in 1980 at a level of 15 per cent (before there had been two sales tax rates) (OECD 1980: 38). In 1981 there was also a sharp increase in some consumption taxes (Institute for Fiscal Studies 2010). Public service recruitment was reduced by 20 per cent and public expenditures were to be kept constant in real terms (Shaw 1983).

Later in the 1980s the government raised more funds through a so-called 'community tax' or poll tax, which was a single flat-rate tax charged on each adult and determined by the local community. The aim was to connect local spending with local taxation, thus local communities which had high spending would be forced to charge a higher poll tax. But this project introduced by Margaret Thatcher proved to be disastrous and very unpopular amongst the electorate. Massive privatisations in this period also worked in favour of budget consolidation, along with the pick-up in economic growth later in the 1980s, which generated more revenues for the government. The revenues collected through privatisations generated more than £27 billion during the 1980s, with more than £7 billion in 1988–1989 alone (Richardson 1994: 71).

The deep recession at the beginning of the 1980s made it difficult to consolidate the budget as tax revenues endogenously declined. Also, expenditure targets could not be realised (Shaw 1983). Overall, the government was not successful in achieving a planned budget surplus even in the period of recovery during the second half of the 1980s.

In 1990 when John Major became Prime Minister he decided to reduce the poll tax and finally abolished it altogether in 1993. Instead, he increased VAT to 17.5 per cent (Institute for Fiscal Studies 2010). During his years in office emphasis was put on reducing government spending through cuts in public sector salaries and cuts in spending for defence, as well as increases in consumption taxes (Zohlnhoefer 2005: 6). However, John Mayor was also unable to consolidate the budget as planned.

After 1997, the Labour government led by Tony Blair also committed itself to lowering the budget deficit, made feasible especially because of higher economic growth in the second half of the 1990s. During this period the important Finance Act of 1998 was brought forward with the following key rules (HM Treasury 2010):

- *The golden rule*: over the economic cycle, the government should borrow only to invest and not to fund current spending (i.e. only public investment will be allowed to be financed by public debt and current expenditure will have to be completely covered by current revenue); and
- *The sustainable investment rule*: public sector net debt as a proportion of GDP should be held over the economic cycle at a stable and prudent level. The debt ratio should not be bigger than 40 per cent of GDP.

Fiscal policy was guided by this act until the outbreak of the subprime crisis when budget deficits in the UK exploded; in 2010 public debt to GDP surpassed 60 per cent. These regulations bear a similarity with the Stability and Growth Pact of the euro zone but leave more room for flexibility and take more into account the current economic situation (Bladen-Hovell 2001: 73). Following this legislature the UK government kept budget deficits in percentage of GDP relatively low and public debt in percentage of GDP at a stable level of below 50 per cent until the subprime crisis hit the country (see Figure 3.8).

All in all, fiscal policy in the UK had a stop-and-go character in the 1970s and, in an inflationary environment, added to inflationary pressures and the currency crisis which hit the UK in that decade. In the early 1980s the economy was still in recession when the government tried a hard 'stop' policy, which intensified the recession and could not balance the budget although the government had tried hard. During the episodes of strong growth in the 1980s budget surpluses would have been more suitable, but the government did not want to increase taxes and cut expenditures further. However, public households kept control of public debt to GDP. Since the late 1980s and throughout the 1990s and 2000s fiscal policy was used in an anti-cyclical way with higher budget deficits in periods of low growth and lower budget deficits or even small surpluses in periods of high growth.

3.2.7 Conclusions

The finance-led growth model of the UK in the 1980s and thereafter is a good example of a bubble-driven economy based on domestic credit and demand creation and a very unequal income distribution. Except for the government sector the debt quotas of the other economic sectors increased to very high levels and created a fragile economic constellation by the end of the 2000s. Household demand was not driven by equal income distribution but by credit; investment was largely carried out by highly leveraged firms. As in the US, the UK macroeconomic policy regime combined relatively high growth with long-term current account deficits, which added stress to the role of domestic demand drivers.

Similarly to the US case, the structural changes under the Cconservative revolution, which in both countries started in the 1980s, led to an unstable regime. The financial system in the UK became very unstable and at the same time deeply integrated into an unstable worldwide financial system. The City of London became an important world business centre in the UK and made the country dependent on a fragile financial system. Labour market reforms in the 1980s led to weaker unions and an uncoordinated wage bargaining system. Wage dispersion expanded and led to a very unequal income distribution. Statutory minimum wages introduced under the Blair government helped to reduce wage dispersion somewhat and added to the stability of the labour market.

Process policies in the 1970s were a complete failure and not ideal for creating growth in the 1980s. The 1990s and first decade after 2000 reflected an interaction between monetary policy, fiscal policy and wage development which allowed relatively high growth. The external sectors, especially after the 1970s and early 1990s, stopped being a restricting factor for macroeconomic policy. However, we should always keep in mind that this positive development was built on a very unstable institutional basis and not on planned coordination. In future decades it may be difficult to build a prosperous development on such a basis.

3.3 The exhaustion of the German export model and the EMU

3.3.1 Overview about the political and economic development

The core structure of the economic policy regime in Germany has been maintained for many years. It was and is still marked by a mercantilist orientation. This means that export successes have always been an important economic policy guideline for the German Federal Republic. In comparison with the US and UK, which have accepted high current account deficits over long periods, in Germany phases of current account deficits are seen as indicators for economic crises and thus as challenges to be dealt with. Since the 1950s, the export success of Germany has essentially been based on an undervaluation of the D-Mark which is associated with moderate nominal wage increases and continuous intervention of the German Bundesbank in foreign exchange markets to prevent a strong appreciation of the D-Mark (Spahn 1988; Herr 1990; Riese 2001). This strategy was supported by all relevant political players including employers' associations and unions.

In the 1950s and 1970s Germany was one of the economic 'miracle' countries with high GDP growth, driven by high export demand, high investment demand and high consumption demand. Compared with other countries and in spite of the deep crisis in 1975 Germany was able to realise relatively high GDP growth rates for most of the 1970s. Similarly, the 1980s showed relatively high growth and low unemployment rates (Table 3.5 and Figure 3.12). Politically, the 1950s and 1960s were shaped by conservative parties with coalitions between the Christian Democratic Union of Germany (CDU) and the Free Democratic Party (FDP). Only in 1966 did the CDU and the Social Democratic Party of Germany (SPD) form a grand coalition. In 1969 under Chancellor Willy Brandt, the SPD started a coalition with the FDP. After Brandt stepped down in 1974, Helmut Schmidt became Chancellor within the same coalition and served until 1982. No substantial neoliberal reform took place during this period. In 1982 the FDP left the coalition with the SPD and a CDU–FDP coalition under Chancellor Helmut Kohl was formed, which lasted until 1998. Under the long period of chancellorship of Helmut Kohl no fundamental changes in the institutional framework of Germany took place. In substance, Helmut Kohl followed a social democratic policy and even the FDP at that time was not market-radical.

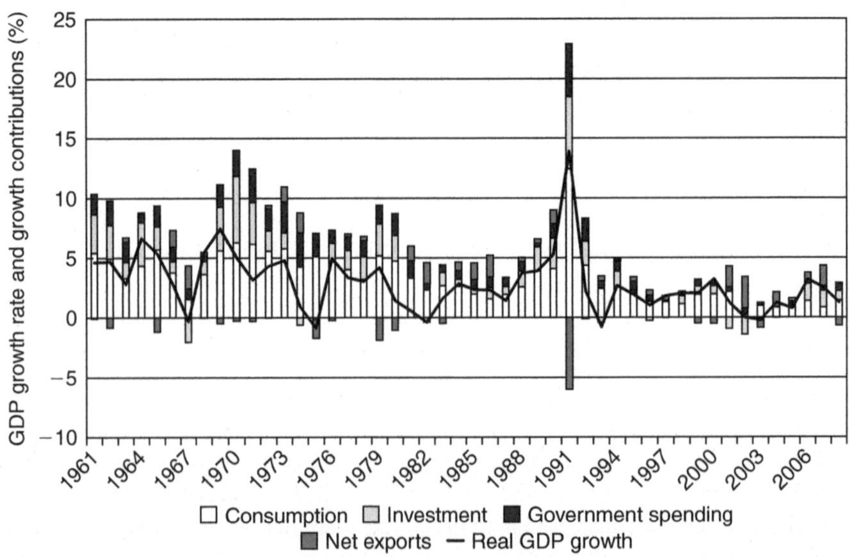

Figure 3.12 Contributions of the different demand aggregates to GDP growth in Germany, 1961–2008 (source: AMECO 2010, authors' calculations).

Table 3.5 Macroeconomic indicators in Germany, 1971–2009 (average values over the business cycle)

Business cycles	*1971–1975*	*1976–1982*	*1983–1993*	*1994–2003*	*2004–2009*
Real GDP growth rate	2.45	2.43	2.71	1.56	0.64
Unemployment rate	1.46	3.50	6.37	8.44	8.95
Inflation rate	6.14	4.54	2.54	1.53	1.67
Percentage change in nominal unit labour costs	7.31	3.82	2.35	0.57	0.76
Percentage change in real wage per employee	3.69	1.64	1.35	1.77	0.00
Budget balance as percentage of GDP	–1.27	–3.06	–1.92	–3.08	–2.11
Current account balance as percentage of GDP	1.30	0.11	2.06	–0.31	5.87
	Mid-1980s	*1990*	*Mid-1990s*	*2000*	*Mid-2000s*
Gini coefficient	0.257	0.258	0.272	0.270	0.298

Source: AMECO 2010, OECD 2009c, authors' calculations.

Kohl became the Chancellor of German unification when the Berlin Wall came down in 1989. He promised 'flourishing landscapes' in the East (Kohl 1990). A year later in 1990 the German Democratic Republic (GDR) legally joined the Federal Republic of Germany. However, the German unification was dominated and driven by political considerations and not by economic needs resulting in a number of inadequate repercussions.[28]

As a consequence of the way the unification process was carried out, industrial production in East Germany collapsed almost completely. Employment dropped from about 9.6 million in 1990 to 6.1 million in 1993. While, after the severe economic crisis in 1990 and 1991, the new federal states showed higher growth rates than West Germany, this process of adjustment ended around 1997. Since then, the growth rates in East Germany have hardly exceeded or have even been below those of West Germany.

German unification also placed a considerable burden on public households. On the one hand, there were high public expenditures caused by the enormous infrastructural backlog. On the other hand, high public transfers became necessary, for example to finance local communities in the East as tax revenues in the East were too low. Additionally, large special write-offs were allowed for investment in the new states.

The deep economic crisis in the new federal states resulted inter alia from the politically chosen conversion of wages and salaries, pensions and so on from GDR-Mark to D-Mark. When East Germany joined the D-Mark area an overnight appreciation of the former GDR area by about 300 per cent took place. In addition to this, nominal wage levels in the new federal states rose rapidly at the beginning of the unification process without corresponding increases in productivity. Consequently, for the first years after unification, increases in unit labour costs were considerably higher in East Germany than in West Germany. Moreover, the lack of East German competitiveness was at least initially aggravated by the absence of working distribution channels for East German products, inadequate marketing of products from the East, and similar factors.

The conversion of monetary wealth and debt at the beginning of German currency union in 1990 was around two GDR-Marks to one D-Mark and did not reflect a realistic exchange rate between the previously separate currency areas. For monetary wealth owners (mainly households) this conversion rate was good and triggered a demand boom. However, this boom did not stimulate production in the East but rather in the West since East German production was not sufficiently competitive and East Germans, at least shortly after unification, had a preference for western goods. At the same time, the conversion rate led to an over-indebtedness of almost all East German companies. This also explains why the German privatisation agency of East German state-owned enterprises (Treuhandanstalt) had to take over most of the debt and after everything was privatised ended up with a loss. For example, in 1995 the government was burdened with the debts of the Treuhandanstalt and some East German public residential-building cooperatives of about 10 per cent of GDP. In this respect, the currency reform in 1990 in the context of the German unification was fundamentally different from that of 1948. Back then monetary wealth in old Reichsmark as well as debt was almost destroyed and gave the enterprise sectors excellent conditions for starting a period of expansion.

Unification has left deep marks in the German social security system. The social cushioning of unification has been financed to a considerable extent by the social security systems of the old federal states. For example, the West German pension system was massively burdened by financing East German pensions. This was due to the conversion rate between the GDR-Mark and the D-Mark that favoured East German over West German pensioners, but also on grounds of the higher participation rate of women in the GDR, as well as the longer average working life in the GDR compared with West Germany, which thus created higher pension entitlements in the East than in the West. As a consequence, the social security systems ran into financial difficulties that created pressure to reform them.

German unification threw Germany into a deep economic shock. The new German states did not develop economically as well as expected. Moreover, attempts to transfer West German institutions to East Germany were unsuccessful. This was especially the case with regard to the labour market; strong unions and employers' associations in a wage bargaining system as was traditional in West Germany could not be established.

In 1998 Helmut Kohl lost the election and a coalition between the SPD and the Green Party (Alliance '90/The Greens) under Chancellor Gerhard Schröder came into power. During this period and after a one-year struggle with Finance Minister Oskar Lafontaine (also SPD) over economic policy strategy, a radical neoliberal reform was implemented in Germany. Especially the labour market and the financial market were affected. In 2005, Angela Merkel (CDU) became Chancellor, again of a grand coalition between CDU and SPD. The coalition more or less continued the economic policies started by the Schröder government. In 2009 Merkel became the head of a ruling coalition between CDU and FDP, of which the latter had begun to follow a much more market-radical policy approach in comparison with the decades before. The party landscape in Germany has changed dramatically since unification, with the two traditional major parties (CDU and SPD) and three smaller parties (FDP, The Greens and The Left – Die Linke) in parliament.[29] In previous decades, the FDP was the only smaller party in the federal parliament.

Low German growth rates in the 1990s and even more so in the 2000s were primarily caused by a stagnation of private consumption, while investment demand was disappointing too. In the 2000s – with the exception of 2006/07 – export demand was more or less the only demand driver and was consequently not enough to create sufficient growth. Germany became the slowest growing country in the European Monetary Union (EMU) and even in the European Union (EU). Low consumption demand was caused by climbing unemployment rates as well as by reforms in the labour markets which increased wage dispersion and triggered precarious jobs. The increasingly unequal income distribution is shown by the rising Gini coefficient in Table 3.5.

After German unification and the neoliberal reforms the EMU, which started in 1999, was the third economic shock for Germany. On the basis of macroeconomic wage coordination, wage increases in Germany were traditionally relatively low. Given the D-Mark exchange rate, low wage increases led to rising price competitiveness and growing export surpluses. Before the EMU was established an increase in exports had typically triggered an increase in consumption and investment demand. Relatively low German wage increases and export surpluses resulted in appreciation pressures of the D-Mark which were fought by the German Bundesbank by means of low interest rates. The latter then provoked domestic demand increases and prevented German exports from becoming too high. Because of this effect, Germany used to have the lowest real interest rates in the EU. In contrast, since the start of the EMU the growth of German exports cannot be stopped by exchange rate adjustments, however, low German wage increases and the resulting low inflation rates led to the highest real interest rate in Germany within the EMU.

3.3.2 Financial system

Germany is a country with a bank-based financial system. Traditionally, investment banks and non-bank financial institutions as well as capital markets did not play an important role. Around one-third of the German banking system is made up of local banks owned by local governments (Sparkassen) and to a lesser extent by collectively owned banks (Volksbanken). In the tradition of the so-called house bank system, companies used to borrow from one major bank that had a long-run relationship with the company. In the German financial system, following Schumpeter (1926), the banker used to be the the ephor of the entrepreneur. Between the three big German private commercial banks (Deutsche Bank, Dresdner Bank and Commerzbank) and the big German insurance company (Allianz) there was a close relationship with major German stock companies. Financial institutions did not only grant credit to big German companies, but as owners also kept large share packages of these enterprises and took over the voting rights from smaller shareholders. There was a dense network of cross-shareholdings and interlocking directorates, also including mostly informal links to governments. The interrelation between major German financial institutions, companies and the state was called Germany Inc. or 'Deutschland AG' and can be considered one of backbones of German development after the Second World War (Streeck 2009: 77).

To a large extent real estate credits were granted by special institutions, however, other banks also granted real estate credits. Real estate financing in Germany was generally conservative and subsidised by the state. Households had to have a relatively high percentage of own capital to buy a house or a flat. Real estate assets were usually not used as collateral for consumption credits. In international comparison the percentage of Germans living in their own house or flat is relatively low (Herr and Stachuletz 2010).

The type of financial system including the 'Deutschland AG' described above existed until the 1990s. In comparison with other developed countries there were not many institutional changes in the German financial system in the 1970s and 1980s. International capital flows had been liberalised in the early 1960s as the D-Mark was a strong currency, but the domestic financial system remained conservative and largely unchanged until the 1990s.

In 1991 the German transaction tax in stock markets was abolished, but the big steps in financial deregulation came under the SPD–Green coalition after 1998 (Hein and van Treeck 2008). Among other changes, in 1998 it became easier for share companies to buy back their own shares. The tax burden of companies was substantially reduced in 2000. Of key importance was the abolishment of the capital gains tax in 2000, which allowed firms to sell the largely undervalued cross-shareholdings of other firms without being taxed. This gave the signal for the mutual disentanglement of financial and non-financial corporations and the end of German Inc. Of course these tax changes were not the only reason for the erosion of German Inc. Many big German financial and non-financial companies wanted to become global players, started to follow the shareholder value corporate governance system and became exposed to unfriendly takeovers by foreign investors. The traditional national model of the German Inc. had simply become too narrow for globalisation strategies. The high profits companies were now making by selling their old stock holdings helped them go global (Streeck 2009). In 2004 the required minimum capital for investment funds in Germany was reduced and hedge funds were allowed. In actual fact, investment funds were allowed to follow largely the same business models as hedge funds. In 2007 the Basel II regulation with all of its pro-cyclical effects was introduced in Germany. In the same and in the following year enterprise taxes were cut again while real estate investment trusts and certain private equity companies were supported by special tax cuts. Thus, Germany was on the way (as was most of continental Europe, pushed by the EU Commission) to establishing a more US and UK type of largely deregulated financial system when the subprime crisis hit the world economy.

Despite the 'old fashioned' nature of the financial system, it started to embrace international characteristics. One effect of this was that German banks in 2008/2009 in the 2000s bought the later toxic papers from the US financial system. Losses and large-scale rescue packages by the German government for German banks were not caused by a domestic real estate bubble, but were the direct consequence of the fact that most German banks had gone global.

The poor growth performance in Germany in the 1990s and thereafter can also be seen in the development of the debt quotas of the different German sectors (Figure 3.13). Enterprise debt to GDP until the late 1990s increased relatively quickly, but then stagnated. In comparison with the US and UK, household debt to GDP remained low in Germany and showed no tendency to increase. This reflects the fact that Germany had neither a real estate bubble (see Section 2.2.2) nor did consumption credits play an important role. Germany did not follow the consumption and real estate credit-driven growth model of the US and UK and realised lower growth rates. Public debt to GDP increased from around 40 per cent of GDP in 1991 to about 80 per cent in 2010. Obviously,

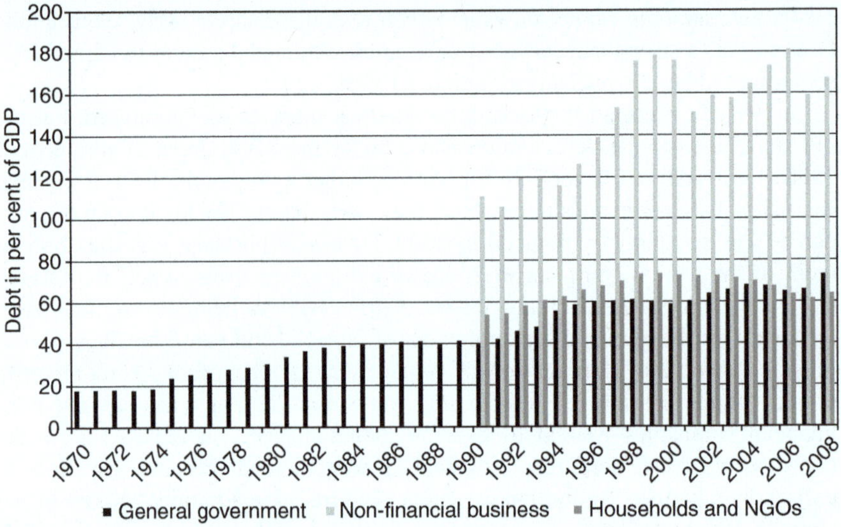

Figure 3.13 Debt in percentage of GDP in Germany, 1970–2009 (source: AMECO 2010, Deutsche Bundesbank 2010).

Germany also did not finance government expenditures sufficiently by increasing taxes. Nor did it stabilise expenditures in boom phases.

3.3.3 Foreign economic policy

Since the beginning of the 1950s the trade balance has never been negative in Germany. Until the late 1980s phases of negative current account balances were very short. However, as a consequence of German unification the German current account slipped into deficit from 1991 to 2001. In contrast, in 2002 and thereafter, Germany achieved vast current account surpluses as a result of record surpluses in the trade balance, on average amounting to nearly 6 per cent of GDP in the period 2004–2009 (see Table 3.5).

From the 1970s until the creation of the euro in 1999 the D-Mark was the second most important reserve currency after the US dollar. The Japanese yen also took over international functions but lost considerable ground after Japan fell into a period of low growth in the early 1990s. The exchange rate movements between the D-Mark, or later the euro, and the US dollar have been extremely volatile. After a long downward trend of the US dollar starting in the early 1970s, between the end of the 1970s and 1985 the US dollar increased strongly in value with respect to the D-Mark. After 1985 the US dollar depreciated sharply, stabilised in the late 1980s and became strong again at the end of the 1990s. In the first two years after its introduction the euro depreciated sharply against the US dollar, then appreciated sharply until it again became weak in

2010 (see Figure 2.10). Overall, the exchange rate movements of the D-Mark and later the euro must be considered excessive and not explainable by economic fundamentals. Such strong exchange rate fluctuations are extremely disturbing, particularly for an export-oriented medium-sized country like Germany.

Germany has followed two strategies to defend itself from exchange rate disturbances. First, not only during the period of the Bretton Woods System did the German Bundesbank intervene extensively to defend the exchange rate (actually the total increase in central bank money in the 1950s and 1960s was created by foreign exchange interventions), it also intervened later to slow down the appreciation of the D-Mark. Before the central banks in developing countries like China started buying foreign currencies, Germany – after Japan – had the second biggest foreign exchange reserve in the world (Herr 1990).

Second, Germany was always one of the drivers of European monetary integration for the purpose of creating stable exchange rates, at least in Europe. This was actually the initiative of not so much the Bundesbank, but of German governments. After the collapse of the Bretton Woods System efforts were soon made to establish a European currency arrangement in order to protect intra-European trade from unpredictable exchange rate movements. In 1973 this led to the 'European Currency Snake' with the D-Mark as the 'head' of the snake. With the European Monetary System (EMS) in 1979, which was very much pushed forward by the then German Chancellor Helmut Schmidt together with his French counterpart Giscard d'Estaing, the D-Mark took on the leading reserve currency role within this fixed exchange rate system, while the other member countries of the system were forced to follow the monetary policy of the Bundesbank.[30] The German 'stability culture' was exported to the other member countries of the EMS and from their viewpoint created an exogenous nominal anchor to bring down the high inflation rates in that period. The logical consequence was that in the course of the 1980s, reduction in inflation rates occurred in all EMS countries. With the start of the EMU a large part of German trade became regional trade within the currency area. This constellation led to exploding German current account surpluses as no exchange rate appreciation could stop the German export hunger any longer.

The more or less permanent trade and current account surpluses show that the external sector set no long-term hard constraints on domestic economic policy for Germany. On the contrary, German economic policy in many cases restricted macroeconomic policy in other countries which had higher inflation rates and/or realised current account deficits. Therefore, the German economic growth weakness from the mid-1990s onwards must be seen as 'home-made'.

3.3.4 Wage policy

Compared with other countries, nominal wages and nominal unit labour costs in Germany increased moderately. With the exception of a few periods wage development from the 1950s to the 1980s was more or less in line with trend productivity increases and a low-targeted inflation rate. However, after the mid-1990s, compared with the wage norm, wages in Germany rose too slowly (see Figure 3.14). Yet, low wage increases in Germany did not create employment. Instead, inflation rates dropped to very low rates so that the threat of deflation began to appear. In the spring of 2003, the IMF expressed its concern that the world economy could slide into a deflationary development. Besides Japan, already gripped by deflation, Hong Kong, Taiwan and especially Germany were classified as facing very severe deflationary threats (IMF 2003). Too low wage increases thus led to a dangerous macroeconomic situation in Germany.

We have to distinguish between the old German model of wage setting which was established after the Second World War and was in place until the early 1990s and the new model which developed afterwards. In the old model wage negotiations were highly coordinated and took into account macroeconomic effects of wage development. Traditionally, the annual wage round started in Baden-Württemberg in the metal industry, a stronghold of the metal industry where, for example, Mercedes Benz and many of its suppliers are located. The German metal workers union, the strongest German union, and the metal industry employers' association in Baden-Württemberg negotiated a pilot agreement. These negotiations were backed by the whole union movement and all the employers' associations. As early as in the 1950s productivity-oriented wage increases had become a guideline for a macroeconomically stabilising wage development, also in the union movement. Defence of the international competitiveness of German companies played a role in the negotiations as well. The outcome of the negotiations in Baden-Württemberg was then adopted more or less automatically by the entire German metal industry. Similarly, the outcome

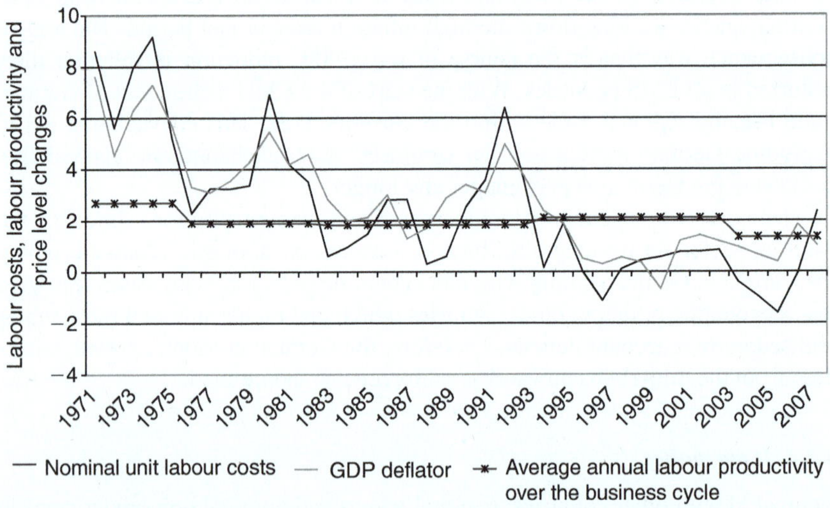

Figure 3.14 Productivity, unit labour costs and price level changes in Germany, 1961–2009 (percentage change to the previous year) (source: AMECO 2010, authors' calculations).

of the negotiations in the metal industry was adopted by all industries with only minor modification, even by industries with weaker unions and employers' associations and by firms without union representation. This informal signalling effect guaranteed a high coordination in German wage negotiations despite formal negotiations on the industry level. As in Scandinavian countries Germany had no statutory minimum wage but the wage bargaining mechanism prevented the development of a low-wage sector (Sockice 1990).

Work councils are the second pillar of worker representation in firms. According to the law work councils can be elected in firms with at least five permanent employees; in bigger firms full-time work councils have to be paid for by firms. Work councils have substantial information rights from management, and consultation rights in matters such as human resource planning, job content, working environment, determination of employees and so on (Gerlach and Meyer 2010). In addition to this, in many cases employees' representatives sit on the board together with owners to control management, albeit with a stronger position on the owners' side. Traditionally, work councils did not negotiate wages and were a controlling arm of unions at the firm level.

There was never any doubt that wage increases which were considered too high would be immediately punished by the German Bundesbank; it was always the invisible party at the wage negotiation table. Wage developments in Germany only went askew in two periods. The first exception was at the beginning of the 1970s during the reform euphoria when the public sector union started the wage round and negotiated double digit wage increases. The Bundesbank immediately reacted with hard, restrictive monetary policy (Scharpf 1987). After the sharp economic recession in 1974/75, which was mainly caused by restrictive monetary policy, German trade unions returned to moderate wage increases. The second period was during the short unification boom in the early 1990s. Unit labour costs in West Germany increased by about 6 per cent during the high growth phase in 1992 and added to the already existing demand inflation. The inflation rate in West Germany in 1992 increased to 5.1 per cent. Nominal wage increases above the wage norm were understandable in that period as employees, especially in West Germany, were feeling the costs of German unification because social security contributions and some taxes were increased. Only two years earlier, Helmut Kohl had told them that flourishing landscapes in the East would allow for unification without any costs. Eventually the Bundesbank reacted with restrictive monetary policy and triggered a crisis in 1993.

It was only in the course of the 1990s that the traditional system of wage bargaining eroded and a dual wage bargaining system in Germany developed. One of the key elements of the new system is that the signalling effect from the metal industry to all industries in all regions broke down. The erosion of the old system came in two waves. First, the West German wage-setting mechanisms could not be established in East Germany. Especially employers' associations remained very weak in East Germany. Unions in the East were discredited from their former function in the GDR and lost most of their members. Companies which did not belong to employers' associations did not have to follow the negotiated wages. Theoretically, local or even central government could have made negotiations binding for all firms – a practice widely used for example in France – but in Germany this instrument was only used in very exceptional cases. Even negotiated wages in some industries, especially service industries, in the East as well as in the West, became very low.

Second, labour market reforms under the Schröder government did not fill the institutional gap by introducing statutory minimum wages and/or policies to strengthen unions and the wage bargaining process; he reformed labour markets in a neoliberal way. In the centre were the so-called Hartz reforms in the years 2003 and 2004. Among other things, the entitlement for unemployment benefits were cut from 32 to 12 months; long-term unemployment benefits and social assistance was amalgamated into a single and flat rate whereas benefits became means-tested; requirements of the unemployed to accept job offers were tightened. At the same time the largely used option of early retirement under the Kohl era to relieve the labour market was abandoned. In 2006 against the explicit will of unions the decision was made to increase the legal age of retirement stepwise from 65 to 67 years (Streeck 2009: 62).[31] Labour market reforms in Germany in the 2000s are comparable with the reform period after Margaret Thatcher became prime minister in the UK (Carlin and Soskice 2007). Due to the absence of statutory minimum wages and long term unemployment benefits, wages in the low-wage sector started to fall to the very low social assistance level of the Hartz reforms.

In the metal industry, the chemical industry and the public sector the old wage bargaining system still exists in a modified way. However, companies have been granted more flexibility to alter industry-wide negotiations. Work councils have become more powerful in negotiation processes and a more firm-based logic of wage development has been developing (Gerlach and Meyer 2010). In addition, independent unions of small groups and professions like airline pilots, hospital doctors or engine drivers have gained strength and have been able to increase wages above the average wage increase. Nominal wage increases in the modified old traditional wage sector has remained low but positive. But, as mentioned, the signalling effect to all sectors has broken down.

Around 40 per cent of German employees are not covered by wage bargaining. As statutory minimum wages do not exist, these employees live under a type of Manchester capitalism without any protection. In 1998, 76 per cent of all employees in West Germany were covered by collective agreements; by 2007 this percentage had declined to 63 per cent. During the same period of time the coverage in East Germany decreased from 63 to 54 per cent (Bispinck and Schulten 2009: 203).

Tables 3.6 and 3.7 show to what extent the reforms and the weakness of labour market institutions in Germany increased wage dispersions. Employees in the increasing low-wage sectors have had to accept substantial cuts in nominal and real wages. The wage dispersion stimulated outsourcing from high-wage sectors to low-wage sectors and precarious jobs. There should be no surprise why consumption demand as well as production has stagnated in Germany.

Table 3.6 Nominal and real hourly wages in Germany in Euro, 1995–2006

	Nominal hourly wages (average)			*Change in nominal hourly wages in %*		*Real wages (in 1995 prices)*	
	1995	*2000*	*2006*	*1995–2000*	*2000–2006*	*Real wages 2006*	*Change 1995–2006 (%)*
1st quartile	6.84	7.23	6.88	5.8	–4.8	5.90	–13.7
2nd quartile	10.39	11.15	11.73	7.3	5.2	10.06	–3.2
3rd quartile	13.11	14.49	16.02	10.5	10.6	13.74	4.8
4th quartile	21.20	22.79	25.58	7.5	12.3	21.94	3.5
Overall	12.88	13.91	15.05	8.0	8.2	12.90	0.2

Source: Bosch *et al.* (2008: 425).

Table 3.7 Share of low, mean and high hourly wages in per cent in Germany, 1995–2006[1]

	1995	*2000*	*2006*
Low (less than 2/3 of median)	15.0	17.5	22.2
Mean (2/3 to 4/3 of median)	63.2	59.0	51.6
High (more than 4/3 of median)	21.8	23.6	26.3

Source: Bosch *et al.* (2008: 425).

Note
1 All employees. Separated calculations for median of East and West Germany.

3.3.5 Monetary policy

With the end of the Bretton Woods System, which imposed an obligation for the central bank to stabilise the exchange rate, the German Bundesbank switched to monetary targeting and followed this monetary policy strategy until the beginning of the EMU. From its formation as an independent central bank after the Second World War it had made it clear that price level stability was the dominant target for monetary policy. In the 1950s and 1960s this policy did not restrict growth as the Bundesbank could count on a coordinated wage bargaining process with overall low increases in unit labour costs which were in line with the inflation target of the Bundesbank. Also monetary policy was not so much focused on price level stability during that time.

Monetary targeting by the Bundesbank cannot be compared with the period of monetary targeting under Paul Volcker at the end of the 1970s in the US. The Bundesbank used monetary targeting more as a communication tool with the public, but to a large degree followed a pragmatic monetary policy. A clear sign of this is that in half of the years between 1974 and 1998 the central bank missed its target. However, the Bundesbank, in comparison for example with the Fed, was quick to increase refinancing rates in cases of inflationary danger and reduced interest rates only relatively slowly even when the inflationary danger was over (Emminger 1986; Spahn 1988; Herr and Spahn 1989; Bofinger 2001).

The recessions in 1974/1975, 1981/1982 and 1992/1993 were all clearly induced by a restrictive monetary policy (Figure 3.15). Restrictive monetary policy in 1974 is understandable and prevented Germany from facing the same fate that so many other countries had encountered in the 1970s when they were caught in an inflationary spiral. The 1981/1982 case is not that clear. First of all, during the late 1970s the Bundesbank followed the very restrictive monetary policy in the US to prevent an even stronger depreciation of the D-Mark against the US dollar. However, in 1981 restrictive monetary policy was intensified as a reaction to a weakness of the D-Mark within the EMS. In this period it might have been possible to accept a weaker D-Mark in the EMS for an exchange of higher growth because there was no danger of inflation. Monetary policy in 1992/1993 was definitely too restrictive and led to unnecessary growth and employment

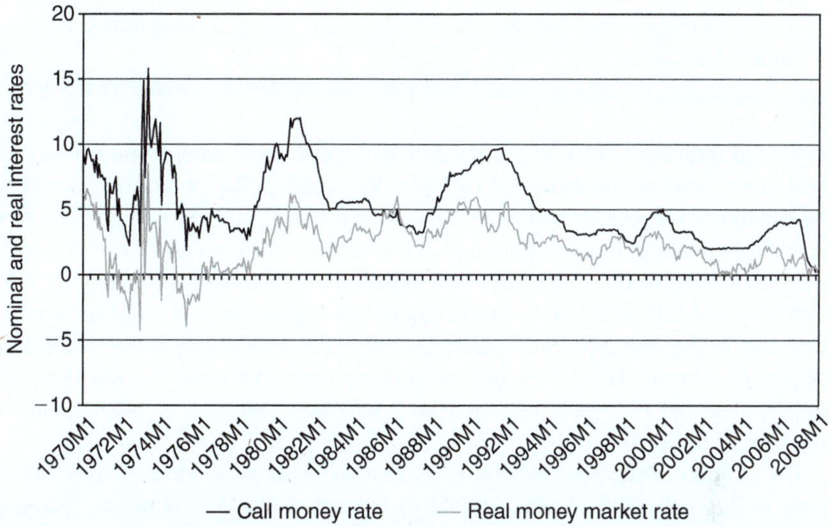

Figure 3.15 Nominal and real money market interest rates in Germany, 1970–2009 (real rate: nominal minus change in CPI), (source: IMF 2010d).

losses. From the beginning of 1991 for 36 months long-term interest rates were lower than the short-term ones. This inverse interest rate structure for such a long time shows how restrictive monetary policy was in that period. Even as early as 1992 it was clear that the unification boom would soon be over and the moderate inflation rates would go down. In spite of this the Bundesbank increased interest rates further and triggered the EMS crisis as the UK, for example, was already in a crisis and was not prepared to increase interest rates even further to follow the policy of the Bundesbank. The UK left the EMS and other countries, for example France, were only able to remain in the EMS because exchange rates were allowed to float ±15 per cent around the central rate. There is the temptation to argue that the Bundesbank wanted to disrupt the EMS in the hope that the already planned EMU could not be realised.

Monetary policy was transferred in 1999 to the European Central Bank (ECB). In its first monthly bulletin the ECB presented its theoretical approach towards monetary policy (ECB 1999). The ECB defined price stability as an inflation rate between 0 and 2 per cent which should be realised in the medium term. For monetary policy a two-pillar strategy was chosen. The first pillar was based on traditional monetarism and considered to be the more important one. M3 should increase according to a so-called reference value with a constant rate of 4.5 per cent per annum. The second pillar followed a completely different approach.

> In parallel with the analysis of monetary growth in relation to the reference value, a broadly based assessment of the outlook for price developments and

risks to price stability in the euro area will play a major role in the Eurosystem's strategy. This assessment will be made using a wide range of economic indicators.

(ECB 1999: 49)

Suggested indicators were wage developments, exchange rates, bond prices and yield curve, various measures of real activity, fiscal policy indicators, business and consumer surveys and so on. This second pillar of monetary policy has discretionary character in the tradition of John Maynard Keynes and Knut Wicksell and has nothing to do with traditional monetarism. The two-pillar strategy was confusing and followed two contradicting policy approaches – a monetarist monetary rule in the first pillar and a discretionary monetary policy in the second. It appears that the ECB in 1999 defined a compromise between the old Bundesbank strategy of monetary targeting and policies suggested by other member countries of the EMU.

The official acceptance by the ECB that the two-pillar strategy had failed came in 2003. In 2001 in the middle of a deep crisis M3 started to increase sharply and continued to increase well above the reference value of 4.5 per cent until the subprime crisis broke out. During the crisis households switched from long-term investment in stocks, debt securities and so on to short-term liquidity. Such portfolio shifts between 'long' and 'short' which affect M3 should have been expected. In the following years when the economy in the euro area recovered M3 continued to increase well above the reference value of 4.5 per cent because of the strong credit expansion. Real expansion in the euro area was moderate and the ECB could almost perfectly realise its inflation target. Finally, in 2003 it was clear that the ECB could not follow M3 targeting. In that year in spite of high M3 growth in the euro area Germany suffered from the danger of deflation; an increase of interest rates which was signalled by the monetarist pillar was simply not possible. The ECB (2003) revised its strategy. First, the inflation target was now defined close to but below 2 per cent. An inflation rate close to 0 per cent was now considered dangerous. Second, the first pillar, the monetary pillar, became the second pillar without any direct relevance for economic policy. Actually, M3 became one indicator for monetary policy among many others (Heine and Herr 2008).

In spite of moderate GDP growth and the absence of inflationary pressure in the euro area in the years 1999 and 2000 the ECB increased refinancing rates following interest rate increases in the US in this period (see Figure 3.15). Higher interest rates in the euro area have to be seen as a reaction to the weak euro, which had depreciated around 20 per cent against the US dollar between 1999 and 2000. The ECB felt that 'the exchange rate of the euro (had) moved out of line with the sound fundamentals of the euro area' (ECB 2001: 85). In autumn 2000 on the initiative of the ECB a concerted intervention in the foreign exchange markets took place by the monetary authorities of the EMU, the US, Japan and the UK. In November 2000 the ECB intervened again to strengthen the euro (ECB 2001: 85). This is a clear sign that the ECB was worried about the weakness of the euro and cared about the exchange rate.[32] Interventions in the foreign exchange markets and higher interest rates in the euro area stopped the depreciation of the euro vis-à-vis the US dollar. This episode is a good example which shows that flexible exchange rates do not automatically increase the national power to follow a domestically oriented monetary policy. Even such a strong currency area like the EMU cannot neglect the nominal exchange rate.

During the year 2001 the economic situation changed as the US headed towards recession. The Fed cut interest rates in several steps from above 6 per cent to below 2 per cent. In this phase the ECB showed for the first time that it would not react to weak GDP growth as quickly and strongly as the Fed and would more or less follow the very cautious policy in the tradition of the Bundesbank. Of course, it should be mentioned that the ECB has a one-goal strategy – price level stability – and is only expected to support other targets if the goal of price level stability is fully realised.

In the years that followed, monetary policy by the ECB adhered to a rather cautious strategy. Opportunities for interest rate cuts were not used even when the euro appreciated strongly against the US dollar by nearly 30 per cent. According to the ECB there was no need to cut interest rates as the inflation rate in the euro area was always around the target of 2 per cent. When the subprime crisis hit the world in 2007 the ECB cut interest rates, as before, very late and hesitantly. However, when the crisis escalated the ECB reacted with very low interest rates and fulfilled its function as lender of last resort to satisfy the liquidity needs of banks when the money market also broke down in Europe.

3.3.6 Fiscal policy

In the 1950s and 1960s high growth rates and low unemployment had led to low budget deficits or in some years even to budget surpluses in Germany. Slight economic slowdowns, as experienced in the middle of the 1960s, were stabilised with active fiscal policy. Since there was a rapid return to high growth and high employment, new debt remained low. This constellation changed with the economic recession of 1975, the first deep economic slowdown after the Second World War in Germany. Despite a fiscal policy that accepted automatic stabilisers and used discretionary additional expenditures, growth rates in general became lower than in the decades before. Public households could not be balanced in the upswing that developed in the second half of the 1970s. In the early 1980s anti-cyclical fiscal policy was carried out again. The consequence was a return to rapidly rising budget deficits throughout the first half of the 1980s (the highest of 3.5 per cent of GDP in 1981). However, the economic recovery as well as subsequent efforts to balance the budget were the reason that budget deficits oscillated between a mere 1 and 2 per cent of GDP in the second half of the 1980s. Small surpluses were even achieved in 1989. Thus, the budget balancing process in the 1980s was more successful in Germany than, for example, in the US or in most of the other EU-12 countries, which had budget deficits of between 4 and 5 per cent throughout the 1980s (see Figure 3.16 and Table 3.8).

Table 3.8 Fiscal policy indicators for Germany, 1971–2008 (average growth rates over the business cycle, unless mentioned otherwise)

Business cycles	*1971–1975*	*1976–1982*	*1983–1993*	*1994–2003*	*2004–2008*
Nominal GDP growth	8.88	6.58	6.73	2.48	2.90
Total expenditures	14.17	6.17	6.67	2.58	0.85
Discretionary expenditure indicator	12.80	5.96	6.42	1.62	1.48
Government consumption	14.55	6.72	6.40	2.29	1.63
Government investment	6.33	1.64	5.95	–2.86	1.86
Subsidies	13.45	6.56	7.76	–0.24	–0.96
Social benefits	15.88	6.32	6.76	4.03	–0.29
Total revenues	11.19	6.91	6.73	2.32	2.57
Social security contributions	14.59	7.87	7.18	2.82	0.59
Direct taxes	11.08	6.63	6.21	1.88	4.55
Direct taxes, cyclically adjusted	11.78	7.46	6.15	1.88	3.39
Indirect taxes	6.95	6.22	6.74	3.03	4.08
Indirect taxes cyclically adjusted	8.28	6.32	6.65	3.00	3.34
Budget balance (% of GDP)[2]	–1.26	–3.06	–1.92	–3.08	–1.79
Budget balance, cyclical adjusted (% of GDP)[2]	–3.73	–4.27	–1.73	–3.07	–1.86

Source: OECD 2009c.

Note
1 Government consumption, government investment and subsidies.
2 Average size over the business cycle.

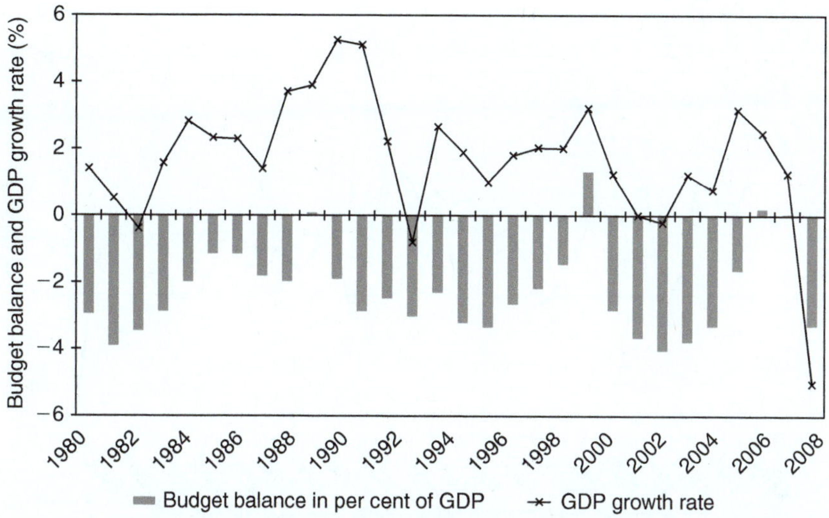

Figure 3.16 Budget balance in percentage of GDP and GDP growth rate in Germany, 1970–2009 (source: OECD 2009c, authors' calculations).

The budget balancing process at the end of the 1980s came to an abrupt halt with German unification. Because of unification, social expenditure, costs for building up public infrastructure in East Germany, tax incentives for private investment in East Germany and so on had to be financed. Between 1991 and 1994 public investment increased sharply (see Figure 3.17). In addition to this, Germany contributed to the costs of the first Gulf War and the withdrawal of Soviet troops from Germany. As a consequence budget deficits rose rapidly up until 1995. Government expenditures as a share of GDP rose from about 40 per cent of GDP in the year 1989 to approximately 56 per cent of GDP in 1995 (Figure 3.16). In the early 1990s this happened in spite of a booming economy in West Germany with inflationary tendencies.

The federal Government tried rather tentatively at first to master these financial challenges by increasing certain taxes and cutting certain expenditures. Last but not least, social insurance contributions of employees were increased substantially to stabilise the social security systems, which ran into financial difficulties after East Germany had been integrated into the German systems.[33] This brief outline shows that fiscal policy endeavours at the beginning of the post-unification period were insufficient and unable to cover the financial costs of unification by means of additional tax revenues. The government also had overly optimistic expectations for future growth in East Germany, which contrasted considerably with opinions of many economists (Heine *et al.* 1990; Westphal *et al.* 1991). All in all, fiscal policy did not achieve a balance in bearing the costs of German unification equitably amongst all social groups. Employees

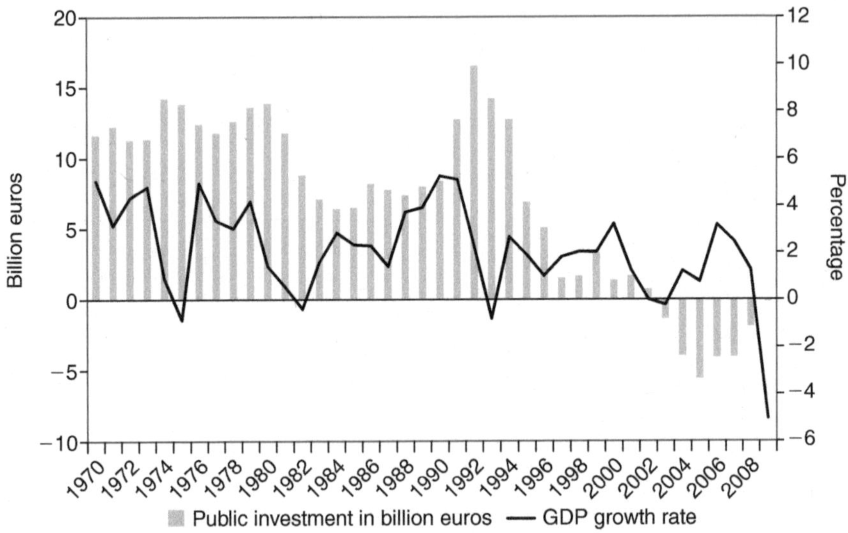

Figure 3.17 Net public investment in billion euros at 2000 prices and GDP growth rate in Germany, 1970–2009 (source: AMECO 2010).

liable to compulsory social insurance have had to carry a particularly high financial burden. Additionally, it must be kept in mind that the tax reforms of 1986, 1988 and 1990 had also favoured higher-income groups. In the early 1990s, the German Institute for Economic Research came to the understandable and valid conclusion that from the beginning the state had made few demands on the West with regard to making sacrifices in the course of unification. It also failed to dismantle privileges and subsidies during the economic boom in West Germany which was brought about by the unification process. Finally, it burdened wages with a one-sided and hardly justifiable tax policy. This repeatedly put the social consensus into question (see Flassbeck 1992).

Budget deficits were reduced gradually from the middle of the 1990s to the end of the decade and in the year 2000 even a small surplus was achieved. Policies to reduce budget deficits were at least partly enforced by the Maastricht Treaty of 1990 which allowed only countries with a budget deficit of below 3 per cent of GDP to join the EMU. According to the Maastricht Treaty the deficit in the year 1997 was taken into account because in 1998 the decision was made to select countries to be allowed to join the EMU in 1999. The Maastricht Treaty, however, had no sanctioning mechanism for deficits after 1997. Germany pushed for the Stability and Growth Pact which was passed in 1997 and contained a sanctioning mechanism if a member country of the EMU were to exceed a budget deficit of more than 3 per cent of GDP. Consolidation of the budget was achieved in Germany by decreasing public investment (Figure 3.17) and by reducing employment in the public sector, which dropped by about half a million from 1993 to 1998. At the same time wage increases in the public sector were below the average (between 1993 and 1998, wage increases in the public sector were 10 per cent compared with 15 per cent in the whole economy) (Teichmann and Vesper 1999). There were also cuts in state social expenditure in the middle of the 1990s (for example, the conditions to be eligible for unemployment benefits became stricter and unemployment benefits were lowered).

In 2000 as part of financial reforms the tax burden of companies was substantially reduced. At the same time public unification costs remained high. Under this condition budget deficits increased sharply with the economic downturn in 2001. As GDP growth remained poor and given the above factors, from 2002 to 2004 budget deficits were above the 3 per cent limit of the Stability and Growth Pact requirements. Taxes were again lowered in 2005 based on the argument that growth and employment should be increased whereas at the same time there was an attempt to consolidate the budget. This is shown in the radical reduction of public investment to very low levels (see Figure 3.17).

When the subprime crisis hit Germany, budget deficits again exceeded the 3 per cent limit of the Stability and Growth Pact – but compared with most other European countries and the US only moderately. In 2008 and early 2009 Germany at first hesitated to use stimulus packages to stabilise the sharp recession in 2009. Then, however, a relatively coordinated fiscal stimulus took place in the EMU which effectively stabilised production and employment in Europe. In 2010 with the outbreak of the debt crisis in Greece and other EMU countries a wave of budget consolidation measures was implemented also in Germany. This policy was definitely too early for a quick or medium-term recovery from the deep crisis that followed the financial disaster in 2007 and 2008.

All in all, fiscal policy in the 1970s and 1980s was basically anti-cyclically oriented. This changed in the early 1990s after German unification. At first, sizeable budget deficits were allowed, driven partly by high public investment even in a period of a booming economy in the West. Fiscal policy was obviously procyclical in this economic phase. Actually, it came to a clash between very expansionary fiscal policy and relatively high wage increase on the one hand and monetary policy on the other hand, whereas the latter stopped the unification boom in 1992/1993. It would have been better to have financed German unification by tax increases and by cuts in subsidies in West Germany. Quick tax increases would also have dampened the demand inflation in West Germany. However, this opportunity was wasted as the Kohl government argued that unification would be possible without substantial burdens.

When the crisis of 1992/1993 was over fiscal policy was immediately oriented towards stabilisation in order to limit further budget deficits. In this phase of economic development it would have been better to maintain expansionary fiscal policy at least in the early phase of recovery in order to give recovery a sufficient impulse. In this phase too early fiscal stabilisation also reinforced by the pressure resulting from the Maastricht Treaty hindered economic recovery (Vesper 2000: 623). In the recession of 2001 and also in the following years no ideal active fiscal policy was followed. Tax reduction for firms and high income groups were paramount and demand effects of these policies were poor. Automatic stabilisers were not allowed to work completely as this would have meant higher budget deficits in the short term. This was not accepted, not least, because of the fear of breaking the Stability and Growth Pact. Taxes were frequently cut and then attempts were made to lower public expenditure. This is most prominently shown in the collapse of public investment in Germany after the first phase of unification. During the 2008/2009 crisis fiscal stimulation was at first anti-cyclical. But in this phase, too, budget consolidation started much too early and tax cuts added to the budget deficit without sufficiently stimulating demand and output. All in all, after unification Germany did not follow a clearly defined anti-cyclical fiscal policy which includes the medium-term stabilisation of discretionary expenditures. In some periods fiscal policy was pro-cyclical, always consolidating too early after recessions. Also the way taxes were cut did not allow for sufficient demand effects.

3.3.7 Germany and the EMU

The creation of the EMU on 1 January 1999 marks a structural break for the member countries of the monetary union. Monetary policy was transferred to the ECB and even more important nominal exchange rate adjustments were no longer possible. Usually, at least in history, monetary unions and states are identical. In the EMU this is not the case. The budget of the central level of the EU compared for example with the budget of the federal state in the US, not a very centralised country, is minuscule and has only the budget volume of a larger German regional state. There are for example no taxes directly levied by the EMU centre. Tax systems, social security systems, labour market institutions and wage bargaining processes are markedly different in the various EMU countries. Indeed the EMU is a unique historical experiment offering the chance to create a prosperous and politically strong Europe, but also with the danger of becoming a monetary union with deep regional problems, economic stagnation and political instability.

Let us look at the role of Germany in the EMU. Since its creation the EMU has had a relatively balanced trade and current account balance. But since the EMU came into being, Germany, Austria, Finland and The Netherlands have built up record trade and current account surpluses, whereas especially the southern members of the EMU have realised huge deficits in the trade and current account balance (Table 3.9). Germany, as the biggest economy in the EMU, has become a burden to the EMU as it increasingly exports unemployment to other EMU countries which are the most important German trade partners.

The imbalances reflect strongly diverging developments within the EMU. In recent years, while in countries such as Ireland, Spain or Greece demand was driven primarily by domestic consumption and a construction boom, economic growth in Germany was based almost exclusively on strong export growth and corporate investments in the export sector. Behind the huge regional imbalances within the EMU are first of all different developments of unit labour costs. Table 3.10

Table 3.9 Trade and current account balances of selected EMU countries (% of GDP), 1999–2008

		1999	*2000*	*2001*	*2002*	*2003*	*2004*	*2005*	*2006*	*2007*	*2008*
Euro Zone	TB	1	1	1	3	2	2	2	1	2	1
	CAB	0	0	0	1	0	1	0	0	0	–1
Belgium	TB	4	3	4	5	4	4	4	3	3	–1
	CAB	5	4	4	5	4	4	3	3	2	–2
Germany	TB	1	0	2	5	4	5	5	6	7	6
	CAB	–1	–2	0	2	2	5	5	6	8	7
Ireland	TB	14	13	16	17	16	15	12	11	11	12
	CAB	0	0	0	0	1	0	–3	–3	–5	–5
Greece	TB	–8	–13	–13	–14	–13	–10	–9	–9	–10	–9
	CAB	–5	–12	–11	–13	–13	–10	–11	–11	–14	–13
Spain	TB	–2	–3	–3	–2	–2	–4	–5	–6	–7	–6
	CAB	–3	–4	–4	–4	–4	–6	–7	–9	–10	–10
France	TB	2	1	1	2	1	0	–1	–1	–2	–3
	CAB	2	1	1	1	0	–1	–2	–2	–3	–4
Italy	TB	2	1	1	1	1	1	0	–1	0	0
	CAB	1	0	0	0	–1	–1	–1	–2	–2	–3
Netherlands	TB	4	6	6	7	6	7	9	8	9	8
	CAB	4	6	5	6	6	9	7	10	10	6
Austria	TB	1	2	2	5	4	4	4	5	6	5
	CAB	–1	–1	–1	3	2	2	2	3	3	3
Portugal	TB	–10	–11	–10	–8	–7	–8	–9	–8	–7	–9
	CAB	–9	–11	–10	–8	–6	–8	–10	–10	–10	–12
Finland	TB	10	10	10	9	7	7	4	5	5	4
	CAB	8	8	9	9	5	7	4	5	4	2

Source: AMECO (2010).

Note
TB: trade balance, CAB: current account balance, plus means a surplus.

Table 3.10 Development of nominal unit labour costs in selected EMU countries, 1999–2008, (2000 = 100)

	1999	*2000*	*2001*	*2002*	*2003*	*2004*	*2005*	*2006*	*2007*	*2008*	*1999–2008*
All EMU countries	98.8	100.0	102.4	105.0	107.3	108.3	109.7	110.9	112.8	116.5	17.7
Belgium	99.7	100.0	104.3	106.5	107.3	106.9	108.5	110.3	113.4	117.7	17.9
Germany	99.3	100.0	100.9	101.8	102.8	102.6	101.8	100.6	101.0	103.1	3.8
Ireland	96.7	100.0	104.6	105.1	108.4	112.5	117.7	121.5	125.9	134.7	38.0
Greece	98.8	100.0	99.7	109.8	110.4	113.1	116.4	114.8	122.0	128.9	30.2
Spain	97.2	100.0	103.2	106.2	109.3	112.0	115.6	119.4	122.8	127.0	29.8
France	98.9	100.0	102.3	105.3	107.1	108.3	110.2	112.4	114.7	117.7	18.9
Italy	99.5	100.0	103.1	106.8	111.5	113.8	116.9	119.4	121.3	126.4	26.8
Netherlands	97.1	100.0	105.0	110.1	113.1	113.3	112.9	113.9	116.3	120.3	23.1
Austria	100.1	100.0	101.4	101.6	103.0	102.4	103.2	104.3	105.1	108.3	8.1
Portugal	95.7	100.0	103.8	107.3	111.3	112.4	116.2	117.7	119.2	123.5	27.8
Finland	99.1	100.0	103.4	104.7	105.8	106.1	108.6	108.4	109.9	116.7	17.6

Source: AMECO (2010).

illustrates that between 1995 and 2008 unit labour costs rose only minimally in Germany. Indeed, between 2004 and 2006, unit labour costs even fell. In Italy, Greece, Spain, Portugal or Ireland, by contrast, labour costs rose rapidly, while France for example was slightly above the EMU average. The overall differences in the development of unit labour costs are enormous and have fundamentally changed the price competitiveness of these countries. German wage increases were much too low as Germany violated the wage norm of nominal annual wage increases according to trend productivity plus the target rate of inflation. Thus the misguided German wage development became not only a problem for Germany, but it added substantially to regional incoherence of the EMU. At the same time wage increases in some of the EMU countries were much too high. The drama of the situation is given by the fact that within the EMU exchange rate adjustments are no longer possible to balance regional imbalances.

If wages increase in one country more strongly than in the rest of the EMU, it means two things: on the one hand, that country will lose competitiveness and on the other, the domestic inflation rate will rise because production costs will increase for non-tradable goods and services and producers will pass on these higher costs to consumers. The uniform nominal interest rate fixed by the ECB for the entire EMU represents a lower real interest rate in the country with a higher national inflation rate. The lower real interest rate works primarily to stimulate the real estate market and the construction sector. This effect led in the EMU to real estate booms in some of the deficit countries which disguised the loss of competitiveness. With the subprime crisis the real estate bubbles in the EMU came to end and with it the growth engine in the current account deficit countries. The regional distortions in the EMU became open.

In order to avoid changing regional price competitiveness, nominal wages in each region should increase according to the regional productivity trend plus the target inflation rate in the monetary union. However, it is not very likely that the market process in the EMU would create regional wage developments according to such a regional wage norm. Established and functioning labour market institutions and coordination and monitoring mechanisms in the whole monetary union are needed to gear regional wage development towards the regional wage norm. In the EMU no such mechanism exists. The EMU countries have different labour market institutions which reduce the chances of wage coordination. There are no European unions and no European employers' associations which could coordinate wages. Some countries have more centralised wage bargaining systems, while others have systems that are more decentralised. There are countries with relatively high union density and others with low union density; some have higher employment protection, some only low protection; some have minimum wages, some do not and so on.

Besides wages there is the problem of fiscal policy. It is highly questionable whether a monetary union without a strong economic centre can enjoy growth-promoting fiscal policy. So far the Stability and Growth Pact has been a failure. It has added to pro-cyclical fiscal behaviour. In spite of frequent attempts to reduce budget deficits in a crisis many EMU countries have violated the rules of the pact for many years. The weakness of the Pact also became clear after the outbreak of the subprime crisis when Greece and other countries in the EMU realised double digit budget deficits which reflect the lack of demand last but not least because of their huge current account deficits. For growth-promoting fiscal policy, EMU taxes such as a fraction of the value-added tax or income tax, and the right at the central fiscal level to carry out active fiscal policy by deficit spending and realising budget surpluses are needed. EMU taxes are also needed to strengthen the financial power of the European centre. Today, the central budget is too small to support economic coherence in the EMU, especially if the aim of the EMU is the creation of more or less equal living conditions in the member states. Finally, to support economic and social coherence there should be a basic EMU welfare state, a common tax system to prevent competition in tax cuts and so on.

In 2010 the EMU has chosen a fiscal coordination in the way that the countries in the biggest crises, the countries with high deficits in the current account and in the public budget are forced to follow very restrictive fiscal policy, whereas the surplus countries and especially Germany follow restrictive fiscal policy too. Such policies in the middle of a deep economic crisis reflect strong pro-cyclical fiscal policy which will deepen the crisis and delay recovery.

3.3.8 Summary

The German macroeconomic policy regime in the 1990s and thereafter cannot be considered growth promoting under any circumstances. Especially the economic and political shock of German unification in the 1990s and the following neoliberal reforms changed the German macroeconomic policy regime fundamentally. With its incoherent macroeconomic policy Germany became one of the key problems for the stability of the euro area.

Monetary policy by the Bundesbank as later by the ECB was conducted too restrictively in many periods compared for example with the Fed. Phases of high interest rates were maintained for too long, as the monetary reaction during the crisis in 1992/1993, after 2001 and 2007/2008 indicate. Interest rates were increased even as production was already declining, as for example in the middle of 1992. Cuts in interest rates were carried out too tentatively by both the Bundesbank and later by the ECB, which more or less copied the monetary policy strategy of the Bundesbank.

Fiscal policy in Germany was even more problematic than monetary policy. For example, at the beginning of the 1990s fiscal policy operated strongly pro-cyclically reflecting at least partly a misled macroeconomic policy of German unification which did not immediately increase taxes to finance the unification burden. In some periods the efforts to stabilise the budget were undertaken too quickly when the economy was not yet out of the crisis. Automatic stabilisers were undermined by fighting against budget deficits in periods of low growth. Under fiscal perspectives the collapse of public investment after the mid-1990s in Germany must be seen as growth and welfare reducing. Additionally, fiscal policy was often based on a perceived necessity to cut taxes, especially for firms and the rich. At the same time Germany was not able to finance public expenditures in a sound way and prevent a long-term increase of public debt to GDP.

Wage policy and neoliberal labour market policies were a disaster in Germany. After the first phase of German unification nominal wage increases were too low and even created deflationary dangers, for example between 2001 and 2004. German wage development became one of the key disturbing factors for the EMU as it has no viable mechanism to solve the problem of different regional developments of unit labour costs. In Germany, which does not have statutory minimum wages, neoliberal labour market reforms led to an extremely quick and widening wage dispersion and to an increase in precarious jobs. Distribution in Germany also changed because of a falling wage share of income. The outcome has been stagnant consumption demand and low GDP growth.

The benefits of a mercantilist policy approach for a relatively large developed country like Germany is questionable for at least three reasons. First, Germany, like Japan, is in danger of subordinating its wage development with the intention of increasing international competitiveness. Deflationary dangers are created, especially when export successes fail to produce a satisfactory economic expansion. Second, the orientation towards export and current account surpluses makes a country dependent on world market developments. In 2009, Germany was one of the most affected countries after the subprime crisis with an annual GDP growth rate of minus 4.9 per cent. Third, the high German surpluses force member countries in the EMU to deflationary policy which could lead to the demise of the currency union. Thus, it would be undoubtedly better for the coherence of the EMU and the world economy if Germany would stimulate its domestic market to trigger growth and even accept moderate current account deficits.

Germany has remained below its economic possibilities since it was not able to create an optimal macroeconomic policy regime. Because of the nature of its institutions, Germany would have had the potential to achieve a growth-promoting interaction between monetary, fiscal and wage policies. However, in terms of process policy as well as Ordnungspolitik the economic shock of German unification was not managed in an optimal way. On the contrary, the neoliberal reforms that followed did not solve the problems of the German economy, they intensified them. In the EMU Germany was also unable to find a policy suitable for a monetary union. Taking all of these points together it is no surprise that economic development in Germany has been one of the worst of all industrial countries throughout the past two decades.

3.4 The Japanese deflation

3.4.1 Overview of political and economic development

Japan is an interesting case as it is a country showing high growth performance from the Second World War until the end of the 1980s which then was interrupted by an asset price deflation. Growth after the bubble has remained sluggish. Before the late 1970s Japan had been a highly regulated economy, the core country of the East Asian Miracle (Stiglitz 1996), which can be referred to as an Asian type of capitalism. The economic model was built on the basis of a broad consensus and strong links among all economic sectors. It was remarkable that the strong informal ties between suppliers and buyers, between banks and companies (within the so-called house bank system), between the Ministry of Finance, the Bank of Japan and the private banks secured an undisrupted development. The financial system was highly regulated and used for industrial policy. Nationwide wage coordination was basically organised by employers' associations whereas firm-based unions usually accepted management's offers (Soskice 1990). Income distribution was exceptionally equal during the Japanese miracle.

One element of the system was the export orientation which affected all levels of policy. In the first decades after the Second World War Japan used high tariff and non-tariff barriers to control trade und implement a development-oriented industrial policy. After Japan joined the OECD in 1966 pressure to liberalise foreign trade increased. However, the Japanese government took only gradual steps in the process of trade liberalisation and until today protects some sectors (for example the agricultural sector) and uses non-tariff barriers to influence the structure of trade.

The country was almost completely governed by the conservative Liberal Democratic Party (LDP) from the party's founding in 1955 until its defeat in the 2009 elections. The LDP was only out of power for 11 months when opposition parties created a coalition after the election in 1993. This one-party rule also seemed to have paved the way for the rigidity of institutional reforms and the inertia of the government towards a more aggressive change in institutions in the aftermath of the collapse of the asset price bubble and the recession and long stagnation that followed.

In the 1980s, Japan experienced big institutional changes. Beginning from 1979 the government started an agenda for the liberalisation of financial markets and foreign trade, when capital controls were also being gradually removed. To some extent these changes reflected international pressure (for example from signing the Louvre and Plaza Agreement, see below). The government also envisioned making Tokyo a big financial centre, like London or New York, and creating a new model closer to that of the US by means of increasing competition and financial innovation in the financial market.

The pace at which Japan managed to re-build its economy, economic growth and productivity increases achieved after the Second World War was remarkable and earns the right to be labelled a miracle. From 1960 to the first big oil price shock in 1973 Japan reached an average growth of more than 9 per cent, which turned out to be the highest growth in all OECD countries coupled with very low unemployment rates, a success that Japan could never achieve in the consecutive years that followed. In 1974 the Japanese economy fell into recession, but recovered quickly. Also, Japan was not affected by the world recession in 1981/1982. But in the early 1990s the positive development changed abruptly and Japan fell into a prolonged period of stagnation with an average growth in the 1990s and 2000s of barely 1 per cent (Figure 3.18 and Table 3.11).

It is worth emphasising that up to the 1970s high Japanese growth was combined with a more or less balanced current account. The Japanese government actively followed a policy to avoid current account deficits (see Herr 1990). Since the 1970s Japan realised current account surpluses which increased to a level of between 3 and 4 per cent of GDP for decades (Figure 2.12).

In the 1980s high growth based on an investment boom in construction as well as in the wholesale and retail sector was combined with an asset price bubble in the real estate sector and in stock markets and low consumer price inflation. As already mentioned, the fall into recession after the bubble bust in the early 1990s brought about a break in this development. Domestic demand lost its dynamic. Consumption demand, usually a driving force for demand also in periods of low investment, became very weak as well as investment demand. Government demand also did not compensate the loss of domestic private demand. Current account surpluses were high, but could not be sufficiently increased to trigger satisfactory growth. The collapse in consumption and investment demand continued to be Japan's Achilles' heel from the end of the bubble until today. Unemployment rates in Japan increased slowly after the break in the early 1990s and reached levels unknown in Japan the decades before.

In the early 1970s Japan had an inflation problem as the oil price shock in 1973 led to a wage–price spiral. This inflationary period quickly came to an end when nominal wages started to increase in line with the wage norm. As early as the 1980s inflation rates in Japan became very low. After the mid-1990s Japan

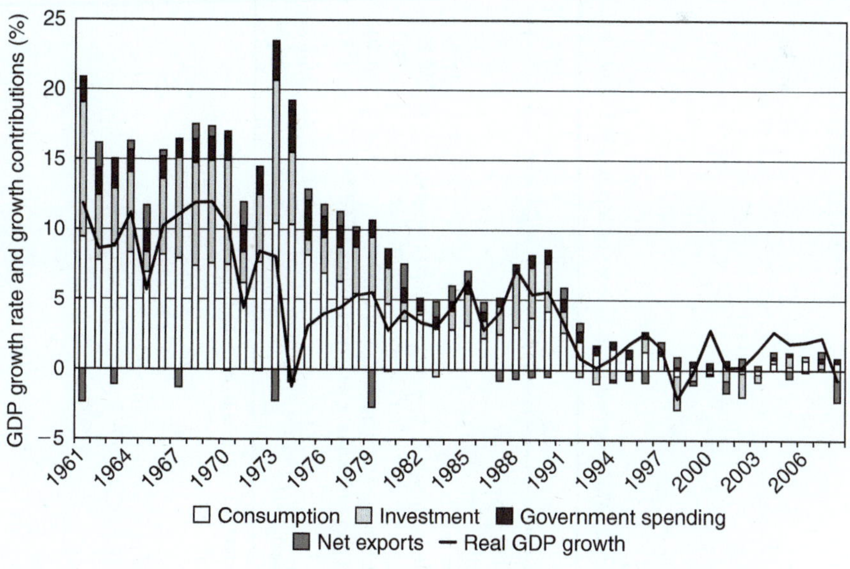

Figure 3.18 GDP growth and growth contributions of its components in Japan in per cent, 1961–2008 (source: AMECO 2010, authors' calculation).

Table: 3.11 Macroeconomic indicators of Japan, 1971–2009 (average values over the business cycle)

	1971–1974	*1975–1986*	*1987–1993*	*1994–1999*	*2000–2009*
Real GDP growth rate	4.90	4.11	3.79	0.79	0.72
Unemployment rate	1.33	2.29	2.33	3.60	4.74
Inflation rate (CPI)	11.54	4.95	1.78	0.47	–0.23
Percentage change in nominal unit labour costs	14.42	3.18	0.90	–0.33	–1.68
Percentage change in real wage per employee	7.07	2.74	2.11	0.98	0.54
Budget balances as percentage of GDP	0.49	–3.55	0.60	–6.17	–5.73
Current account balance as a percentage of GDP	0.96	1.28	2.52	2.37	3.19
	Mid-1980s	*1990*	*Mid-1990s*	*2000*	*Mid-2000s*
Gini coefficient	0.304	–	0.323	0.337	0.321

Source: AMECO 2010, author's calculations.

slipped into a long-lasting deflationary development which became a serious burden for Japanese development.

3.4.2 Developments in the financial system

Traditionally, the financial sector in Japan was structured as a bank-based, highly regulated system (Stiglitz and Uy 1996). The main source of funding for firms was banks, whereby a very small share of credit was raised through the capital market, the latter being poorly developed. The Japanese banks were heavily regulated and supervised by the Ministry of Finance and the Bank of Japan within the so-called convoy system. This means, first, the Ministry of Finance had very close and often informal links to financial institutions. A big part of credit allocation was influenced by policy decision (Amyx 2004: 61–104). Second, the Bank of Japan was not independent but a department of the Ministry of Finance. Furthermore, the Policy Board, the highest decision-making body of the central bank, was staffed mostly by officials from the Ministry of Finance (Cukierman 1992: 396–411; Tachi 1993: 73). Under this system, not only banks' liquidity but also their solvency was implicitly guaranteed by the government. Banks were willing to build long-term credit relationships with firms and keep big share packages of large companies. Firms in this environment were safeguarded from being cut off from credit markets, realised very high debt quotas (see Table 2.1) and followed the 'high debt model' typical for Asian countries (Wade and Veneroso 1998). Part of the model was also the long-term relations in the labour market with job guarantees for a majority of employees (Aoki 2001).

The types of business that banks and other financial institutions could engage in were harshly restricted under the Banking Law of 1927 and Article 65 of Japan's Securities and Exchange Law of 1948.[34] The real estate market was also a specific segment of the financial system and only certain financial institutions (called jusen, cooperatives established as subsidiaries of banks, brokerages and insurance companies specialising in real estate) were allowed to give real estate credit. Deposit and lending rates were controlled by the Bank of Japan, which secured a low level of competition between banks and prudent bank lending (Amyx 2004: 41–60). Moreover, after the Second World War the Foreign Exchange Control Law set limits for international capital movement and thus created a borderline between the domestic and the international financial market (Suzuki 1986: 148).

Until 1991 the Bank of Japan used the so-called window guidance system to set credit ceilings for commercial banks. As firms more or less only had the option to take credit from banks, the window guidance system gave the Bank of Japan an efficient and strong instrument to control the credit volume going to firms. This specific structure of the financial system was an important determinant for the success of the Japanese model until the 1980s. Undoubtedly, for the existence of this type of financial system capital controls are necessary to prevent credit controls from becoming endangered by foreign capital.

The end of the 1970s brought some reforms. In 1977 the secondary market for bonds was opened. Interest rate controls were phased out between 1979 and

1983. A further institutional change was the removal of foreign exchange controls in 1980.[35] In 1980 Japanese banks only held 4 per cent of international lending, while in 1989 this amount had risen to 40 per cent.[36] These events marked the start of financial market liberalisation in Japan which was executed throughout the decades that followed. The last big liberalisation step, the so-called Big Bang, started at the end of the 1990s. This was a package whereby, under the Foreign Exchange Control Law in 1997, international capital controls and restrictions for foreign ownership were completely phased out by 2001 (Wallace 2002, Patrikis 1998). The fundamental institutional changes in the financial system encouraged a changing behaviour by companies and gave financial institutions and the public much more freedom to invest and to take credits.

In the 1980s the exaggerated optimism produced by the liberalisation led financial institutions, firms and private wealthowners to engage in higher-risk, higher-return activities. Non-financial sector debt rose tremendously between the 1980s and 1990s as the financial sector became more deregulated (see Figure 3.19). However, credit expansion was also stimulated by expansionary monetary policy especially in the second half of the 1980s.

In Japan the break from a growth regime to a stagnation regime in the late 1980s/early 1990s is clearly shown in the shrinking quota of non-financial business debt in relation to GDP in the 1990s and 2000s. Household debt measured in percentage of GDP increased slowly, starting from a low level in the 1970s, reaching its peak in the late 1990s and then starting to fall moderately. Compared with the US and UK, Japan is not characterised by a credit-driven consumption model of households. This did not lead to a precarious indebtedness of households but to a lack of domestic consumption and demand. The

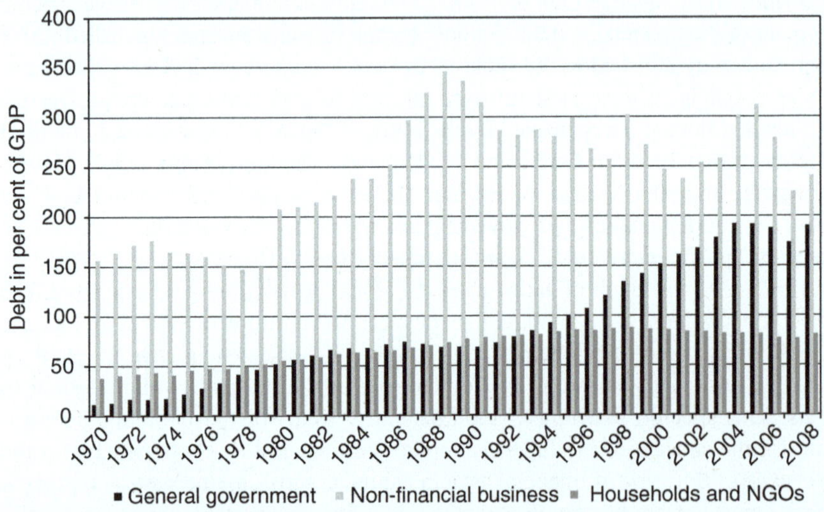

Figure 3.19 Debt in percentage of GDP in Japan, 1970–2009 (source: AMECO 2010, Bank of Japan, Flow of Funds Accounts 2010).

government's indebtedness, however, increased to spectacular heights. Starting from around 10 per cent of GDP in the early 1970s it increased to over 200 per cent in 2010. Public debt started to explode when the economy entered its stagnation phase in the early 1990s.

On the basis of financial liberalisation and also the expansionary policy of the Bank of Japan (see below) a huge asset price bubble developed in the second half of the 1980s. Real estate prices in Tokyo, Yokohama, Nagoya, Kyoto, Osaka and Kobe more than doubled between 1985 and 2000 (see Figure 2.5), while stock price inflation was about the same. The asset bubble followed the usual sequence. At the beginning asset price inflation seemed to be justified by fundamentals and driven by the financial liberalisation. In the last stages of the bubble asset prices in Japan increased to irrational levels driven by speculation which to a large extent was financed by credit.

With the unavoidable collapse of stock prices (starting in 1990) and real estate prices (starting in 1991), real estate companies could not sell their real estate assets at expected prices and began experiencing problems; banks found themselves in financial distress as credit and interest by debtors could not be paid and the value of collateral and equity was soaring. Non-performing loans started to increase and continued to be problematic throughout the 1990s and escalated after the Asian crisis in 1997 when Japan was hit by a recession. In 1998 non-performing loans amounted to 29.9 trillion yen and increased to 43.2 trillion yen in 2002, which represented about 8.4 per cent of total bank loans (see Figure 3.20). There is one particularity in the Japanese development of asset

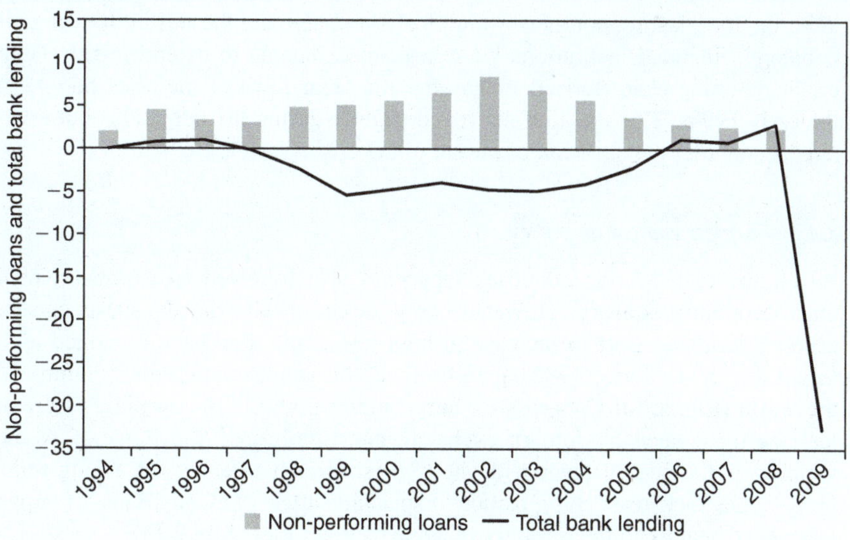

Figure 3.20 Non-performing loans (in percentage of total loans) and total bank lending (as percentage change over the previous year) in Japan, 1994–2009 (source: Bank of Japan 2010, authors' calculation).

markets. After its collapse real estate prices started to fall continuously and by the mid-2000s had reached about the same level as in the late 1970s. Since its sharp fall in the early 1990s the stock market has never recovered. The long-term stagnation and low level of asset prices certainly added to the stagnating consumption demand as well as to the low credit expansion as the value of collaterals and equity remained low.

The non-performing loan problem was aggravated as banks did not write-off bad loans in time and did not clean their balances with their own resources or government help. Financial institutions seemed to have expected that the crisis would only be temporary and a recovery of the economy as well as asset prices would allow them to grow out of the problem. Government was also reluctant to address the problem adequately as it did not want to use tax-payers' money to help financial institutions. In the first stage mergers and organised takeovers of institutions were thought to be a way to solve the problem. However, non-performing loans did not disappear and since the late 1990s, when financial institutions were additionally hit by the Asian crises in 1997, several credit cooperatives, securities companies and banks have found themselves in an extremely difficult financial position. Also, the deflationary development created permanent additional debt burdens. After the Asian crisis rescue mergers were organised again, but it became obvious that the actual problem was bigger than assumed. Now very late, the government stepped in. In 1998 two large banks (Long Term Credit Bank of Japan and Nippon Credit Bank) were nationalised and a revitalisation package was promoted by the government to inject capital into the financial system and help financial institutions.

The problems in the financial system had repercussions on the real economy. With the long-lasting non-performing loans problem and the fall in the value of collateral, financial institutions were hesitant or unable to extend credit. Tight credit rationing characterised Japan after the breakdown of the asset bubble in the early 1990s. The situation improved slightly during the late 2000s but escalated again after the outbreak of the subprime crisis (see Figure 3.20).

3.4.3 Foreign economic policy

As all successful Asian countries Japan has also followed an export-oriented macroeconomic strategy. However, only in the 1980s did Japanese current account surpluses start to increase to high levels and they have remained high (see Table 3.11). Since 1988 Japan has been the largest net creditor country in the world (Library of Congress Country Studies 2009).[37] The surpluses were at least partly created by foreign exchange interventions by the Bank of Japan, which was the central bank with the highest foreign reserves for a long time, until China took over this position. Especially after 1993 the Bank of Japan intervened heavily in the foreign exchange market (see Figure 2.13).

The Japanese current account surpluses in percentage of GDP became especially high during the depreciation of the yen against the US dollar in the first half of the 1980s. The Yen–Dollar Accord, signed in 1984, aimed to curb US current account deficits which were to a large extent caused by Japan. Among other things the liberalisation of the Japanese financial system should support the reduction of US current account deficits. It was hoped that the removal of entry restrictions for foreign financial institutions and interest rate controls in Japan would lead to higher Japanese capital imports and an upward pressure on the yen (Hsu 1999: 495). However, the desired appreciation of the yen was not achieved, nor could the current account deficit in the US be decreased. Thus, a new agreement – this time including all the G-5 countries – called the Plaza Agreement, was signed in 1985. The agreement aimed at coordinated monetary policy actions to bring exchange rates more in balance. The increase of the money market interest rate of the Bank of Japan in 1985 should be seen in this context (see Figure 3.22). The US dollar started to fall sharply in 1985. The yen appreciation after 1985 reduced the Japanese current account surpluses moderately, albeit not enough to reduce the pressure on Japan to follow policies to reduce the surpluses further, especially from the US. The US dollar collapsed more than had been intended and the Louvre Accord in 1987 was meant to bring a halt to the now destabilising depreciation. This time the Bank of Japan was pressed to reduce interest rates, which it did. Low interest rates and expansionary policy were seen as serving the aim to stabilise the US dollar and to stimulate growth in Japan and, via higher imports, reduce Japanese current account surpluses. External pressure was at least partly responsible for the expansionary monetary policy during the asset price bubble at the end of the 1980s in Japan.

3.4.4 Wage policy

Before the economic break at the end of the 1980s/early 1990s unemployment in Japan was traditionally very low. But even after the break, unemployment did not exceed 6 per cent, even in the deepest recession. There were several reasons why the official unemployment rate did not increase to the extent which could be expected from low GDP growth and productivity development. First, bonuses and wages were reduced during the recession rather than an immediate lay-off of workers. Second, early retirement as well as high flexibility in working hours prevented open unemployment (Hiwatari 2002: 17; Freeman and Weitzman 1987: 96). Third, the Japanese labour market has traditionally been divided into regular and non-regular employees. Regular employees used to have life-long employment guarantees in the company where they had started work, long-term career perspectives, relatively high wages and good fringe benefits. Non-regular employees are short-term contract employees, temporary employees and part-time employees; they earn less than regular employees and their termination is relatively easy. The number of regular workers dropped from 83 per cent of all workers in 1982 to 68 per cent in 2002, and 66 per cent in 2008 (Nakata and Miyazaki 2010). The big group of non-regular workers with precarious working conditions, much lower wages than regular employees and no union representation have functioned as a buffer for changes in economic growth.

Japan is an exemplary case for the argumentation used earlier in this book in that the major causes for a prolonged deflation are falling nominal unit labour costs. Nominal wage increases after the end of the bubble in the 1980s became very low and wages even fell after the shock of the Asian crisis. Only after 2005 did nominal wages stop falling, and increased only very slightly before the subprime crisis began. Taking trend productivity development into account it is not a surprise that unit labour costs in the second half of the 1990s started to decrease substantially in Japan and led to a long period of moderate deflation (see Figure 3.21).

Why did the nominal wage anchor in Japan break down? Of key importance is the wage bargaining system in Japan and the orientation of labour unions. There are mainly firm-level unions that organise only regular employees. Regular employees often automatically become members of the corresponding company union. Firm-level unions are members of the national union federation, but wage negotiations de facto take part at the company level. Nationwide wage coordination is traditionally undertaken by employers' associations and not by unions. A small number of big firms on an industry or multi-industry basis mainly coming from the export sector, government and union federations discuss wages and recommend a certain wage development. Union federations are weak and do not play an important role in this process. Wage recommendations are more or less passively accepted by firm unions. The employers' associations, government and unions all follow a corporatist mercantile strategy, while wage developments take into account international competitiveness. Expected exchange rate developments, for example, play an important role for wage developments (Soskice 1990: 41; Hiwatari 2002: 14). Union orientation in Japan is

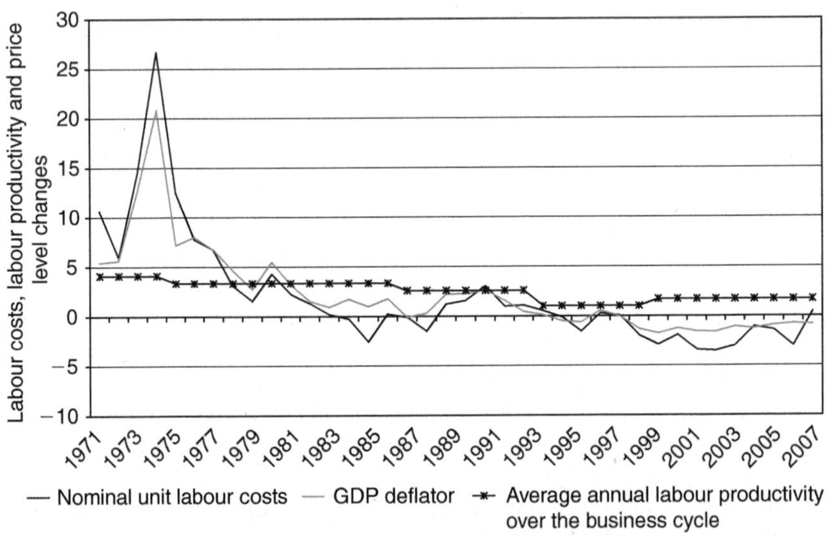

Figure 3.21 Productivity, unit labour costs and price level changes in Japan, 1961–2009 (percentage change to the previous year) (source: AMECO 2010).

not unlike the one in Germany. However, unions in the German export sector which negotiate with the employers' associations are likely to be less willing in following mercantilist wage restraint than the Japanese unions which follow wage guidelines more or less given by a handful of big export-oriented firms. In addition, firm-level wage negotiations in a situation of severe economic crisis always have the tendency to lead to wage cuts, as the microeconomic logic to improve the firm's competitiveness by undercutting costs of other firms becomes bone-crushing.

The function of minimum wages to prevent a deflationary development has not been exercised in Japan. During the deflation the National Council, which recommends the annual changes of minimum wages, almost froze. Between 1999 and 2006 they only increased very moderately minimum wages (Nakakubo 2009: 27; Kambayashi *et al.* 2008). Thus, minimum wage policy was not used to fight against deflationary developments.

Income distribution became slightly less equal in Japan; shown by the increasing Gini coefficient (Table 3.11). The wage quota dropped dramatically in Japan from around 75 per cent in the mid-1970s to around 60 per cent before the outbreak of the subprime crisis in the late 2000s (see Figure 2.24). Changes in distribution, but first of all increases in precarious jobs, and falling and depressed asset prices led to stagnating consumption in Japan.

3.4.5 Monetary policy

As in the other spheres of economic activity, monetary policy was also embraced by institutional changes. The first big institutional change for Japanese monetary policy was the collapse of the Bretton Woods System. Then international capital controls were abolished as well as direct interest rate controls of lending and deposit rates and credit ceilings. Finally, in 1997, the New Bank of Japan Law gave the central bank more independence (Amyx 2004: 185).

Until 1991 the main monetary policy instrument was the window guidance system, which was then abolished. Under this system the central bank allowed commercial banks to give a certain percentage of additional credits to the public in a specified period of time. Commercial banks followed the guidance more or less 100 per cent, giving the Bank of Japan a very powerful instrument for controlling credit expansion. As mentioned above, different international agreements pressured Japan to follow an expansionary economic policy, especially in the second half of the 1980s. Indeed, in the second half of the 1980s the Bank of Japan allowed commercial banks to increase credits annually by well above 10 per cent, much higher than in the 1970s and early 1980s. In 1991 the credit expansion was then reduced to below 5 per cent (Werner 2003: 133). In addition, other liberalisation steps allowed firms to get even more credit. It was a fatal mistake by the Bank of Japan and the government not to stop the asset price bubbles and even push the banks to give more credit. Instruments to influence credit allocation and to stop asset price inflation and too much credit going to the real estate sector would have been available, however, there was no political will to stop the bubble.

To this first mistake a second mistake was added. The Bank of Japan did not respond quickly enough to fight against the asset price deflation and the crisis in the real economy which followed. By 1992 at the latest the danger of a deep recession had become unequivocal. Given the relatively low inflation at that time and the perspective of a sharp drop in GDP growth, a sharp cut in interest rates would have been appropriate – especially as the window guidance system did not exist any longer. Bernanke and Gertler (2001), Mussa (2003) and Ferguson (2003) all argue correctly that monetary policy during the development of the bubble was too loose and after the implosion of the bubble too restrictive. In spite of low GDP growth and very low inflation rates, the Bank of Japan kept interest rates relatively high until the mid-1990s. Only in April 1995 was the interest rate cut to 1 per cent (see Figure 3.22).

Under the pressure of increasing deflationary problems after the Asian crisis in 1997, in 1999 the central bank explicitly declared it would pursue a zero interest rate policy until deflationary concerns subsided (see Bank of Japan 1999). The economy recovered modestly and the Bank of Japan gave up its zero interest rate policy in August 2000. However, this proved to be too early as recession came back to Japan after the worldwide economic crisis at the end of the Internet bubble in 2000/2001. In March 2001 the refinancing rate was again reduced to zero and kept at this level until 2006. To give the economy an additional expansionary push a so-called quantitative easing policy was implemented in 2001. The idea was to increase the money supply and pump liquidity into the banking system. Various instruments were used such as outright purchases of government bonds, purchases of corporate bonds and commercial papers, as well as

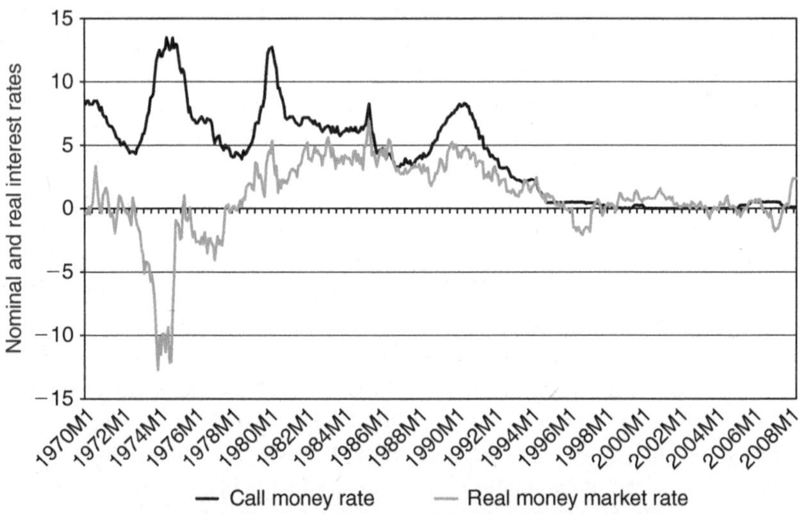

Figure 3.22 Nominal and real money market interest rates in Japan, 1970–2009 (real rate: nominal minus change in CPI), (source: IMF 2010d).

purchases of stocks by the Bank of Japan and the government (OECD 2005). After 2005, the situation improved slightly. In 2006 the Bank of Japan lifted its main refinancing rate to 0.4 per cent and 0.75 per cent in 2007. As a response to the subprime financial crisis, the Bank of Japan reduced the discount rate in two steps back to 0.1 per cent in December 2008 and kept this rate during the crisis. It also reapplied quantitative easing by purchasing corporate and government bonds as well as stocks held by banks with the aim to recapitalise banks and increase the stability in the financial system (OECD 2009a).

Monetary policy proved to be largely ineffective in Japan. The zero interest rate policy and later the aggressive pumping of liquidity into the economy were not sufficient to stimulate credit expansion and private demand. Because of deflation real interest rates remained positive, but what seemed to be even more important was that the distortions in the financial system in the form of non-performing loans, lack of equity and changing behaviour of banks could not be overcome (Baba *et al.* 2005).

3.4.6 Fiscal policy

Since 1975 Japan has been running deficits in the public budget almost continuously except for the period between 1988 and 1992 when the economy was booming and government made efforts to consolidate the budget. Even the big annual budget deficits of 6.17 per cent of GDP on average between 1994 and 2003 and 5.51 per cent between 2004 and 2008 did not seem to give the necessary stimulus to overcome the long period of low growth (see Figure 3.23; Table 3.12).

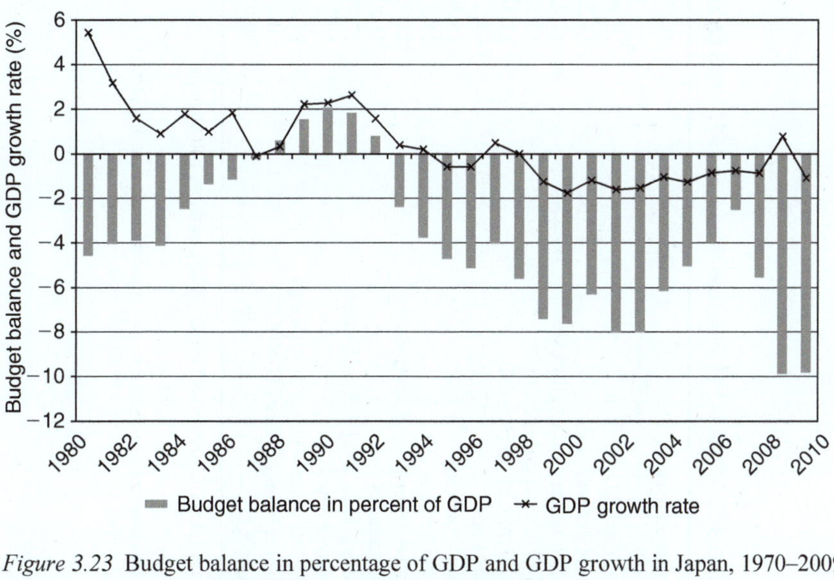

Figure 3.23 Budget balance in percentage of GDP and GDP growth in Japan, 1970–2009 (source: OECD 2009c, authors' calculations).

Table 3.12 Fiscal policy indicators for Japan 1971–2008 (average growth rates over the business cycle, unless mentioned otherwise)

Business cycles	*1971–1974*	*1975–1986*	*1987–1993*	*1994–1999*	*2000–2008*
Nominal GDP growth	16.40	8.00	5.17	0.49	0.23
Total expenditures	23.22	10.59	5.56	2.74	–0.18
Discretionary expenditures[1]	22.42	8.06	6.42	1.92	–0.34
Government consumption	22.52	8.60	5.57	2.88	1.51
Government investment	21.10	7.51	9.84	–0.29	–6.94
Subsidies	30.21	5.34	2.62	1.65	–3.46
Social benefits	25.50	13.92	5.58	5.17	2.37
Total revenues	21.33	10.05	5.08	0.08	1.41
Social security contributions	21.73	12.53	6.38	2.99	1.57
Direct taxes	25.81	8.91	4.72	–4.35	1.28
Direct taxes, cyclically adjusted	27.42	9.24	4.04	–3.65	0.50
Indirect taxes	15.57	8.75	5.68	2.81	0.12
Indirect taxes, cyclically adjusted	15.85	8.85	5.30	3.38	–0.36
Budget balance (% of GDP)[2]	0.49	–3.55	0.60	–6.17	–5.51
Budget balance, cyclically adjusted (% of GDP)[2]	–0.72	–3.06	–0.44	–6.52	–5.25

Source: OECD (2009c) AMECO (2010), authors' calculations.

Note
1 Government consumption, government investment and subsidies.
2 Average size over the business cycle.

In late 1991 in the light of the coming recession, budget surpluses were reduced and Japan switched from a budget surplus to a budget deficit. In retrospect, similar to monetary policy a quicker and more substantial switch to expansionary fiscal policy would have been desirable. Japan started to realise higher budget deficits as the economy did not recover during the 1990s. However, the fiscal stimuli were not structured in an optimal way. Most of the budget deficits throughout the years that followed the end of the bubble were caused by tax reductions to stimulate private demand. The timing of fiscal policy was also not always good. In 1997 when the Asian crisis hit Japan the consumption tax was increased from 3 to 5 per cent. At that time the Japanese government thought that the recession had been overcome and the Fiscal Structural Reform Act was implemented which aimed to reduce the debt-to-GDP ratio to 60 per cent and the budget deficit to 3 per cent of GDP. In 1998 when the country was hit by a new slowdown of growth the government took a decisive step to increase spending again (Kuttner and Posen 2002: 9). In the following years the government encountered the conflict of stabilising the economy with fiscal stimuli and consolidating the budget. After 2003 GDP growth recovered moderately and a period of fiscal consolidation started. In 2009 fiscal deficits exploded again.

After the bubble burst in Japan fiscal policy would have had more room for expansionary stimuli. Over the business cycle from 1994 to 1999 inflation was not a problem for fiscal policy as the inflation rate was very low and would have allowed massive demand creation by government. The deflationary development would have suggested a very expansionary fiscal policy. However, the increase of discretionary expenditures in this period was very modest. Tax revenues stagnated and were the main reason for the budget deficits. As expected, social benefit expenditures increased quite strongly during the crises years. In the period 2000–2008, with regard to inflation, fiscal policy also did not make use of its options. Discretionary expenditures even declined over the cycle, especially government investment dropped by nearly 7 per cent annually. Also, social benefits did not increase much during the period, whereas tax revenues increased quite substantially (see Table 3.12).

Looking at the need for expansionary fiscal policy during the 1990s and 2000s and the options that existed for fiscal policy, fiscal stimulation was not expansionary enough for Japan to come out of stagnation. The policy was furthermore characterised by stop-and-go as the government decided to cut back spending and increase taxes and social security contributions as soon as the economic performance looked better (as for example in 1997 and throughout the period between 2005 and 2009). Early consolidation efforts added to low growth and stagnation. However, government fiscal stabilisation was big enough to prevent a development similar to the 1930s. A balanced budget policy would definitely have pushed Japan into an extreme demand deflation and a cumulatively shrinking GDP. It also should be taken into consideration that there was no guarantee that a more expansionary fiscal policy would have led to a sustainable economic recovery based on private demand. Government debt would probably have become even higher than today and unsustainable.

As mentioned, during the subprime crisis public debt reached over 200 per cent in 2009. If Japan comes back into a constellation with normal positive interest rates, this high debt will become a big burden for public households and a challenge for structuring taxes and expenditures in a social way.

3.4.7 Conclusions

After the end of the bubble in the early 1990s, Japan was on the verge of sliding into a deflationary constellation, comparable with the development in so many countries in the 1930s. This time monetary and fiscal policy prevented such a scenario. Falling unit labour costs substantially added to the economic problems.

Japanese economic leaders should never have allowed the asset price bubble in the 1980s to occur. They would have had the instruments at that time to control credit expansion to the real estate sector and reduce speculative activities. After the implosion of the bubble, interest rates were lowered too hesitantly. Later, when the Bank of Japan was following a zero interest rate policy, all possibilities of reducing real interest rates were lost within the context of deflation. The lesson which had already been taught decades before and also applies to Japan is that in a deflationary situation monetary policy loses power.

Fiscal policy was expansion oriented and prevented a cumulative drop in demand. But fiscal policy was ambiguous, with the government consolidating the budget too early when it thought the crisis had been overcome. Such a policy is understandable as public debt to GDP exploded, but it would have been worthwhile testing whether stronger fiscal stimuli would have been strong enough to overcome the stagnation. Demand could also have been stimulated almost limitlessly by interest-free central bank loans to the government. However, such an unconventional combination of monetary and fiscal policy was not followed.

It was a fatal mistake for the government not to clear the balance sheets of financial institutions from non-performing loans quickly and in a comprehensive way. It waited too long and even then did not solve the problem quickly. Rapid intervention in the early 1990s would have helped to revive the distorted credit-investment mechanism. The best strategy would have been to nationalise banks whenever governments had to stabilise them. Later the banks could have been privatised again.

Wage development in Japan was glaringly dysfunctional. After the bursting of the asset price bubble and half a decade of low growth, the nominal wage anchor started to erode. Japan's example shows how important labour market institutions are in preventing insufficient wage increases or, even worse, cuts in nominal wages. The misled wage development can be at least partly interpreted as an element of a mercantile strategy and wage coordination aimed at cutting costs to become more competitive. The Japanese example is also instructive, as it shows that a strong position on world markets does not guarantee successful growth and employment, especially when domestic demand remains weak. The deflationary development permanently increased the real debt burden, intensified the lack of equity and collateral, stimulated credit rationing, added to the lack of demand and depressed asset prices further. Japan shows that deflation is not something from the past; it can happen again. Also, developments as in the 1930s can occur whenever the macroeconomic policy regime leads to a dysfunctional interaction of macroeconomic policies and economic developments.

4 A new globalisation

A wage-led and investment-led reform strategy

The finance-driven globalisation

Throughout recent decades economic development has been based on a range of unsustainable structures. Thus, many economies are characterised by volatile asset markets that are associated with volatile exchange rates, stock market and real estate markets bubbles, unstable prices of natural resources, and unsustainable credit expansion that was not only targeted at productive investment.

Moreover, consumption demand deviated from its role as the core engine of stable and sustainable demand. In some cases consumption demand was unable to create sufficient economic growth, while in others it was financed by unsustainable private household indebtedness and wealth created by increasing asset prices. Germany and Japan are good examples of the first case. In the past decades both have been unable to create sufficient economic growth to prevent high and/or increasing unemployment. Both countries have stabilised demand by means of high exports, but have suffered from a lack of domestic demand. Without export surpluses their growth performance would have been even worse. However, it has also become clear that the mercantilist orientation of these countries that was successfully combined with high domestic demand in the past has broken apart. While consumption demand in the US and the UK was extensive, it was unsustainably financed. Albeit both countries achieved relatively high growth and employment creation, they experienced huge stock market bubbles and even greater real estate bubbles as well as large increases in household indebtedness. Countries like Ireland, Spain and other southern European countries also fit this scenario.

Sometimes asset price bubbles went along with high credit expansion and high investment in the real sector. An example is the new economy bubble of the 1990s in most developed countries. However, to increase returns on equity, corporations increased their leverage to historically high levels. Sometimes asset price bubbles led to credit expansion without investment in the productive sector. Examples are from the frequent real estate bubbles after the 1970s.

Last but not least, during the past decades unstable international capital flows built up huge international imbalances which frequently led to violent adjustments. The long list of currency and financial crises in developing countries shows this very clearly. Developed and developing countries furthermore suffered from large exchange rate adjustments which turned the international financial system into a worldwide shock machine. The ballooning and subsequent shrinking of current account imbalances can be considered boom–bust cycles that express international bubbles caused by capital flows.

Asset price bubbles and unsustainable credit expansion are always two sides of one coin. The bubble economies in the US, the UK, Spain, Greece, Ireland, the Baltic countries and others were able to realise relatively high growth despite frequent asset market shocks. However, in western countries a new bubble, which would lead again to a strong increase in investment and/or consumption demand, seems highly unlikely in the foreseeable future. What we have found in recent decades in the bubble countries is not an economic cycle which turns on the same level, but a cycle of bubbles turning on a higher level – a metaphorical cycle of asset price inflations following asset price deflations that changes its level upwards. A clear sign of this is the increase of credit quotas measured in percentage of GDP of almost all economic sectors in all countries. In the tradition of Hyman Minsky (1975, 1982) and Irving Fisher (1933) it can be argued that escalating leverages of all types of economic agents have created a fragile economic constellation. The historically high indebtedness of the enterprise sector, private households, governments and sometimes whole states makes it extremely unlikely that a new bubble with new credit expansion and a new growth phase will be triggered, at least not in an appreciable number of countries. And even if this were the case, the fragility of the economic system would be increased even further and a new crisis like the subprime crisis would be the outcome. Without fundamental institutional and structural changes (Ordnungspolitik) western economies will most likely fall into a medium- or even long-term phase of low growth or even stagnation. The most recent and best example of such a development is Japan, which fell into a long phase of stagnation after its stock market and real estate market had suffered an asset price deflation following the bubbles in the second half of the 1980s. There is the danger that a period of low growth in the US, Europe and other countries will lead to the Japanese deflationary constellation.

Four scenarios seem to be possible in the medium term. First, as mentioned, new bubbles are theoretically possible. They could lead to a new phase of unsustainable credit expansion and relatively high GDP growth and after some time to a new financial crisis with again deep, negative effects on growth, employment and distribution. However, this scenario is not very likely as indebtedness of all economic sectors is already very high and new credit expansion difficult. And even if this first scenario were to materialise, it would eventually lead to the scenarios discussed below.

The second scenario describes economies trapped in long-term stagnation. In this case GDP growth is low and unemployment rates are high. There is a lack of demand dynamics from earned wages or other income as well as from bubbles. Such a scenario is characterised by highly or increasingly unequal income distribution and a high or increasing population living from precarious work and living in unstable personal conditions in high relative poverty. The results are lost decades for societies. Such a scenario is not theoretical. The Latin American development in the 1990s was characterised by the expression 'lost decades'; both Japan and Germany in the 1990s and 2000s to a certain extent fit the scenario. We can easily imagine that long-term stagnation could even lead to substantially lower economic dynamics than in the past decades in Japan and Germany.

Third, we cannot exclude that a scenario of low growth and long-term or ever-increasing unemployment problems combined with weak unions and deregulated labour markets could lead to nominal wage cuts and deflation. In the Japanese case deflationary developments started a period of more than half a decade of low GDP growth and high pressure in the labour market. Expansionary fiscal policy leading to a ratio of public debt to GDP of over 200 per cent in 2010 and current account surpluses in the background of an expanding world market prevented deflation from getting out of control in Japan. It does not look as if all countries after the subprime crisis are willing or able to follow a fiscal policy as in Japan, which was forced to accept high budget deficits for a long period of time. Hard deflationary policies have been forced upon Greece, Ireland and other countries after the outbreak of its sovereign debt crisis in 2010. These policies combine hard fiscal austerity programmes with nominal wage cuts in the public sector. The latter will most likely spill over to the private sector quickly. The therapy applied to these countries is similar to the public sector wage reductions of 1930–1932 implemented by German Chancellor Heinrich Brüning (with his emergency decrees) that paved the way for Nazism. Portugal, Spain and Italy are in the same constellation within the European Monetary Unions and may also follow a Brüning policy in upcoming years. Countries outside the currency union in Europe, such as Hungary and the Baltic countries, have applied similar policies too. It remains an open question as to how long countries like the US can follow medium-term oriented expansionary fiscal policies with escalating public debt. But even without public expenditure cuts and nominal wage cuts in the public sector, we cannot exclude deflationary developments. Unions and employers' associations have become weak since the neoliberal era and the microeconomic logic for firms to survive as well as neoclassical thinking demand wage cuts. This third scenario is destabilising for the economy and unsustainable. It may lead to the last scenario.

In our fourth scenario debt quotas of all economic sectors are high and may even increase further. Public debt to GDP increased substantially throughout recent decades in almost all western countries and as a result of the subprime crisis quickly increased further. Japan is only the tip of the iceberg. Imagine interest rates jumping to 10 per cent in Japan; given the 200 per cent public debt to GDP this would mean a frightening public interest rate burden of 20 per cent of GDP. Other economic sectors in some of the countries have extremely high indebtedness too. Examples are private households in the US and the UK or the enterprise sector in Japan and in the UK. High debt can lead to constellations in which 'non-market' policies become attractive for policy-makers. For example, budget deficits can be directly financed by the central bank, either because private agents do not give credit to the government or in case the public debt has curtailed the room for manoeuvre of public households. To a certain extent the financing of public households by printing money is possible. However, excessive money creation to finance governments involves the danger of destroying the reputation of the currency. Capital flight may bring about higher import prices and can trigger nominal income increases which lead to a cumulative inflation and even hyperinflation. When public budgets are financed by money creation, inflationary developments as a result of capital flight in real assets like real estate or even durable goods are also possible. Yet, high public debt does not automatically lead to inflation – a good example for this is Japan from the 1990s to the 2000s – but it can lead to constellations in which governments see taking credit from the central bank as the only possibility to keep society functioning. In a critical situation this seems better than sacking policemen and closing hospitals or schools. A currency reform is a second instrument for reducing public debt and domestic debt in general. It means that the stock of domestic debt and monetary wealth is depreciated in comparison with flows like wages, rents or tax payments. A high inflation rate without central bank's adjustments in the nominal interest rate and a currency reform destroy monetary wealth and thus the savings of private households. Both of these 'non-market' measures have deep distributional effects and can hardly be carried out without political destabilisation. The scenario described here is not a short-term one. But without deep reforms similar to those implemented by the New Deal in the 1930s, the likelihood of its occurrence is high.

A fundamental reform agenda is needed

In this book we have made clear that we are convinced that a deregulated type of capitalism is unacceptably unstable and is only preferable for a small proportion of society. It produces a very unequal income distribution. In such a regime most people are pushed around by markets and live in high uncertainty, even if their income situation is acceptable. Unemployment is high and volatile. Last but not least firms are also exposed to high uncertainty as well as to shocks in financial markets and goods markets. However, as just mentioned, even such a radical market-based macroeconomic policy regime privileges some groups in society, for example agents in the financial sector or top income earners. It would also be a misunderstanding to assume that such a regime automatically breaks down. Scenario one and two (see above) are possible and guarantee the continuation of the existing macroeconomic policy regime even if it becomes less dynamic.

To change the present macroeconomic policy regime, fundamental changes are needed. However, we are convinced that in the foreseeable future there is no realistic alternative to a regulated type of capitalism. Even radical ecological reforms based on completely different production and consumption patterns must be kept together by a macroeconomic policy regime. Macroeconomic policy regimes cannot be established or changed easily. Deeply embedded traditions, norms, informal institutions and so on make it difficult or even impossible to shape societal structures. However, the 1930/1940s as well the 1970/1980s prove that 'Ordnungspolitik' or fundamental changes of institutions as well as rules and changes in key macroeconomic policies are well able to profoundly change economies and societies.

What can be done to establish a positive macroeconomic policy regime which is able to avoid the negative scenarios outlined above? We call such a new model, following the New Deal, the *New Globalisation*. This approach is built on the assumption that the market mechanism is not a wonderful machine to coordinate the millions of economic actions of firms and households in a harmonious way and lead to the welfare of nations or even all economic agents. Our analysis has led us to the conclusion that market economies are endogenously unstable and must be embedded in institutions and active government policies. Karl Polanyi (1944) taught us that money, labour and nature cannot be left to markets. In this book we concentrate on money and labour. We shall discuss the different elements of a New Globalisation step by step as follows.

Sustainable development of demand and its components

Of importance for a new macroeconomic policy regime is a combination of fundamental institutional and structural changes *and* a process policy which stimulates prosperous economic development. A key element for the creation of a prosperous economy is a stable income creation process that exists within a stable institutional framework and is based on sufficient and sustainable investment and consumption demand. Both of these demand elements must stay in a proportional relationship and must stimulate each other. However, even a positive interrelation of investment and consumption demand does not guarantee automatically full employment.

Investment only makes sense when the capacities created can be used. This implies sufficient goods market demand apart from investment demand. This brings us to *consumption demand* (including demand for private housing) as the quantitatively most important demand element. Without sufficient consumption demand capitalist societies will suffer the fate of Midas – in spite of being rich enough to produce much more and employ many more people, the lack of consumption demand brings unemployment and hardship. However, the potential fate of Midas only exists if the different demand elements in society are left to purely market-based processes. ‘This disturbing conclusion depends, of course, on the assumption that the propensity to consume and the rate of investment are not deliberately controlled in the social interest but are mainly left to the influences of *laissez-faire*.’ (Keynes 1936: 219). What is indeed needed is deliberately controlled consumption and investment demand in the social interest.

This leads us to the basic idea of a sustainable wage-led prosperity, which includes a sustainable recovery of economies after the subprime crisis. Wage-led recovery means that household demand must be sufficiently high to allow satisfactory GDP growth. As outlined above, in the neoliberal era of recent decades some western countries were not able to stimulate sufficient consumption demand to have satisfactory growth; other countries had sufficient household demand, but this demand was based on credit and led to an unsustainable increase of household debt in percentage of GDP. The key point of a wage-led prosperity is high consumption demand that is based on income. Wages are stressed here as a source of income and demand because they have the biggest share in national income and wage earners are the group in society with the highest propensity to consume. The lower the income of a household, the higher the likelihood that the household will not save a high percentage of its income. Thus, low-income households tend to have a high propensity to consume.

A nominal increase in the wage level is not the policy which can lead to a wage-led prosperity. Ultimately, changes in the wage level do not affect real wages and real opportunities to consume. The nominal wage level should increase according to the wage norm, which implies wage level increases in line with the sum of trend productivity and the target inflation rate. Wage-led prosperity must first of all be based on changes in income distribution. The changes in income distribution in favour of rich households undertaken during the neoliberal era must therefore be reversed.

A first area of policies to change income distribution is the reduction of wage dispersion. One instrument available here includes statutory minimum wages. Higher minimum wages compress the wage structure from below and in this way change income distribution. In addition, an active minimum wage policy can act as a dam against deflationary pressures in a situation of high unemployment. Social transfers can be interpreted as reservation wages as nobody would like to enter gainful employment being paid an amount below them. Statutory minimum wages should sufficiently exceed this reservation wage to prevent the unsatisfying situation that wages of full-time employees fall to the level of social transfers. The latter case can be observed in Germany, which lacks a statutory minimum wage.

However, wage dispersion should not be reduced only by fighting against a low-wage sector. Adjustments in the high-wage sectors are similarly important.

The best policy to find a wage structure which allows sufficient incentives for employees and at the same time limits wage dispersion (also by achieving a development of the nominal wage level according to the wage norm) is collective bargaining that takes into account macroeconomic repercussions of wage development. Thus, strengthening unions, employers' associations and industry-wide wage bargaining systems is an element of paramount importance of a wage-led prosperity strategy. Also, patterns like compulsory membership of companies in employers' associations, and making the outcome of wage negotiations binding for all companies in an industry are examples of institutional changes in the right direction.

A change in functional income distribution can support a wage-led prosperity too. While, as already mentioned, changes in the nominal wage level cannot affect functional income distribution, polices to reduce the profit mark-up are promising. Since profit mark-up increases during the Neoliberal Globalisation mainly reflected changes in the financial system, the latter has to be reformed again in such a way that excessively high profits in the corporate sector and their payout to the financial sector are made impossible.

Last but not least, governments can change tax and expenditure structures in such a way that the market-given income distribution is modified. For example, high income tax rates reduce overly high market-given incomes, whereas the government's supply of public goods in the field of education or health care improves the income situation of poorer households.

Consumption by households does not only depend on income distribution, but also on the level of uncertainty individuals are exposed to. If people live under precarious conditions without stable employment, incentives for high savings rates are high. The same is true when insufficient pension payments after retirement or insufficient protection against health risks or unemployment are expected. Also, when households anticipate substantial expenditures for the education of their children, saving is stimulated. Thus, a comprehensive welfare state and social security system as well as the delivery of public goods by the state stimulate consumption. Assuming that private households tend to save a part of their income whereas governments spend all their revenues, a high difference between gross and net income respectively a higher government share on total demand also increases and stabilises demand (this is the so-called Havelmoo effect).

Let us come to *investment demand*, the second important pillar of a prosperous economy. Investment in productive capital is not only important for current demand. In this function it could be theoretically substituted by other demand elements. However, investment is of key importance for capacity development in the economy and the technological progress which is almost always embedded in investment goods. Investment demand depends on low interest rates including sufficient availability of credit and on positive long-term expectations by investors in productive capital. Typically, a stable economic expansion path with high market demand and high capacity utilisation stabilises expectations. Virtuous cycles are also based on a self-fulfilling prophecy: high investment demand leads to high income creation which, provided that income distribution is relatively equal, is the basis for high income-based consumption demand. A virtuous cycle is created with productivity increases and innovations, high aggregate demand, relatively equal income distribution and stable expectations. The Golden Age of the 1950s and 1960s is an example of such a virtuous cycle. Of course, both investment and consumption demand must be deliberately influenced and controlled in such a way that this prosperous cycle does not break down.

So far we have not mentioned *government demand*. There is no doubt that fiscal policy has to play an important role in stabilising the business cycle and in this way in improving the overall performance of the economy. However, fiscal policy is not able to create a prosperous economy when the other parts of goods market demand are insufficient. Public budgets over the business cycle should be balanced. There is no advantage of increasing public debt to GDP in the long term. Public consumption expenditures in the medium term should be financed out of public revenues and not by loans. Public investment can be financed by credit, but in this case investments with direct future cash flows like building roads and introducing tolls should be preferred.

Export demand in the form of exports/current account surpluses as a demand engine are possible for individual countries but not for the world as a whole. In the framework of a New Globalisation, current account imbalances should be limited. This also implies that export-led growth should not be used by countries to stimulate the economy in the medium- and even long term. At most, developing countries should be allowed an export-led development strategy to a certain extent.

A New Globalisation can be grouped around a big project to transform the existing production and consumption structure including the existing structures of cities towards ecologically sustainable means of production, consumption and life. Such a project is frequently called a 'Green New Deal' (see for example The Green New Deal Group 2008). A 'big project' like this seems a suitable instrument to help trigger a new virtuous cycle in the logic described above. However, it cannot be primarily based on fiscal expansion. Rather, it should rest upon investment of enterprises. A big public enterprise sector, especially in the field of public services, can play an important role to determine the investment dynamics of a society. Nevertheless, public households should support such a project by infrastructure investment and delivery of public goods. This should be done without increasing government debt to GDP.

The financial system

The financial system fulfils an important coordination function in a market-based economic system. It has to support economic development by delivering cheap and sufficient credit first of all for the corporate sector. However, the financial and economic system which developed under the Neoliberal Globalisation after the 1970s has not fulfilled this function and was not able to support a sustainable path of economic development. The opposite is the case, the financial system has been producing all types of harmful shocks. Asset price bubbles in real estate markets and stock markets became as frequent as huge exchange rate shocks or highly volatile prices of natural resources from oil to gold. Debt to GDP quotas of almost all economic sectors in almost all countries in the world made the financial system and economics more and more fragile. Such shocks in a fragile constellation increase the level of uncertainty of all economic agents. The result is low-scale and more short-term investment. Partly, and as far as possible, agents try to protect themselves from increasing uncertainty by using future contracts. However, while the quantitatively exploding derivative markets certainly reduced the individual uncertainty of some agents, at the same time they increased the uncertainty and fragility of the whole financial system. Future markets exploded quantitatively in a way which cannot be explained by the need to protect productive activities. They became highly speculative and their own source of instability and uncertainty.

On the other hand, a relatively simple financial system with commercial banks focusing on credits to enterprises is well able to deliver cheap and sufficient credit to firms. In such a system proprietary trading of commercial banks should not be allowed and commercial banks should furthermore be prohibited to give credit to non-bank financial intermediaries like investment banks, hedge funds or private property funds. Such a banking system does not feed non-bank financial intermediaries with almost unlimited funds for risk-oriented and speculative activities. Rather, risk-loving and speculative investors then are forced to use their own capital or that from private households – funds that are still more than sufficient for financing very risky investment projects. Should such funds taper off there is no systemic risk for the entire financial and economic system. The basic business model of commercial banks should be in giving credit and holding it until it is paid back. This implies that the selling of credit (securitisation) is strictly controlled and limited. Should the equity of banks not be enough for expansions – as banks have to keep a certain percentage of their credits as equity – there is no sound argument against asking banks to issue new shares to increase their equity. Part of the banking system could be owned by the public sector. In Germany, for example, the big sector of state banks owned by local governments has traditionally given credit to small- and medium-sized companies and was not very much affected by the subprime crisis. Such publicly owned local banks are very close to the highly praised idea of the microfinance model. In developed countries a microfinance sector can equally support the development of the small- and medium-sized enterprise sector. Smaller banks should not be allowed to invest worldwide. Their business model could be to finance national activities in the real economy.

The equity holding of financial institutions has to be increased. Since the mid-1990s, banks, rating agencies and so on have been using microeconomically oriented risk models that led to a drastic decline in equity holdings in proportion to given credits. This development added to the fragility of the financial system and has to be reversed. In general the role of microeconomic risk models for equity holding should be reduced as they exhibit pro-cyclical effects. Such models, which are based on historical data, signal low risks during expansionary periods with asset price inflations and high risks in periods of contractions and asset price deflations. Policies to prevent such pro-cyclical effects include the requirement of equity holdings for certain types of credit independent of historical development and risk models. Central banks should also be allowed to increase the need for equity holding for certain types of credit, for example real estate or consumption credits, in a discretionary way according to the historical situation. Such regulations can be extended to all types of credit to influence credit allocation in a preferable way. Also the percentage of own capital needed for real estate investments or other investments could be amended in a discretionary way according to the macroeconomic situation.

Credit expansion to households should only be tolerated as prime loans and should be limited during a period of destabilising credit expansion. This should not only be the case for real estate credits but for consumption credits in general. Such a policy reduces the likelihood of non-performing loans and at the same time prevents poor households from becoming over-indebted.

All financial institutions taking over commercial bank functions have to be regulated in the same way. This implies that there should be no insufficiently regulated shadow banking systems. Even if there is a wall between commercial banks and non-bank financial institutions, the latter have to be regulated to guarantee transparency and to protect investors to a certain extent. All of these institutions have to be forced to use a certain percentage of their own capital for their economic activities. Moral hazard problems escalate if risk-loving institutions are allowed to act with a low amount of own capital as this stimulates economic activities where possible profits are very high and privatised while own potential losses are low.

Derivative markets have to be cut down in volume and structure. Just like medical products, financial products are dangerous. Before their introduction they should be standardised and approved by a public agency. Moreover, financial products should only be bought and sold in organised and transparent exchanges which ask for a percentage of the contract value (margin) as a deposit.

Rating agencies, which play a major role in modern financial markets, are organised like a private cartel. This has to be changed. First, public rating agencies need to be established to compete with private ones that did such a poor job before the subprime crisis. Second, the role of ratings, for example for equity holdings of banks, has to be reduced. Third, rating agencies should not be allowed to advise institutions in cases in which they are responsible for evaluating the financial products of these institutions.

The definition of international accounting standards cannot be left to a private institution like the International Accounting Standards Board (IASB) that determines accounting standards according to partisan interests. Fair-value accounting became popular in the 1990s and led to pro-cyclical accounting rules as assets had to be booked according to current and volatile market prices. As this system added substantially to the subprime crisis and its transformation into a general financial and real economy crisis, like banking supervision, accounting standards have to be regulated by governmental authorities.

Because of its importance for the financial system and its social function, real estate financing should become a special segment of the financial market and separately regulated. For example the macroeconomic volume for real estate credits should be controlled. The amount of own capital in percentage of the value of a real estate investment can be fixed by financial authorities and (even regionally) adjusted if needed. Or, as mentioned, equity holding for real estate credits by financial institutions and the selling of such credits to other institutions can be adjusted in a discretionary way. Speculative gains in the real estate market could be taxed with the aim to reduce speculative activities.

All financial transactions could be taxed in the tradition of a Tobin tax. Such a financial transaction tax does not prevent bubbles and other instabilities in the financial sector. For example, in the real estate sector relatively high transaction costs exist and at the same time real estate bubbles, as one of the most dangerous kinds of bubbles, developed in past decades one after the other. However, a financial transaction tax does punish very short-term oriented speculation with intensive selling and buying on the basis of low speculative margins. Such transactions will be suppressed without changing the functioning of financial markets. Besides, the main purpose of a financial transaction tax is to raise revenue and for this it is a useful instrument.

Revitalisation of stakeholder corporate governance system

One aspect of financial system reform is to overcome corporate governance in the tradition of shareholder value which became popular in the 1980s. The shareholder value system subordinates the larger firms' strategies solely under the interest of the owners. To solve the principal-agent problem between owners and managers, stock market development is used as a measure for the management's performance. However, as stock markets are driven by unclear fundamentals – to be precise, even if agents search for fundamentals, different fundamentals are found and are interpreted with different models – and in addition by short-term speculation, in the shareholder value system corporate governance is linked to the volatile and not predictable developments of stock markets. Thus, for corporate strategies the shareholder value system leads to suboptimal developments. It prevents the long-term orientation of firms and hinders the use of the most efficient technologies if these imply long-term investment. Besides, the shareholder value system has led to extremely high salaries and bonuses for managers and in this way is one of the factors which led to the more unequal income distribution during the period of Neoliberal Globalisation. Bonuses are usually not paid according to relative performance, but according to the stock price developments in general. The system perverted the function of stock markets to mobilise new capital for firms as managers to a large extent bought back the own shares of their companies to increase share prices and bonuses.

To reverse the negative tendencies of the shareholder value system corporate governance must become more democratic. Other stakeholders' interests in addition to those of owners must be reflected in management decisions. The old model of corporate governance from the 1950s and 1960s where management had to search for a compromise between the different interests in a firm has to be revitalised. In a stakeholder system salaries of management are controlled and set in perspective to the overall wage structure within the firm. A key role has to be played here by trade unions which express the interest of the workers. Strong unions automatically force management to compromises. Institutional changes which give workers' representatives more power to influence the management can lead to a preferable stakeholder model.

Different ownership models can coexist at the same time. Large and medium-sized companies should usually be owned by private owners in the form of stock companies. But large state-owned companies, especially in the field of public services, as well as companies with mixed ownership can also play an important role. In all cases of natural monopolies (high economies of scale, network effects, etc.) markets have to be heavily regulated. In this traditional sector of public enterprise, private companies did not really produce an advantage. In many cases privatisation in this area only led to the erosion of working conditions and to monopoly profits without improving services. Cooperatives can play a role in smaller- and medium-sized companies.

Even under a stakeholder model in normal markets firms independent of their ownership compete with each other and follow individual strategies. The competition created by this behaviour of firms is an important element of a market economy and leads to productivity increases and innovations. However, even in such stakeholder capitalism with many different forms of ownership a macroecnomic policy regime is needed to stabilise the economy and guarantee a sustainable development.

Global governance

Global governance is an important part of a New Globalisation. The New Deal in the 1930s was created after the world market broke down and even added to the breakdown of the world market by nationally oriented policies. Only after the Second World War was the Bretton Woods System built as a framework of a global economy. Today, a national option that would include the breakdown of globalisation does not seem feasible for a good reform agenda. What is needed is a global governance system which satisfies three needs.

First, global imbalances have to be controlled. There must be a mechanism to prevent current account surpluses and current account deficits. In his proposal for the Bretton Woods System, John Maynard Keynes recommended an exchange rate system with fixed but adjustable exchange rates, a stimulation of economic growth in surplus countries and a slowdown in deficit countries as well as an adjustment of the exchange rate if growth stimulation or slowdown does not work or is economically too costly for the countries involved. The aim of his proposal was to prevent an asymmetric adjustment process mainly born by deficit countries. Both surplus and deficit countries should be forced to contribute to the balance of their current accounts. Such a system involves international capital controls. Otherwise the stabilisation of the exchange rates is not possible or forces monetary policy to a harmful interest rate policy (Keynes 1942).

Second, in his proposal Keynes demanded an international reserve currency (the bancor) issued by an international institution (clearing union) as international reserves of central banks. To a small extent such money was created when the IMF introduced the Special Drawing Rights. While private capital flows are not stabilised by such supranational money of central banks, it can eliminate the destabilising shifts in reserve holdings by central banks. Moreover, it can reduce the problem of countries like the US, which was pushed into current account deficits as the outcome of the high demand for international reserves. Reform preferences along the lines of Keynes' Bretton Woods proposals are still valid today and can be used as a starting point for solving global governance problems in the field of the international financial and exchange rate system.

Third, the world financial and exchange rate system can help poor countries to accelerate their development. This implies that developing countries are not pushed in current account deficit constellations. For development it is even positive if developed countries realise moderate current account deficits and developing countries moderate current account surpluses. Developed countries should open their markets for imports from developing countries while developing countries should be given the right for one-sided protection in the tradition of Friedrich List to protect and support their infant industries.

All these proposals for a new global governance system do not sound politically very realistic. But this does not mean that nothing can be done. Big countries or currency areas like the US, Japan and the European Monetary Unions can switch immediately to a combination of a managed floating exchange rate mechanism which implies an exchange rate policy that not only smoothes exchange rate volatility but also moves the exchange rate in such a way that the current account is more or less balanced. This can only be achieved by using selective capital controls and, if needed, heavy foreign exchange interventions.

Working time as a policy instrument

Even highly regulated market economies may find it challenging to guarantee full employment. But full employment is a precondition for a fair society and sufficient power in the hands of workers and trade unions. Labour demand given by GDP growth and productivity development together with population growth and labour market participation rates determine the unemployment rate. The traditional model for achieving full employment has been to stimulate growth. Growth stimulation is without a doubt a necessary strategy to create a new prosperous phase. But in a medium- and long-run perspective, major societies may chose to reduce GDP growth rates. Probably ecological considerations will even force societies to reduce growth rates. At the same time productivity increases should continue to develop. It would be foolish to prevent technological progress also for ecological reasons. However, GDP growth rates below productivity growth rates reduce employment and thus labour demand.

Additional instruments to guarantee full employment are needed. Controlling population growth to guarantee full employment is not only difficult but also undesirable. The same is true for labour market participation rates. For example, going back to family models where one partner stays at home and the other is the breadwinner is no longer a feasible policy. While productivity can be decreased to a certain extent by reducing the intensity of excessive work, it is misleading to decelerate productivity increases by suppressing innovations and technological development.

Only one variable is left: working time. Changes in working time can be used as a rational macroeconomic instrument to reduce unemployment if GDP growth is insufficient or not wanted. Of course, working time cannot be changed every few years. But it is an adequate instrument as soon as labour market disequilibrium becomes a medium-term problem. All types of working time changes are possible (weekly working time, yearly working time, pension age, etc.). It should be mentioned that working time reductions in a situation of no productivity increases are only possible without inflationary effects without wage compensation. Of course, working time can also be reduced without inflationary effects by productivity increases and unchanged nominal wages. In such a case working time reductions can take place without real wage reductions.

We have tried here to give a comprehensive vision of how a New Globalisation might look. There may be many controversial arguments concerning details and/or the entire vision we advocate. But we feel that the neoliberal model which developed in the 1980s and thereafter is becoming more and more unstable and harmful for societies and the people living in them. Given the wealth of developed nations, developments could have been better and improvements are possible. Ideas can become very powerful and change the way of thinking and actions of agents. To contribute to theoretical debates and in this way to changing ideas and policies is what academia can and should do. This is what continues to motivate us and sustains our interest in making a contribution to positive change.

Notes

2 Macroeconomic policy regimes and their assessment

1 The new classical model, for example, also speaks about regimes (see Lucas 1973, 1981).

2 Ordnungspolitik as a term was used by Eucken (1939) to explain economic policy that shapes the economic order of an economy. He and his followers stand for a special version of liberal policies, so-called ordoliberal principles such as: freedom for private economic activities, no price controls, competition policies to prevent monopolies and oligopolies, free trade and open international markets, policies for reducing uncertainty, etc. We do not subscribe to the ideas of this version of liberal thinking. Ordnungspolitik is used here to denote a policy conducted by government with the aim to change institutions to achieve certain results and to shape the behaviour of the agents.

3 'There are two steps one can take. One is to take expectation formation as exogenous and to restrict attention to short period equilibria. ... The other route is to invoke Rational Expectations' (Hahn 1981: 181).

4 Keynes (1937: 215) expresses the instability of expectations very clearly:

> The practice of calmness and immobility, of certainty and security, suddenly breaks down. New fears and hopes will, without warning, take charge of human conduct. The forces of disillusions may suddenly impose a new conventional basis for valuation. All these pretty, polite techniques, made for well-panelled Board Rooms and a nicely regulated market, are liable to collapse. ... I accuse the Classical economic theory of being itself one of these pretty, polite techniques which tries to deal with the present by abstracting from the fact that we know very little about the future.

5 There are additional problems with macroeconomic production functions and models based on them. A macroeconomic production function does not exist if there are many capital goods since the 'K' (which stands for the value of the capital stock) in the production function varies with every change in distribution (interest rate movements). Thus a macroeconomic production function is only possible under the extremely unrealistic assumption of only one capital good (Sraffa 1960; Samuelson 1966).

6 The classical paradigm also follows this logic.

7 The system becomes even more regulated when the central bank channels credits in certain industrial sectors or regions. Moreover, industrial policy can be carried out via the financial system.

8 Up until today (2010) China has applied controls on deposit and lending rates of banks.

9 See the Japanese case study below. For the Chinese example, see Herr (2010).

10 This shows that the so-called capital market in neoclassical models that equalises savings and net investment by adjusting the interest rate is based on the assumption that there is no default risk of debtors. Moreover, savings and net investment are flow categories (representing values in a period of time) whereas credit markets are typical stock categories (representing values at point of time).

11 In 1999 the Glass–Steagall Act after several reforms was completely abolished.

12 For example in the US the stock markets crashed by over 22 per cent on Monday 19 October, 1987 without explanation (Shleifer 2000: 20).

13 In contrast with exchange-traded derivatives, OTC derivates are directly negotiated between two parties. Due to the missing intermediary body and extensive deregulation, the market is highly opaque.

14 A business cycle starts with the first year of recovery measured in real GDP growth rates and ends with the deepest slowdown of real GDP growth rates.

15 The index covers three dimensions: separate exchange rates for capital transactions or not, restrictions on payments to current account transactions and restrictions on payment to capital transactions (see IMF 2010a).

16 The so-called absolute purchasing-power-parity theory can be transformed into a relative purchasing-power-parity theory using the changes in the price levels in different countries instead of the absolute levels.

17 Isard (1995: 63) wrote: 'Direct evidence on the behaviour of real exchange rates strongly confirms that PPP is not a valid hypothesis about the relationship between nominal exchange rates and national price levels in the short-run.' In a similar vein Krugman and Obstfeld (2000: 406) stated:

> How well does the PPP theory explain actual data on exchange rates and national price levels? A brief answer is that all versions of the PPP theory do badly in explaining the facts. In particular, changes in national price levels often tell us little or nothing about exchange rate movements.

18 Assuming a slower adjustment in the goods market than in the asset market, the interest rate parity in combination with the PPP theory can lead to short-term deviations of the exchange rate from the long-term equilibrium given by the PPP theory. Overshooting exchange rates during the adjustment process are possible (Dornbusch 1976). But also in this case in the medium-term the PPP theory will be realised. Empirically, the failure of the PPP theory to explain exchange rate movements cannot be cured by adding the interest-rate-parity theory and assuming slow adjustments in the goods market. Actual exchange rate movements are too far away from movements forecasted by the PPP to be explained by differentials in the interest rate. For example, analysing movements of the external value of the US dollar, Dornbusch and Frankel (1988: 164) came to the following conclusion: 'It appears that the dollar overshot the overshooting equilibrium.'

19 In a similar way Mundell (2000) stated:

> Volatility of the exchange rates aggravates instability of the financial markets, disrupts trade and the efficiency of capital flows. Exchange rate uncertainty is an immediate cause of gross, excessive volatility in financial markets and the massive shifts in cross-border funds today.

20 'Costly adjustments to exchange rate fluctuations serve no useful purpose, and substantial real resources will be wasted along the way' (Obno 1994: 8).

21 So-called hysteresis effects follow from large exchange rate movements.

22 Besides Japan and Germany, after 2000 China became the third big surplus country. Also, some natural resource exporting countries realised high current account surpluses during periods of high natural resource prices.

23 It is no surprise that there is no positive correlation between capital account liberalisation and economic growth in developing countries (Stiglitz 2004).

24 These are reserves held by central banks.
25 We speak about international contracts if debtors and creditors act in different currency areas.
26 Local foreign liabilities of banks are deposits inside the country kept in foreign currency. Local assets of banks in foreign currency are domestic credits given in foreign currency. In these cases foreign currencies take over domestic functions.
27 In the Bretton Woods System, as mentioned, central banks with appreciating currencies were forced to intervene in the foreign exchange market to prevent the appreciation of their currencies. In the EMS in the very short term it was the same. However, in the EMS central banks with strong currencies could quickly demand hard currencies from central banks issuing weak currencies. Thus, in the end the EMS had an asymmetric adjustment process.
28 This also occurs in countries with high dollarisation. Domestic debt in a foreign currency can also lead to currency mismatch and to the same problems as foreign debt in foreign currency (Priewe and Herr 2005).
29 Especially for developing countries, there are two more reasons why real depreciations are problematic. First, if import and export elasticities are low a real depreciation will increase the trade deficit (the Marshal–Lerner condition must be fulfilled to depreciate successfully). Second, a real depreciation may push a large proportion of the population below the poverty line and might be politically and socially unacceptable.
30 US foreign debt is nearly 100 per cent of GDP. At the end of 2008 US foreign debt was US$13.75 trillion, GDP in 2008 was US$14.44 trillion (CIA *World Factbook* 2009).
31 At the end of the 1970s restrictive monetary policy was unavoidable in the US. However, Paul Volcker, who followed monetary targeting with mixed success when he became president of the Fed in 1979, adhered to an unnecessarily restrictive policy and in this way maximised the cost to bring inflation down.
32 As far as the disposable income of households is concerned the effect is clear. But positive net income flows to firms can also stimulate investment, for example, when firms have difficulties getting (cheap) credit.
33 For simplification in the following debate we assume current account imbalances and trade imbalances to be identical.
34 Only if capital imports take the form of foreign direct investment or equity portfolio investment is no foreign debt built up.
35 Gross debt can be much bigger than net debt as some sectors in the economy can take foreign credit and other sectors can invest abroad.
36 For the calculation of the index and the weights see Bofinger (2001, chapter 7).
37 Bofinger (2001: 219) also calculated indices of central bank independence for the Swedish central bank (1.1), the Canadian central bank (0.81) and the Reserve Bank of New Zealand (0.51).
38 M2 usually is defined as notes and coins in circulation, demand deposits and other checkable deposits, saving deposits and certain time deposits. M3 is M2 plus money market funds and other liquid assets.
39 Also, central banks in many other countries implemented inflation targeting: Chile in 1991, Brazil, Poland, Colombia and Mexico in 1999, South Africa and Thailand in 2000, South Korea, Hungary and Iceland in 2001, the Philippines and Peru in 2002 (Samimi and Motameni 2009: 1321).
40 It is difficult to calculate a basic interest rate (see below). The monetary policy description would also work without a basic interest rate.
41 Compare Mishkin and Posen (1997), Bernanke *et al.* (1999), Goodhart (1989), Blinder (1998), Bernanke and Mishkin (1997) and Bernanke and Gertler (2000).
42 Owing to the space limitations of this text, we refrain from a deeper discussion about the specifics of the New Consensus and the Post-Keynesian model regarding

monetary policy. Carlin and Soskice (2006), Clarida *et al.* (1999), McCallum (2001) and Taylor (2000) among others give a description of the New Keynesian model. A detailed criticism of the New Consensus from the Post-Keynesian perspective is given in Arestis and Eichner (1988), Arestis and Sawyer (2004, 2006), Fontana (2002, 2004), Fontana and Palacio-Vera (2002, 2004), Hein (2004, 2006) and Palley (2006a).

43 Institutionalists, as well as Marxist and Neo-Ricardians, can also be found in the group of Post-Keynesians. For some of them money is not important. We only discuss here the streams that are important for our topic.

44 For a debate see Robinson (1956), Arestis and Eichner (1988), Parguez and Seccareccia (2000) and Rochon and Rossi (2006).

45 For a debate see Kriesler and Lavoie (2005), Epstein (2005), Epstein and Yeldan (2009: 3–28), Lavoie (1996, 2006), Moore (1988), Palley (2002, 2006b) Fontana and Palacio-Vera (2002, 2004), Fontana (2006b) and Hein (2001).

46 Some suggest real exchange rates as an additional target (Epstein and Yeldan 2009; Debelle 2001).

47 Keynes (1936: 376) even believed that the equilibrium interest rate tends to a value of zero in the long run.

48 As already mentioned in Section 2.1 any change in distribution changes the structure of relative prices and thus the value of the capital stock. A macroeconomic production function must assume a world with only one capital good, otherwise the neoclassical parable breaks down.

49 Wicksell fought his whole life to explain the natural rate of return. He criticised the usual neoclassical argument of a (marginal) productivity of physical capital. He thought the more roundabout production processes were, the more productive they became. This way of thinking led him down a blind alley.

50 Keynes (1936: Chapter 11) discusses explicitly that the marginal efficiency of capital has nothing to do with (marginal) productivity of physical capital, which is the key explanation of a rate of return on capital by neoclassical economists. It is clearer to call the marginal efficiency of capital an expected interest rate for investment in productive capital (Heine and Herr 2003).

51 Whether the Fed should have prevented the stock market bubble at that time is another story. We think a second central bank instrument should have been used to slow the bubble at that time and not interest rate policy.

52 Portfolio shifts between long-term debt-securities and shares as long-term investment and short-term bank deposits have already been discussed in detail by Keynes (1930b).

53 The liquidity and investment traps can actually be found in Keynes (1936). However, Keynes only referred to the liquidity trap as a theoretical possibility, which was not likely to occur in his opinion. Keynes emphasised the investment trap.

54 Monetarists such as Friedman who were fighting against Keynesian 'fiscalists' prove themselves to be better 'Keynesians' when they emphasise the effectiveness of monetary policy with respect to the Neoclassical Synthesis (Friedman 1968).

55 For support of this argument, see Minsky (1982), Bernanke and Gertler (1989) and Bernanke *et al.* (1994).

56 It was also shown that interest rate policy of the German Bundesbank from the beginning of the 1970s up to the year 2003 was even more effective in recessions than in periods of economic expansion (Kuzin and Tober 2004). Such findings are not only restricted to Germany but can also be found in the euro area (Peersman and Smets 2001; María-Dolores 2002). Similar results were observed by Garcia and Schaller (2002) for the US. According to their investigations, interest rate changes in the US appear to be two to three times more effective during recessions than they are in boom phases.

57 The situation is different in regions within one currency area. If German unit labour

costs more or less stay the same over long periods while in other regions of the European Monetary Unit (EMU) unit labour costs increase substantially, German firms will crowd out firms that are permanently confronted with increasing unit labour costs. Exchange rate adjustments in such cases cannot compensate for higher increases in unit labour costs.

58 We assume monopolistic competition, as under pure competition firms are not able to influence prices. But there is a general problem with the assumption of pure competition. If firms have no influence on prices the question is: Who changes prices? In the absence of pure competition this problem does not exist.

59 In national accounting categories profit inflation exists if, and here for simplicity we omit governments and foreign countries, net investment is greater than households' savings and firms react with price increases.

60 In the 1970s stagflation became the stumbling block to the Neoclassical Synthesis which assumed that the Phillips curve, which states a trade-off between decreasing unemployment rates and increasing inflation, is stable. In comparison with Keynes the Keynesians from the Neoclassical Synthesis were hard put to explain stagflation.

61 We follow Mankiw (2001: 41): 'As a practical matter, Fed policy of the 1990s might well be described as "covert inflation targeting" at a rate of about 3 per cent.'

62 The neoclassical paradigm in all its standard models assumes that a worker can stay at home and consume her or his leisure time when real wages are very low. The firm in this vision of the economy is forced, so to speak, to offer good wages as otherwise a utility-maximising worker simply is not interested in working.

63 The Treaty of Detroit was a contract negotiated between the United Auto Workers and the big three car producers in the US in 1950. It was a long-term contract which was aimed at reducing strikes in exchange for stable medium-term wage increases, extensive health, unemployment and pension benefits and increased vacation time. The Treaty was used as a model for other industries.

64 In addition, the non-existence of strong employers' associations leads to poor vocational training on the corporate level as firms have the incentive to let the others train workers and then to hire them.

65 See Ball and Mankiw (2002), Layard *et al.* (1994), Gordon (1993) and Franz (1996). For a critical discussion see Stiglitz (1997) and Hein (2002, 2003).

66 Legally fixed expenditures are primarily social security expenditures. Discretionary expenditures are combined under the three titles 'defence budget', 'international' and 'domestic' and are fixed each year and can vary. Each of these expenditure titles are brought together with certain taxes into what are called pay-as-you-go (PAYGO) pools. When a fixed upper expenditure limit is exceeded, it must be financed by tax increases and/or expenditure reductions in another position in the corresponding pool (Blinder and Yellen 2001).

67 Smithin (2007) and Wray (2007) argue in this direction. Also compare Hein (2004, 2006) as well as Hein and Truger (2008).

68 Functional finance as a concept was first developed by Lerner (1943).

69 This argument also makes clear that public debt does not lead to redistribution between generations but to a redistribution within future generations.

70 We should keep in mind that the marginal product is derived from a macroeconomic production function, which only exists under the assumption of one capital good.

71 We assume that variable costs depend only on labour inputs. Marginal costs are then labour input for one additional output unit multiplied by the wage rate, $(\partial Hr/\partial Yr)\cdot w$. As $\partial Yr/\partial H$ gives the marginal product of labour we get as marginal costs w/MP_L.

72 Compare for example Bhaduri (2008), Bhaduri and Marglin (1990), Lavoie (1995) or Hein and Vogel (2008).

73 For example Thomas Palley (1998: 67) draws an arrow from bargaining power to distribution and writes: 'Thus, profits in these sectors were high, and with the help of unions, workers were able to capture some of these profits in the form of higher

wages.' On p. 115 in the same book he stresses the relationship between wages and prices and writes that after a supply shock like increasing oil prices 'the inflation is self-sustaining as the price increases feed into wages, which then feedback into costs and prices'. Levy and Temin (2010: 42) also argue that the deterioration of the bargaining power of workers reduced the wage quota. The same problem can be found in Hein and Truger (2010).

74 Mathematically it has one degree of freedom. This is the difference to the neoclassical General Equilibrium Model which determines relative prices and distribution at the same time.

75 The capital coefficient depends on existing technology and also on distribution as any profit rate leads to a unique system of relative prices and to a unique value of the aggregated capital stock.

76 Above, it was argued that Keynes (1936: chapter 17) with l as liquidity premium, i as interest rate and q as profit rate draws the following sequence: $l = i = q$. We can also interpret l as the rate of return financial agents demand from productive investment independent of the interest rate. Then we get $l = q$ without the interest as a necessary link.

77 In this case the demand curve for labour for skilled workers shifts to the right while the demand curve for unskilled workers shifts to the left.

78 This is known as the Amoroso–Robinson Relation.

79 When the price elasticity of demand approaches minus infinity the equation becomes identical with the condition to maximise profit under pure competition. In the latter case the price cannot be changed by a firm.

80 This argument adheres to the tradition of Sraffa (1960) and the so-called Cambridge-Cambridge debate.

81 In Figure 2.25 D1 stands for the bottom 10 percent of wage earners, whereas D9 stands for the top 10 per cent of wage earners.

82 However, there were also countries which were able to reduce wage dispersion. The most successful countries were Spain, coming from a state of an underdeveloped economy with huge wage differentials, but also France. In Austria, wage polarisation was decreased by reducing wage dispersion among high earners.

83 Only female employees with a BA degree were able to improve their relative wage position in the US (Levy and Temin 2010: 23).

84 In 2007, the bottom 90 per cent of households were those with incomes below about US$110,000. The next 9 per cent were those with incomes between US$110,000 and about US$400,000, and the top 0.1 per cent were those with incomes above about US$2,000,000. Calculations are in current 2007 dollars (Feller and Stone 2009).

85 The Gini-coefficient expresses deviation from a situation of completely equal distribution, at which its value would be zero. The higher the coefficient, the more marked the inequality.

86 The 1950s show the same picture.

87 Economists like Minsky (1975) and Kindleberger (1996) analysed such credit-driven expansion long ago. For arguments in the same direction among many others compare Palley (1998, 2009) or Hein and Schoder (2009).

88 For a similar approach and for more details see Dullien *et al.* (2009, 2011).

89 There are different possibilities for such a regulation. For example, equity holding of banks (and other financial institutions) could at least partly follow a standard approach as was the case in Basel I. That means different asset classes can be created, preferably more than in Basel I, and for each class a certain percentage of assets should be kept as equity independent of the business cycle and asset price developments. However, equity holdings by financial institutions could also be made anti-cyclical. Goodhart (2009: 53ff.) recommends anti-cyclical capital adequacy requirements which vary with asset price developments. Palley (2004) demands asset-based reserve requirements to reduce credit expansion in periods of asset price

bubbles and stimulate credit expansion in periods of asset price deflation. The best way would be that the central bank has the discretionary power to change such requirements or risk models could relate equity holding positively with asset price changes.

90 The regulation depends on the tradition of the financial system. In financial systems with universal banks the banking system traditionally kept big share packages but as a long-term investment. In the US under the Glass–Steagall Act (1932/33), which was in place until the 1990s, commercial banks were not allowed to keep shares.

91 For more details of such reforms see also Fitoussi and Stiglitz (2009), Bofinger (2009) or Hein and Truger (2010).

92 Countries that face high foreign debt in foreign currency or other problems to depreciate could in addition be granted the right to use a general tariff on all imports to protect themselves from high current account deficits. For the price competitiveness an increase in tariff has the same effects as depreciation.

93 This is a way to organise collective action and to produce the public good of a stable price level (Olson 1965). Calmfors and Driffill (1988) and Soskice (1990) argue in the same logic.

94 Employers' associations in many countries used to support equal wages for equal work. However, this changed. Two interpretations are possible. First, small companies or companies with relatively low productivity started to dominate employers' associations. Second, employers' associations were against collective bargaining to weaken unions and valued this aim more highly than the removal of the dysfunctional situation of having different wages for one type of work in one industry.

95 We prefer a pension system on the basis of pay-as-you-go, where expenditures are financed by the currently employed generation, and not a capital-based system. A pay-as-you-go system is more stable and makes distribution conflicts between the young and elderly more open and politically debatable. Of course, in addition to a pay-as-you-go system private savings are always possible but should not be subsidised by the state. Switzerland, for example, has a pension system where all persons who live in the country and are employed (or self-employed), from the unskilled worker to the general manager, have to become members.

96 This idea of functional finance became popular again among some Post-Keynesians (see Section 2.6).

97 Keynes was always in favour of an international solution to stabilise currencies and financial markets. As second best he suggested national solutions. For a global solution see Keynes (1942), for a national solution Keynes (1933).

98 In the Congressional testimony on 23 October, 2008, Alan Greenspan acknowledged that he was 'partially' wrong in opposing regulation and stated: 'Those of us who have looked to the self-interest of lending institutions to protect shareholder's equity – myself especially – are in a state of shocked disbelief.' (cited in Lanman and Matthews 2008). Stiglitz (2008) correctly stated that Greenspan 'didn't really believe in regulation; when the excesses of the financial system were noted, [he and others] called for self-regulation – an oxymoron.'

99 This would also reduce the incentive to use all types of tricks to reduce profits with the aim to cut the tax burden.

100 We could add here migration which changes population and the supply of labour.

3 Case studies

1 Initially, interest rate ceilings were restricted to the commercial banking sector. However, facing rising competition among thrifts Regulation Q was extended to the savings and loan associations in 1966 in order to prevent deposit rate wars. Nevertheless, ceilings for thrifts were allowed to be higher than for commercial banks (FDIC 1997: 217).

2 Hellmann *et al.* (2000) show in a formal model that deposit-rate ceilings are appropriate since imprudent gambling strategies are prevented.

3 In addition, the act established uniform reserve requirements for all depository institutions and the right for all depository institutions to borrow from the Fed.

4 The CFMA was preceded by provisions of the CFTC issued in 1989 and revised in 1993 that exempted swaps that met several conditions from regulation under the CEA. However, in 2000 most of the swaps did not meet these conditions (Jickling 2003: 6–7).

5 The Texas energy company Enron that collapsed in 2001 was actively engaged in OTC derivative trading. In November 2008 the New York Times published E-mails written by Enron executives showing the way in which they influenced negotiations on the CFMA. According to these E-mails Enron officials advocated exempting provisions for energy trading by paying particular attention to the Republican Senator from Texas Phil Gramm who had a key role in writing the act (Lipton 2008).

6 Also called Food, Conservation, and Energy Act of 2008. The bill was vetoed by the then president George W. Bush but the veto was overridden by the House and the Senate.

7 Also called Gramm–Leach–Bliley Act (GLBA).

8 In a speech in 2008, US Finance Secretary in the Obama government, Timothy Franz Geithner argued:

> This non-bank financial system grew to be very large, particularly in money and funding markets. In early 2007, asset-backed commercial paper conduits, in structured investment vehicles, in auction-rate preferred securities, tender option bonds and variable rate demand notes, had a combined asset size of roughly \$2.2 trillion. Assets financed overnight in triparty repo grew to \$2.5 trillion. Assets held in hedge funds grew to roughly \$1.8 trillion. The combined balance sheets of the then five major investment banks totalled \$4 trillion. In comparison, the total assets of the top five bank holding companies in the United States at that point were just over \$6 trillion, and total assets of the entire banking system were about \$10 trillion.

9 In Table 2.7 nominal wage increases in the 1990s and 2000s are shown to be around 1 per cent too low. However, we should keep in mind that the target inflation rate in the USA was taken as 3 per cent and not as 2 per cent as in the other countries.

10 For a comparison of this: 10 per cent of US citizens do not have a high school diploma.

11 'For example, increased domestic and international competition, a decline in unionisation, and increased concern about job security are possible reasons why, at current levels of unemployment, wage and price pressures have been so subdued' (CEA 1996: 53).

12 That monetary policy was too restrictive in 1979–1982 can for example be indicated by a Taylor rule. Using such a rule Mankiw (2001) shows that interest were much too high in most of the time in the period.

13 The Council of Economic Advisors particularly emphasised the functionality of the automatic stabilisers in the Budget Enforcement Act:

> A balanced budget amendment would throw the automatic stabilizers into reverse. The Congress would be required to raise taxes or cut spending programs in the face of a recession, to counteract temporary increases in the deficit. Rather than moderate the normal ups and downs in the business cycle, fiscal policy would be forced to aggravate them.
>
> (CEA 1995: 30)

14 Among other changes, the lowest income tax rate was lowered from 15 to 10 per cent, the 27 per cent rate went to 25 per cent, the 30 per cent rate to 28 per cent, the 35 per

cent rate to 33 per cent, and the top marginal tax rate decreased from 39.6 to 35 per cent.

15 See also Mankiw (2001: 51):

> Despite this environment, and the fact that a prominent conservative headed the U.S. central bank, the FED during the 1990s avoided any type of commitment to a policy rule. Conservative economists are sceptical about policies that rely heavily on the judgments of any one man. But that is how monetary policy was made over this decade, and it was hailed as a success by liberals and conservatives alike.

16

> From France to the Philippines, from Jamaica to Japan, from Malaysia to Mexico, from Sri Lanka to Singapore, privatisation is on the move … The policies we have pioneered are catching on in country after country. We Conservatives believe in popular capitalism – believe in a property-owning democracy. And it works! … The great political reform of the last century was to enable more and more people to have a vote. Now the great Tory reform of this century is to enable more and more people to own property. Popular capitalism is nothing less than a crusade to enfranchise the many in the economic life of the nation. We Conservatives are returning power to the people. That is the way to one nation, one people.
>
> (Speech delivered by Margaret Thatcher at the Conservative Party Conference on 10 October 1986 in Hampshire)

17 Also over the post-war period the growth rate in UK was much slower than in the other industrialised countries (Crafts and Woodward 1991: 8).

18 Secondary banks consisted of accepting houses (which set the foot for the Eurobond market in London, were involved in foreign trade, and in underwriting foreign securities), overseas banks (with the majority of their assets abroad) and foreign banks.

19 Secondary banks owned 46 per cent of the total assets in the financial sector in 1970, up from 13 per cent in 1960 (Gola and Roselli 2009: 8).

20 The assets of insurance and pension funds as a share of the total UK financial assets increased from 12.5 per cent in 1990 to 17.5 per cent in 1999 (Gola and Roselli 2009: 21).

21 For only six weeks in 1972 the UK was a part of the so-called 'snake' where some European currencies pegged one-sided to the D-Mark to reduce exchange rate fluctuations.

22 Empirical studies have shown that the British pound at the entry into the European Monetary System was 10 per cent overvalued (Cobham 2001: 75).

23 Union density increased from 42 per cent of the work force in 1969 to 52 per cent in 1979. Afterwards the process of a steady decline started, reaching a level of below 30 per cent in 2007 (OECD 2009d).

24 See Freeman and Pelletier (1989) for a more articulate overview of the regulatory changes in the labour market in the 1970s and 1980s.

25 In 2007, approximately 4.5 per cent of all employees were covered by the minimum wage (Low Pay Commission 2008: 67).

26 One way to show this is the annual change in the ratio minimum wage/average wage. This ratio was from 1998 onwards (except 2003) steadily increasing and reached a level of 51.1 per cent in 2007 (Low Pay Commission 2008: 67).

27 As an illustration, the cyclically adjusted budget deficit in 1973 was 5.7 per cent compared with the actual deficit of 4.2 per cent.

28 For the theoretical debate about German unification see Heine *et al.* (1990) and Westphal *et al.* (1991).

29 Oskar Lafontaine left the SPD and from 2007 until 2010 was one of the two party leaders of Die Linke.

30 The EMS was a fixed exchange system with the possibility of realignments. Compared with the Bretton Woods System, the leading currency of the system was not institutionally fixed but was determined by markets.

31 Wolfgang Streek (2009) delivers an excellent analysis of the institutional changes in Germany. The shortcoming of his analysis is that he sticks theoretically to the neoclassical labour market model.

32 This also becomes clear by the following statement by the ECB:

> The exchange rate of the euro depreciated further during this period. The Governing Council took the view that such a prolonged phase of depreciation combined with the significant oil price increase could have medium-term inflationary consequences in a period of strong economic growth, as this could give rise to second-round effects on consumer prices via wage increases.
>
> (ECB 2001: 84f.)

33 A solidarity tax (a temporary surcharge of 7.5 per cent on income and corporate tax payments from the middle of 1991 to the middle of 1992) was introduced; mineral oil tax and insurance tax were raised in the middle of 1991; and the tax on tobacco was increased in 1992. At the beginning of 1993 VAT was raised and again the tax on oil. In contrast, top income tax rates and corporation tax rates were lowered in 1994. Finally in 1995, the solidarity tax of 7.5 per cent was reintroduced. It was reduced to 5.5 per cent at the beginning of 1999 and has been levied ever since.

34 More specifically, there were entry licences which were granted on a discretionary basis by the Ministry of Finance, which also controlled the expansion of existing banks, for example the opening of new branches. The restrictions were particularly strong for insurance companies, whereby no new entrant was allowed in the period after the Second World War until the 1990s. The banks were allowed to hold government bonds, but were not allowed to underwrite, distribute or trade them until 1981 when the Banking Law of 1927 was amended (Kimura/Pugel 1993: 30).

35 It was the Foreign Exchange and Foreign Trade Control Law and the Foreign Investment Law of 1949 that set the institutional framework for controlling international capital flows. Government had the discretionary power to control capital flows on a case-by-case basis. Also, an individual foreign bidder could acquire only 10 per cent of the total shares of a Japanese company, or in a case of a group bidder, the ownership could be extended to 25 per cent (Wallace 2002: 214f.).

36 See Tabb (1995) and Kitamura (1991) for a more detailed description about the development of the post-war Japanese financial system.

37 Japan switched from being a net debtor to a net creditor in 1967.

Bibliography

Abdul, A, Detragiache, E and Tressel, T 2008, 'A new database of financial reforms', IMF (International Monetary Fund) Working Paper No. 08/266.

Akerlof, G, and Shiller, RJ 2008, *Animal spirits*, Princeton University Press, Princeton.

Alfaro, L 2002, *Capital controls: a political economy approach*, Harvard Business School, viewed 14 June 2010, www.people.hbs.edu/lalfaro/kcontrols.pdf.

AMECO 2010, Annual macro-economic database of the European Commission's Directorate General for Economic and Financial Affairs.

Amyx, J 2004, *Japan's financial crisis: institutional rigidity and reluctant change*, Princeton University Press, Princeton.

Aoki, M 2001, *Toward a comparative institutional analysis*, The MIT Press, Cambridge, MA.

Arestis, P and Eichner, AS 1988, 'The Post-Keynesian and Institutionalist theory of money and credit', Journal of Economic Issues, vol. 22, no. 4, pp. 1003–1021.

Arestis, P and Sawyer, MC 2004, *Re-examining monetary and fiscal policy for the 21st century*, Edward Elgar, Cheltenham, UK.

Arestis, P and Sawyer, MC 2006, 'The nature and role of monetary policy when money is endogenous', *Cambridge Journal of Economics*, vol. 30, no. 6, pp. 847–860.

Artis, MS and Lewis, MK 1981, *Monetary control in the United Kingdom*, Phillip Allan, Oxford.

Atkinson, AB, Piketty, T and Saez, E 2009, 'Top incomes in the long run of history', NBER (National Bureau of Economic Research) Working Paper No. 15408.

Auerbach, AJ 2008, 'Federal budget rules: the US experience', *Swedish Economic Policy Review*, vol. 15, no. 1, pp. 57–82.

Baba, N, Nishioka, S, Oda, N, Shirakawa, M, Ueda, K and Ugai, H 2005, 'Japan's deflation, problems in the financial system and monetary policy', Bank for International Settlements (BIS) Working Papers No. 188.

Ball, L and Mankiw, NG 2002, 'The NAIRU in theory and practise', *Journal of Economic Perspectives*, vol. 16, no. 4, pp. 115–136.

Balls E and O'Donnel, G 2002, *Reforming Britain's economic and financial policy: towards greater economic stability*, Palgrave, Basingstoke, Hampshire, England.

Bank of England 2010, *Explanatory notes – wholesale*, Interactive database, viewed 2 July 2010, www.bankofengland.co.uk/mfsd/iadb/notesIADB/wholesale_baserate.htm.

Bank of Japan 1999, *On recent monetary policy*, Excerpt of a speech given by Masaru Hayami, 22 June 1999, viewed 2 July 2010, www.boj.or.jp/en/type/press/koen/kako/ko9907b.htm.

Bank of Japan 2010, Flow of funds accounts time series database.

Barro, RJ 1974, 'Are government bonds net wealth?', *Journal of Political Economy*, vol. 82, no. 6, pp. 1095–1117.

Berger, H, de Haan, J and Eijffinger, SCW 2000, 'Central bank independence: an update of theory and evidence', CESifo Working Paper No. 255.

Bernanke, BS and Gertler, M 1989, 'Agency costs, net worth, and business fluctuations', *American Economic Review*, vol. 79, no. 1, pp. 14–31.

Bernanke, B and Gertler, M 1995, 'Inside the Black Box: the credit channel of monetary policy transmission', *Journal of Economic Perspectives*, vol. 9, pp. 27–48.

Bernanke, BS and Gertler, M 2000, 'Monetary policy and price volatility', NBER (National Bureau of Economic Research) Working Paper No. 7559.

Bernanke, BS and Gertler, M 2001, 'Should central banks respond to movements in asset prices?'; *American Economic Review*, vol. 91, no. 2, pp. 253–257.

Bernanke, BS and Mishkin, FS 1997, 'Inflation targeting: a new framework for monetary policy', NBER (National Bureau of Economic Research) Working Paper No. 5893.

Bernanke, BS, Gertler, M and Glichrist, S 1994, 'The financial accelerator and the flight to quality', NBER (National Bureau of Economic Research) Working Paper No. 4789.

Bernanke, BS, Laubach, T, Mishkin, FS and Posen, AS 1999, *Inflation targeting: lessons from the international experience*, Princeton University Press, Princeton NJ.

Bhaduri, A 2008, 'On the dynamics of profit-led and wage-led growth', *Cambridge Journal of Economics*, vol. 32, no. 1, pp. 147–160.

Bhaduri, A and Marglin, S 1990, 'Unemployment and the real wage: the economic basis for contesting political ideologies', *Cambridge Journal of Economics*, vol. 14, no. 4, pp. 375–393.

BIS (Bank for International Settlements) 2007, *Triennial Central Bank Survey: Foreign Exchange and Derivatives Market Activity in 2007*, Bank for International Settlements, Basel.

BIS (Bank for International Settlements) 2009, Semiannual OTC derivatives statistics at end-December 2009.

BIS (Bank for International Settlement) 2010a, BIS effective exchange rate indices.

BIS (Bank for International Settlement) 2010b, *BIS Quarterly Review: International banking and financial market developments*, Bank for International Settlements, Basel.

Bispinck, R and Schulten, T 2009, 'Re-Stabilisierung des deutschen Flächentarifvertragssystems', WSI (Wirtschafts- und Sozialwissenschaftliche Institut) Mitteilungen, vol. 62, pp. 201–217.

Bladen-Hovell, RC 2001, 'Fiscal policy and the budget', in *The UK economy: a manual of applied economics*, ed. M Sawyer, Oxford University Press, Oxford, pp. 70–92.

Blanchard, O, Dell'Ariccia, G and Mauro, P 2010, 'Rethinking macroeconomic policy', IMF (International Monetary Fund) Staff Position Note No. 10/03.

Blinder, A 1998, *Central banking in theory and practice*, The MIT Press, Cambridge, MA.

Blinder, A and Yellen, J 2001, *The fabulous decade, macroeconomic lessons from the 1990s*, The Century Foundation Press, New York.

BLS (US Bureau of Labor Statistics) 2010, Current Population Survey database.

Bofinger, P 2001, *Monetary policy: goals, institutions, strategies, and instruments*, Oxford University Press, New York.

Bofinger, P 2009, 'Public sector credit rating agencies: more stable financial architecture', in *Re-defining the global economy*, Friedrich Ebert Foundation, Dialogue on Globalisation, Occasional Paper No. 42, New York, pp. 33–36.

Bosch, G, Kalina, T and Weinkopf, C 2008, 'Niedriglohnbeschäftigte auf der Verliererseite', WSI (Wirtschafts- und Sozialwissenschaftliche Institut) Mitteilungen, vol. 61, pp. 423–429.

Brown, C, Eichengreen, B and Reich, M 2010, 'Introduction: labour in the era of globalisation', in *Labour in the era of globalisation*, eds C Brown, B Eichengreen and M Reich, Cambridge University Press, Cambridge, pp. 1–15.

Bubula, A and I Ötker-Robe 2002, 'The evolution of exchange rate regimes since 1990: evidence form de-facto policies', IMF (International Monetary Fund) Working Paper No. 02/155.

Buckle, M and Thompson, JL 2004, *The UK financial system*, 4th edn, Manchester University Press, Manchester.

BulwienGesa AG 2009, *Immobilienindex 1975–2009*, viewed 9 July 2010, www.bulwiengesa.de/fileadmin/user_upload/PDFfiles/Firmenbroschueren/ImmoIndex_dt.pdf.

Calleo, DP 1981, 'Inflation and American power', *Foreign Affairs*, vol. 59, no. 4, pp. 781–812.

Calmfors, L and Driffill, J 1988, 'Centralisation of Wage Bargaining: bargaining structure, corporatism and macroeconomic performance', Economic Policy, vol. 3, no. 1, pp. 13–61.

Card, D 1992, 'The effect of unions on the distribution of wages: redistribution or relabelling?', NBER (National Bureau of Economic Research) Working Paper No. 4195.

Cardarelli, R, Igan, D and Rebucci, A 2008, 'The changing housing cycle and the implications for monetary policy', in *World economic outlook: financial stress, downturns, and recoveries*, International Monetary Fund, Washington DC, pp. 103–132.

Carlin W and Soskice, D 2006, *Macroeconomics: imperfections, institutions and policies*, Oxford University Press, Oxford.

Carlin, W and Soskice, D 2007, 'Reformen, Makroökonomische Politik und Wirtschaftsentwicklung in Deutschland', in *Aufschwung für Deutschland*, eds R Schettkat and J Langkau, Dietz Verlag, Frankfurt aM, pp. 105–165.

CEA (Council of Economic Advisors) 1995, *Economic Report of the President*, United States Government Printing Office, Washington DC.

CEA (Council of Economic Advisors) 1996, *Economic report of the President*, United States Government Printing Office, Washington DC.

CIA (Central Intelligence Agency) 2009, *The world factbook*, Washington DC, viewed 14 June 2010, www.cia.gov/index.html.

Clarida, R, Galí, J and Gertler, M 1999, 'The science of monetary policy: a New Keynesian perspective', NBER (National Bureau of Economic Research) Working Paper No. 7147.

Clark, T and Dilnot, A 2002, 'Long-term trends in British taxation and spending', The Institute for Fiscal Studies (IFS) Briefing Note No. 25.

Clarke, M 1986, *Regulating the city: competition, scandal and reform*, Open University Press, Philadelphia.

Cobham, D 2001, *The making of monetary policy in the UK: 1975–2000*, Series in Financial Economics and Quantitative Analysis, John Wiley & Sons, Chichester, England.

Colander, DC and Matthews, PH 2006, 'Integrating sound finance with functional finance', in *The means to prosperity: fiscal policy reconsidered*, eds PG Berglund and M Vernengo, Routledge, London, pp. 52–66.

Collins, M 1988, *Money and banking in the UK: a history*, Croom Helm, London.

Crafts, NFR and Woodward, NWC 1991, *The British economy since 1945*, Clarendon Press, Oxford.

Cukierman, A 1992, *Central bank strategy, credibility, and independence*, The MIT Press, Cambridge, MA.

Curry, T and Shibut, L 2000, 'The cost of the savings and loan crisis: truth and consequences', *Federal Deposit Insurance Corporation (FDIC) Banking Review*, vol. 13, no. 2, pp. 26–35.

Daniel, WW and Millward, N 1983, *Workplace industrial relations in Britain*, Heinemann, London.

Davidson, P 1991 'Is probability theory relevant for uncertainty? A Post Keynesian perspective', *Journal of Economic Perspective*, vol. 5, no. 1, pp. 129–143.

Debelle, G 2001, 'The case for inflation targeting in East Asian countries', in *Future directions for monetary policies in East Asia*, eds D Gruen and J Simon, Reserve Bank of Australia, Planet Press, Condell Park NSW, Australia, pp. 65–87.

Deutsche Bundesbank 2010, Time series database.

Dimsdale, NH 1991, British monetary policy since 1945, in *The British economy since 1945*, eds NFR Crafts and NWC Woodward, Clarendon Press, Oxford, pp. 89–140.

DiNardo, J, Fortin, NM and Lemieux, T 1996, 'Labor market institutions and the distribution of wages, 1973–1992: a semiparametric approach', *Econometrica*, vol. 65, no. 5, pp. 1001–1046.

Dixit, A and Pindyck, RS 1994, *Investment under uncertainty*, Princeton University Press, Princeton NJ.

Dodd, R 2007, 'Subprime: tentacles of a crisis', *Finance and Development*, vol. 44, no. 4, pp. 15–19.

Dooley, M, Folkerts-Landau, D and Garber, P 2003, 'An essay on the revived Bretton Woods System', NBER (National Bureau of Economic Research) Working Paper No. 9971.

Dornbusch, R 1976, 'Exchange Rate Expectations and Monetary Policy', *Journal of International Economics*, vol. 6, 231–244.

Dornbusch, R and Frankel, J 1988, 'The flexible exchange rate system: experience and alternatives', in *International finance and trade in a polycentric world*, ed. S Borner, Palgrave Macmillan Press, London, pp. 151–197.

Dow, JCR and Saville, ID 1990, *A critique of monetary policy: theory and British experience*, Oxford University Press, Oxford.

Dullien, S, Herr, H, and Kellermann, C 2009, *Der gute Kapitalismus*, Transcript, Bielefeld, North Rhine-Westphalia, Germany.

Dullien, S, Herr, H, and Kellermann, C 2011, *Decent Capitalisms*, London, Pluto.

ECB (European Central Bank) 1999, *Monthly Bulletin January 1999*, European Central Bank, Frankfurt aM.

ECB (European Central Bank) 2001, *The Monetary Policy of the ECB*, European Central Bank, Frankfurt aM.

ECB (European Central Bank) 2002, *Monthly Bulletin November 2002*, European Central Bank, Frankfurt aM.

ECB (European Central Bank) 2003, *Monthly Bulletin May 2003*, European Central Bank, Frankfurt aM.

ECB (European Central Bank) 2010, Statistical data warehouse.

Economic Report of the President: 2009 Report Spreadsheet Tables 2009, B-73: Bond yields and interest rates, 1929–2008, viewed 9 July 2010, www.gpoaccess.gov/eop/tables09.html.

Economists' statement opposing the Bush tax cuts 2003, Economic Policy Institute, viewed 14 June 2010, www.epi.org/page/-/old/stmt/2003/statement_signed.pdf.

Eichengreen, B 2004, 'Global imbalances and the lessons of Bretton Woods' NBER (National Bureau of Economic Research) Working Paper No. 10497.

Eichengreen, B and Hausmann, R (eds) 2005, *Other people's money: debt denomination and financial instability in emerging market economies*, University of Chicago Press, Chicago.

Emminger, O 1986, *D-Mark, Dollar, Währungskrisen: Erinnerungen eines ehemaligen Bundesbankpräsidenten*, Deutsche Verlags-Anstalt, Stuttgart.

Epstein, GA (ed.) 2005, *Financialization and the world ecomomy*, Edward Elgar, Cheltenham, UK.

Epstein, GA and Yeldan, AE 2009, *Beyond inflation targeting: assessing the impacts and policy alternative*, Edward Elgar Publishing, Cheltenham, UK.

Eucken, W [1939] 1992, *The foundations of economics: history and theory in the analysis of economic reality*, Springer, Berlin.

Ewing, KD 2006, *The right to strike: from the Trade Disputes Act 1906 to a Trade Union Freedom Bill 2006*, Institute of Employment Rights, Liverpool.

Fama, E 1970, 'Efficient capital markets: a review of theory and empirical work', *Journal of Finance*, vol. 25, no. 2, pp. 383–417.

Farber, H 2003, 'Job loss in the United States: 1981–2001', Princeton University, Industrial Relations Section, Working Paper No. 471.

FDIC (Federal Deposit Insurance Corporation) 1997, *An examination of the banking crises of the 1980s and early 1990s*, vol. 1, History of the eighties: lessons for the future, viewed 28 April 2010, www.fdic.gov/bank/historical/history/vol. 1.html.

Fed (Federal Reserve Board) 2010, Flow of funds accounts of the United States.

Federal Reserve Bank of St. Louis 2010, Federal reserve economic data.

Feller, A and Stone, C 2009, *Top 1 percent of Americans reaped two-thirds of income gains in last economic expansion*, Centre of Budget and Policy Priorities, viewed 14 June 2010, www.cbpp.org/files/9–9–09pov.pdf.

Ferguson RW 2003, *Uncertain times: economic challenges facing the United States and Japan*, viewed 2 July 2010, www.federalreserve.gov/boarddocs/speeches/2003/200306112/default.htm.

Financial Trend Forecaster 2010, InflationData.com.

Fischer, S, Sahay, R and Végh, CA 2002, 'Modern hyper- and high inflations', *Journal of Economic Literature*, vol. 15, no. 3, pp. 837–880.

Fisher, I 1933, 'The debt deflation theory of great depressions', *Econometrica*, vol. 1, no. 4, pp. 337–357.

Fitoussi, JP and Stiglitz, J 2009, 'The ways out of the crisis and the building of a more cohesive world', OFCE (Observatoire Français des Conjonctures économiques) Document de Travail No. 2009–17.

Flassbeck, H 1992, 'Verfehlte Geldpolitik', *DIW (German Institute for Economic Research) Wochenbericht*, no. 31–32, pp. 385–389.

Fontana, G 2002, 'The making of monetary policy in endogenous money theory: an introduction', *Journal of Post Keynesian Economics*, vol. 24, no. 4, pp. 503–509.

Fontana, G 2004, 'Post Keynesian approaches to endogenous money: a time framework explanation', *Review of Political Economy*, vol. 15, no. 3, pp. 291–314.

Fontana, G 2006a, 'The "New Consensus" view of monetary policy, a New Wicksellian connection?' The Levy Economics Institute of Bard College, Working Paper No. 476.

Fontana, G 2006b, 'The Federal Reserve and the European Central Bank: a theoretical comparison of their legislative mandates', *Journal of Post Keynesian Economics*, vol. 28, no. 3, pp. 433–450.

Fontana, G and Palacio-Vera, A 2002, 'Monetary policy rules: what are we learning?', *Journal of Post Keynesian Economics*, vol. 24, no. 4, pp. 547–568.

Fontana, G and Palacio-Vera, A 2004, 'Monetary policy uncovered: theory and practice', *International Review of Applied Economics*, vol. 18, no. 1, pp. 25–42.

Franz, W 1996, 'Theoretische Ansätze zur Erklärung der Arbeitslosigkeit: Wo stehen wir 1995?', in *Arbeitslosigkeit und Möglichkeiten ihrer Überwindung*, eds B Gahlen, H Hesse and HJ Ramser, J.C.B. Mohr (Paul Siebeck), Tübingen, pp. 3–46.

Franzese, RJ 2001, 'Strategic interaction of monetary policy makers and wage/price bargainers: a review with implications for the European Common-Currency Area', *Emperica*, vol. 28, no. 4, pp. 457–486.

Freeman, R and Pelletier, J 1989, 'The impact of industrial relations legislation on British union density', NBER (National Bureau of Economic Research) Working Paper No. 3167.

Freeman, R and Weitzman, M [1987] 1999, 'Bonuses and employment in Japan', in *The Japanese economy*, part 2, vol. 6, eds P Drysdale and L Gower, Routledge, London, pp. 221–246.

Friedman, M 1953, 'The case for flexible exchange rates', in *Essays in Positive Economics*, eds M Friedman, University of Chicago Press, Chicago, pp. 157–203.

Friedman, M 1968, 'The role of monetary policy', *The American Economic Review*, vol. 58, no. 1, pp. 1–17.

Friedman, M 1969, *The optimum quantity of money and other essays*, Aldine, Chicago, IL.

Galati, G and Wooldridge, P 2006, 'The Euro as a reserve currency: a challenge to the pre-eminence of the US Dollar?', BIS (Bank of International Settlements) Working Paper No. 218.

Galbraith, K 1967, *The New Industrial State*, Princeton University Press, Princeton.

Garcia, R and Schaller, H 2002, 'Are the effects of monetary policy asymmetric?', *Economic Inquiry*, vol. 40, no. 1, pp. 102–119.

Gerlach, K and Meyer, W 2010, 'Wage effects of work councils and collective agreements in Germany', in *Labour in the era of globalisation*, eds C Brown, B Eichengreen and M Reich, Cambridge University Press, Cambridge, pp. 295–316.

Gola, C and Roselli, A 2009, *The UK banking system and its regulatory supervisory framework*, Palgrave Macmillan, Basingstoke, UK.

Goodhart, C 1989, 'The conduct of monetary policy', *Economic Journal*, vol. 99, no. 396, pp. 293–346.

Goodhart, C 2009, *The regulatory response to the financial crisis*, Edward Elgar, Cheltenham, UK.

Goodman, A and Shephard, A 2002, 'Inequality and living standards in Great Britain: some facts', Institute for Fiscal Studies (IFS) Briefing Note No. 19.

Gordon, RJ 1993, *Macroeconomics*, Harper Collins, New York.

Gosling, A and Lemieux, T 2001, 'Labour market reforms and changes in wage inequality in the United States and the United Kingdom', NBER (National Bureau of Economic Research) Working Paper No. 8413.

Grady, J and Weale, M 1986, *British banking 1960–1985*, Palgrave Macmillan, Basingstoke, UK.

Haavelmo, T 1945, 'Multiplier effects of a balanced budget', *Econometrica*, vol. 13, no. 4, pp. 311–318.

Hahn, F 1981, 'General equilibrium theory', in *The crisis in economic theory*, eds D Bell and I Kristol, Basic Books, New York, pp. 123–138.

Hall, PA 1994, 'Central bank independence and coordinated wage bargaining: their interaction in Germany and Europe', *German Politics and Society*, vol. 31, pp. 1–23.

Hall, PA and Franzese, RJ 1998, 'Mixed signals: central bank independence, coordinated wage bargaining, and European Monetary Union', *International Organisation*, vol. 52, no. 3, pp. 505–535.

Hall, PA and Sockice, D (ed.) 2001, *Varieties of capitalism: the institutional foundations of comparative advantage*, Oxford University Press, Oxford.

Hatton, TJ and Chrystal, KA 1991, 'The budget and fiscal policy', in The British economy since 1945, eds NFR Crafts and NWC Woodward, Clarendon Press, Oxford, pp. 68–90.

Hein, E 2001, 'Institutions and macroeconomic performance: central bank independence, labour market institutions and the perspectives for inflation and employment in the European Monetary Union', WSI (Wirtschafts- und Sozialwissenschaftliche Institut) Diskussionspapiere No. 95.

Hein, E 2002, 'Geldpolitik und Lohnverhandlungssysteme in der EWU', in *Neues Geld – alte Geldpolitik: Die EZB im makroökonomischen Interaktionsraum*, ed. A Heise, Metropolis-Verlag, Marburg, Germany, pp. 199–228.

Hein, E 2003, 'Die NAIRU – eine post-keynesianische Interpretation', Hans Böckler Foundation, WSI (Wirtschafts- und Sozialwissenschaftliche Institut) Diskussionspapier No. 113.

Hein, E 2004, *Verteilung und Wachstum*, Metropolis-Verlag, Marburg, Hesse, Germany.

Hein, E 2006, 'Wage bargaining and monetary policy in a Kaleckian monetary distribution and growth model: trying to make sense of the NAIRU', *Intervention. European Journal of Economics and Economic Policies*, vol. 3, no. 2, pp. 305–329.

Hein, E and Schoder C 2009, 'Interest rates, distribution and capital accumulation: a Post-Kaleckian perspective on the US and Germany', IPE (Institute for International Political Economy) Berlin Working Paper No. 4.

Hein, E and Stockhammer, E 2007, 'Macroeconomic policy mix, employment and inflation in a Post-Keynesian alternative to the New Consensus Model', IMK (Macroeconomic Policy Institute) Working Paper No. 10/2007.

Hein, E and van Treeck, T 2008, *Finanzmarktorientierung – ein Investitions- und Wachstumshemmnis?*, IMK (Macroeconomic Policy Institute) Report No. 26, Düsseldorf, Germany.

Hein, E and Truger, A 2008, 'Fiscal policy in the macroeconomic policy mix: a critique of the New Consensus Model and a comparison of the macroeconomic policies of France, Germany, the UK and Sweden from a Post-Keynesian perspective', IMK (Macroeconomic Policy Institute) Working Paper No. 03/2008.

Hein, E and Truger, A 2010, 'Finance-dominated capitalism in crisis: the case for a Keynesian Global New Deal', IPE (Institute for International Political Economy) Berlin Working Paper No. 2/2010.

Hein, E and Vogel, L 2008, 'Distribution and growth reconsidered: empirical results for six OECD countries', *Cambridge Journal of Economics*, vol. 19, no. 32, pp. 479–511.

Heine, M 2004, 'Wie Deflationen entstehen – und was (nicht nur) die SPD von Brüning gelernt hat', *Prokla*, vol. 134, pp. 105–122.

Heine, M and Herr, H 2003, *Volkswirtschaftslehre: Paradigmenorientierte Einführung in die Mikro- und Makroökonomie*, 3rd edn, Oldenbourg, München.

Heine, M and Herr, H 2008, *Die Europäische Zentralbank: Eine kritische Einführung in die Strategie und Politik der EZB*, 3rd edn, Metropolis-Verlag, Marburg, Hesse, Germany.

Heine, M, Herr, H and Kaiser, C 2006, *Wirtschaftspolitische Regime westlicher Industrienationen*, Nomos, Baden-Baden, Baden-Württemberg, Germany.

Heine, M, Herr, H, Westphal, A, Busch, U and Mondelaers, R (eds) 1990, *Die Zukunft der DDR-Wirtschaft*, Rowohlt, Reinbek, Germany.

Hellmann, TF, Murdock, KC and Stiglitz, JE 2000, 'Liberalization, moral hazard in banking, and prudential regulation: are capital requirements enough?', *The American Economic Review*, vol. 90, no. 1, pp. 147–165.

Herr, H 1990, 'Der bundesdeutsche und japanische Merkantilismus', in *Wirtschaftspolitische Strategien – Probleme ökonomischer Stabilität und Entwicklung in Industrieländern und der Europäischen Gemeinschaft*, ed. HP Spahn, Transfer Verlag, Regensburg, Germany, pp. 84–98.

Herr, H 1992, *Geld, Währungswettbewerb und Währungssysteme. Theoretische und historische Analyse der internationalen Geldwirtschaft*, Campus, Frankfurt a. M./New York.

Herr, H 1997, 'The international monetary system and domestic policy', in *Regime changes: macroeconomic policy and financial regulations in Europe from the 1930s to the 1990s*, eds DJ Forsyth and T Notermans, Berghahn Books, Providence, RI.

Herr, H 2009, 'The labour market in a Keynesian economic regime: theoretical debate and empirical findings', *Cambridge Journal of Economics*, vol. 33, no. 5, pp. 949–965.

Herr, H 2010, 'Credit expansion and development: a Schumpeterian and Keynesian view of the Chinese miracle', *Intervention. European Journal of Economics and Economic Policy*, vol. 7, no. 1, pp. 71–90.

Herr, H and Hübner, K 2005, *Währung und Unsicherheit in der globalen Ökonomie*, edition sigma, Berlin.

Herr, H, Kazandziska, M and Mahnkopf-Praprotnik, S 2009, 'The theoretical debate about minimum wages', Global Labour University Working Paper No. 6.

Herr, H and Priewe, J 2005, 'Development strategies beyond the Washington Consensus', *International Politics and Society*, vol. 2/2005, pp. 72–97.

Herr, H and Spahn, HP 1989, *Staatsverschuldung, Zahlungsbilanz und Wechselkurs. Außenwirtschaftliche Spielräume und Grenzen der Fiskalpolitik*, vol. 5, Studien zur monetären Ökonomie, Metropolis Verlag, Regensburg, Germany.

Herr, H and Stachuletz, R 2010, 'Die Immobilienbubble – Makro- und mikroökonomische Entstehungsmuster nachhaltiger Instabilität und Weg aus der Krise', in *Immobilienbewertung. Mehtoden und Probleme in Rechnungswesen, Besteuerung und Finanzwirtschaft*, eds M Kühnberger and H Wilke, Schäffel-Poeschel Verlag, Stuttgart, pp. 365–394.

Hicks, J 1979, *Causality in economics*, Blackwell, Oxford.

Hiwatari, N 2002, 'Economic downturn, unemployment, and policy reform in Germany and Japan: wage moderation and compensation policies in coordinated market economies', in *Conference Papers – American Political Science Association*, 2002 Annual Meeting, Boston, MA, pp. 1–23.

HM Treasury 2010, *Fiscal policy*, viewed 3 July 2010, http://webarchive.nationalarchives.gov.uk/+/www.hm-treasury.gov.uk/fiscal_policy.htm.

Horn, G and Scheremet, W 1999, 'Erfolgreiche Konsolidierung des amerikanischen Staatshaushalts – ein Beispiel für Europa?', *DIW (German Institute for Economic Research) Wochenbericht*, no. 12, pp. 227–233.

House of Commons Treasury Committee 2008, *The Run on the Rock*, Fifth Report of Session 2007–2008, vol. 1, House of Commons Treasury Committee, London.

Hsu, R 1999, *The MIT encyclopedia of Japanese economy*, 2nd edn, The MIT Press, Cambridge, MA.

ILO (International Labour Organization) 2008, *Global Wage Report 2008/09: Minimum*

Wages and Collective Bargaining. Towards Policy Coherence, International Labour Organization, Geneva.

ILO (International Labour Organization) 2009, Global wage database.

IMF (International Monetary Fund) 2003, *Deflation: determinants, risks, and policy options – Findings of an international task force*, International Monetary Fund, viewed 14 June 2010, www.imf.org/external/pubs/ft/def/2003/eng/043003.pdf.

IMF (International Monetary Fund) 2009a, International financial statistics.

IMF (International Monetary Fund) 2009b, World Economic Outlook database.

IMF (International Monetary Fund) 2010a, *Annual Report on Exchange Arrangements and Exchange Restrictions* (issues from 1966 until 2010), International Monetary Fund, Washington D.C.

IMF (International Monetary Fund) 2010b, Annual Report, Washington D.C.

IMF (International Monetary Fund) 2010c, Financial Soundness Indicators (FSIs), Washington, http://fsi.imf.org/

IMF (International Monetary Fund) 2010d, International financial statistics.

IFS (Institute for Fiscal Studies) 2010, *Summary of the main tax measures introduced in each budget and PBR*, viewed 3 July 2010, www.ifs.org.uk/ff/budget_measures.xls.

Isard, P 1995, *Exchange rate economics*, Cambridge University Press, Cambridge, UK.

Jacoby, SM 2010, 'Finance and labor: perspectives on risk, inequality, and democracy', in *Labour in the era of globalisation*, eds C Brown, B Eichengreen and M Reich, Cambridge University Press, Cambridge, pp. 94–152.

Japan Real Estate Institute 2009, JREI Data, Urban Land Price Index, www.reinet.or.jp/docs/outline/sigaiti-zennkoku.pdf.

Jickling, M 2003, 'The Commodity Futures Modernization Act of 2000: derivatives regulation reconsidered', Congressional Research Service, Report RL30434.

Jickling, M 2008, 'The Enron Loophole', Congressional Research Service, Report RS22912.

Johnson, HG 1972, 'The case for flexible exchange rates', in *Further essays in monetary economics*, ed. HG Johnson, George Allen and Unwin, London, pp. 198–222.

Kaldor, N 1985, *The scourge of Monetarism*, 2nd edn, Oxford University Press, Oxford.

Kalecki, M 1971, 'The distribution of national income', in *Selected essays on the dynamics of the Capitalist economy: 1933–1970*, ed. M Kalecki, Cambridge University Press, Cambridge, pp. 63–77.

Kambayashi, R, Kawaguchi, D and Yamada, K 2008, Minimum wage in a deflationary economy: the Japanese experience 1994–2003', Institute of Economic Research, Hitotsubashi University, Global COE Hi-Stat Discussion Paper No. 074.

Kaminsky, GL and Reinhart, C 1999, 'The twin crises: the causes of banking and balance-of-payments problems', *The American Economic Review*, vol. 89, no. 3, pp. 473–500.

Kastendiek, H and Stinshoff, R 2006, 'Kontinuität und Umbruch: Zur Entwicklung Großbritanniens seit 1945', in *Länderbericht Großbritannien*, eds H Kastendiek and R Sturm, Bundeszentrale für politische Bildung, Bonn, pp. 95–116.

Keynes. JM 1930a, 'Economic possibilities for our grandchildren', in *Essays in persuasion*, ed. JM Keynes, W.W. Norton & Co., New York, pp. 358–373.

Keynes, JM 1930b, *The pure theory of money*, vol. 1, Treatise on money, Cambridge University Press, Cambridge, UK.

Keynes, JM 1930c, *The applied theory of money*, vol. 2, Treatise on money, Cambridge University Press, Cambridge.

Keynes, JM [1933] 1982, 'National self-sufficiency', in *Activities 1929–39: world crisis and policies in Britain and America*, vol. 21, The collected writings of John Maynard Keynes, eds E Johnson and D Moggridge, Palgrave Macmillan, London, pp. 233–246.

Keynes, JM 1936, *The general theory of employment, interest and money*, Cambridge University Press, Cambridge, UK.

Keynes, JM 1937, 'The general theory of employment', *Quarterly Journal of Economics*, vol. 51, no. 2, pp. 209–223.

Keynes, JM [1942] 1969, 'Proposal for an international clearing union', in *The International Monetary Fund 1946–1965*, eds JK Horsfield, vol. 3, International Monetary Fund, Washington DC.

Kimura, Y and Pugel, TA 1993, 'The structure and performance of the Japanese securities industry', in *The Japanese financial system and the cost of capital*, eds Walter, Ingo and Hiraki, Takato, New York University.

Kindleberger, C 1981, 'Dominance and leadership in the international economy: exploitation, public good, and free riders', *International Studies Quarterly*, vol. 25, no. 1, pp. 242–254.

Kindleberger, C 1986, 'International public good without international government', *American Economic Review*, vol. 76, no. 1, pp. 1–13.

Kindleberger, CP 1996, *Manias, panics, and crashes: a history of financial crises*, 3rd edn, Wiley and Sons, New York.

Kitamura, T 1991, 'Investment in financial services', in *Japanese direct investment in Europe: motive, impact and policy implications*, eds M Yoshitomi, I Akimuar and T Kitamura, Avebury, Aldershot, England, pp. 86–117.

Kohl, H 1990, 'Fernsehansprache von Bundeskanzler Kohl anlässlich des Inkrafttretens der Währungs-, Wirtschafts- und Sozialunion am 1. Juli 1990', *Bulletin des Presse- und Informationsamts der Bundesregierung*, vol. 86, pp. 741–742.

Kregel, JA 1980, 'Markets and institutions as features of a capitalistic production system', *Journal of Post Keynesian Economics*, vol. 3, no. 1, pp. 32–48.

Kriesler, P and Lavoie, M 2005, 'The new view on monetary policy: the New Consensus and its Post-Keynesian critique', University of Ottawa, Research On Banking International and National Systems Or Networks Working Paper No. 05–01.

Krugman, P 2002, 'For Richer', *New York Times Magazine* 20 October, p. 62.

Krugman, P 2009, *The conscience of a Liberal: eschatology of lost decades*, The New York Times Blog, viewed 14 June 2010, http://krugman.blogs.nytimes.com/2009/06/09/eschatology-of-lost-decades/.

Krugman, P and Obstfeld, M 2000, *International economics: theory and policy*, 5th edn, Addison-Wesley Longman, Reading, MA.

Kuttner, K and Posen, A 2002, 'Passive savers and fiscal policy effectiveness in Japan', Peterson Institute Working Paper No. 02–2.

Kuzin, V and Tober, S 2004, 'Asymmetric monetary policy effects in Germany', DIW (German Institute for Economic Research) Discussion Paper No. 397.

Kydland, FE and Prescott, EC 1977, 'Rules rather than discretion: the inconsistency of optimal plans', *The Journal of Political Economy*, vol. 85, no. 3, pp. 473–492.

Laffer, A 2004, *The Laffer Curve: past, present, and future*, The Heritage Foundation, viewed 14 June 2010, www.heritage.org/Research/Taxes/bg1765.cfm.

Lanman, S and Matthews, S 2008, 'Greenspan concedes to "flaw" in his market ideology', *Bloomberg* 23 October, viewed 14 June 2010 www.bloomberg.com/apps/news?pid=20601087andsid=ah5qh9Up4rIg.

Latter, T 1997, *Causes and management of banking crisis*, vol. 12, Handbooks in central banking, Centre for Central Banking Studies, Bank of England, London.

Lavoie, M 1995, 'The Kaleckien model of growth and distribution and its Neo-Ricardian and Neo-Marxist critiques', *Cambridge Journal of Economics*, vol. 19, no. 6, pp. 789–818.

Lavoie, M 1996, 'Monetary policy in an economy with endogenous credit money', in *Money in motion: the Post Keynesian and Circulation approaches*, eds G Deleplace and EJ Nell, Palgrave Macmillan, London, pp. 532–545.

Lavoie, M 2006, 'A Post Keynesian amendment to the New Consensus on monetary policy', *Metroeconomica*, vol. 57, no. 2, pp. 165–192.

Layard, R, Nickell, S and Jackman, R 1994, *The unemployment crisis*, Oxford University Press, Oxford.

Lee, D 1999, 'Wage inequality in the United States during the 1980s: rising dispersion or falling minimum wage?', *Quarterly Journal of Economics*, vol. 114, no. 3, pp. 977–1023.

Lerner, A 1943, 'Functional finance and federal debt', *Social Research*, vol. 10, pp. 38–51.

Levy, F and Temin, P 2010, 'Institutions and wages in Post-World War II America', in *Labour in the era of globalisation*, eds C Brown, B Eichengreen and M Reich, Cambridge University Press, Cambridge, pp. 15–51.

Library of Congress 2009, *Japan: Country Case Studies*, Washington DC.

Lipton, E 2008, 'Gramm and the 'Enron Loophole', *New York Times* 17 November, p. 1.

Low Pay Commission 2008, *National Minimum Wage: Low Pay Commission Report 2008*, The Stationery Office, Norwich, UK.

Lucas, RE Jr. 1973, 'Some international evidence on output-inflation trade-offs', *American Economic Review*, vol. 63, no. 3, pp. 326–334.

Lucas, RE Jr. 1981, *Studies in business-cycle theory*, The MIT Press, Cambridge, MA.

Lucas, RE Jr. 1996, 'Nobel lecture: monetary neutrality', *Journal of Political Economy*, vol. 104, no. 4, pp. 661–82.

Machin, S 1996, 'Wage inequality in the UK', *Oxford Review of Economic Policy*, vol. 12, no. 1, pp. 47–64.

Mankiw, GN 2001, 'U.S. monetary policy during the 1990s', NBER (National Bureau of Economic Research) Working Paper No. 8471.

Mankiw, GN 2008, New Keynesian Economics, The Concise Encyclopedia of Economics, Library of Economics and Liberty, viewed 9 July 2010, www.econlib.org/library/Enc/NewKeynesianEconomics.html.

Mankiw, NG and Romer, D (ed.) 1991, *New Keynesian economics*, 2 vol. The MIT Press, Cambridge, MA.

María-Dolores, R 2002, 'Asymmetries in the cyclical effects of monetary policy on output: some European evidence', Fundación de Estudios de Economía Aplicada (FEDEA) Working Paper No. 02–04.

Marx, K [1867] 1992, *A critique of political economy*, vol. 1, Capita, Penguin Classics, London.

McCallum, BT 2001, 'Monetary policy analysis in models without money', *Review*, vol. 83, no. 4, pp. 145–164.

Merton, RK 1949, *Social theory and social structure: toward the codification of theory and research*, Free Press, Glencoe, IL.

Minsky, HP 1975, *John Maynard Keynes*, Columbia University Press, New York.

Minsky, HP 1982, *Can 'It' happen again? Essays on instability and finance*, M.E. Sharpe, Armonk, NY.

Mishel, L, Bernstein, J and Allegretto, S 2006, *The State of Working America 2006/2007*, ILR Press, an imprint of Cornell University Press, Ithaca, NY.

Mishkin, FS and Posen, AS 1997, 'Inflation targeting: lessons from four countries' *Economic Policy Review*, vol. 3, no. 3, pp. 9–110.

Moore, BJ 1988, *Horizontalists and verticalists: the macroeconomics of credit money*, Cambridge University Press, Cambridge.

Morrison, I, Tillett, P and Welch, J 1979, *Banking Act 1979*, Butterworths, London.

Mundell, R 1968, *International economics*, Macmillan, New York.

Mundell, R 2000, 'Currency areas, exchange rate systems and international monetary reform', Universidy of CEMA Working Paper No. 167.

Mussa, M 2003, 'Asset prices and monetary policy', in *Asset price bubbles: the implications for monetary, regulatory, and international policies*, The MIT Press, Cambridge, MA, pp. 41–50.

Muth, JF 1961, 'Rational expectations and the theory of price movements', *Econometrica*, vol. 29, no. 3, pp. 315–335.

Nakakubo, H 2009, 'A new departure in the Japanese minimum wage legislation', *Japan Labor Review*, vol. 6, no. 2, pp. 22–38.

Nakata, YF and Miyazaki, S 2010, 'Increasing labour flexibility during the recession in Japan: the role of female workers in manufacturing', in *Labour in the Era of Globalisation*, eds C Brown, B Eichengreen and M Reich, Cambridge University Press, Cambridge, pp. 191–210.

Nationwide Building Society 2009, House price database.

Obno, K 1994, 'The case for a new system', in *Bretton Woods: looking to the future*, Commission Report, Staff Review, ed. Bretton Woods Commission, Washington DC, pp. C5-C12.

OECD (Organisation for Economic Co-operation and Development) 1980, *Economic Surveys: United Kingdom 1980*, OECD, Paris.

OECD (Organisation for Economic Co-operation and Development) 2005, *Economic Surveys: Japan 2005*, OECD, Paris.

OECD (Organisation for Economic Co-operation and Development) 2009a, *Economic Surveys: Japan 2009*, OECD, Paris.

OECD (Organisation for Economic Co-operation and Development) 2009b, OECD – Society at a Glance 2009, OECD Social Indicators.

OECD (Organisation for Economic Co-operation and Development) 2009c, Economic Outlook No. 85 database.

OECD (Organisation for Economic Co-operation and Development) 2009d, Trade union density (%) in OECD countries, viewed 9 July 2010, www.oecd.org/dataoecd/25/42/39891561.xls.

Office for National Statistics 2010, *Public sector May: £14.1bn budget deficit*, viewed 9 July 2010, www.statistics.gov.uk/cci/nugget.asp?id=206.

Olson, M 1965, *The logic of collective action: public goods and the theory of groups*, Harvard University Press, Harvard.

Palley, TI 1996, *Post Keynesian economics: debt, distribution and the macro economy*, Palgrave Macmillan, London.

Palley, TI 1998, *Plenty of nothing: downsizing of the American dream and the case for Structural Keynesianism*, Princeton University Press, Princeton.

Palley, TI 2000, 'The backward-bending Phillips Curve and the minimum unemployment rate of inflation: wage adjustment with opportunistic firms', Paper presented at the Post Keynesian economics workshop, Knoxville, TN, July 2000.

Palley, TI 2002, *Why inflation targeting is not enough: monetary policy in the presence of financial exuberance*, viewed 9 July 2010, www.thomaspalley.com/docs/research/MoneyControlPosenSubmission.pdf.

Palley, TI 2004; 'Asset-based reserve requirements: reasserting domestic monetary control in an area of financial innovation and instability', *Review of Political Economy*, vol. 16, no. 1, pp. 343–358.

Palley, TI 2006a, 'A Post Keynesian framework for monetary policy: why interest rate operating procedures are not enough', in *Post Keynesian principles of policy*, eds C Gnos and LP Rochon, Edward Elgar, Cheltenham, UK, pp. 81–101.

Palley, TI 2006b, 'The fallacy of the revived Bretton Woods Hypothesis: why today's system is unsustainable and suggestions for a replacement', University of Massachusetts Amherst, Political Economy Research Institute Working Paper No. 114.

Palley, TI 2009, 'America's exhausted paradigm: macroeconomic causes of the financial crisis and great recession'. IPE (Institute for International Political Economy) Berlin Working Paper No. 2.

Parguez, A and Seccareccia, M 2000, 'The credit theory of money: the monetary circuit approach, in *What is money?*, ed. J Smithin, Routledge, London, pp. 101–123.

Patrikis, E 1998, 'Japan's Big Bang financial reforms', Speech delivered at Brooklyn Law School, Center for the Study of International Business Law, 27 April, 1998.

Peersman, G and Smets, F 2001, 'The monetary transmission mechanism in the Euro area: more evidence form VAR analysis', ECB (European Central Bank)Working Paper No. 91.

Piketty, T and Saez, E 2006, 'The evolution of top incomes: a historical and international perspective', NBER (National Bureau of Economic Research) Working Paper No. 11955.

Piketty, T and Saez, E 2009, Income inequality in the United States: data series 2009, viewed 9 July 2010, http://elsa.berkeley.edu/~saez/TabFig2007.xls.

Polanyi, K [1944] 2001, *The great transformation: the political and economic origins of our time*, Beacon Press, Boston.

Priewe, J and Herr, H 2005, '*The macroeconomics of development and poverty reduction: strategies beyond the Washington Consensus*', Nomos, Baden-Baden, Baden-Württemberg, Germany.

Rappaport, A 1986, *Creating shareholder value: the new standard for business performance*, Free Press, New York.

Reich, M 2010, 'Minimum wages in the United States: politics, economics, and econometrics', in *Labour in the era of globalisation*, eds C Brown, B Eichengreen and M Reich, Cambridge University Press, Cambridge, pp. 353–374.

Reitan, EA 2002, *The Thatcher revolution: Margaret Thatcher, John Major, Tony Blair, and the transformation of modern Britain 1979–2001*, Rowman and Littlefield Publishers Inc, Oxford, UK.

Revell, J 1973, *The British financial system*, Palgrave Macmillan, London.

Richardson, JJ 1994, 'The politics and practice of privatization in Britain', in *Privatization in Western Europe*, ed. V Wright, Pinter, London, pp. 57–82.

Richardson, R 1991, 'Trade unions and industrial relations', in *The British economy since 1945*, eds NFR Crafts and NWC Woodward, Clarendon Press, Oxford, pp. 417–442.

Riese, H 1986, *Theorie der Inflation*, J.C.B. Mohr (Paul Siebeck), Tübingen.

Riese, H 2001, *Das Dilemma der Ökonomie der Bundesrepublik Deutschland. Retrospektive und Vision*, vol. 2, Grundlegungen eines monetären Keynesianismus: Ausgewählte Schriften 1964–1999, Metropolis, Marburg, Germany.

Robinson, J 1938, 'The economics of hyper-inflation', *The Economic Journal*, vol. 48, pp. 507–513.

Robinson, J 1956, *The accumulation of capital*, Palgrave Macmillan, London.

Rochon, LP and Rossi, S 2006, 'Endogenous money: the evolutionary versus revolutionary views', Centro di Studi Bancari Working Paper No. 14.

Rochon LP and Setterfield, M 2007, 'Post Keynesian interest rate rules and macroeconomic performance: a comparative evaluation', paper presented at the Eastern Economic Association Annual Conference 2007, 23–25 February.

Rochon, LP and Settlerfield, M 2008, 'The political economy of interest rate setting: inflation and income distribution', International Economic Policy Institute Working Paper No. 2008–01.

Rogoff, K 1985, 'The optimal degree of commitment to an intermediate monetary target', *Quarterly Journal of Economics*, vol. 100, no. 4, pp. 1169–1189.

Rogoff, K 2003, *Globalisation and global disinflation*, IMF, Washington DC.

Rosen, S 1981, 'The economics of superstars', *American Economic Review*, vol. 71, no. 5, pp. 845–858.

Ruckstad, MG 1985, 'Paul Volcker and the Federal Reserve: 1979–1982', Harvard Business School (HBS) Case No. 9–386–055.

Sachs, JD 1985, 'The dollar and the policy mix: 1985', *Brookings Papers on Economic Activity*, no. 1, pp. 117–186.

Safford, J 1998, *Staatsverschuldung im Vereinigten Königreich: Die öffentliche Verschuldung unter der konservativen Regierung von 1979–1994, Ursachen und Wirkkungen*, Lang, Frankfurt/Main.

Samimi, AJ and Motameni, M 2009, 'Political stability and of inflation targeting: new empirical evidence', *Australian Journal of Basic Applied Sciences*, vol. 3, no. 2, 1319–1322.

Sargent, TJ 1979, *Macroeconomic theory*, Academic Press, New York.

Samuelson, P 1966, 'A summing up', *Quarterly Journal of Economics*, vol. 80, no. 4, pp. 568–583.

Scharpf, FW 1987, *Sozialdemokratische Krisenpolitik in Europa*, Campus Verlag, Frankfurt a.M./New York.

Schmitt, J 2008, *The union wage advantage for low-wage workers*, Center for Economic and Policy Research, Washington, viewed 21 May 2010, www.cepr.net/documents/publications/quantile_2008_05.pdf.

Schumpeter, J [1926] 1983, *The theory of economic development: an inquiry into profits, capital, credit, interest, and the business cycle*, Transaction, Piscataway, New Jersey.

Schumpeter, J 1976, *Capitalism, socialism, and democracy*, Harper Colophon Books, New York.

Shaw, GK 1983, 'Fiscal policy under the first Thatcher administration 1979–1983, *Finanzarchiv*, vol. 41, pp. 312–342.

Shiller, RJ 1978, 'Rationale expectations and the dynamic structure of macroeconomic models', *Journal of Monetary Economics*, vol. 4, no. 1, pp. 1–44.

Shiller, RJ 2001, *Irrational exuberance*, Broadway Books, New York.

Shiller, RJ 2008, *The subprime solution*, Princeton University Press, Princeton, NJ.

Shleifer, A 2000, *Inefficient markets: an introduction to behavioural finance*, Oxford University Press, Oxford.

Smithin, J 2007, 'A real interest rate rule for monetary policy?', *Journal of Post Keynesian Economics*, vol. 30, no. 1, pp. 101–118.

Soros, G 2008, *The new paradigm for financial markets: the credit crisis of 2008 and what it means*, Public-Affairs Ltd, London.

Soskice, D 1990, 'Wage determination: the changing role of institutions in advanced industrial countries', *Oxford Review of Economic Policy*, vol. 6, no. 4, pp. 36–61.

Spahn, HP 1988, *Bundesbank und Wirtschaftskrise: Geldpolitik, gesamtwirtschaftliche Finanzierung und Vermögensakkumulation der Unternehmen*, Transfer, Regensburg, Germany.

S&P/Case-Shiller Home Price Indices (Composite-10 CSXR) 2009.

Sraffa, P 1960, *Production of commodities by means of commodities*, Cambridge University Press, Cambridge.

Stevenson, T 2008, *Stock market history puts 2008 into relief*, Telegraph, viewed 9 July 2010, www.telegraph.co.uk/finance/newsbysector/banksandfinance/2785830/Stock-market-history-puts-2008-into-relief.html.

Stiglitz, JE 1996, 'Some lessons from the East Asian Miracle', *The World Bank Research Observer*, vol. 11, no. 2, pp. 151–177.

Stiglitz, JE 1997, 'Reflections on the natural rate hypothesis', *Journal of Economic Perspectives*, vol. 11, no. 1, pp. 1–10.

Stiglitz, JE 2003, *The roaring nineties: a new history of the world's most prosperous decade*, W. W. Norton & Company, New York.

Stiglitz, JE 2004, 'Capital-market liberalisation, globalisation, and the IMF', *Oxford Review of Economic Policy*, vol. 20, no. 1, pp. 57–71.

Stiglitz, JE 2008, 'How to prevent the next Wall Street crisis', CNN commentary, viewed 24 June 2010, www.cnn.com/2008/POLITICS/09/17/stiglitz.crisis/.

Stiglitz, JE and Greenwald, B 2003, *Towards a new paradigm in monetary economics*, Cambridge University Press, Cambridge.

Stiglitz, JE and Uy, M 1996, 'Financial markets, public policy, and the East Asian miracle', *World Bank Observer*, vol. 11, pp. 249–276.

Stone, MR 2003, 'Inflation targeting lite', IMF (International Monetary Fund) Working Paper No. 03/12.

Streeck, W 2009, *Re-forming capitalism: institutional change in the German political economy*, Oxford University Press, Oxford.

Summers, L 1991, 'How should long-term monetary policy be determined?', *Journal of Money Credit and Banking*, vol. 23, no. 3, pp. 625–631.

Suzuki, Y 1986, 'A comparative study of financial innovation, deregulation and reform in Japan and the United States', *Bank of Japan Monetary and Economic Studies*, vol. 4, no. 2, pp. 147–159.

Tabb, W 1995, *The postwar Japanese system: cultural economy and economic transformation*, Oxford University Press, New York.

Tachi, R 1993, *The contemporary Japanese economy*, University of Tokyo Press, Tokyo.

Tarling, R and Wilkinson, F 1985, 'Mark-up pricing, inflation and distributional shares: a note', *Cambridge Journal of Economics*, vol. 9, no. 2, 179–185.

Taylor, J 1993, 'Discretion versus policy rules in practice', *Carnegie-Rochester Conference Series on Public Policy*, vol. 39, pp. 195–214.

Taylor, J 1998, 'The ECB and the Taylor Rule: how monetary policy could unfold at Europe's new central bank', *The International Economy*, no. 12/5, p. 24ff.

Taylor, J 1999, 'A historical analysis of monetary policy rules' in *Monetary policy rules*, ed. J Taylor, University of Chicago Press, Chicago, pp. 319–348.

Taylor, J 2000, 'Teaching modern macroeconomics at the principles level', *American Economic Review*, vol. 90, no. 2, pp. 90–94.

Teichmann, D and Vesper, D 1999, 'Öffentliche Haushalte 1999/2000: Keine Abkehr von der restriktiven Linie' *DIW (German Institute for Economic Research) Wochenbericht*, no. 34–35, pp. 619–632.

The Green New Deal Group 2008, *A Green New Deal*, new economics foundation, London.

The National Archives 2010, *The miners strike and the social contract*, viewed 9 July 2010, www.nationalarchives.gov.uk/cabinetpapers/themes/miners-strike-social-contract.htm.

Tinbergen, J 1956, *Economic policy: principles and design*, North-Holland Publishing Company, Amsterdam.

Tobin, J 1998, *Money credit, and capital*, McGraw-Hill, Boston.

Traxler, F 1999, 'Wage-setting institutions and European Monetary Union', in *The role of employer associations and labour unions in the EMU*, eds G Huemer, M Mesch and F Traxler, Ashgate Publishing, Aldershot, Hampshire, UK, pp. 115–135.

UNCTAD (United Nations Conference on Trade and Development) 2009, *The Global Economic Crisis: Systemic Failures and Multilateral Remedies*, UNCTAD, New York.

UK Office for National Statistics 2010, Economic accounts database.

US Bureau of Economic Affairs 2010, National income and product accounts.

Vesper, D, 2000, 'Finanzpolitische Stabilisierung im föderalen Staat: Deutsche Erfahrungen aus den 90er Jahren' *DIW (German Institute for Economic Research) Wochenbericht*, no. 38, pp. 615–623.

Wade, R and Veneroso, F 1998, 'The Asian Crisis: the high debt model versus the Wall Street-Treasury-IMF Complex', *The Left Review*, vol. 228, March/April, pp. 3–23.

Wagner, A 1893, *Grundlagen der Volkswirtschaft*, vol. 1, Grundlegung der Politischen Ökonomie, 3rd edn, C.F. Winter'sche Verlagshandlung, Leipzig.

Wallace, CD 2002, *The multinational enterprise and legal control: host state sovereignty in an era of economic globalization*, Kluwer Law International, The Hague.

Westphal, A, Heine, M, Herr, H and Busch, U (eds) 1991, *Wirtschaftspolitische Konsequenzen der deutschen Vereinigung*, Campus Verlag, Frankfurt a.M.

Werner, RA 2003, *Princes of the Yen: Japan's central bankers and the transformation of the economy*, M.E. Sharpe, New York.

Wicksell, K [1898] 1962, *Interest and prices*, Augustus Kelley, New York.

Williamson, J 2005, *Curbing the boom-bust cycle: stabilizing capital flows to emerging markets*, Institute for International Economics, Washington DC.

Wray, R 2007, 'A Post Keynesian view of central bank independence, policy targets, and the rules versus discretion debate', *Journal of Post Keynesian Economics*, vol. 30, pp. 119–141.

Yahoo! Inc. 2010, Yahoo! Finance Market Statistics.

Yarrow, A 2006, 'The challenges facing investment banking in the UK', in *Big Bang 20 Years on*, ed. Centre for Policy Studies, City of London, pp. 42–50.

Zohlnhoefer, R 2005, 'The politics of budget consolidation in Britain and Germany: the impact of blame-avoidance opportunities', CES Germany and Europe Working Paper No. 05.2.

Index

Page numbers in *italics* denote tables, those in **bold** denote figures.